BOOKS
CHILDREN
LOVE

BOOKS
CHILDREN
LOVE

A GUIDE TO THE BEST
CHILDREN'S LITERATURE

ELIZABETH LARAWAY WILSON

CROSSWAY BOOKS

A PUBLISHING MINISTRY OF
GOOD NEWS PUBLISHERS
WHEATON, ILLINOIS

Library of Congress Cataloging-in-Publication Data

Wilson, Elizabeth Laraway.
 Books children love : a guide to the best children's literature /
Elizabeth Laraway Wilson.—Rev. ed.
  p. cm.
 Includes index.
 ISBN 13: 978-1-58134-198-0 (alk. paper)
 ISBN 10: 1-58134-198-9
 1. Children—Books and reading—United States. 2. Children's
literature—Bibliography. 3. Christian literature for children—Bibliography.
4. Best books. I. Title.
Z1037 .W745 2002
011.62—dc21   2002013455

VP		16	15	14	13	12	11	10	09	08	07	
18	17	16	15	14	13	12	11	10	9	8	7	6	5

For my dear and loving family—
John, Wendy, Anna, Andrew, Mary, Katy;
Rick, Peter, Maria, and Nicolas—
and those who are yet to come.
You are God's forever-gifts to me.

CONTENTS

FOREWORD

"Please read me a story," says the eager little person. Or, "Can I sit on your lap?" "Oh, you're stopping at a good place! Couldn't you read just a bit more?" Familiar pleas in any family. The speaker could be a young child who has pulled out a favorite book or an older child speaking for the whole family as they sit sprawled, relaxed and content, one evening in the family room with mugs of hot chocolate steaming beside each one. The Lord of the Rings has drawn everyone into its world, and nobody wants to stop.

Books! Books contain the throb of human life; the magic entrances, fascinates, sets alight imagination, opens doors of interest and curiosity, informs, and triggers questioning. Restless bodies become still and concentrated—thinking is encouraged. Reading out loud together fosters warm ties in human relationships. The experience is shared, and then interesting and meaningful conversation ensues. Developing the ability and desire to pursue reading *is* education. That's why in English universities you don't "study history"; you "read history," or law, or whatever.

Unfortunately, our generation suffers from the presence of a compulsive box that spews out time-consuming, addictive fare. TV! The personal growth possible through reading, conversation, *life,* is not possible for many children and adults today. The priorities are wrong. Often there is no time left for the really important things in life.

Concerned families and teachers know that the number one priority in society is a functional family unit. This doesn't mean merely a location called "home" where meals are served and the car garaged. Parents have to create something; they have to give priority to "family life"—which takes time, energy, and discipline. Family life includes, for instance, routines such as mealtimes with shared conversation, cleaning up the yard together, reading through a whole book as a family, time spent with one child, etc. This is life. This is education. I'm personally very encouraged by the growing numbers of people who realize this, who realize they don't have to be dragged along by the patterns of our increasingly confused society. They realize they are responsible, and there are good alternatives that work. One indication of this trend is the increase of home-educated children. Another is the fact that new ways of organizing more flexible schools are being found, within which the parents share the responsibility and activities. Then we must consider the children whose parents can't or won't give them these riches at home. Can teachers help? *Yes.* With books! Magic that gets through to the most bored and restless child! Yet they cannot be "dry" books, such as many textbooks. They must be open doors that woo children into something living. This guide to good children's books will indicate many such choices.

"Today we'll not start with any schoolwork. Let's put our chairs in a circle. I have such a good story, I want to share it with you." And the group will bite the bait as you read, say, *The Lion, the Witch and the Wardrobe* by C. S. Lewis. Maybe the class will come alive to the love, romance, and fascination of books. What did they come to school for? To be bored by pages and pages of workbooks? To decide they hate learning? To be tested so that grownups can be satisfied making graphs about them or analyzing them on computers? Meanwhile our children perish. That greatest and most beautiful resource—the *child*—is lost, having been allowed to waste away with a malnourished mind. Atrophied brains! That is what I see around me in my country. Poor America! And we enjoyed such a good heritage.

This is where our Christian roots gave us a priceless infrastructure. We had the firm undergirding of truth: God's reality as communicated in His Word. Human life with value and love, knowing where we're going and why there is evil and what to do about it. We were given responsibility, free choice, and creativity, all of life—abundant life. God is the God of life, love, and reality. We can enjoy the creativity of other persons, and we are to do so. That was what education was all about, and Christians should look for the "real thing," not some shoddy copy. So the child should be led to truly good books—the originals, or classics, if you will.

We live in a fallen world; that is what those of us who accept the Christian faith think. But God's people, as we read about them in the Bible, could face what *other* people think—their ideas, their mistakes. So we needn't be afraid of other cultures, other viewpoints, when reading books to children.

It is a sin to brainwash another person. We are to inform people and teach them the truth. If you are a Christian, then you have a responsibility to communicate God's Word to others. It means living as God intended. But we *aren't* to insist on blinders so that children can't understand what other people think. In other words, go ahead and read a wide spectrum of books. Talk over together ideas you don't think are right. Many times children will comment *themselves* on the content and ideas in a book. This is strengthening.

Interested? Tired of jaded, nonthinking kids and falling literacy statistics? Discouraged about education that doesn't educate? My husband and I searched for answers and came across a great British educator who worked at the turn of the century: Charlotte Mason. She discarded most textbooks in favor of "living books" and life itself. The children thus "brought up" went on to become thinkers, writers, lovers of learning, contented persons. I was so excited by the way these ideas helped our own children that I wrote a book about it, *For the Children's Sake*. Although written with a Christian worldview, the book's ideas are *true* to all children and life, and many have found these applicable in any case. I believe these ideas are needed more than ever by the children in our inner cities, those with "low self-esteem," those with no "identity" or inner riches—the children of today.

After writing the book, I was inundated with pleas from parents and teachers and adults who said, "I missed out as a kid. Please, I want to start now myself." They all asked: "Can you tell me which are living books? What can we read? Where do we start?"

Elizabeth Wilson spent a year researching books of quality in many categories. Books for younger children, books for older children. *Not* textbooks, but books that they'll *enjoy* reading. And now she has added the best books that have been written since the first edition was published. Here they all are.

Keep the treasure hunt going! Once bitten, you'll want to discover many other books *you'll* love. One other caution: We're all different. Each person is attracted by slightly different books, different writers. Don't expect each book to be right for everybody!

If you're new to all this, choose from the literature section first. And good reading to you!

Susan Schaeffer Macaulay

CHILD LIGHT
(CHILD LIFE)

Charlotte Mason's practical ideas were *so* good we've tried to go one step further than merely explaining them in the book *For the Children's Sake* (Crossway). Hence this guide to the best children's books available. *Books Children Love* will go a long way in helping you begin to put the ideas in my book into practice in your family or classroom. You can even safely stop school for a few years and feast on good books and right living! Your children or students would experience childhood with a lot more zest and vigor. And they would not lose out, by the way.

In time comprehensive guides to grade-related curriculum will be available, published also by Crossway Books. These guides will be invaluable to schools and home schools wishing to implement Charlotte Mason's principles.

We had to rename "Child Life" due to an unrelated magazine already using that name. We are continuing under the new name Child Light. If you wish information on other material available (including tapes on home education, etc.), newsletter, and future seminars, write to:

Child Light (Child Life)
Sound Word Association
P. O. Box 2035
Michigan City, IN 46350, USA

Susan Schaeffer Macaulay

INTRODUCTION

During the fifteen years since *Books Children Love* was first published, it has been good to learn that many parents, teachers, and others have continued to find it helpful and have taken the book to their hearts. This newly revised edition combines the timeless classics and other fine books of the original edition with a wealth of wonderful new selections, each of which I read in its entirety.

To say that it is even more difficult today than it was in 1987 to find well-written books that reflect traditional Judeo-Christian values simply states a reality consistent with cultural trends—but fine books are still being written. Finding these books and introducing them to parents, teachers, and others concerned with the whole-person needs of children is the reason for this book's existence.

Readers already familiar with *Books Children Love* may recall the role in its background of Charlotte Mason, an inspired educator of the past, and of Susan Schaeffer Macaulay and her husband, Ranald Macaulay, who were developing an educational philosophy that would meet the often-expressed needs of parents and children. The Macaulays were drawn to Charlotte Mason's recognition of the crucial importance of fine books in the education and character formation of children. Susan Macaulay is the daughter of Edith Schaeffer and the late Dr. Francis Schaeffer, founders of L'Abri Fellowship and internationally known writers. Both of the Macaulays have also written several widely read books. In *For the Children's Sake* (Crossway, 1984) Mrs. Macaulay has effectively discussed the basis for their approach to childhood learning.

My own involvement in the project came about as the Macaulays and I shared our mutual interest in the education and nurture of children and of the significant part worthwhile books should have in their lives. With my own background in literature, researching and writing an extensive children's book list was a project I undertook with great enthusiasm.

One of Charlotte Mason's foundational concepts was that it was of primary importance for all children to be comfortably at home with books and to be provided with excellently written, interest-holding books on as wide a range of topics as possible—books that also embodied ideas and ideals in harmony with traditional values. She called such works "living books," and her own extensive experience an educator had demonstrated conclusively that when a child has an ongoing relationship with such books, he or she is willingly participating in the most effective form of education.

Books Children Love was written to provide information on a broad range of books. Hundreds of books from more than two dozen subject areas are listed, with comments on each book designed to give readers a clear idea of its tone and content. A variety of books provide fine literature and its insights into human nature and experience; knowledge about places, people, events, processes, causes, effects—all absorbed as the child reads. This happens whether the book is a well-told story, an equally well-written biography or history, a book showing great artists' paintings, or simply a well-crafted book on how to successfully grow a vegetable garden. At the same time, the "nuts and bolts" kind of knowledge is also being absorbed: Vocabulary is built, reading and spelling skills are greatly aided, and repeated exposure to various models of good writing help the reader learn to put his or her own thoughts into an effective written form.

Of even more significance are the moral and ethical (and often spiritual) values conveyed by books. When a child identifies with either a real or a fictional character who demonstrates courage, faith, honesty, determination, kindness, or any one of the qualities so important to nurture in a child's own character, all those values are reinforced in the child's consciousness. When the effects of dishonesty, unkindness, carelessness, hypocrisy, and other wrong behavior are observed in the course of a story or a nation's history, the truth is learned with lasting effectiveness.

The story itself (whether fact or fiction), its setting, and fine writing combine to hold the interest of the young reader; but at the same time solid values are reinforced, helpful ideas are introduced, and the child's lifelong supply of general knowledge is enjoyably increased. Other living books show a child how to prepare for a camping trip, how to care for pets, how to learn more about nature, how to create a great variety of crafts. Still others share exciting discoveries or enter the world of artists and their work.

The examples just given mention only a few of the list's subject areas, and in that connection it is important to emphasize that any list such as this one is essentially unfinished—both because it cannot possibly include all the fine books available, and because more excellent new books are written each year.

It is hoped that this book will be used simply as a start, and that once readers become more aware through the book's pages of the richness and diversity waiting for their children in the world of books, they will continue to seek out on their own the kind of books to which they have been introduced, or reminded of, in this volume.

Another matter of significance is the criteria used in the selection of the books. The first criterion was the essential starting point that a book must readily catch and hold a reader's interest. Then, depending upon the category and purpose of the book, it should do some or all of the following—provide a "magic carpet" to transport a child to faraway places; offer fascinating insights into lives different from his or her own; give sheer joy or wholesome entertainment; increase understanding of that which is true and real; incorporate significant ideas or issues in a natural and credible manner; stimulate imagination and creativity; encourage logical thought, curiosity, and questions; provide clear, accurate information on a specific topic.

The second criterion relates to the literary quality of the writing itself. This is, of course, inextricably bound up with the qualities mentioned above, for it is writers with gifts of imagination, understanding, and vision, a superior grasp of language use and a pleasing style, who are able to create books that do the things we have just talked about. In this regard it has been important to distinguish between "good intentions" and fine writing. The fact that a writer may wish to convey either some worthwhile truth or some exciting experience (or both) does not in itself qualify his or her work as good, and I have excluded books of any category in which the writing is poor. This does not mean that I have confined the list only to books of the very highest literary excellence; there is a good proportion of such books, but also a solid representation of material that is very good in relation to its function and that, though it may not be timeless literature, is well-crafted and effective.

The final criterion applied has to do with the implied values of the writer as revealed in his or her work. The list includes books by both Christian and non-Christian writers, and a wide range of people in varying circumstances are found in the books—some of them children in very difficult situations. It is important for children to have an informed awareness and an ever-growing understanding of reality as it exists outside their own immediate experience. I have, however, chosen not to include books that reflect a perverse view of human life, that exploit deviant behavior, or that undermine or attack basic Judeo-Christian moral and ethical values. Parents and others involved in caring for, teaching, and nurturing children do need to be aware of what children are reading.

In conclusion, I would like to speak from my heart and from my own experience. It is difficult to emphasize enough just how important parents (or other caregivers) are in helping children to be at home with books, to become a part of this ongoing relationship that can be so significant in a child's life. Reading "living books" with ease and joy is not simply a means of success in school and later career enhancement, not just a valuable aid to building character and to learning important truths. It is a gift that enriches life always in countless ways and that strengthens family relationships—the shared joys of favorite stories, of discussions about ideas and people, of skills learned together with a book's help, of faraway places brought into the home as Mom or Dad reads aloud. Such times are never forgotten and become a part of the bonds between parent and child, between sisters and brothers, long after children become parents themselves. Homes should overflow with good books; libraries should be loved and often visited; from the very beginning of life children should see and hear their parents reading. Parents need to read to little ones as often as possible; children should be encouraged to talk about what they have read. And if parents haven't had happy reading experiences in their own childhood, they need to determine that this will not happen to their children. To be at home with books, children need book-loving homes.

If *Books Children Love* brings children and fine books together, it will have served its essential purpose. It is a book that was written with love— love for children with their wonderful questing minds, their lives of yet-undreamed, unshaped possibilities; love for language, for ideas, for imagination, for knowledge, for all that is a part of the inexhaustible richness of the world of books; and, above all, with a love for God and for all He has made and done and given—truth, beauty, love, infinite diversity—for He called it very good.

NOTES ON THE
BOOK'S ORGANIZATION

As the Table of Contents indicates, the books are divided into subject areas. In each category books are arranged alphabetically as in a library, with the author's name first. The one exception to this is in the *Biography* section in which, also as in a library, the books are arranged alphabetically by the last name of the subject of the biography (that name appears in a heading above an entry, or entries, related to the biographical subject).

Following the author's name is the name of the book and then various brief informational items. The last of these items (shown in parentheses) are suggested grade levels—for example, (ps=preschool). These levels, however, are not to be taken in a rigid sense or as a restricting guide as to when a child should be ready for a certain book. Readiness varies widely with individual children, and suggested grade levels shouldn't be used in a way that will either discourage or limit a child's reading—or, on the other hand, attempt to urge him or her on ahead of individual readiness.

In the main Literature sections the books are grouped in three grade levels for the convenience of the reader: Level I—ps-grade 2; Level II—grades 3-4; Level III—grades 5-6-up. As to the categories of literature, a few words of explanation about two of them may be helpful. *Fantasies, Talking Animal Stories* includes stories (other than fairy tales, myths, and legends, which have categories of their own) that are not limited by pragmatic reality. In addition to stories that transcend space, time, or the world as we know it, this section also includes all stories about animals who behave as human beings. This latter group may be largely realistic in events and interaction of characters but is complete fantasy in its use of animals who function as human beings—even if in some stories they are animals in most respects but talk together as only humans can. The *Historical* category includes all realistic stories written either about or during any time before 1930. In other words, books by writers such as Louisa May Alcott or Lucy Maud Montgomery were not historical when they were written, but they have now become so, whereas stories by Rosemary Sutcliff or Elizabeth George Speare have been written in modern times about the past and are also historical.

It should be noted that most of the older children's classics are published by a number of different publishers, sometimes changing many times. Most of the entries include the original publication date in parentheses. A quick check of *Books in Print* in your library's reference department will show all currently published editions. A current problem is that some of the finest of the old classics have been issued in a variety of abridged, condensed, and revised forms that trivialize, "dumb down," and often destroy the basic character and atmosphere of the originals. While there are a very few cases in which minimal changes made by a qualified editor of great intelligence and literary skill make a particular book more accessible without changing its essential nature, this is not the case with the mass of the above kinds of alterations. Whether it involves a book in the library or one in a bookstore, it should be looked at carefully to be sure it contains the text as the author wrote it; otherwise it is unlikely to contain the qualities that make it unique and that are the most rewarding to its readers. Many libraries still have the older books with original texts even when they add some of the simplified editions, but some collections are increasingly at risk as old books are sometimes ruthlessly discarded to make way for the new.

As to whether a book is in or out of print, while some titles remain consistently in print, others drop out (and sometimes back in) every year. Fortunately, a great many out-of-print titles still remain on library shelves. In this revised edition of *Books Children Love* I have retained some especially fine books that are currently out of print but are readily available in many local libraries and through interlibrary loan requests. Finally, a good book is worth trying to track down. The Internet has put many smaller bookstores out of business, but it has also made it easier to search for books, including titles that are out of print. Websites such as alibris.com feature listings from thousands of used-book dealers.

1

ANIMALS
Domestic Animals, Pets, Zoo Animals

Burnford, Sheila. *The Incredible Journey*. Yearling Books, 1996 (1960), 148 pp. (5-up).
> Primary listing under *Literature: Level III, Realistic Stories—Modern*
> It is Burnford's wonderful portrayal of the character and personality of each of the lost pets (two dogs and a Siamese cat) that has made the book a modern classic and sustained its popularity for four decades. As the three make their hazardous way home, their suspenseful adventures reveal the distinctive nature of each pet and the interaction among them—something the film based on the story couldn't adequately do. A very special story for animal lovers.

Engfer, LeeAnne. *My Pet Hamster and Gerbils*. Lerner Publications, 1997, 64 pp. (2-up).
> Small, furry animals that can live comfortably in a moderately-sized cage have become increasingly popular pets for children in today's more than busy households. Engfer's practical and clearly written book helps children take a large share of responsibility themselves for the selection and care of hamsters or gerbils (though some adult oversight is, of course, always needed). The species types to choose from are described and pictured in color photographs, as are the details of care and feeding, what to look for in monitoring the pets' health, and what activities the animals enjoy. A glossary of terms related to these animals is included, as well as a list of several organizations that can provide additional information. One group, for example, advises schools in creating classroom displays of rodent pets.

Gutman, Bill. *Becoming Your Bird's Best Friend*. Illus. by Anne Canevari Green. The Millbrook Press, 1996, 64 pp. (4-6).
> This general survey of the nature and needs of pet birds focuses especially on how to establish a loving and rewarding relationship between a young owner and his or her pet bird. The writer profiles several different types of birds and includes practical care and feeding information and guidelines. He wants primarily, however, to help the owner understand the bird, to know why it does specific things, and most of all to learn how to meet the bird's emotional need for attention and company. Gutman writes with warmth and humor, and the text is further enlivened with amusing drawings in color. A note for prospective bird owners: Even if you plan to acquire a manual on your particular species of bird, this book

is the one to read before you select your bird—and to keep handy to refer to as you try to develop a happy, trusting friendship with your pet.

Hansard, Peter. *A Field Full of Horses*. Illus. by Kenneth Lilly. Candlewick Press, 1994, 24 pp. (ps-4).

There is something about horses that strongly appeals to most children. Is it the way they move and their glossy coats and swishing tails? Is it the proud way they hold their heads, gazing calmly out of large, beautiful eyes? Or is it the way they look when they trot and gallop, rear and buck? As the narrative proceeds, horses of varying colors and types are seen in a great variety of stance and movement. The author speaks conversationally about the horses, wonders about the horses, and involves the reader in wondering and asking too. So seemingly casual, the writer's just-right choice of words is matched perfectly with the illustrator's outstanding drawings, many of which are accompanied by little hand-printed informational notes. This book will satisfy children's eyes, answer many questions about one of their favorite animals, and give them new ideas to wonder about.

Herriot, James. *James Herriot's Treasury for Children*. Illus. by Ruth Brown and Peter Bennett. St. Martin's Press, 1992, 246 pp. (ps-up).

Real-life Yorkshire veterinarian James Herriot didn't just take care of a great variety of animals, both pets and "working" farm animals—he wrote about them too. Eight of his books are written especially for children, and this beautiful, big volume contains all of them. Eventful and often suspenseful, the stories all reflect Herriot's endless love for the animals he spent his life among. This book is well seasoned with his inimitable humor—a wonderful choice for the whole family to enjoy together.

Lee, Barbara. *Working with Animals*. Lerner Publications, 1996, 112 pp. (4-8).

Working with animals is often an appealing idea to children. Some dream of becoming a veterinarian, a wildlife specialist, or a zookeeper. Others simply have a lively interest in what such people do in their day-to-day jobs. Writer Barbara Lee interviewed and observed a dozen people who work with animals (each in a different branch of the field) and provides a well-balanced picture of what each one does—often in his or her own words. None of them glamorizes the work, which in every case is demanding and often requires specific college and graduate-level preparation. Competition for such jobs is usually intense. Particularly in the less educationally demanding areas, many of the people profiled were able to enter the field only after volunteering and becoming familiar with the work on their own time. But all of these people are doing what they love to do—and doing it with determination, commitment, and immense satisfaction.

MacClintock, Dorcas. *Animals Observed: A Look at Animals in Art*. Charles Scribner's Sons, 1993, 56 pp. (Art, all ages; text, 5-up).

Primary listing under *Art*

This collection of drawings, paintings, and sculptures by artists who were especially interested in animals is almost in the "something for everyone" category. The pictures are wonderful, from the page facing the introduction with its colorful painting of a wildcat gazing with narrowed eyes from its secure perch in a tree, to the little sculpture on the last page of a calf nonchalantly scratching its neck with a hind foot. In between are giraffes, zebras, bears, dogs, monkeys, horses, and many more. Then there is the very readable text, which not only puts each animal and its portrayal in the context of its era, its setting, and its artistic creator, but also succinctly provides information about the particular kind of animal. In the case of animals that have been moved from their natural homes, the book tells their individual stories. Younger children will love the pictures and mini-stories, and all other ages, including adults, will find much of interest.

Maxwell, Gavin. *The Otter's Tale*. Dutton, 1962, 124 pp. (4-up).

A warm, appealing story of Mijbil, Edal, and Teko, pet otters, and their life with writer Gavin Maxwell. This true account is not only excellent because of its interesting story and irresistible photographs, but it indirectly makes an important point about the amazing possibilities that exist in relationships between people and animals—when the people are informed, concerned, and willing to meet the animals' needs. The lengths to which Maxwell goes make it quite clear that the ownership of an animal should involve a serious commitment. Fortunately, most pets don't have the extensive needs of an otter, but as a child reads of Maxwell's responsible care of his delightful pets, he or she can also see in a new way that whether one has a hamster, a lizard, a dog, cat, or other pet, a choice should always be made—either a faithful commitment to learn about and meet the animal's needs or a decision not to have a pet at all.

Maze, Stephanie and Catherine O'Neill Grace. *I Want to Be a Veterinarian*. I Want to Be . . . Series. Harcourt Brace and Co., 1997, 48 pp. (5-up).

The first step for an animal-loving child toward finding out if he or she would like to become a veterinarian might be to read a book like this one. Offering a broad range of introductory information, the book briefly surveys the work of veterinarians, from small-animal community practices, such as the one to which a reader's family might take their pets, to medical care for farm animals and riding horses. The work of veterinary specialists—as wide-ranging as that of doctors who treat people—is discussed. Included are veterinarians working at aquariums and zoos and those in research and in wildlife programs both in the United States and abroad that work to save endangered species of animals and birds. Veterinarians also teach in the veterinary medicine programs of universities and colleges—and a few multitalented vets go on to become authors as well. Also a variety of careers are open to those who want to become veterinary technologists. The text is accompanied throughout by a wealth of colorful, informative photographs. A useful section offering sources of additional information concludes the book.

Morley, Christine and Carole Orbell. *Me and My Pet Fish*. Illus. by Brita Granström. World Book Inc., 1997, 32 pp. (3-up).

An enjoyable and practical little guide to the care of goldfish. Colorful drawings and photographs enliven every page. Starting with background information and a brief discussion of the many varieties of colors, shapes, and distinguishing features among goldfish, the book then takes the reader step by step through the essentials—what to look for in buying a healthy fish, the size a tank needs to be in relation to the number of fish, the needed (and optional) accessory equipment, and guidelines for feeding. One requirement that will surprise many people is that the fish tank should not simply be filled with tap water. The water must be treated with a liquid dechlorinator (available in pet stores), as chlorine is harmful to fish. Concluding the book is a little section on the care of goldfish in an outdoor pond and a brief glossary of relevant words.

Muir, John. *Stickeen*. Heyday Books, 1990 (1909), 96 pp. (4-6).

A true and unusual dog story by the mountain man/naturalist of Yosemite fame. Unlike many dog stories, particularly those written some years ago, this one is not even slightly sentimental and is out of the ordinary both in the nature and actions of the dog and in the amazing experience Muir recounts of the perilous walk on the glacier. (A good biographical preface on Muir is included.)

Owl Magazine Editors. *The Kids' Cat Book*. Greey de Pencier Books, rev. ed. 1990 (1984), 96 pp. (3-8).

Put together by editors of *Owl, the Discovery Magazine for Children,* this is an informative and entertaining mélange. Its varied content includes a range of background facts about types of cats, cats in the wild, a look at various kinds of pet cats, suggestions on choosing a kitten, and care and feeding tips. There are cat-related puzzles and brief cat stories, with a wealth of drawings and photographs illustrating the text. This is a great book for a youngster to read either in preparation for having a pet cat or simply to enjoy its extensive and pleasing content.

Owl Magazine Editors. *The Kids' Dog Book*. Greey de Pencier Books, rev. ed. 1990 (1984), 96 pp. (3-8).

A companion book to *The Kids' Cat Book* (above), this compilation includes a similar diversity of content, providing factual background information about the canine family in general and about specific types of dogs. Practical pet-related advice and training tips are given clearly and often in a humorous vein. Readers may especially enjoy a section on "Real Life Wonder Dogs." The book is lavishly illustrated throughout with photographs and drawings. The material in this and its companion book is not simply informative and entertaining, but it also provides helpful models for young students as to how to research a specific subject, clearly categorize and organize each part, and then supply supporting details and examples for each part of the topic.

Patent, Dorothy Hinshaw. *Miniature Horses*. Cobblehill Books/Dutton, 1991, 48 pp. (4-up).

Few children can resist the appeal of miniatures—especially those that bear a faithful, accurately proportioned likeness to whatever larger object they represent. In the world of animals, there are few true miniatures to be found, but over the years one animal successfully miniaturized has been the horse. (It should be noted that miniature horses are not the same species as ponies.) Patent's well-written book tells of the creation and development of these tiny horses no larger than a big dog, discusses the two types of horses the miniature breeders have chiefly worked on developing, and goes on to provide a wealth of information about the little horses, both as show favorites and also as pets. Miniature horses are not just enjoyable to see, but they have gentle, people-friendly natures that make them ideal pets. A mini can be ridden by a child up to sixty pounds and can pull a small cart and its passenger. Excellent color photographs illustrate every aspect of the text.

Pullein-Thompson, Diana, editor. *Classic Horse and Pony Stories*. Illus. by Neal Puddephat. DK Publishing, 1999, 96 pp. (4-up).
   Primary listing under *Literature: Anthologies*
   A number of the selections in this beautifully illustrated collection are excerpted from favorite classic books. Horse and pony stories are among most youngsters' favorites, and these are some of the best. Well written, full of action and suspense, and exemplary of fine values, each story is a pleasure to read. For more details, see the entry under its primary listing category shown above.

Rosen, Michael J., editor. *Purr . . . Children's Book Illustrators Brag About Their Cats*. Harcourt Brace and Co., 1996, 42 pp. (k-5).
   In this lighthearted collection, forty-three well-known illustrators of children's books each contribute a page of drawings and a little story about their most memorable cat. From Scaredy Kate who had kittens in the closet among the sneakers (the kittens were promptly named Adidas, Nike, Converse, Etonic, and Reebok) to Tuxedo who simply wouldn't learn any social skills, from Zazou and Pearl to Wendy and Groucho, each cat is a unique individual whose whimsical stories amaze and amuse. Beyond the fun of it all is a serious and worthwhile purpose: The book royalties and a portion of the publisher's profits are donated to The Company of Animals, a fund that provides grants for veterinary services, homes for stray animals, and aid for the pets of the elderly and the ill.

Schmidt, Jeremy. *Village of the Elephants*. Walker and Co., 1994, 30 pp. (2-5).
   Primary listing under *History and Geography*
   In a tiny village near India's southern tip, each family has an elephant. Owned by the government, the elephants work in India's logging industry, and the men of each family are their drivers (mahouts), fully responsible for their care. The relationship between the elephants and their human working partners is one of the closest such alliances known in our world. The elephants are not grouped together in their non-working hours; each one is tethered to a tree beside its mahout's small home, a vital part of that family's life. Traveler and writer Jeremy Schmidt, along with photographer Ted Wood, introduces the reader to a village full of elephants, to one in particular, Mudumalai, and to the boy, Bomman, who is learning to be a mahout and who gives Mudumalai his bath every morning. This view of elephants is very different from the usual zoo or circus perspective—one well worth seeing.

Schomp, Virginia. *If You Were a . . . Veterinarian.* If You Were . . . Series. Benchmark Books, 1998, 32 pp. (2-4).

This introduction to the work of a veterinarian is put together well. The approach is brief and simple, well suited to children in the early grades. Illustrated with an effective selection of color photographs, the book, in a conversational, informal tone, shows and tells about veterinary work in a variety of settings. These range from the city offices where family pets make up most of the patient list, to the rural practices with their treatment of cows, horses, goats, and sheep. Both in the city and the country, vets may care for injured wildlife brought in by good Samaritans. Finally, zoos and wild animal parks require veterinarians who can treat the wide range of animals in their care. Young readers will enjoy learning about the interesting variety in veterinary practice and will gain understanding of how the work is done.

Simon, Seymour. *Pets in a Jar: Collecting and Caring for Small Animals.* Puffin Books, 1979 (1975), 96 pp. (4-up).

A child who likes to observe the behavior of a small species of wildlife, and who would enjoy creating an environment in which such a little creature could thrive, will find this book most helpful. The two opening chapters focus on general selection, collection, and care notes. Simon then goes on, in six separate chapters, to focus individually on fifteen kinds of possible "pets in a jar." Planarians, tadpoles, earthworms, crickets, and hermit crabs are just a few of the possibilities. An experienced elementary and junior high science teacher, Simon brings a good background of factual knowledge to his writing. All the animals discussed in the book have been kept and observed in either Simon's classrooms or at his home.

Smith, Roland. *Inside the Zoo Nursery.* Cobblehill Books, 1993, 58 pp. (4-up).

When visitors at a zoo see the baby animals in the zoo nursery, some may not realize that every little creature there represents a problem of one kind or another. Because, of course, if everything has gone perfectly in the baby's birth and infancy, it won't be in the nursery at all, but with its mother. The nurseries are there to meet the zoo babies' needs when something goes wrong for them, and this informative book discusses a variety of circumstances that can put a baby animal in the nursery. The writer describes how each problem is handled, what equipment is used, and how each baby is prepared to get back into the mainstream life of the zoo—or to be sent to a new home—when the baby is ready. Excellent color photos complement the substantial, well-researched text. When young readers next visit a zoo, they will enjoy knowing more about the nursery and its care of the problem babies.

Wegman, William. *ABC.* Hyperion, 1994, 56 pp. (ps-up).

Primary listing under *Language*

An unusual and entertaining ABC in which photographs of Weimaraner dogs, meticulously posed, form each letter. Still more dogs are used in amplifying the book's instructional aspect. The author's clever text and often hilarious photographs make this an effective as well as enjoyable alphabet book. At the same time the book offers children many pages of pictures of the dogs Wegman uses so innovatively.

Ziefert, Harriet. *Let's Get a Pet*. Illus. by Mavis Smith. Viking, 1993, 32 pp. (all ages).
Both practical and entertaining, this well-thought-through book is an excellent source of help for anyone considering getting a pet. Colorful, informative, and amusing illustrations accompany every detail of the text. Using a two-parent, two-children family as her examples, the writer starts with a series of questions prospective pet owners should ask themselves. Then she specifies the commitment involved and the range of care various pets require, discusses the general characteristics of a variety of possible pets, tests the extent to which each prospective owner would be willing to do necessary but unpleasant tasks in pet care, and concludes with the fictional family's final analysis and choice of a pet.

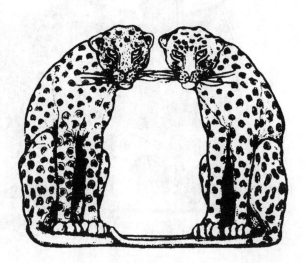

Wittenberg & Sother St.

2

ART AND
ARCHITECTURE

Aaseng, Nathan. *Building the Impossible*. The Oliver Press, 2000, 144 pp. (5-8).

Today the new record-breaking heights of buildings, lengths of bridges, and sheer immensity of a project's scope receive little lasting attention and bring little fame to individual architects and builders. Such undertakings now involve a number of equally responsible professionals, all of whom rely heavily on complex computer calculations and the bank of technical knowledge accumulated over time. This is very different from the work of the great builders of the past, the "innovators" who, without any of our contemporary technology, launched out into unknown territory and created structures that had previously seemed impossible. Writer Nathan Aaseng has profiled eight builders and their precedent-making structures, from Imhotep (of about 2700 B.C.) and the Step Pyramid of Egypt to William Lamb and the Empire State Building in twentieth-century New York. Aaseng enriches his narrative with relevant—and often fascinating—biographical information about these builders with extraordinary vision. He puts each project in a clearly described context of related political and economic conditions, and he provides a lively recounting of the building techniques, obstacles overcome, and often surprising events along the way.

Corbishley, Mike. *The World of Architectural Wonders*. Peter Bedrick Books, 1996, 45 pp. (4-8).

An attractively presented survey of fourteen noted architectural sites of the ancient world, the book ranges from Roman and Greek ruins to the deserted Incan city of Machu Picchu; from Jordan's stone city of Petra to the American cliff dwellings of the Anasazi. Illustrated with excellent photographs and precisely detailed drawings (all in color), the book includes a surprising quantity of well-coordinated information on each entry. Pleasure and wonder are reason enough to experience this book, but, in addition, learning of the existence of each of these historic structures (or group of structures) and having an idea of what they are like is part of the general knowledge with which children need to be equipped. This book provides an enjoyable and informative introduction to ancient buildings and cities that they will see pictured and hear mentioned throughout their lives—and which they will encounter in a variety of classes as they move through their education.

Curlee, Lynn. *Liberty*. Atheneum Books for Young Readers, 2000, 42 pp. (2-6).

Primary listing under *History and Geography*

A comparatively small number of those who can identify pictures of the Statue of Liberty—or even of those who have seen this national monument for themselves—know its full story. First proposed by a French professor, Édouard de Laboulaye, the statue became the creative passion of a gifted young sculptor, Frédéric-Auguste Bartholdi. Laboulaye envisioned the sculpture as "a monument to the first 100 years of American independence and a gesture of friendship between two nations"—America and France. This concept fit Bartholdi's taste perfectly, for he was strongly attracted to monumental art and to classic Greek or Roman sculpture. This heroic mode, in turn, was eminently suited to Laboulaye's vision of the statue as a symbol of the freedom for which America had fought.

The entire project was immense—not only in size but in complexity. The statue's exterior was to be fabricated of sheets of copper done in sections. The hollow interior would, of course, need a complicated support framework to hold the statue up. Just the copper shell weighs more than thirty-two tons, and the finished statue is more than 151 feet high. Curlee's account of how this problem was solved is fascinating. Other equally intriguing and often surprising aspects of the statue's creation are included, and the writer's clear and lively narrative makes for both enjoyable and informative reading.

de Treviño, Elizabeth Borton. *I, Juan de Pareja*. Farrar, Straus and Giroux, 1987 (1965), 192 pp. (4-7).

Primary listing under *Literature: Level III, Realistic Stories—Historical*

This fine story of Juan de Pareja (fictionalized but based on reality), who spent most of his life with the famed Spanish artist Velázquez and his family, provides wonderful insights into the work of an artist and much information about art in general. The account of Juan's life is in itself fascinating. Born into slavery in early seventeenth-century Spain, he endured great hardship as a young child. But later he became a trusted member of the Velázquez household, a knowledgeable assistant and friend to the artist, an artist in his own right—and a free man.

Fisher, Leonard Everett. *Alphabet Art*. Simon and Schuster Children's Books, 1984 (1978), 64 pp. (5-up).

Primary listing under *Language*

An unusual compilation, the book includes large two-page spreads of thirteen different alphabets (Arabic, Gaelic, Thai, for example) and is rich in a variety of artistic qualities. Each alphabet is introduced with an illustration and an inscription written out in the related language. The layout of the alphabets invites the reader to attempt to graphically duplicate these fascinating, strange symbols. An excellent choice for an art unit related to calligraphy.

Greenberg, Jan and Sandra Jordan. *Frank O. Gehry: Outside In*. Dorling Kindersley Publishing, 2000, 47 pp. (5-9).

Primary listing under *Biography*

This lively picture biography takes the reader into the life and work of Frank Gehry, one of today's most notable architects. For years he was a successful cutting-edge designer of innovative buildings. But it was his creation of the Guggenheim Museum in Bilbao, Spain (opened in 1997), that catapulted Gehry into worldwide recognition and acclaim. The museum's outside surface is of titanium, glowing in sun and shade, creating ever-changing reflected hues; its swooping, free-flowing forms and calculatedly slanted angles rivet the gaze; the effect is breathtaking even in photographs.

As a graduate student, Frank Gehry saw an exhibit of paintings by the French architect Le Corbusier and observed that the forms Le Corbusier used in his architecture were based on organic shapes he had used in his paintings. Gehry realized that as an architect, he wouldn't *have* to stay within the rigid shapes followed by most buildings. "That's when I threw the grid away," he exulted, "and said, 'Man, there's another freedom out there, and that's the place I want to be.'"

Children are especially open to unconventional and imaginative forms. Thus innovative shapes in architecture in this book provide another opportunity for a creative stretching of the mind and the vision, a vital part of growing and learning. This is an enjoyable, exciting, and informative book in its writing, photography, and typography. A glossary, bibliography, and list of locations where some of Gehry's work can be seen complete the volume.

Guarnieri, Paolo. *A Boy Named Giotto.* Translated by Jonathan Galassi. Illus. by Bimba Landmann. Farrar, Straus and Giroux, 1998, 24 pp. (2-5).

A fictional story about a real person, the famed Florentine painter and architect Giotto di Bondone, known simply as Giotto (Jôt´tō), c.1266-c.1337. As is often the case with famous people of the distant past, we know few details of Giotto's life. It is thought that while still a shepherd boy, he met the artist Cimabue, who later became his teacher. However, there is no absolute evidence even of that, only that he *was* Cimabue's student. Giotto did leave behind his sheep-tending and did become a noted artist, considered by art scholars to have been a major influence for positive changes in art that continued long after his death. His paintings and buildings can still be seen in various locations. In this, Guarnieri's first book for children, he makes up a story about little Giotto out on the hillsides with his father's sheep, drawing pictures on stones and in the sand. Giotto longs to spend his life as an artist. When the noted painter Cimabue visits their little town, Giotto sees one of the artist's beautiful paintings, manages to talk with him about his hopes, and eventually becomes Cimabue's student. Landmann's wonderful illustrations glow with golden tones, rich, deep color, and fascinating detail. A feast for the eyes.

Haldane, Suzanne. *Faces on Places: About Gargoyles and Other Stone Creatures.* Viking, 1980, 40 pp. (3-7).

An attractive introduction to architectural ornaments. Combining history and anecdotes, the writer tells how some of the fanciful creatures and comic faces seen on buildings are made. Excellent photographs illustrate each part of the concise text, and children will thoroughly enjoy applying the knowledge newly gained from Haldane's book as they start focusing on gargoyles and other carvings on the buildings of their own communities or those seen in family travels. Not currently in print, this book is still on many library shelves and is worth looking for and requesting through interlibrary loan if necessary.

Hill, Lee Sullivan. *Towers Reach High*. Carolrhoda Books, 1997, 32 pp. (ps-3).

The simple format of this book, with its one sharply delineated photograph on each page and its brief text, will be enjoyed by young children. There is, however, the potential for a wider learning experience, which an adult sharing the reading with a child can develop. A tower of any kind, reaching up beyond the level on which we commonly live, appeals to the imagination and immediately signals a significance and purpose beyond the familiar routines of our lives. Each of the towers in the book—a lighthouse, an airport tower, a church steeple, and more than twenty others—can open up as wide a range of questions and conversational learning as the child and adult who share the experience may wish. Just starting with the key questions as to why the tower was built, how it was used, and whether it is still being used that way will provoke much thought, some research—and perhaps many more questions. A concluding feature of the book will be helpful in this regard—a photo-index with a tiny picture of each of the book's tower subjects and a short paragraph of additional information about it.

Hines, Anna Grossnickle. *Pieces: A Year in Poems & Quilts*. Greenwillow Books, 2001, 30 pp. (all ages).

Primary listing under *Literature: Poems and Rhymes*

This delightful collection of seasonal poems illustrated with photographic reproductions of tiny theme-related quilts offers a blend of written, visual, and textural art. A riot of color and flowing form within the exquisite design and craftsmanship of the miniature quilts is an unusual and rewarding artistic experience. Two pages about "The Story Behind the Quilts" complete this irresistible book.

Isaacson, Philip M. *Round Buildings, Square Buildings, Buildings That Wiggle Like a Fish*. Alfred A. Knopf, Inc., 1988, 121 pp. (5-up).

With a loving enthusiasm for the beauty and artistry of the world's architectural treasures, the writer says, "A building has harmony when everything about it—its shape, its walls, its windows and doors—seem just right. . . .When each suits the other so well that they come to belong to one another, the building is a work of art." Isaacson takes the reader on a guided tour through a fascinating diverse collection of pictures he has taken of buildings that are beautiful with that special harmony. The photographic quality of his pictures is outstanding. Some of the buildings are famous; others are not widely known. Some are magnificent; others quietly restrained. All are a delight to see.

The author shares his appreciation of the buildings' characteristics in clear, unpretentious language, providing basic guidelines for understanding the principles of architecture and looking at buildings perceptively. The joy he feels in each example is contagious, and one couldn't find a more pleasurable or effective introduction to architecture. The book concludes with a dozen pages of concise notes about each building—a splendid way of offering these details without slowing the flow of the book's text.

Kurelek, William. *Lumberjack*. Tundra Books, 1996 (1974), 48 pp. (4-8; all ages for art).

Also listed under *Biography* and *History*

A highly regarded Canadian painter, Kurelek created a vibrant gallery of paintings to accompany his story of what it was like to be a lumberjack more than fifty years ago. Vivid colors, simplicity of line, and authentic detail all characterize Kurelek's warm, realistic portrayals. This artist's work is a good choice to be included in a study of modern painting, not only because of the quality of his work, but because the personal faith that informs his perspective gives his work a dimension to which many readers can especially relate.

Kurelek, William. Companion volumes: *A Prairie Boy's Winter*. Houghton Mifflin, 1984 (1973), 48 pp. *A Prairie Boy's Summer*, Tundra Books, 1996 (1975), 48 pp. (4-8; all ages for art).

Also listed under *Biography* and *History*

As in *Lumberjack* (above), colorful full-page paintings face each page of text in these reminiscences of the artist's boyhood on the Canadian prairie near the United States border. Visual and verbal pictures combine to make the world of the 1930s live again.

Kurelek, William. *A Northern Nativity*. Tundra Books, 1976, 48 pp. (4-8; all ages for art).

Twenty striking paintings accompany the unique text of this lovely book. Each scene pictures Joseph, Mary, and the baby Jesus set in the era of the Great Depression in the United States. At a long-ago Christmastime when he was twelve, the artist dreamed that Christ had come bodily to other places, other cultures. The radiant paintings symbolize the truth that Jesus did indeed come to all peoples for all times.

Kurelek, William, paintings and comments; Margaret Engelhart, additional text. *They Sought a New World: The Story of European Immigrants to North America*. Tundra Books, 1985, 48 pp. (4-8; all ages for art).

Primary listing under *History*

This distinguished Canadian artist was impelled by a deep longing to preserve the heritage from immigrant forebears for future generations. In the *Prairie Boy* books and *Lumberjack* (listed above), Kurelek captured the experiences of his youth growing up in Canada, the son of immigrants. In this story of the European immigrant experience, his insightful art brings the accompanying narration to life. In twenty-eight paintings the account is spread before us in all its patient enduring, grinding effort, and frequent isolation—but also with its festive gatherings and its hopes for the future. Kurelek wanted the children and grandchildren of these courageous people to remember and literally to see the reality in which they were rooted. In his intensely felt paintings Kurelek left them—and all of us—the poignant evidence of what it meant to seek a new world.

Lewis, Marguerite. *Randolph Caldecott, the Children's Illustrator*. Alleyside Press, 1992, 48 pp. (4-up).

Primary listing under *Biography*

Quiet, cheerful, and patient, Randolph Caldecott (1846-1886) had as intense a passion for artistic expression as any of history's stormy artists known for their moodiness. Without any background for becoming an artist, he drew from the time he could control a pencil or charcoal stick, with an inborn talent that showed in his efforts when he was just a boy. He spent as much time as he could in the woods and fields outside the ancient English town of Chester, drawing the little animals he watched for hours at a time. His joy in this pursuit was reflected in the liveliness and subtle humor of his art. For years Randolph worked as a bank clerk, becoming known as an artist through the frequent appearance of his work in a variety of publications. It was, however, his work as the increasingly popular illustrator of a series of children's books that firmly established him as an artist, and he was then able to devote all his time to the work he loved. When the American Library Association instituted an annual award more than sixty years ago to honor the illustrator of each year's best picture book, the award was named for Randolph Caldecott. Marguerite Lewis's biography includes many of the artist's captivating illustrations for long-ago children's books.

Linder, Leslie and Enid. *The Art of Beatrix Potter*. Frederick Warne, 1955, 336 pp. (all ages).

This lovely book on Beatrix Potter's art includes more than 300 reproductions of her drawings and paintings. Each section of the book is opened with notes on the history of the specific group of pictures and on the development of Potter's work. Selections from her childhood art are followed by later work in several categories: interiors, landscapes, plant studies, microscope work, fungi drawings, and animal studies. These, in turn, are followed by drawings that represent fantasies and a variety of ideas Potter had for stories. Not in print, but still available in many libraries, the Linders' book is more effectively done than some other compilations covering similar material.

Macaulay, David. *City*. Houghton Mifflin, 1974, 112 pp. (5-up).

Author/artist Macaulay has created detailed drawings and descriptions of the building of a Roman city. The construction specifications are so clear and complete that the reader can fully visualize the roads, aqueducts, and buildings taking shape. A miniature model city could be built from the information given. Along with his architectural approach, Macaulay conveys a broad range of information about the culture and daily customs of the first-century Romans. The accompanying text is as clear and crisp as the splendid drawings.

Macaulay, David. Three books: *Castle; Cathedral; Pyramid*. Houghton Mifflin, 1977, 74 pp.; 1973, 77 pp.; 1975, 80 pp. (5-up).

See the above listing for Macaulay's book *City* for a description of his technique and the broad purpose of this splendid series of books. On all levels Macaulay's work is superb, capable of both informing and inspiring.

Macaulay, David. *Unbuilding*. Houghton Mifflin, 1980, 78 pp. (5-up).

Using the same meticulous techniques as in his other books, Macaulay reveals both architectural and historical/cultural reality. In this case, instead of showing initial construction, he depicts what would be revealed if the Empire State Building were dismantled step by step. This innovative reversal of the usual sequence in the building process stimulates the reader's visualization of the architectural processes (and related social and cultural elements) involved in the creation of the famous building.

Macaulay, David. *Mill*. Houghton Mifflin, 1983, 128 pp. (5-up).

Another wonderful joining of architecture and history is further seen in this book of David Macaulay's. Spanning the years from 1810 to 1974, Macaulay focuses on four imaginary but typical textile-related mills built in New England at intervals during that time. The writer can take even such apparently unexciting subject matter and render it fascinating. Not only are his drawings and descriptions so lucid that models of the earlier structures he depicts could be constructed simply by following his text, but also the reader is made aware of the technological and social changes taking place with the passing years.

Macaulay, David. *Building Big*. Houghton Mifflin, 2000, 192 pp. (5-up).

The acclaimed creator of a number of fine books on significant types of buildings has written another splendid volume. Packed with detailed architectural descriptions, drawings, and diagrams, the book also provides background information on some of the world's structures that are "big"—both in size and significance. Thirty-five outstanding bridges, tunnels, dams, domes, and skyscrapers are looked at inside and out. Macaulay discusses the reasons for their being built, the special problems encountered and how they were overcome, and the details of technologies and innovative decisions developed to meet unique conditions. Each aspect of *Building Big* inspires young readers to look differently at the world around them and to become aware of the ways in which the structures of that world affect our lives.

MacClintock, Dorcas. *Animals Observed: A Look at Animals in Art*. Charles Scribner's Sons, 1993, 56 pp. (5-up; all ages for art).

The drawings, paintings, and sculptures presented here are the works of artists who cared strongly about the animals they portrayed. In her introduction, MacClintock writes: "The animals themselves were *well observed* [author's italics]. They are portrayed both lovingly and skillfully by artists who had in common an intense interest in animals and who observed with empathy." The artists are from various countries and span many centuries. The book is full of wonderful pictures but is not simply a "picture book"; the writer's comments address not only each work of art itself but provide all sorts of information about the kind of animals represented by the particular work. Yet the book is not a natural history text. Included are many delightful and illuminating anecdotes (some highly humorous), but the central focus remains on each animal itself. Readers will find the book unusual, enjoyable, and rewarding.

Marcus, Leonard S. *A Caldecott Celebration: Six Artists and Their Path to the Caldecott Medal.* Walker Publishing Co., 1998, 49 pp. (4-up).

For over sixty years the American Library Association has awarded a medal to "the artist of the most distinguished American picture book for children published during the preceding year." Known as the Caldecott Medal, its bestowal is a prestigious honor. In celebration of the medal's sixtieth anniversary, children's historian Leonard Marcus has written this highly readable account. After a concise introduction on the background of the coveted award, he goes on to write about six Caldecott Medal artists—one from each decade of the award's existence.

Marcus takes the reader into the lives and studios of the artists, focusing on the things readers would most want to know: How did each one become an artist? Why did they start illustrating children's books, and how do they go about the process of creation that brings a story to life? Within a few pages each, Marcus provides a surprising amount of information, including samples of the artists' preliminary sketches for their award-winning books, insights into the interaction between the artists and their book editors, anecdotes about how they develop the visions they first see mentally, and descriptions of the different kinds of artists' materials and techniques each one uses. (And don't miss the handy glossary of terms used in the text.)

Marshall, Catherine. *Catherine Marshall's Story Bible.* Avon, 1985 (1982), 200 pp. (ps-up).

Primary listing under *Bible*

Children will be inspired by the imagination and creativity shown in the seventy-seven vivid illustrations of the Bible stories, all done by children six to ten years old. All the children were members of a Geneva, Switzerland, art class conducted by Michéle Kenscoff. See primary listing for more information.

Merrill, Yvonne Y. *Hands-On Rocky Mountains.* Kits Publishing, 1996, 83 pp. (2-6).

Primary listing under *Crafts*

The chief focus of this book is on the artifacts of several people-groups (the Anasazi, American Indians, settlers, trappers, and cowboys) that lived in what the author calls the "Rocky Mountain West." (In addition to the attention given to the various artifacts, each group is also briefly profiled as to its history and culture.) The craft projects of the book involve making adapted replicas of utensils, clothing, and miscellaneous accessories used by each of the groups. Many of these items reflect the particular group's characteristic art forms in decoration and shaping. All the artifacts referred to are shown in colorful photographs. Children wanting to create art objects or design-drawings will find a number of interesting ideas and models in Merrill's book.

Reynolds, Graham. *Constable's England.* The Metropolitan Museum of Art, New York/George Braziller, 1983, 184 pp. (all ages).

Published in connection with a special exhibition of Constable's paintings at New York's Metropolitan Museum of Art, Reynolds's book offers excellent color plates of more than sixty of Constable's superb English landscapes. Each is accompanied on the facing page with information about the painting and its setting. Next to repeated visits to a museum or art gallery to view a specific artist's work, such a book is the best way for a child (or adult) to become familiar with that artist's choice of subject and medium (oils, watercolors, pastels, for example), his or her distinctive painting techniques, and the unique vision conveyed by the artist. A substantial introduction to the book provides information on Constable's life and work. The book is no longer in print but well worth looking for in libraries.

Richardson, Joy. *Looking at Pictures: An Introduction to Art for Young People.* Harry N. Abrams, Inc., Publishers, 1997, 80 pp. (all ages—with guidance).

An attractive and effectively presented introduction to ways of seeing and understanding art. The material is organized into sections dealing with the twelve major themes involved in a study of art. For example, the treatment of light, use of color, perspective, and other specific ways in which an artist has dealt with his or her subject. Key artistic concepts and the vocabulary used when talking about painting are included and discussed. Each section of the book focuses on one major work, with a reproduction of the painting and enlarged insets of the work's significant detail analyzed clearly and understandably. The paintings used are in the National Gallery, London, and include works of Rembrandt, Van Eyck, Constable, Cezanne, and a number of others. Most children enjoy learning how to look intelligently at paintings, and after absorbing the helpful guidance of a book such as this, are delighted to try out their new knowledge in museums and art galleries.

Roop, Peter and Connie, editors. *Capturing Nature: The Writings and Art of John James Audubon.* Illus. by Rick Farley. Walker Publishing Co., 1993, 39 pp. (4-up).

Primary listing under *Biography*

In his own words, the great American naturalist-artist tells of his virtual obsession to portray the birds of America, not only as accurately and perfectly as possible, but in the natural patterns of their lives—flying, perching, eating, caring for their young. This brief but admirable book, perceptively presented by the editors, speaks from the artist's own consciousness and makes sense of a life that involved long trips to observe birds in all their movements, changing plumage, and choices of food; that meant endless hours of drawing and redrawing, of repeated financial losses, and years when few others were interested in his work. Audubon wrote candidly of his struggles, even detailing the painstaking ways he discovered to improve the naturalness of appearance in the birds. His words reveal the singleness of his purpose, the preeminence in his life of his artistic vision—a vision he amply fulfilled, as evidenced by the heritage he left. The dozen reproductions of his paintings in the book reward careful observation in the light of his own comments about his work.

Rosen, Michael J., editor. *Down to Earth*. Harcourt Brace and Co., 1998, 64 pp. (4-6).

Primary listing under *Growing Plants: Outdoors and Indoors*

In this delightful book, forty-one children's book authors and illustrators have contributed little stories and pictures about their joyful experiences with things that grow in the earth. While reading this book with a child, or children, observe together the differing ways the artists depict plants: the bold, bright colors and brush strokes of some; the soft, delicate shades and misty effects of others. Discussion of the contrasts or similarities, the feelings evoked by the varying styles, will encourage thoughtful observation of art and a growing ability to see it in greater depth and in new ways. Many of the drawings also offer wonderful models children can attempt to copy in paintings of their own.

Rosen, Michael J., editor. *Purr . . . Children's Book Illustrators Brag About Their Cats*. Harcourt Brace and Co., 1996, 42 pp. (k-5).

Primary listing under *Animals*

In this enjoyable collection, a number of children's book illustrators draw pictures of, and tell a story about, their most memorable cat. Aside from being a fun-filled read about cats, the book offers children an opportunity to see the many different ways artists portray similar subjects. Some children may be inspired to follow the artists' examples, drawing and writing about their own pets, perhaps deciding to try to do their illustration in the style of one particular artist. Check the *Animals* listing for more details about the book.

Rudstrom, Lennart. Three books: *A Family; A Home; A Farm;* paintings by Carl Larsson. Putnam, 1979, 32 pp.; 1974, 31 pp.; 1976, 34 pp. (all ages).

These books offer splendid paintings of family, home, and farm scenes in the artist's homeland of Sweden. Simple text comments on Larsson's life and the subjects of his paintings. The text is suited to young readers, but the books can be used with all ages in relation to the art. The work of this prominent Swedish artist of the late nineteenth and early twentieth centuries became very popular in the United States more than a decade ago. A number of his paintings were reproduced on calendars, note cards, and a variety of other materials. In the manner of popularization, the commercial interest largely ran its course, and today it is less easy to find Larsson reproductions, though they have not disappeared. This fact does not diminish the very real artistic value of his work, however, and these now out-of-print books merit searching for.

Rubin, Susan Goldman. *There Goes the Neighborhood: Ten Buildings People Loved to Hate*. Holiday House, 2001, 96 pp. (3-7).

Bitter controversy over the innovative design of a building is not unusual, but the writer has chosen ten especially interesting and notable structures—each one quite different from any of the others—to write about. The result is a lively, well-researched, often amusing account. Included among the ten are the Washington Monument, the Eiffel Tower, New York's Solomon Guggenheim Museum, and the home of architect Frank Gehry, whose biography *Outside In* is listed above and also under *Biography*. (Years ago some of his neighbors hated his house so much that one of them shot a bullet through the living room window. The bullet remains in the wall.)

Samoyault, Tiphaine. *Alphabetical Order: How the Alphabet Began*. Translated by Kathryn M. Pulver. Penguin Books, 1998, 30 pp. (4-7).

Primary listing under *Language*

In Samoyault's amply illustrated book on the origins and development of the alphabet, the role of visual art in the history of written communication is graphically demonstrated. The emphasis of the book is on language, but the link with art is clearly seen as people turned first to drawings to convey facts and ideas and to keep records. Although pictographs gave way eventually to stripped-down letters that symbolized specific sounds of language, art continued to be involved—in the calligraphy of handwritten, pre-printing press material and in the later focus on typography. Early hieroglyphics viewed at the dawn of the third millennium A.D. are amazingly like the work of some of our late twentieth-century artists. With its vivid range of pre-alphabet pictographs (cuneiform and hieroglyphics, for example) and its brilliant charts of world alphabets, this book is one to put into the hands of a creative and artistic young person.

Sanderson, Ruth. *Tapestries*. Little, Brown and Co., 1998, 32 pp. (3-6).

Primary listing under *Bible*

A rich feast of color and texture enhance Sanderson's retelling of the stories of women of the Bible. Using "oil paint instead of thread," the artist perfectly complements her assertion that each woman's life is a part of the weaving of the tapestry of faith. The artist's portrayals of her subjects against intricate tapestry-like backgrounds are vibrant examples of the significance in art of texture and pattern—and symbolically of the weaving of each life. Young artists may be inspired to try for themselves to create similar fabric-like drawings with luminous colors and graceful designs.

Thomson, Ruth. *Drawing*. Get Set . . . Go! Series. Children's Press, 1994, 24 pp. (2-4).

The relaxed, experimental atmosphere of this little book encourages children to feel comfortable about trying new ways to use pens, pencils, crayons, and water-color paints. Ten simple—and fun—drawing projects are modeled, each of which could be varied to suit the young artist once he or she has grasped the concept. Younger children will need some initial guidance from an adult in getting their materials together and getting started, but the text is uncomplicated and easy to read. The book provides a good way of helping children find that they can do art projects on their own, using a variety of materials and subjects. Three other books in this series are *Painting, Printing,* and *Collage.*

Tudor, Bethany. *Drawn from New England: Tasha Tudor.* Putnam, 1979, 96 pp. (5-up).

Primary listing under *Biography*

This is a lavishly illustrated biography of the famed artist (widely known for her delightful illustrations of children's books), written by her daughter. The book contains many examples of Tasha Tudor's work, as well as a wealth of family photographs and snapshots. Particularly significant from the artistic perspective are the descriptions of Tudor's love of her work, of its growth and development, and of the way in which she fulfilled her artistic promise without compromising her determination to live a simple country life.

Turner, Robyn Montana. *Rosa Bonheur.* Little, Brown and Co., 1991, 32 pp. (2-6).

From childhood on, Rosa Bonheur had two dominant areas of interest in her life: art and animals. Born in 1822, Rosa lived at a time when girls were not encouraged to become artists. In spite of that, she immersed herself in study and painting and became a noted artist of her era. Today her paintings are seen in museums and other collections throughout the world. Author and art education consultant Robyn Turner has created an appealing and informative picture biography. The writer combines the story of Rosa Bonheur's life (a much happier and more successful one than is often the case with artists) with comments on her work and reproductions of a number of her paintings. In her work, Bonheur was able to bring her two loves, art and animals, together. Young readers will especially enjoy the book's many paintings of horses, oxen, sheep, and wild animals, often pictured in vigorous motion. *The Horse Fair,* a huge canvas depicting a colorful mass of rearing, plunging horses, is one of her most famous paintings.

Unlike the vision of many later artists, Bonheur's intent was to present for viewers as accurate a representation as possible of how her subjects looked. "The eye is the route of the soul," she wrote, "and the pencil or brush must sincerely and naively reproduce what it sees." Rosa had her first exhibit in the Salon, the annual Paris art show, when she was just nineteen. Her realistic portrayals delighted the public, and by the time she was twenty-six, she was famous—and well off financially. This enjoyable book is one of a series, Portraits of Women Artists for Children.

Venezia, Mike. *Monet.* Children's Press, 1993, 32 pp. (ps-4).

As one of the founders of impressionism, French artist Claude Monet was not only a major influence in the late nineteenth-century art world, but his work remains lastingly popular with many people today. Monet is an artist children can easily relate to, with his love of nature and his desire for immediacy and everyday-life reality in his painting. Author Mike Venezia has written an attractive and perceptive book that includes reproductions of seventeen of the artist's paintings and a number of clever little illustrations of his own that amplify the text. Venezia's comments on the artist's technique are particularly helpful. For example, he discusses the painting *The Cliff Walk Pourville*, pointing out the use of many slashing "colorful brush strokes" that, when seen close up (and he shows an example), don't seem to form a recognizable effect. He then shows the whole picture as it is seen from a normal viewing distance, and the scene is effectively there. The writer's approach is excellent for getting kids and art together. At the end of the book, Venezia lists the museums where the paintings discussed may be seen.

Watt, Fiona. *The Usborne Book of Art Ideas.* Designed by Amanda Barlow and Non Frigg. Usborne Publishing Ltd., 2000, 96 pp. (1-8).

An appealing book that combines creativity, clarity, and helpful organization. The more than 200 ideas for things to do with art offer something for everyone. The book deals with a wide range of artists' materials: acrylic paints, chalk and oil pastels, inks, poster paints, tissue paper, wax crayons, and watercolors. Instructions are effectively given on such topics as the basics of color and tone, and perspective. The text is simply stated but comprehensive, and the overall effect is colorful, imaginative, and enjoyable. All ideas and suggestions are fully described and illustrated.

Additional sources for art study may be found among adult materials and used with children by parents or teachers. Following are some possibilities.

The Library of Great Painters. Harry W. Abrams, Inc. This series offers large, extensive (and expensive) volumes about such artists as Rembrandt, Vermeer, Velázquez, Michelangelo, da Vinci, and many others. Each volume contains brief biographical information on the artist and a number of reproductions of his paintings with accompanying commentary. For example, the Rembrandt volume includes 108 reproductions, forty-eight of them in color. The cost of this type of book makes it impractical for many families to own it, and when libraries have them, they will usually be on the reference shelves rather than available for borrowing. An adult with perhaps two children at a time, however, could make good use of such books at a table or reading nook in the library.

A good many books focusing on a specific artist are published each year. Some of these are in paperback as, for example, *Leonardo da Vinci* by Bruno Santi, Scala/Harper, 1990 (1981), 80 pp. Any large general bookstore has an art section. Look these shelves over periodically for possible finds. Also browse in the art sections of both the children's and adult departments of your local library. Many works now out of print are still on library shelves.

Next best to haunting major art museums, the ideal way to familiarize children with a particular artist's work would be the small portfolios that were used in art study by the English schools directed by Charlotte Mason (see this book's Introduction). Each portfolio measured approximately 8 x 10 inches and contained brief biographical information, small but excellent color reproductions of six or so of the artist's most representative work, and brief comments on each painting itself. These fine materials were published in England but are no longer available there. Nor did I find anything of the kind being published in the United States. But a parent or teacher could create portfolios by ordering small folio prints and combining them with informational materials researched in a library. (Unfortunately, even publishers of folio prints seldom offer as many as six different reproductions of each artist's work.)

Finally, do try query letters to major art museums, such as the Metropolitan Museum of Art, New York, which might provide helpful sources of small reproductions of specific artists' work. Find out about art museums in large cities in your part of the country and write to them, or plan a family expedition and ask a reference person for helpful suggestions. (Remember to send a stamped, self-addressed envelope with any written query.) Try also using the Internet for a search. The book listed in this section on Constable's painting, *Constable's England* by Graham Reynolds (Metropolitan Museum of Art, New York/George Braziller), is exactly the sort of thing found in the little portfolios I have described above, except that the book, of course, is on a grand scale. Try to see this book or one you think is similar in a library and use it (on a small scale) as your model. It is the closest thing I have seen to embodying the spirit of those marvelous little portfolios of the past.

3

BIBLE/SPIRITUAL AND MORAL TEACHING

Aylward, Gladys (as told to Christine Hunter). *Gladys Aylward, the Little Woman.* Moody Press, 1970, 150 pp. (6-up).

Primary listing under *Biography*

There are many lessons in faith, endurance, and obedience to God's purposes in this story of courageous Gladys Aylward and her missionary work in China. See the biographical entry for details.

Bennett, William J., editor. *The Children's Book of Virtues.* Illus. by Michael Hague. Simon and Schuster, 1995, 111 pp. (ps-up).

This is one of those special books that belongs in every family library. After Bennett's best-selling *Book of Virtues* was published, he received many requests to compile a book of selections for children, and this book is the result. Replete with wonderful Michael Hague illustrations, the book contains thirty-one entries in all: beloved poems, fables, and stories that are part of our traditional literary heritage. Parents (and grandparents) often fondly remember a particular story from their own childhood that emphasized some fine character quality and want to share it with their children, but have difficulty finding it. Can any of us who heard the story as children ever forget the little Dutch boy who put his finger into the hole in the dike and kept it there for many hours, thereby keeping the sea from ravaging his town and its people? "The Little Hero of Holland" is one of the stories included in this collection. The book's entries are grouped under specific headings: Courage; Perseverance; Self-Discipline; Honesty—to name only a few. The book is ideal for family read-aloud times, but it is also a splendid way to reinforce the core values and virtues that children still need to make their own.

Bennett, William J., editor. *The Children's Book of Heroes.* Illus. by Michael Hague. Simon and Schuster, 1997, 111 pp. (2-6).

One frequently hears the term "role model," but the specific qualities that entitle a person to that status are often not clearly defined and appear to differ from one speaker or writer to another. As William Bennett comments in the book's introduction, ". . . children imitate what they see and hear. They naturally look for examples to follow. Today's popular culture offers plenty. Countless 'stars' and 'superstars' are put on pedestals for children to idolize and mimic. The problem is that most are celebrities, not heroes (it has been said that the difference between the two is that while the hero is known for worthy actions, the celebrity is known for being well known)." Bennett believes that parents, friends, and teachers need to point out to children on an ongoing basis what it is that "heroes"—people who truly merit admiration and imitation—*do* that stands out, and who some of these people are. This enjoyable and vividly illustrated collection of twenty-one poems, stories, and biographical accounts is all about heroes who embody a wide range of heroic qualities: courage, endurance, compassion, faith, gratitude, honor, and vision—behaviors worth copying. When children become well acquainted with such examples, they soon realize that it is not being famous, powerful, wealthy, or idolized by crowds that makes a hero. Instead, it is living out fine values in response to the needs of others and in surmounting adversity, danger, or evil.

Bennett, William J., editor. *The Book of Virtues for Young People*. Silver Burdett Press, 1996, 378 pp. (5-up).

    Similar in organization to *The Children's Book of Virtues* (listed above), this much more extensive volume serves the same purpose for older children and young people. The 116 stories, poems, and folk tales are grouped in categories: Self-Discipline, Compassion, Responsibility, Honesty, Faith, and five other indispensable qualities. Each section opens with a brief introduction that describes what is meant by self-discipline, compassion, and so on. The selections are all treasured readings valued for decades, centuries, and even millenniums. Full of wisdom and truth, they provide many clear insights into right ways of dealing with the realities of human existence. Effectively written, challenging, and inspiring, this is a valuable collection for every family library.

Brumbeau, Jeff. *The Quiltmaker's Gift*. Illus. by Gail de Marcken. Pfeifer-Hamilton Publishers, 2000, 44 pp. (ps-4).

    Primary listing under *Literature: Level II, Fables, Folk Tales, and Fairy Tales*

    This colorful fantasy about a mysterious quiltmaker and a king so selfish that he orders his subjects to celebrate his birthday twice a year (with lavish gifts) is not only entertaining but offers a built-in moral worthy of *The Book of Virtues*. Can this selfish king actually discover that it is more blessed to give than to receive? Turn to the primary listing of the book to read more about it—and about the quilt blocks pictured throughout the book.

Carlson, Melody. *The Lost Lamb*. Illus. by Steve Björkman. Crossway Books, 1999, 40 pp. (ps-3).

    An appealing story told in lively rhyme. A modern-day shepherd loses Zebedee, one of his flock of 100 young sheep, and looks for the lost one all night until he finds him. Based on Jesus' parable of the lost sheep, the heartwarming story conveys the strength of the shepherd's love, the persistence of the search, and the joy of the finding. Young listeners and readers are helped to understand the kind of love God has for each of them in the story's personalizing of the sheep, with each one given a name. Björkman's delightful illustrations perfectly complement the tone, the emotion, and the profound truth of the warmly told story.

Crossway Books Editors. *In the Beginning: The Story of Creation.* Crossway Books, 1998, 48 pp. (ps-3).

The story of creation in the majestic words of Genesis 1 is presented against a background of remarkable photographs: the earth seen from the moon; a crashing wave; still, reflective waters; towering skies awash with sunset's fire; crystal drops of water hanging from the tips of leaves; a dimly visible whale with her calf, submerged in the sea's depths; the glow of molten lava, and a thundering mass of zebras in migration. Sheer magnificence and stunning power seen in God's masterworks evoke awe and reverence, even as the consummate artistry in the coloration of a tropical toucan's beak reminds us of the Creator's loving interest in each creature he has brought into being. Sit with your child and turn the pages slowly: "In the beginning God created the heavens and the earth." Speak together of Him and share the timeless wonder and truth of God, the creator.

Everett, Betty Steele. *Freedom Fighter: The Story of William Wilberforce.* Christian Literature Crusade, 1994, 114 pp. (5-up).

Primary listing under *Biography*

It would be hard to find a more outstanding role model or a more authentic hero than William Wilberforce. A member of the British Parliament for forty-five years, he probably did more than any other one man to end slavery across the world. A gifted and wealthy young man, he became a Christian in his mid-twenties. He was already a member of Parliament, but now his commitment to public service deepened and became more focused. During almost half a century in the House of Commons, Wilberforce was a significant force for good in the British government. A model of absolute integrity and great compassion, he both initiated and/or strongly supported many laws to improve the lives of the British people, especially the poor. But the long-range undertaking to which he felt most deeply committed was his work against slavery. The Wilberforce story is significant not simply for what he accomplished in Parliament or for the worldwide recognition he won for his fight against slavery, but for the spiritual commitment of his life and the pattern of conscious choices he made through the years as he tried before all else to serve God faithfully and show God's love for others.

Ferguson, Sinclair B. *The Big Book of Questions & Answers: A Family Guide to the Christian Faith.* Christian Focus Publications Ltd., 1997, 192 pp. (all ages—a book for adults to use *with* children).

This lively and well-organized book answers questions children ask about spiritual and biblical matters and suggests activities that add to their understanding of the ideas being discussed. The helpful format and brief, direct style of the writing hold attention and make concepts easy to grasp. Each of the book's ten chapters focuses on a specific topic: "God Is Our Creator," "How Things Went Wrong," "God Had a Plan," for example. Each chapter asks and answers significant questions: "What is God like?" "Is there only one God?" "What is sin?" "What was God's plan to save us?" A question, answer, and related activities occupy one page. Each section is clearly presented, with enough "white space" throughout to ensure a crisp, uncluttered format. The author has served as Professor of Systematic

Theology at Westminster Seminary, Philadelphia, and the theological perspective is conservative and evangelical.

French, Fiona. *Bethlehem: With Words from the Authorized Version of the King James Bible*. HarperCollins Publishers, 2001, 24 pp. (all ages).
   Primary listing under *Celebration Days and Seasons*
   Inspired by the magnificent stained-glass windows of England's cathedrals, Fiona French has created a glorious celebration of Jesus' birth. The Christmas story is told in the beloved words of the King James Bible from the Gospels of Luke and Matthew. Each part of the unfolding events is pictured as though seen in the brilliance of a multicolored stained-glass window. This is a family treasure book that will fill hearts with joy and special memories.

Halperin, Wendy Anderson. *Love Is . . .* Simon and Schuster Books for Young Readers, 2001, 22 pp. (k-3).
   The timeless words of the apostle Paul in 1 Corinthians 13 are the text of this heartwarming little book. Acclaimed illustrator Wendy Halperin has applied each of Paul's definitions of what love is *not*, and what love *is*, to some of the day-to-day realities of life. Each large two-page spread is filled with wonderful little pictures. The scenes for "Love . . . is patient. Love is kind" depict (on the left) a variety of ways in which people are showing impatience or unkindness, and on the facing page the same individuals or groups are embodying love through their patience and kindness. The colorful and appealing pictures are full of wonderful details, a hallmark of Halperin's art. A special book to look at and talk about with your children.

Hunkin, Oliver. *Dangerous Journey: The Story of Pilgrim's Progress*. Illus. by Alan Perry. Eerdmans, 1985, 126 pp. (3-up).
   This lavishly illustrated adaptation of *Pilgrim's Progress* is a good way to introduce children to Bunyan's vivid depiction of the Christian journey from the "City of Destruction" through "the wilderness of this world" to the joys of the "Celestial City." Hunkin has edited with care, and the result is a readily understandable narrative that uses Bunyan's own words and preserves a clear sense of the original's dramatic action, its shrewd depiction of human nature, and the many guises of temptation. There is suspense, peril, and humor aplenty, with each page illuminated by Alan Perry's splendid full-color illustrations.

Johnson, James Weldon. *The Creation: A Poem*. Ed. by Paul Edwards. Illus. by Carla Golembe. Little, Brown and Co., 1993, 30 pp. (ps-up).
   Primary listing under *Literature: Poetry*
   Children will respond especially well to this poem's celebration if it is read aloud to them as they follow the artist's imagery page by page. There is an energy and power in the unexpected word pictures and in the book's striking graphics that inspire awe. Yet at the same time there is a playfulness when, for example, the ball of brightness that is the sun is flung out like a cosmic baseball into the darkness of space. The awe-inspiring Creator-God has in that flashing image been personal-

ized. He has thrown the sun into its place as we, created in His image, might toss out a ball. God's power is joyously celebrated.

Karon, Jan. *Miss Fannie's Hat.* Illus. by Toni Goffe. Augsburg, 1998, 32 pp. (1-4).
    Primary listing under *Literature: Level I, Realistic Stories—Modern*
    Lovable Miss Fannie, a sprightly ninety-nine, has a closetful of wonderful hats that she has worn for years. She loves every one of them, but most of all the beautiful pink one with the silk roses that she has worn each Easter for thirty-five years. When Miss Fannie's church decides to have an auction to raise money for some needed repairs, she is asked to give one of her hats for the sale. The difficult choice of the hat and the outcome of her decision give young readers a wonderful opportunity to think about loving and giving, about unselfishness and the joy of doing something special for God. The warmth and humor Jan Karon (author of the greatly loved Mitford novels) brings to her writing are much in evidence, complemented by Toni Goffe's delightful illustrations.

Larcombe, Jennifer Rees. *The Baby in the Basket.* Illus. by Steve Björkman. Crossway Books, 1999, 19 pp. (ps-3).
    Larcombe's lively, effective retelling of the baby Moses' story, with its use of extra-large type size for emphasis on key phrases, begs to be read aloud with appropriate drama. Colorful, entertaining illustrations full of details of the Egyptian setting bring a new zest to a favorite Bible story. Faithful to the biblical account, the writer has brought the familiar people and events to life in a most enjoyable way.

Levete, Sarah. *How Do I Feel About Being Jealous.* Copper Beech Books, 1999, 24 pp. (1-up—see comments below).
    The author has used a group of five fictional children of diverse backgrounds around which to structure discussion about jealousy—a frequent problem both at school and at home. The material is interestingly presented, well organized, to the point, and attractively illustrated in color. Jealousy is clearly defined and explained, helping readers to realize that a person can be jealous over things that belong to others and can also be jealous of people themselves. The wrong and unkind things jealousy can cause a person to do are discussed and the question, "How can you stop feeling jealous?" is answered.
    It is because the book does such an excellent job of dealing with its subject that it is included here—in spite of one major difficulty: *all* of the illustrations (including, of course, the kinds of activities the children are engaged in, the related playthings, and the whole visual atmosphere of the book) are of children who are clearly first through third graders, while the maturity of the discussions and dialogue is just as clearly geared to grades four to six. Thus, if simply handed the book, the children who could most fully grasp and benefit from the book's content would be put off by the illustrations of "little kids." The younger group, who would relate happily to the "kiddy-land" illustrations, need a simpler approach and more time on each jealousy-related concept. (A few especially perceptive and advanced younger children could be exceptions to the general response.)

A solution is for an adult to be closely involved with a child in the initial reading of the book. Appropriate simplification by the adult for the younger children and an "You older kids can see how on-target the jealousy problems discussed are, and you can just overlook the little-kid pictures" approach for upper elementary youngsters could make the book helpful for all grades one-to-six kids.

Lucado, Max. *Just the Way You Are.* Illus. by Sergio Martinez. Crossway Books, 1999 (1992), 31 pp. (ps-5).

Long ago in a faraway village an orphaned family of five children were overjoyed to hear that the king wanted to be a father to them and was going to adopt them. The village people advised the children: They must impress the king with their special gifts. Only then, people said, would he be pleased with them and take them to live with him. Four of the children began spending all their time improving their talents, but the youngest one knew of nothing she could do to impress the king. She just went on as she had been, giving help and encouragement to weary travelers at the city gate. One day the king came looking for the children. He was alone, riding on a donkey, and very simply dressed. The four gifted ones were too busy enhancing their abilities even to talk graciously to the stranger. It was the little girl who greeted him at the gate who learned who he was and what mattered to him, and heard him say, " 'Of course you'll be my child. I love you just the way you are.' " A beautiful allegory of God's unconditional love and acceptance.

Lucado, Max. *The Song of the King.* Illus. by Toni Goffe. Crossway Books, 1995, 29 pp. (1-4).

Primary listing under *Literature: Level II—Fables, Folk Tales, and Fairy Tales*

Set in a traditional fairy-tale form, this allegory is developed around the triumph of Cassidon the wise over Carlisle the strong and Alon the swift—all knights seeking the hand of the king's daughter. In setting the test for the three, the king sends his son to give the king's message to the knights. The one who overcomes the dangers and difficulties of the way leading to the king's home, reaching it safely, will be given the hand of the princess in marriage. By the terms of the king's directions, each knight is allowed to choose a companion to help him on his journey. It is Cassidon's crucial choice of the king's son (a choice only revealed at the end of the story) that enables him to traverse the menacing paths without losing his way or being destroyed by the sinister Hopenots of the dark forest. Cassidon arrives in joy and triumph at the king's castle. A timeless message in an appealing story.

MacArthur, John. *I Believe in Jesus: Leading Your Child to Christ.* Illus. by Melinda MacArthur. Tommy Nelson, 1999, 29 pp. (ps-up).

Parents or grandparents sometimes feel at a loss for words when they want to tell a child about God's plan of salvation. They know there is more involved than just saying, "Jesus loves you, and He wants you to give your heart to Him," but they don't know how to put it all into clear, understandable words. With four grown children and ten grandchildren of his own, Pastor John MacArthur cares deeply about children's spiritual needs and has lent a helping hand in this effective book. Simply worded, in language children can readily understand, the writer has explained comprehensively and yet concisely God's wonderful plan, just as it is found in the Bible. Each brief section of text is accompanied by a relevant Scripture verse from a child-friendly translation. The book's pages are enhanced throughout by the artist's fresh, appealing drawings, which glow softly in a particularly attractive palette of colors.

Macaulay, Susan Schaeffer. *How to Be Your Own Selfish Pig*. Chariot Victor, 1982, 128 pp. (6-up).

Written primarily for teenagers, this cogent, lively book can also be helpful for preteens who are particularly thoughtful, questioning, and mature. The bottom-line realities of Christian belief are explored in an appealing and direct way. Valid questions are raised—and answered—not with pat formulas but with reasoned biblical truth that can be lived out in the nitty-gritty of everyday life.

Magnusson, Sally. *The Flying Scotsman*. Charles River Books, 1981, 191 pp. (5-up).

Primary listing under *Biography*

This inspiring story of the life and work of Eric Liddell, Olympic runner and missionary widely known through the film *Chariots of Fire*, embodies important spiritual truths. These are not in any sense "preached" at the reader. Liddell lived his faith in a remarkable way, and the writer has conveyed most effectively the beliefs and principles on which the runner's life was based.

Marshall, Catherine. *Catherine Marshall's Story Bible*. Avon, 1985 (1982), 200 pp. (ps-5).

An unusual book that combines the colorful art (seventy-seven unique illustrations) of six- to ten-year-old students of a Geneva, Switzerland, art class and thirty-seven favorite Bible stories told in Marshall's vivid style. Children will not only find the stories freshly appealing, but will have their own creativity inspired as they see the graphic interpretations of other children.

Nystrom, Carolyn. *Who Is God?* Illus. by Eira Reeves. Moody Press, 1993, 30 pp. (ps-up).

Children often have questions about God that sound simple but are surprisingly difficult for adults to answer with biblical accuracy and in a way that children can understand. How can I know God? What does God look like? Is God always fair? Can God be in more than one place at a time? Does God know what I think? The writer answers these and many more questions with an insight honed by her experience in answering many such questions posed by children from widely varying backgrounds. Lively, colorful illustrations brighten each page and help young readers see some of the many ways in which the nature of God relates to their here-and-now lives.

St. John, Patricia. A number of books by this writer. Moody Press.

See listings under *Literature: Level III, Realistic Stories—Modern*

These stories have a clear, specifically Christian message that is well integrated into the flow of events in natural, credible ways. Young people see how to apply belief and a commitment to do God's will to the problems and decisions they must deal with in daily life.

Sanderson, Ruth. *Tapestries*. Little, Brown and Co., 1998, 32 pp. (3-6).

In an "Author's Note," Ruth Sanderson speaks of her love of tapestries, those intricately woven wall hangings so rich in color and design. In retelling directly from the biblical accounts the stories of twenty-three women of the Bible, the artist/writer sees the women as part of the tapestry of faith, each one contributing the varied threads of her life to the overall design. Portrayed in softly glowing colors against lavishly detailed backgrounds, each woman and her story are woven into the whole. A deeply beautiful tapestry indeed.

Spier, Peter. *Noah's Ark*. Doubleday, 1977, 44 pp. (ps-3).

Spier's wonderful illustrations are a feast for the eye and the imagination. Except for a brief frontispiece quotation ("But Noah found grace in the eyes of the Lord") and a delightful translation of the poem "The Flood" by Jacobus Revius (1586-1658), Spier's book is without text. But his unique, incredibly detailed drawings make the beloved story live again in a fresh, vivid evocation. Not intended as a complete recounting of the biblical story, the book's focus on the graphic aspects of the ark, the flood, and the animals provides a supplement to the complete story that will delight readers of all ages.

Vos, Catherine F. *The Child's Story Bible*. Eerdmans, 1983 (1935), 382 pp. (1, 2— or up to 4 if desired).

All of the narrative portions of the Bible are told in a way children can understand. The stories are completely true to the Scriptures on which they are based, but the writer has also included some explanatory material, just as a parent would do in making the story clear to a child. An excellent way to begin to instill a comprehensive knowledge of the Bible as a whole in the minds of children.

4

BIOGRAPHY

ADAMS, ABIGAIL

Bober, Natalie S. *Abigail Adams.* Atheneum, 1995, 248 pp. (6-up).

If Abigail Adams had not been a constant letter-writer throughout her life, this enthralling biography with its wealth of details about her life and times could not have been written. Wife of the nation's second president, John Adams, and mother of sixth president John Quincy Adams, Abigail was at the heart of momentous, historic years. The author has made extensive use of her letters and, along with other wide-ranging research, takes us into the personal world of a remarkable and warmly human woman. National events are an intrinsic part of her life, but we see them with a personal perspective. Deeply in love with her husband (and he with her) for all of the fifty-four years of their marriage, Abigail endures many long periods of intense loneliness while he is away serving the needs of the young, struggling nation. Devoted mother, faithful friend, woman of faith, advocate of education for girls, outspoken critic of slavery and racial prejudice, energetic homemaker, skilled manager of the always-meager family finances, avid reader, articulate conversationalist—the reader enjoys her company all through the book.

ALCOTT, LOUISA MAY

Meigs, Cornelia. *Invincible Louisa.* Little, Brown and Co., 1968 (1933), 260 pp. (6-up).

This is the classic biography of Louisa May Alcott, the much-loved author of *Little Women* and other favorite stories that are still read and treasured more than 130 years after their first appearance. In her life Alcott quietly embodied the strong, loving qualities of family devotion so evident in her writings. At the same time, she was far ahead of her day in supporting the right of young women to make independent choices and to live useful, authentic lives, free of the strictures of artificial and oppressive social patterns. By nature active and impatient, Louisa was also intelligent and acutely sensitive. As a child of only eleven, she began to realize that her family needed care of the sort that her beloved but ineffectual father never managed to provide. Louisa took upon herself the responsibility of someday being able to give each one the security and opportunity so desperately needed. She not only fulfilled this childhood dream, but she left in her books the heritage of a strong, idealistic response to living that continues to inspire successive generations of readers.

Ryan, Cary, editor. *Louisa May Alcott: Her Girlhood Diary*. Troll Associates, 1993, 42 pp. (5-up).

When Louisa May Alcott was ten years old, she began a diary in which she recorded not only daily activities but also her inner struggles and hopes. Although she wrote intensively over a number of years in what she called her "journal," she later destroyed most of the diaries. Some childhood entries have survived, however, and writer Cary Ryan has compiled these and provided a brief but comprehensive narrative background placing the entries in their setting and illuminating Alcott's early life. Much of *Little Women* is based on Louisa's own experiences, and she herself was the real-life Jo whom Louisa referred to as "a struggling human girl, like hundreds of others." She says ruefully, "I don't talk about myself, yet must always think of the willful, moody girl I try to manage, and in my journal I write of her to see how she gets on." Ryan's slim volume offers contemporary readers an opportunity to know Alcott better through the touching vulnerability of her inmost thoughts.

As an adult Alcott, through her widely read stories, undoubtedly did more than any other person of her time to combat wrongful social attitudes in the rearing of both boys and girls. Unfortunately, in narrator Ryan's desire to emphasize Louisa's independence, she frowns on the aspect of Louisa's training that encouraged her to recognize her own weaknesses and to learn to control them. Yet without the development of self-discipline and unselfishness in her life, the world would never have known Alcott's stories—and their reforming influence—that came from the heart of the woman she became. Overall, however, Ryan has done readers a welcome service in making easily accessible the poignant (and often amusing) outpourings from the heart of a remarkable young girl.

ANDERSON, MARIAN

Patterson, Charles. *Marian Anderson*. Franklin Watts, 1988, 159 pp. (6-up).

Marian Anderson, born in 1902, was not only blessed with the gift of magnificent song, but she also demonstrated in her life and musical career qualities of character that make her an inspiring role model for any young person. Surprisingly thorough for a biography written for middle school youngsters, Patterson's account takes the reader into the background of Anderson's life and the development of her career. Woven into the biography is the writer's consistent emphasis on the growth of Marian's character—the choices made; the unflinching dedication to work and the study of her art; the loyalty to, and love for, her family; her integrity and fairness in the business aspects of her career. Marian's poise and dignity when she encountered racial prejudice were unshakable, and she became one of the most admired women of her day. The first African-American to sing at the Metropolitan Opera in New York, Anderson also spent much time abroad and was acclaimed internationally. One of her greatest joys, however, was in the recognition she won in America, the homeland she dearly loved—a recognition crowned when she was awarded the Presidential Medal of Honor.

Note: Marian Anderson's music is available in recorded form, and the story of her life would have special meaning if the reader were able to hear her incomparable voice. Such tapes or CDs may sometimes be borrowed from public libraries and are, of course, generally available for purchase.

ANGOULÈME
Powers, Elizabeth. *The Journal of Madame Royale.* Walker and Co., 1976, 150 pp. (5-up).

This moving account is based largely on the journal kept by Marie Thérèse Charlotte (her married name was Angoulème), daughter of Louis XVI and Marie Antoinette, and on firsthand writings of others close to the royal family. The princess (as the daughter of the king, the French titled her Madame Royale) was fourteen when the French Revolution started, and she and her family were imprisoned. Three years later she was released to exile in Austria. Her parents had been guillotined, and her young brother had died under mysterious circumstances. In her journal Marie Thérèse writes not only of her present experiences but also of the past and her life with her family before the violence of the Revolution. Hers is a view of those tragic events from an unusual and enlightening vantage point. The perspective is personal, and thus largely subjective, but whatever the political failings or cultural and moral blind spots of the French royalty, it seems unarguably true that they were subjected to degrading and inhumane treatment, behavior that was particularly unjust in the case of helpless children. The book is no longer in print, but because of its unique perspective, it is worth searching for in libraries.

ANTIN, MARY
Wells, Rosemary. *Streets of Gold.* Illus. by Dan Andreasen. Dial Books for Young Readers, 1999, 39 pp. (3-6).

In 1894 almost-thirteen-year-old Masha Antin (thereafter known as Mary) sailed into Boston Harbor with her family. Their dream had come true; they had reached America. The Antin family's home had been in Russia, but because they were Jewish, their lives were made very difficult; they had longed for freedom. Bad as things were, people were not prevented from leaving (as they often would be in future years under communism). Drawing from Mary's own written account, Wells vividly portrays the family's life in Russia, the long journey, and the new life they found in Boston. (Each episode of the narrative includes a quotation in Mary's own words, set in large type in the page margins.) Mary had always longed to go to school, but Jewish girls were not allowed to attend in Russia. Entering first grade knowing only the Russian language, Mary learned English well enough to transfer to the fifth grade within six months. An assignment given during her first year in school to write a poem about George Washington inspired her to write thirty-five stanzas. Mary's teacher, impressed with the accomplishment of her young pupil, took Mary and the poem to the *Boston Herald* newspaper. Calling the poem a tribute to freedom, the paper published it—all thirty-five verses. A charming, beautifully illustrated true story and a reminder of freedoms often taken for granted today.

ARCHIMEDES

Bendick, Jeanne. *Archimedes and the Door of Science.* Living History Library. Bethlehem Books, rev. ed. 1995 (1962), 143 pp. (5, 6-up).

Not a great deal is known about the details of the life of the great third-century-B.C. Greek mathematician Archimedes. Records of his discoveries and inventions and of a few personal characteristics remain, however, and the biographer has fitted these into the known material on the period's customs and events. Although mathematics was the subject in which Archimedes immersed himself, he made many related scientific discoveries and invented a number of practical machines and processes, copies of which are still being used today. In many ways, Archimedes helped to establish the scientific mode of inquiry, and thus all branches of science are strongly indebted to him. Good literary quality and a lively, humorous style characterize this well-told biography.

Note: Originally part of the old Immortals of Science Series published by Franklin Watts, the above title has been revised and reprinted. Copies of the books in this series (others of which we also list) are still on the shelves of many libraries. It is well worth making an interlibrary loan request for any of these books if your library does not have them.

AUDUBON, JOHN

Roop, Peter and Connie, editors. *Capturing Nature: The Writings and Art of John James Audubon.* Illus. by Rick Farley. Walker Publishing Co., 1993, 39 pp. (4-up).

Selected from various sources, some of Audubon's own writings about himself and his art (here effectively complemented by Farley's illustrations) have been brought together with reproductions of a number of his superlative paintings of birds. This autobiography is satisfying because it leaves the reader with some understanding of the life and purpose of the great naturalist-artist. Like many of those who have been gifted with unique creativity in a specific area, only one thing mattered supremely to Audubon—portraying the birds of America as perfectly as possible in the natural patterns of their lives. The years of traveling the country to observe birds; the endless hours of drawing, self-criticizing, redrawing; the financial disasters; the neglect of wife and home and the long wait for interest from others in his work— these all made sense to him because he fulfilled the purpose that had motivated his life. Today just the one word *Audubon* resonates with the heritage he left.

AYLWARD, GLADYS

Aylward, Gladys (as told to Christine Hunter). *Gladys Aylward, the Little Woman.* Moody Press, 1970, 150 pp. (6-up).

This version of the story of Gladys Aylward and her missionary work in China is Aylward's own account as told to Hunter, a professional writer. Shorter, less dramatized, and with a much stronger emphasis on Aylward's evangelistic work than Alan Burgess's *The Small Woman* (see below), this book, written later, adds a new dimension to her story. Both books should be read to fill in the complete picture. Burgess, a more gifted writer, includes much more material and wonderfully re-creates scenes, settings, and atmospheres. He conveys far more of the feel of China than does Hunter. On the other hand, Hunter focuses more fully on Aylward's primary purpose in being in China—winning people to personal faith in Christ. A recommendation would be to first read (or read aloud sections from) *The Small Woman* and then go on to *Gladys Aylward, the Little Woman*, which is more complete as to the spiritual aspects of Aylward's life and work but less rewarding in the literary sense.

Burgess, Alan. *The Small Woman.* Buccaneer, 1996 (1957), 256 pp. (adv. 5, 6-up or parent/teacher read-aloud).

The enthralling story of Gladys Aylward, a young English parlor maid who believes God is calling her to go as a missionary to China. Rejected at the end of a three-month probationary period at the China Inland Mission Training School in England (Gladys did not do well in the theology class, for example), she finally decides to go on her own. Hearing of an elderly, widowed independent missionary in North China who needs help, Gladys writes. The reply indicates that if Gladys can get herself there, they can try working together. Unable to afford steamship fare, Gladys pays three pounds down on a train ticket to China via Siberia. Each month the amount paid toward her ticket increases, and finally in October 1932, she is on her way. On the long journey danger, hardship, fear—and amazing deliverances—become everyday occurrences, a fitting prelude to her unique ministry in China. An absolutely gripping story, with the authentic flavor of a China that no longer exists.

BELL, ALEXANDER GRAHAM

Fisher, Leonard Everett. *Alexander Graham Bell.* Atheneum Books for Young Readers, 1999, 28 pp. (4-7).

This brief but comprehensive account of the life and accomplishments of one of America's foremost inventors and humanitarians does more than just tell about Bell. In the cogency, energy, and focused enthusiasm of his writing, Fisher conveys those same qualities in the character and life of his subject. Brilliant, gifted, and empowered with a desire to make life better and more effective for everyone, Aleck Bell, as he was called for most of his adult life, worked tirelessly on the creation of technological devices (with the telephone the most widely known) that became the basis for an endless stream of life-enhancing innovations and communication systems. Moreover, as he eventually became a man of wealth, he contributed generously to launch the careers of other promising and gifted people. An intensely caring man, Bell was involved for years in trying to help the deaf and was reportedly the one who brought Anne Sullivan into the life of the blind and deaf Helen Keller. This is an especially effective biography of a man whose life was full of achievement and inspiration.

BENTLEY, WILSON

Martin, Jacqueline Briggs. *Snowflake Bentley.* Illus. by Mary Azarian. Houghton Mifflin Co., 1998, 26 pp. (1-6).

Most children who live in cold-winter climates welcome the snows of winter. They love to see snowflakes falling, to watch the whiteness spread and deepen, to throw snowballs, make snowmen, and slide downhill on their sleds. But to Wilson Bentley, snow wasn't just something to play in. It was the most wonderful and beautiful thing in his life. Born February 9, 1865, in Jericho, Vermont—where annual snowfall is about 120 inches a year—Willie loved all of nature that surrounded him on the family farm—the flowers, butterflies, grasses, insects, and animals. But it was snow he wanted to study and the fragile, ephemeral beauty of each flake that he wanted to share with the world. But how could he do this when every snowflake he caught on a black tray simply melted away before he could draw the lovely designs? Martin's engagingly written picture biography tells how Wilson solved this problem and describes his life's work of capturing on film the unique beauty of countless snowflakes. Azarian's unusual woodcut illustrations are the ideal enhancement of Martin's story of this unusual man and his gift to the world.

BONHEUR, ROSA

Turner, Robyn Montana. *Rosa Bonheur.* Little, Brown and Co., 1991, 32 pp. (2-6).

Primary listing under *Art*

Robyn Turner's enjoyable picture biography tells the story of Marie Rosalie Bonheur (1822-1899), who was known as Rosa for most of her life. Her last name, Bonheur, means in French "happiness," "prosperity," "good fortune." And unlike the lives of so many artists, full of intense struggle, poverty, and turmoil—often without gaining recognition—most of Rosa's life echoed the joyful meanings of her name. Circumstances were often difficult during her childhood. Money was scarce, and her mother died when she was only eleven. Rosa, however, knew exactly what she wanted to do even though she lived in an era in which girls were not encouraged to become artists. She drew and painted for hours at a time, day after day. Her father, a competent but not outstanding artist, was happy to teach his daughter to draw, but because she was a girl, he feared she would not be able to make her living as an artist. Rosa simply persisted; she had always loved animals and was increasingly drawn to portraying them so perfectly that they looked ready to walk out of the painting. At nineteen Rosa had her first exhibit at the Salon, the annual art show in Paris. Continuing to study and paint tirelessly, she created paintings that had a great appeal for the lovers of both art and animals. By the time Rosa was twenty-six, she had become famous. Her paintings were selling for substantial sums, and for the rest of her life Rosa Bonheur continued painting and was, like her name, happy, prosperous, and blessed by good fortune.

BOWDITCH, NATHANIEL

Latham, Jean Lee. *Carry On, Mr. Bowditch.* Houghton Mifflin, 1955, 251 pp. (5-6).

A biography in story form, this account of the life and achievements of sea captain and mathematician Nathaniel Bowditch (born in New England in 1773) reads like fiction. But in addition to holding the reader's interest with the suspense, tragedy, and triumph of Nathaniel's life, the book also offers excellent historical background on the young American nation. Fine values are reflected throughout. Still in print after forty-five years, this excellent and enjoyable book has become a classic.

BOYLE, ROBERT

Sootin, Harry. *Robert Boyle: Founder of Modern Chemistry.* Immortals of Science Series. Franklin Watts, 1962, 133 pp. (6-up).

Primary listing under *Nature, Science, and Technology*

In Sootin's well-researched biography, Boyle emerges not just as a scientist, but as a human being, a man living in the seventeenth century with a family intimately involved with the turbulent issues of the day. Many interesting sidelights in this regard, and on his family in general, are included. In addition to his dedication to scientific inquiry and to the open dissemination of all new scientific discoveries, Boyle was also a devout Christian who believed there was no conflict between religion and science, but that on the contrary it was God who had designed the natural laws people were slowly discovering. Boyle's work more than 300 years ago is still an integral part of the basis for today's chemistry and physics. Long out of print, this biography is well worth a special request at the library.

BRAILLE, LOUIS

Freedman, Russell. *Out of Darkness: The Story of Louis Braille.* Illus. by Kate Kiesler. Houghton Mifflin, 1997, 81 pp. (4-6).

The inspiring story of the man who invented the system of raised dots that enables the blind to read. Accidentally blinded as a small child, Louis Braille was not only gifted intellectually and musically, but was also blessed with an exceptionally kind and giving nature. As a student in France's only school for the blind, Louis learned readily from hearing material read to him. However, he longed for access into the wider realms of printed materials—and he wanted this for others as well. Previous systems employing raised letters or dots and dashes had proved completely unworkable, but Louis believed that the basic concept of using fingertip touch and some system of raised dots was sound. Years of work resulted in an effective system; yet it was more years before the government would develop its potential. Recognition finally came in 1844. Although Braille died of tuberculosis eight years later at forty-three, his remarkable work lives on as sightless people the world over are enabled to read because of Braille.

Neimark, Anne E. *Touch of Light: The Story of Louis Braille.* Harcourt, Brace, Jovanovich, 1970, 186 pp. (4-6).

Out of print, perhaps permanently, this fine biography is still on the shelves in some libraries or obtainable through an interlibrary loan request. For the in-depth reader it offers a more detailed and extensive coverage of Braille's life than does Freedman's *Out of Darkness* and also includes the spiritual dimension in Braille's life. From early boyhood on, he had a sense of mission, believing that God wanted him to find a way to make it possible for other sightless people to be able to read.

BRAND, PAUL

Wilson, Dorothy Clarke. *Ten Fingers for God*. Zondervan, 1989 (1965), 304 pp. (6-up).

The enthralling story of Dr. Paul Brand and his work in restorative surgery and related rehabilitation of leprosy victims. The son of missionary parents in India, Brand was educated in England. In his early years he felt that the last thing he would ever do would be to become a doctor. But in an unusual pattern of events, his mind changed, and he was prepared for the remarkable contribution he was to make to thousands of lives. This biography wasn't written for children and is too long and too detailed for a majority of fifth or sixth graders, but some advanced readers might enjoy it. In general, a broader use with children would be to read sections aloud, something the book lends itself to quite well in its narrative that moves from one specific phase of Brand's life to another. Older children will be fascinated by Brand's medical discoveries and by the dramatic changes his surgery made in his patients' lives.

BRIDGMAN, LAURA

Hunter, Edith Fisher. *Child of the Silent Night: The Story of Laura Bridgman*. Houghton Mifflin, 1963, 128 pp. (1-4).

Simply but effectively written, this is the story of how a little deaf and blind girl learned to read and to communicate. At that time the use of Braille had not yet been accepted even in its inventor's own country, France, and was unknown in America. Using raised letters of the alphabet on labels attached to familiar objects (a cumbersome and limited method), teachers at the Perkins School for the Blind began the difficult task of educating Laura Bridgman. This was in 1837, preceding Helen Keller by some years. The book is excellent reading for young students and a fine way to encourage greater understanding of those handicapped in vision or hearing.

BURBANK, LUTHER

Quackenbush, Robert. *Here a Plant, There a Plant, Everywhere a Plant Plant! A Story of Luther Burbank*, rev. ed. 1998 (1982), Luther Burbank Home, 36 pp. (1-5).

A brief, contemporary-style biography of Luther Burbank (1849-1926), the American plant genius who developed many new varieties of fruits, vegetables, and flowers. The most widely known of these are probably the Burbank potato and the Shasta daisy. The writer's fast-moving, humorous approach serves to introduce Burbank and his work in an easy-to-read, appealing way.

CALDECOTT, RANDOLPH

Lewis, Marguerite. *Randolph Caldecott, the Children's Illustrator.* Alleyside Press, 1992, 48 pp. (4-up).

More than sixty years ago a new annual award was instituted by the American Library Association. This honor was to go to the illustrator of the chosen picture book of the year and was named for the nineteenth-century English artist Randolph Caldecott (1846-1886). He is considered by many to be the first children's book illustrator. The initial Caldecott Medal was awarded in 1938, and receiving the award continues to be a prestigious honor. Randolph's love for drawing was so inborn and so strong that it shaped and defined his life. His father was a tailor and hatter, widowed when the boy was only six. A serious bout with rheumatic fever left Randolph with fragile health, and he was allowed to stay in school (rare in working-class families of the day). Randolph spent as much time as he could in the woods and fields. Even then he could make the pictures of the little animals he loved to draw look amazingly lifelike, with subtle touches of humor and personality. Starting as a young teenager, he worked patiently and cheerfully for some years as a bank clerk, drawing when he could. His passion for drawing never lessened, and eventually his work was increasingly used by papers and magazines. A series of children's books that he illustrated established him as an artist and especially as a children's illustrator. Finally he was enabled to draw full time. Randolph never became entirely well and strong, and he died a month before his fortieth birthday.

CARVER, GEORGE WASHINGTON

Adler, David A. *A Picture Book of George Washington Carver.* Illus. by Dan Brown. Holiday House, 1999, 30 pp. (ps-3).

This colorfully illustrated picture biography provides a brief but informative overview of the life and remarkable achievements of George Washington Carver. Born into slavery near the end of the Civil War, he was orphaned at an early age. Although he was still a small child when slaves were freed, George had to struggle not only to survive, but also to gain the education he wanted more than anything else. The story of how he accomplished this is an inspiring one.

Even as a child, Carver loved plants and animals, and he developed a talent for drawing and painting them. As he matured, however, a lifelong desire to help his own people caused him to focus on the practical uses of plants, and this became his life work. It was Carver who recognized the potential value of peanuts and yams in the agricultural South. Over the years he made discovery after discovery about how to improve and use these and other plants. (Children enjoy learning that it was Carver who developed peanut butter.) He became one of the first African-Americans to bring widespread and permanent economic help to many of his people. A man of great faith, Carver believed that each discovery was a message from God and refused to accept money for any of them. He lived frugally as a teacher and researcher at the Tuskegee Institute for fifty years, until his death in 1943.

Carey, Charles W., Jr. *George Washington Carver*. The Child's World, Inc., 1999, 39 pp. (2-6).

Written for older children, Carey's account offers substantially more text than Adler's (above) and many additional details about Carver's life and work. Moving chronologically through Carver's life, the book offers a wealth of photographs with captions that do not simply identify the picture but include related material as well. Carey goes into Carver's life in some depth; for example, his enlightening comments on Carver's work at the Tuskegee Institute include a description of his relationship with students and methods he devised for effective communication with young people who arrived ill-prepared for college studies. Carver was a loved mentor whom his students never forgot.

Note: The above two books nicely complement each other, and it would help older children in acquiring a good, basic knowledge of Carver's life and work to read both.

COLUMBUS

d'Aulaire, Ingri and Edgar Parin. *Columbus*. Illus. by author. Beautiful Feet Books, 1996 (1955), 64 pp. (k-6).

As in their other large picture-and-text biographies, the d'Aulaires have combined literary excellence with art in a delightfully effective way. Lively and realistic, Columbus's story is told with wonderful little touches that encourage analysis and thought. For example, near the end of the book we read, "Many people say that Columbus was poor and forsaken in his old age. That is not true. He wasn't poor, but he was bitter because he was not the richest and mightiest seaman in the world. Columbus was a great man. But he was not a modest man. He wanted too much, and so he did not get enough."

DOUGLASS, FREDERICK

Douglass, Frederick. *Escape from Slavery: The Boyhood of Frederick Douglass in His Own Words*. Ed. and illus. by Michael McCurdy. Alfred A. Knopf, 1994, 61 pp. (5-up).

Frederick Douglass had longed for freedom from the moment he was old enough to understand his enslavement until he finally escaped when he was twenty-one. Douglass became one of the most powerful voices speaking for the abolition of slavery and equality for all. He felt it was important for everyone to realize what it meant to be a slave and what a slave's everyday life was like. For that reason he wrote his own story, describing the brutality, cruelty, and hopelessness of life as a slave. This particular edition of Douglass's autobiography is designed to make its contents more accessible to young readers. Retaining the writer's own words, it has excerpted sections just as they were written, briefly summarizing events that occurred between them. Abridgements and edited versions of books are often better avoided, but in this case the editor has done an excellent job of presenting a coherent account of Douglass's experience in his own words. Children may want to read the complete biography of this remarkable man in the future. In the meantime, this edition provides a vivid account of what it meant to live as a slave and of the power of the human spirit to transcend seemingly hopeless circumstances.

EDISON, THOMAS ALVA

Cousins, Margaret. *The Story of Thomas Alva Edison*. Random Books for Young Readers, 1981 (1965), 160 pp. (5-9).

The life of Edison (certainly one of history's most gifted—and nonconforming—men) makes highly interesting reading in this full-length biography. From early childhood on, Edison was uniquely his own person. Strong-willed, vigorous, curious, and not at all concerned about what other people thought of him, he fit no mold. Had he lived in the highly structured society of today, one can only speculate what might have become of him. As it was, he spent just three months in school, was tutored informally by his mother for about three years, and at twelve was out working a full day. Afflicted most of his life by deafness, he developed a tendency toward living a solitary life of preoccupation with his intense interest in scientific experiments and study. There was nothing planned, ordered, or conventional about Edison's life; his restless, questioning mind constantly drove him on. He drifted from job to job; at every opportunity he plunged into research, worked night and day, made remarkable discoveries, and took on new projects. Eventual recognition, continuing fame and honors, marriage, children, periods of wealth—nothing essentially changed this unique man and his burning compulsion to know more and to develop more and more devices that would contribute to people's comfort and enjoyment.

EQUIANO, OLAUDAH

Equiano, Olaudah. Adapted by Ann Cameron. *The Kidnapped Prince: The Life of Olaudah Equiano*. Alfred A. Knopf, 1995, 136 pp. (4-9).

An unusual true story of a young African boy from a ruling family sold into slavery in 1757 when he was twelve. Cameron has put into more contemporary language Olaudah's own story that he wrote in England in 1789. In a quiet, low-key way Equiano tells of his harrowing experiences. This story brings home the horror of slavery and of racial bigotry. No effort to be sensational is needed—the realities speak for themselves. Full of suspense and hope, the narrative builds to its triumphant climax when Equiano buys his own freedom.

Note: Ann Cameron's adaptation is based on the writer's own book, *The Interesting Narrative of the Life of Olaudah Equiano, or Gustavus Vassa, the African, Written by Himself*. (The name Gustavus Vassa was given to Equiano during his time of enslavement, but he kept and commonly used that name.) To preserve the flavor of the author's time, Cameron used Equiano's own words when possible, simplifying some of the language for today's readers. Speaking of the adaptation, Cameron says, "I did not add any ideas of my own to his story or fictionalize it in any way." An abridged version of Equiano's original book is currently in print, published by Heinemann in 1997, part of the African Writers Series.

ERATOSTHENES

Lasky, Kathryn. *The Librarian Who Measured the Earth*. Illus. by Kevin Hawkes. Little, Brown and Co., 1994, 48 pp. (3-up).

More than two thousand years ago a very intelligent Greek boy named Eratosthenes was full of questions about the natural world around him. He grew up to become a teacher, writer, and the chief librarian of the ancient world's great center of learning in Alexandria, Egypt. He never stopped wondering and learning. Questions about geography fascinated Eratosthenes, especially one: How big around was the earth? No one knew. Finding the answer—and the ingenious method he used to do so—are the heart of this biography. With the use of basic materials and his own gift for mathematics, Eratosthenes solved the problem. When the circumference of the earth was re-measured in the 1900s, there was a difference of only 200 miles between the modern-day figure and the one Eratosthenes calculated before the birth of Christ. Colorful illustrations on every page, filled with authentic details of ancient Greek and Egyptian settings, bring to life Lasky's captivating, excellently written text. Young readers will especially enjoy the warmth and humor in the account of this significant person who lived so long ago—and will perhaps, like Eratosthenes, never stop asking questions and finding answers.

FARRAGUT, DAVID

Latham, Jean Lee. *Anchors Aweigh: The Story of David Glasgow Farragut*. Harper and Row, 1968, 273 pp. (5-9).

The adventurous, action-filled life of Farragut, the famous American naval officer, is splendidly told here. Farragut's navy career began in 1810 when he was only nine years old. Captain David Porter, a friend of the boy's father, began the youngster's training, and others who saw his ability and promise were later instrumental in teaching him mathematics, foreign languages, and seamanship. Daring, cool in the face of danger, and exceptionally determined, Farragut was put in positions of leadership from his youth onward. A Civil War hero, he became a rear-admiral when Congress created the new rank and bestowed it on him. Two years later he was made a full admiral. Qualities of courage, determination, and loyalty are reflected throughout this story of Farragut's life. This is another splendid out-of-print book, retained here in the hope that parents and teachers will search their public libraries and make interlibrary loan requests if necessary to find it.

FIBONACCI, LEONARDO

Gies, Frances and Joseph. *Leonard of Pisa and the New Mathematics of the Middle Ages*. New Classics Library, 1983 (1969), 128 pp. (6-up).

Primary listing under *Mathematics*

A fascinating account of the life and work of Leonardo Fibonacci, brilliant thirteenth-century Italian mathematician. His book on the use of the Hindu/Arabic system of numbers, the system we use today, played a significant part in the mathematical revolution that made so many modern concepts possible. The book is well written and full of colorful sidelights on the culture of the time.

FRANKLIN, BENJAMIN

d'Aulaire, Ingri and Edgar Parin. *Benjamin Franklin*. Illus. by author. Doubleday, 1985 (1950), 48 pp. (1-4).

This splendid biography of Franklin is lively, accurate, and beautifully written, with a wealth of fascinating detail about this famous American. The large, lavishly illustrated picture-book format includes substantial text as well. Franklin was not only one of our nation's founders and a gifted diplomat who worked tirelessly for many years both at home and in Europe for the benefit of the United States, but he was also gifted in his scientific vision and his wide-ranging inventiveness.

Franklin, Benjamin. *The Whistle*. Illus. by George Overlie. Lerner, 1974 (1779), 32 pp. (3, 4-up).

A wonderful little autobiographical story about not paying too high a price—for either objects or men's regard. The woodcut illustrations and attractive over-all graphics pleasingly enhance the words of wisdom written more than 200 years ago by one of early America's legendary figures. Out of print, but well worth searching for at libraries.

Giblin, James Cross. *The Amazing Life of Benjamin Franklin*. Illus. by Michael Dooling. Scholastic Press, 2000, 48 pp. (3-7).

The essence of Benjamin Franklin's character and significant highlights of his life are effectively captured in this concise, highly readable picture biography. Even for those who eventually want to know more details about Franklin's life, Giblin's book provides an ideal introduction to this unique man: printer, writer, inventor, civic reformer, humanitarian, and an American founding father who spent years of his life in public service. The author's excellent text is splendidly complemented by Dooling's fine, meticulously researched illustrations.

Note: The d'Aulaire biography (above) has been retained, along with adding Giblin's book. Not only are they both well worth reading, but in some cases small, low-budget libraries might have only one of the two books.

FRITZ, JEAN

Fritz, Jean. *Surprising Myself*. Richard K. Owen Publishers, Inc., 1992, 32 pp. (3-6).

Popular children's author Jean Fritz has written a warm, informal autobiographical sketch that introduces herself: She grew up in China and now lives in Dobbs Ferry, New York; she takes her vacation every year on an island in the Caribbean; she has a daughter and son and two grandsons. She also tells young readers something about how a writer does her work. Fritz speaks of how she "finds" stories, telling what triggered the idea behind several of hers. She speaks also of visits to story-site places, note-taking, research in libraries, reading, and her choice to write first by hand, crossing out and rewriting as she goes, and finally typing up the finished copy. Excellent photographs abound. Having read this little autobiography, children may better appreciate reading her books and will also have a new awareness of what is involved in an author's work. Some of Jean Fritz's books are listed elsewhere in *Books Children Love*.

GALILEO

Hightower, Paul. *Galileo: Astronomer and Physicist.* Enslow Publishers, Inc., 1997, 128 pp. (5-up).

Primary listing under *Nature, Science, and Technology*

Galileo had one of history's brilliant minds. His life (1564-1642) was defined by his work. Early in his study of science, he emphasized the importance of demonstrating theories with practical experiments and established evidence, rather than simply believing unquestioningly the unproven views of some accepted authority. Like all such thinkers, he encountered frequent opposition and was never one of the "good old boys" of the university faculties where he taught. The author recounts the controversies in Galileo's professional life, which were intensified by his feisty nature and lack of tact and diplomacy. The fact that he was repeatedly proven right didn't add to his popularity, though his scientific reputation grew steadily over the years.

The most significant controversy of Galileo's life was his repudiation of Aristotle's view of the centrality of the planet earth and his own correct belief that the earth revolved around the sun. This issue is briefly discussed in the primary listing and thoroughly covered in the book itself. A clear, readable account of the life and work of one of the pillars of scientific thought.

GEHRY, FRANK

Greenberg, Jan and Sandra Jordan. *Frank O. Gehry: Outside In.* Dorling Kindersley Publishing, 2000, 47 pp. (5-9).

Twenty years ago architect Frank O. Gehry and his family had outgrown their small apartment. Not affluent enough at that time to build his "dream house," Gehry bought a modest old house that to him was unbearably conventional. "I didn't want to destroy it," he said. "I thought if I built a house around it so you could look inside and see the old house, there would be some historical continuity for the neighborhood." At the time, the unquestionably *un*conventional "wrap" that he created was viewed with outrage. Yet today, say the writers of this beautiful and splendidly-written picture biography, "The . . . house fits in somehow. . . . Part of the job of artists and architects is to show us what we will like next year or in ten years, not what we already like." "Think differently" is a concept Gehry embodies, and it is this ability to envision forms never before seen in architecture that has made him a groundbreaker in his field. Architect of the widely acclaimed Guggenheim Museum in Bilbao, Spain (opened in 1997), and of other spectacular contemporary buildings in the United States and Europe, Frank Gehry and his work graphically demonstrate the worth of pursuing a valid inner vision. Excellent, engaging writing, wonderful photography, and appealing typography characterize this book. A glossary of architectural terms, a bibliography, and a list of locations where some of Gehry's work can be seen all enhance this lively biography.

GRAHAM, MARTHA

Garfunkel, Trudy. *Letter to the World: The Life and Dances of Martha Graham.* Little, Brown and Co., 1995, 92 pp. (6-up).

Primary listing under *Dance, Drama, and Other Performances*

From the age of seventeen until her death at almost ninety-seven, Martha Graham's life was dance, and it is dance that is the focus of this biography. Graham's feeling about her work had an almost religious quality. As the writer comments, "[W]hen asked why she chose to become a dancer, she answered, 'I did not choose. I was chosen.'" Graham always possessed an urgency to communicate universal human experiences and emotions through dance. She was one of the pioneers of modern dance and came to be considered by many its foremost creator and arbiter.

Martha was in her last year of high school when she saw a poster advertising the performance of a notable dancer/choreographer. Although Martha had never had a dance lesson in her life, seeing just one of this dancer's programs set her on a path from which she never deviated. Dancer, choreographer, teacher, known the world over and showered with honors and recognition, Martha Graham was one of those rare people with an early and absolute commitment to specific work that completely fills, and at the same time absorbs, their lives.

GREENE, BETTY

Benge, Janet and Geoff Benge. *Betty Greene: Wings to Serve.* YWAM Publishing, 1999, 193 pp. (5-up).

Not many people know the adventure-filled story of Betty Greene. Born in 1920, she was completely captivated as a small child by the thought of flying a plane. When she was seven, Charles Lindbergh made history with his solo flight across the Atlantic and became her hero of heroes; she knew that somehow she had to fly. Understanding parents and an uncle's generous sixteenth-birthday gift provided the flying lessons. A few weeks later Betty was soloing. But in 1936 only a few wealthy women could fly planes on a regular basis; careers in aviation for women were virtually nonexistent. Betty conscientiously tried to fit the mold of "suitable" career training, but her heart was not in it. Then a conversation with an elderly family friend sparked a dream in her that combined flying with serving foreign missions. At the same time, world-changing events were on the horizon that would play a large part in making what had seemed an impossible dream come true.

The writers' fast-moving narration includes a lot of flying—about which they speak knowledgeably and well—and also concerns a vision of service fulfilled. Most of all, this is the story of a remarkable woman of courage and commitment and the amazing series of opportunities that prepared her step by step for the work God had for her. Even Greene's ahead-of-her-time vision couldn't have pictured what lay ahead. An exciting and inspiring book from the Christian Heroes Series.

HARRIOT, THOMAS

Staiger, Ralph C. *Thomas Harriot, Science Pioneer*. Clarion Books, 1998, 128 pp. (6-up).

> Primary listing under *Nature, Science, and Technology*

> This story of Thomas Harriot and his work is as unusual as Harriot himself. A gifted thinker with a wide-ranging interest in the natural world, Harriot was well known during his lifetime and could have left a substantial legacy of carefully documented discoveries and frequently their practical application, had he chosen to do so. Instead, he is largely unknown today. It has taken the persistent detective work and painstaking research of a loosely organized group of scholars across the world (who call themselves the Harrioteers) to ferret out the evidence of Thomas Harriot's substantial and broad-spectrum contributions to science. Ralph Staiger has recounted a truly fascinating story of this enigmatic man: Oxford graduate, dedicated researcher and discoverer, keen observer, and questioner. In addition to the account of Harriot and his work, Staiger brings to life the Elizabethan era with its simmering ideas and bold ventures. Moving between the old world and the as-yet-unknown future, the thinkers and doers of Harriot's time were in the midst of profound change in the making—on the threshold of the modern world.

HUGHES, ARIZONA HOUSTON

Houston, Gloria. *My Great-aunt Arizona*. Illus. by Susan Condie Lamb. HarperCollins, 1992, 32 pp. (1-4).

> A teacher and writer, author Gloria Houston has written a loving and inspiring picture biography of her great-aunt, Arizona Houston Hughes. Growing up in the beautiful hills and hollows of North Carolina's Appalachian Mountains, Arizona loved her world of trees and flowers, school and chores—and Saturday night square dances. More than anything else, she loved to read and to picture all the faraway places she hoped to see someday. Yet Arizona never left the mountains; instead, she became a teacher. At first she taught children not so many years younger than she was. As the years went by, she taught *their* children—and then their grandchildren. She loved each child and shared her joy in reading and her dreams of faraway places with them all. Beautifully told and brought to visual life with Lamb's wonderful illustrations glowing on each page, this true and lovely story will not only warm hearts but also remind many of the special teacher who will never be forgotten and who, as Houston writes, "goes with us in our minds."

JACKSON, WILLIAM HENRY

Lawlor, Laurie. *Window on the West: The Frontier Photography of William Henry Jackson*. Holiday House, 1999, 132 pp. (5-up).

This splendid book brings together a breathtaking collection of photographs, a broad-spectrum view of the development of the American West during the last half of the nineteenth century, an "inside" look at the art and technology of photography as it became increasingly significant, and the life story of photographer William Henry Jackson (1843-1942). He missed by just ten months living for an entire century. Lawlor has done a remarkable job of balancing her material as she presents Jackson's life and work in an appealing and always interesting way, while at the same time relating it to the larger historical and cultural context.

Jackson's artistic vision was inborn. Almost entirely self-taught, by the time he was seventeen (in 1860), he was working as a retouching artist in a little Rutland, Vermont, photography studio. (At that time photography in America was just over twenty years old.) Jackson soon left retouching behind, but photography itself became his passion as he explored the West, wrestling the heavy, bulky, yet fragile photographic equipment up rocky mountainsides, taking pictures of a beauty and grandeur as yet largely unknown to Americans—or to the world. Not long before his death, Jackson spoke of the early years of his experience in the West as the most interesting period of his life, as he sought "to make all known to others." A glossary of photographic terms, a time-line of events, and an extensive bibliography are included.

JEFFERSON, THOMAS

Ferris, Jeri Chase. *Thomas Jefferson: Father of Liberty*. Carolrhoda Books, 1998, 112 pp. (4-8).

Quite apart from his notable achievements in public life (author of the Declaration of Independence, secretary of state, vice president and president of the United States—to name only a few), Thomas Jefferson was a man well worth reading about. Intellectually brilliant and with an exceptionally wide range of interests, he was also graciously human, full of concern for the welfare not only of his own family, but for that of the nation's people. He was a lifelong advocate of democracy and opposed the idea that only the elite should control government. Although he owned slaves (as did all but the poorest of Virginia's population), he tried repeatedly during his government service to initiate measures to limit and then phase out the practice. He was fiercely opposed and without the support of others was unable to achieve his goal. His hope remained that the next generation would realize the wrongness of slavery and end it forever.

During Jefferson's presidency he had the foresight to act quickly and decisively when the opportunity came to buy the Louisiana Territory from France in 1803. That purchase doubled the size of the existing United States. His final legacy to the nation he loved was his design and oversight of the building of the University of Virginia, opened the year before his death at age eighty-three on July 4, 1826. Excellently written, the book is a fine introduction to one of our nation's most influential early leaders.

KELLER, HELEN

Davidson, Margaret. *Helen Keller*. Illus. by Vicki Fox. Scholastic, 1989 (1973), 96 pp. (k-3).

A lively account of the life of Helen Keller written for early readers. The writer has focused effectively on the highlights of Keller's life, with a high proportion of the book dealing with her childhood and youth. Children are given a good introduction to the inspiring story of the little blind and deaf girl who became an educated and articulate woman.

Graff, Stewart and Polly Anne Graff. *Helen Keller*. Illus. by author. BDD Books for Young Readers, 1980 (1966), 80 pp. (2-6).

The Graffs' approach to the life of Helen Keller has a somewhat broader scope than Davidson's (see above) and tells more about Keller's adult life. Since these were such significant years, reading both books would round out the picture, and many early-grades children would be comfortable with the Graffs' book. The language in this account is not demanding, though a bit more sophisticated than that of Davidson.

KURELEK, WILLIAM

Kurelek, William. 2 books, companion volumes: *A Prairie Boy's Winter*. Houghton Mifflin, 1984 (1973), 48 pp.; *A Prairie Boy's Summer*. Tundra Books, 1996 (1975), 47 pp. (4-up, read to some in 2, 3).

Also listed under *Art* and *History*

Fine evocations of what it was like to grow up on a Canadian prairie farm in the 1930s. The son of a Ukrainian immigrant family, Kurelek went on to graduate from college and then, to the dismay of his father, to become a painter. From the other side of the years of struggle and conflict, the renowned artist remembers his boyhood and a distinctive way of life unknown to today's children.

Kurelek, William. *Lumberjack*. Houghton Mifflin, 1974, 48 pp. (4-up, read to some in 2, 3).

Primary listing under *Art*

The noted Canadian artist describes life in the lumber camps of another era. Working as a lumberjack in 1946 and again in 1951, Kurelek's memory retained even small details of that life. Simply, yet vividly told, the account preserves verbally (and pictorially) a way of life forever gone. (Lumbering is one of those processes that has completely changed since the early 1950s.) Both the fine text and the wonderfully realistic paintings (one on each facing page) take the reader to another time and place.

LA FLESCHE, SUSAN

Brown, Marion Marsh. *Homeward the Arrow's Flight*. Field Mouse Productions, 1995 (1980), 185 pp. (5, 6-up).

A moving biography of Susan La Flesche (1865-1915), who was raised on an Omaha Indian reservation, member of a remarkable family dedicated to helping their people. Susan finds that her calling is to aid the reservation Indians medically. Graduating from medical school at the head of her class, she becomes the first Native American woman doctor in history. One of the most appealing aspects of the book is the lively, strong-willed, warm-hearted personality of its central character, the indomitable Dr. Susan. But Brown's account of Susan's years of education in the East also includes much about the lives of Susan's family members: her father, Iron Eyes, her sisters and brother—gifted, dedicated people all.

LEATHERS, BLANCHE

Gilliland, Judith Heide. *Steamboat! The Story of Captain Blanche Leathers.* Illus. by Holly Meade. Dorling Kindersley Publishing, Inc., 2000, 32 pp. (ps-3).

Blanche is eight years old. Two years after the end of the Civil War, peacetime traffic moves again on the mighty Mississippi River. Her plantation home is near the river, and Blanche spends hours on the riverbank. She already knows many things about this sometimes wild, sometimes deceptively calm flow of water and the ships that navigate their way along its often treacherous surface. Blanche already knows what she wants to be when she grows up—a steamboat captain. The entertaining account of how her "impossible" dream comes true isn't a record of wishful thinking but of purpose, preparation—and some good fortune along the way. Vibrant with energy, the book's illustrations perfectly complement Blanche's story. Bursting with color and spiced with a myriad of fabric-pattern details, the pictures are not only enjoyable to see, but the effect is enhanced when the reader is aware that they were created with paper cutouts and bold splashes of paint. The concluding page tells more about the historical Blanche Douglas Leathers and includes a photograph of this unusual and far-seeing woman.

LEE, ROBERT E.

Marrin, Albert. *Virginia's General: Robert E. Lee and the Civil War.* Atheneum, 1994, 218 pp. (5-up).

Writer-educator Albert Marrin combines biography with an insightful study of a significant era in American history. Although Robert E. Lee's name is vaguely familiar to many contemporary Americans, few know much about him. Lee was a remarkable figure in our history, not simply because of his role in the Civil War but because of the goodness and integrity of his character. Marrin illustrates this with details of Lee's kindness, sense of justice, and unwavering faithfulness to duty. A devout Christian, he often prayed for God's guidance.

Marrin interweaves his account of Lee's life with a description of the tragic war in which he played a significant part. A graduate of West Point, Lee had spent his adult life as an officer in the Union army. On April 18, 1861, President Lincoln asked Lee to head the Union military forces. The most painful decision of his life now faced Lee. He hated slavery and was personally committed to the Union. Had Virginia not chosen to join the other southern states, he would have agreed to the president's request and led the fight for the Union. But when his state seceded, Lee believed the generations-long bond between his family and their state demanded his loyalty to Virginia. He resigned from the army and prepared to stand with the

Confederacy. Marrin's account of General Lee and of the Civil War as engaged in by the South is clear, balanced, and full of the human details that make history live. *Virginia's General* is plentifully illustrated and annotated and has an extensive bibliography and index.

Note: Marrin has also written with equal excellence of the Civil War as engaged in by the North: *Unconditional Surrender: U. S. Grant and the Civil War.*

LIDDELL, ERIC

Magnusson, Sally. *The Flying Scotsman*. Charles River Books, 1981, 191 pp. (5-up).

An inspiring biography of Olympic runner and missionary Eric Liddell (known most widely through the fine motion picture *Chariots of Fire*). The approach is journalistic rather than literary, but the writing is good journalism, treating its subject with integrity and accuracy. Liddell's warmth, Christian commitment, transparent simplicity, and unselfish love for others comes through strongly—yet there is nothing stuffy, self-righteous, or preachy either in Liddell himself or in the tone of the book. He was a remarkable man, one who truly lived his deeply held faith. Liddell's life story is both highly interesting and spiritually challenging to read.

LINCOLN, ABRAHAM

Harness, Cheryl. *Young Abe Lincoln: The Frontier Days, 1809-1837*. Illus. by the author. National Geographic, 1996, 32 pp. (3-6).

What kind of boy born to poor, unschooled parents grows up to become one of America's two greatest presidents? What could have started him on a path so different from any followed by those around him? These and other questions about Lincoln's early years are answered in an attention-holding text and bursting-with-life illustrations that take the reader right into the heart of Abe Lincoln's boyhood and youth. Both illustrations and text have been carefully researched, with the informative material smoothly woven into the appealing narrative, surrounded by authentic scenes and people who look as though they had just walked onto the pages from Midwestern America in the early 1800s. Thus, along with Lincoln's own story, readers see a vivid picture of a significant part of American life, an important scene in the drama of United States history.

Marrin, Albert. *Commander in Chief: Abraham Lincoln and the Civil War*. Dutton Children's Books, 1997, 246 pp. (5-up).

This excellent account of President Lincoln, on whom the responsibility rested most heavily both to preserve the Union and bring a decisive end to slavery, shows him as a very human man rather than as a remote historical figure. Marrin's writing is always meticulously researched, but his work is far more than an account of factual events. The writer injects a story quality that makes the book highly readable, while maintaining historical accuracy. Vivid description, personal details of Lincoln's life, and lively narrative all benefit from the author's fine use of language and overall literary skill.

As war in all its horror becomes a reality, Lincoln struggles with enemies in the Congress, problem generals on the battlefield, and his own constant, compassionate awareness that every battle—even if a victory for the Union—means the death of many mothers' sons on both sides of the conflict. Marrin gives a balanced picture of Lincoln, the determined commander-in-chief, and Lincoln, the weary, burdened man, conscious of his own human weaknesses, wondering if he has made a wise decision in this or that situation, grieving the terrible consequences of all-out military assaults. A wealth of illustrations, many end notes, an extensive bibliography, and complete index add to the breadth and usefulness of the book.

LINDBERGH, CHARLES A.

Giblin, James Cross. *Charles A. Lindbergh: A Human Hero.* Houghton Mifflin, 1997, 212 pp. (4-up).

Charles Lindbergh barnstormed through the Midwest in the early 1920s—wing-walking on an old biplane and parachuting from perilously low altitudes. He was one of a handful of restless and often reckless young men enthralled with the newness and excitement of flight and glad to be making a risky livelihood doing something that would let them fly. Lindbergh had dropped out of his mechanical engineering program in his sophomore year of college, unable to find interest in his classes. He headed for an aviation company in Nebraska that had advertised a flight instruction program. There he had his first plane ride and, completely unaware of what lay ahead, began the ascent that within five years catapulted him into worldwide fame, superhero status, and the pages of history. But there was much more than that to the young aviator's life, and the author tells it well—from Charles's family, his earliest days, the transition into his preoccupation with flying, and his meteor-like rise to fame. The chronicle continues through later flying achievements, personal joys and tragedies, and the further complexities of his mature years—issues undreamed of by the "Lucky Lindy" of the solo flight from New York to Paris in May 1927. An even-handed and perceptive biography about one of America's best-known, yet often puzzling twentieth-century heroes.

LOBEL, ANITA

Lobel, Anita. *No Pretty Pictures: A Child of War.* Greenwillow Books, 1998, 193 pp. (6-up).

For years children's book illustrator and author Anita Lobel resisted suggestions and urgings to write about her childhood experiences during World War II. Living in the United States since 1951, Lobel has never gone back to her native Poland. Long-past trauma can keep its "no revisiting" signs up for many years—sometimes permanently. Now a grandmother, the writer finally goes back—not literally, but in the kind of remembering that re-creates the years of bewilderment, separation, danger, hardship, and overwhelming anxiety that began for the five-year-old Jewish girl and her three-year-old brother when the Nazis invaded Poland. This massive aggression not only triggered the war but began the infamous persecution and slaughter of Polish Jews.

Lobel's brilliant re-creation speaks quietly of the years of flight and pursuit, of fear and capture, of imprisonment and eventual release at war's end for her brother, their nanny, and herself—all recalled in the way it was perceived in her childhood mind. It is important for older children today in their free and sheltered lives to know what can be unleashed when evil becomes the law of a nation and what wanton hatred and brutality was poured out on men, women, youths, and little children—simply because they were Jews. When the allied armies defeated Hitler's Nazis, freedom was restored to Anita and her family—eventually reunited. One story among millions (and with a more fortunate ending than many)—a story worth knowing.

LONGFELLOW, HENRY WADSWORTH

Holberg, Ruth Langland. *An American Bard: The Story of Henry Wadsworth Longfellow*. Harper and Row, 1963, 168 pp. (6-up).

The most popular American poet of his day, Longfellow is still read in some schools, though literary critics have not looked kindly on his work for many years. Simple, straightforward, usually strongly rhymed and often sentimental, the poetry of Longfellow is largely seen as belonging to the past. Yet a real part of our American literary heritage, and linked closely with our history and national legends are such treasured pieces as "The Village Blacksmith," "Paul Revere's Ride," "The Courtship of Miles Standish," "Evangeline," "The Story of Hiawatha," and others. Holberg tells the story of the gentle, book-loving man whose chief desire from boyhood on had been to write poetry. For some years it was necessary for Longfellow to earn a living as a professor of modern languages, first at Bowdoin, then for many years at Harvard. Then his writing of poetry had to be done as he could find the time. His life was darkened twice by the death of a loved wife, but in spite of tragedy and loss, he retained his warm, outgoing spirit. Before he was fifty, his poetry had become so popular that he was able to leave teaching and devote himself solely to his literary career. He was honored widely both in Europe and at home. Now out of print, this enjoyable biography is still worth looking for on library shelves or through interlibrary loan.

MANJIRO

Blumberg, Rhoda. *Shipwrecked!: The True Adventures of a Japanese Boy*. HarperCollins Children's Books, 2001, 80 pp. (3-7).

Manjiro, born in 1827 on the smallest of Japan's main islands, expected to spend his life in the dismal poverty of a little fishing village. When he was nine, his father died, leaving him responsible for the support of his mother, four younger siblings, and an invalid older brother. There was no possibility for a young man, regardless of his abilities, to rise above the level of society in which he had been born. Such an attempt was illegal, and punishment for an infraction of any of the hundreds of suffocating laws was very harsh. At fourteen, after five years of labor on fishing boats, Manjiro was able to join a group of three brothers and their friend as a full-fledged crew member on their small fishing boat.

Unknowingly, Manjiro was embarking on an adventure that would take him across much of the world, put him in America for some time, and reveal his undreamed of brilliance of mind and ability. One day he would help Japan move out of the dark ages and into the world of nations from which it had isolated itself for centuries. Beautifully written and illustrated; filled with action, suspense, and amazing people, *Shipwreck!* is the fascinating true story of a remarkable (and most likable) person.

MOODY, RALPH

Moody, Ralph. *Little Britches.* W. W. Norton and Co., 1962 (1950), 250 pp. (5-up).

This remarkable account of three years in the author's boyhood reads like fiction but reflects authentic experience and emotion. Ralph's father has been fighting illness, his lungs severely damaged by work in the woolen mills of New Hampshire. A well-meaning but not fully reliable relative in Colorado urges the sight-unseen purchase of a ranch near Denver. In 1906 the Moody family—father, mother, Ralph, and his four brothers and sisters—move to what turns out to be marginal land and a tumbledown shack. Ralph has just had his eighth birthday, but in the difficult circumstances he, the eldest son, is soon seriously involved, along with his father, in the work of family survival. A father and mother of remarkable character and the often self-willed, sometimes mischievous, and wholly lovable young Ralph are the central figures in this saga of courage, determination, ingenuity, and family devotion.

Life in Colorado is not only full of exhausting toil, danger, suspense, and crisis but of loyal friendships and family celebrations as well. In the world of the ranches around him, Ralph learns a somewhat hazardous but wonderfully satisfying new skill and finds his own special niche. An unusual and enthralling true story that underscores the strength and value of family bonds and bone-deep integrity.

Note: Parents will want to be aware that there are a few brief and scattered instances of mild profanity used by some occasional characters in the story. Just one notable instance occurs in the latter part of the book in which the cowboy/rancher group express intense emotions with a cluster of profanity. In a family read-aloud project, parents can omit these sentences.

NIGHTINGALE, FLORENCE

Armentrout, David and Patricia. *Florence Nightingale.* People Who Made a Difference Series. Rourke Publishing, 2002, 24 pp. (1-3).

This brief but effective biography outlines the life of Florence Nightingale (1820-1910), the English nurse who made remarkable changes in the care of ill and injured people. Born into an affluent family, Florence never wanted a life of luxury and social prominence. At seventeen she wrote in her diary that God had called her to a life of service. She began visiting the sick in hospitals, and in her early twenties felt sure that nursing was the work she was called to do, even though her family opposed her for some time. Whether it was nursing badly wounded British soldiers in a dirty, ill-managed hospital in Turkey during the Crimean War, opening a nurses' training school in London, or writing books on health care and the importance of cleanliness and high nursing standards in hospitals, Florence was true to her calling. She inspired many others to follow her example. Young children will enjoy being able to read a biography for themselves, a good introduction to learning about the world's true heroes and heroines.

OWENS, JESSE

Streissguth, Thomas. *Jesse Owens*. Lerner Publications Co., 1999, 112 pp. (5-8).

The last of ten children in their struggling family, James Cleveland Owens was born in 1913. Called "J. C." when he was small, he became Jesse when a teacher misunderstood the "J. C." The boy adopted the new name. Sharecropping in Alabama offered little for the future. Jesse's mother, Mary Emma, wanted better opportunities for her children. A move to Cleveland, Ohio, in the early 1920s wasn't a magical solution, but it did improve the quality of life for the Owens family. Jesse especially enjoyed the running in some of his physical education classes. A junior high teacher/track coach noticed the boy's running and jumping talents and began helping him train effectively. During the next few years, Jesse greatly improved his skills. By 1932 his coaches were preparing him for Olympic tryouts. The highlight of Jesse Owens's career was his stunning success in the 1936 Olympics in Berlin. He won four gold medals and set three new world records, but the most significant triumph was the refutation of Hitler's racist theories through these victories by an African-American.

PAIGE, SATCHEL

Cline-Ransome, Lesa. *Satchel Paige*. Illus. by James Ransome. Simon and Schuster, 2000, 30 pp. (1-5).

Satchel Paige would have been the last person to think of himself as a role model. As an individual, he was an example of the uniquely talented person who discovers at an early age that he can do one thing supremely well and finds great satisfaction in developing and using his gift to the full. Born in 1906, the seventh of the twelve Paige children, Satchel was always large for his age. The youngster soon learned that he needed to find ways to help his family meet their needs. He began carrying passengers' luggage at the local train station, acquiring his lifelong nickname "Satchel." Meanwhile, in his free time he was practicing a skill that would be lastingly significant to him. Satchel had found that he loved to pitch a baseball more than anything else. He moved into the Negro League majors at eighteen. (This was before the regular major leagues had any African-American players.) Satchel had already gained a following and loved the life of a professional player. He even enjoyed the travel and played in a number of other countries. By 1948, when he was forty-two, the color barrier had come down. He was recruited by the Cleveland Indians and became the first African-American to play in a World Series—a tremendous milestone on the road to equality for blacks. Inducted into the Baseball Hall of Fame in 1971, Satchel Paige remains a landmark figure not only in the annals of baseball, but as a symbol of one more area of this nation's culture from which African-Americans were no longer excluded.

PASTEUR, LOUIS

Smith, Linda Wasmer. *Louis Pasteur: Disease Fighter*. Enslow Publishers, Inc., 1997, 128 pp. (4-8).

Primary listing under *Nature, Science, and Technology*

Louis Pasteur's parents, and later his wife and children, were all-important to him. But in company with almost all outstanding scientists, his life was his work. Writer Linda Smith has done an excellent job of providing extensive background information and of describing and explaining just what it was that Pasteur accomplished, relating it effectively to him as a person. Most of us today take for granted Pasteur's great discoveries and interventions in science, particularly in the area of infection and disease. We may know, for example, that he is responsible for pasteurization and for the rabies vaccine, but we may never stop to think of the lives saved and the human misery averted by just these two of Pasteur's many achievements. As we read of Joseph, the nine-year-old boy badly bitten by a rabid dog, and of Pasteur's deep concern and anxiety for him, the human side of the often stern, work-obsessed scientist is revealed.

The writer's clear, well-organized account brings to life the problems confronting Pasteur as he and others were trying to find answers to how disease is spread and how infection could be successfully treated. This volume is one of the biographies in the Great Minds of Science Series.

PATERSON, KATHERINE
Cary, Alice. *Katherine Paterson.* The Learning Works, Inc., 1997, 136 pp. (4-8).

A lively, insightful biography that gives the reader a true sense of getting to know this well-liked writer. The middle child of Raymond and Mary Womeldorf, missionaries in China, Katherine lived a happy, carefree life until her fifth year. Within that period her two younger sisters were born, and the family was called back to America for an indefinite stay. This was 1937, and Japan's pre-World War II incursions into China, along with China's own internal conflicts, made conditions unsafe. Katherine had already been struggling with her displacement as the family's youngest child and fear at the upheaval in the country. Now she had to learn to live in a very different country and to be the "new kid"—not just once, but in a succession of schools. Overwhelmed by the thoughtless—sometimes even malicious—cruelties children often inflict on a small, shy newcomer and frightened by a lack of warmth and encouragement in her teachers, Katherine entered a long, difficult period of her life. One day Katherine would draw upon her experience of childhood suffering to write stories—and even to win a coveted Newbery Medal. The little girl who was made to feel stupid and unworthy became a gifted woman for whom the demonstration of acceptance and unconditional love is of utmost importance. An inspiring life story.

POTTER, BEATRIX
Aldis, Dorothy. *Nothing Is Impossible.* Peter Smith, 1988 (1969), 156 pp. (3-7).

Shy, lonely, and dominated by self-centered parents who had little or no understanding of a child's needs, Beatrix Potter nonetheless had an inner core of strength and determination—and a well of interest and talents that overflowed in spite of her narrowly restricted life. From the time she had been a small girl, Beatrix had kept little animals as pets. She also had a great love for the natural world and a remarkable talent for drawing. All of these aspects of her life came together with the delightful, whimsical quality of her imagination. Dorothy Aldis has written a warm and sympathetic account of the life and work of one of the most famous of children's writers, long beloved for her endearing stories, beginning with *The Tale of Peter Rabbit*.

Johnson, Jane. *My Dear Noel: The Story of a Letter from Beatrix Potter*. Illus. by the author. Dial Books, 1999, 30 pp. (1-3).

This lovingly illustrated and gently told story of Beatrix Potter and her friendship with Noel Moore and all his family adds richness to the background of Potter's first-published story, *The Tale of Peter Rabbit*. A friend of the Moore family before she became a noted children's writer, Potter was a favorite of the Moore children. She and Noel, the eldest, were especially close. While still quite young, Noel had a long illness during a time when Beatrix was traveling. Wanting to cheer and entertain the little boy even though she couldn't come to see him, she wrote him an illustrated letter that was the very first version of the Peter Rabbit story. Noel delightedly realized that the family of little rabbits was based on himself and the other children of his family. The Moores and Beatrix Potter remained friends over the years, and as Johnson tells us at the end of the book, Noel himself spent his adult life helping slum children as a priest in London.

RÖNTGEN, WILLIAM CONRAD

Cherman, Beverly. *The Mysterious Rays of Dr. Röntgen*. Illus. by Stephen Marchesi. Atheneum, 1994, 23 pp. (4-6).

Primary listing under *Nature, Science, and Technology*

One night in November 1895, German physicist William Conrad Röntgen (often spelled "Roentgen" in this country) was very slow in answering a call to dinner. Absorbed in his laboratory project, he finally came upstairs and ate hastily, muttering abstractedly, "I have found something interesting." Then he rushed back to his lab. He was testing electrical measurements and magnetic effects, and in the process he had just discovered a short-wave ray that he labeled "X" for "unknown." He found that these invisible rays passed through wood, flesh, or other nonmetallic objects and made possible the photographing of the internal structures of objects.

Recruited as a guinea pig for his experiments, Röntgen's wife felt distinctly queasy as she saw for the first time an unusual picture of her hand—like a photographic negative but showing each bone and looking uncomfortably like the hand of a skeleton. Describing his work with the mysterious ray at a scientific meeting, he demonstrated with the hand of one of the professors. Cheers broke out, and the "ray" (commonly called simply "X-ray") entered history. In 1901 Dr. Röntgen was awarded the first Nobel prize in physics. Unlike many people, he had no desire for personal gain and donated the prize money for university research. Author Cherman offers an effective portrayal of a dedicated scientist, the value of whose work is incalculable.

Note: For more details on Dr. Röntgen's process of discovery and a mention of the X-ray's many uses, see the primary listing.

ROOSEVELT, THEODORE

Harness, Cheryl. *Young Teddy Roosevelt.* Illus. by author. National Geographic Society, 1998, 38 pp. (3-6).

It would be difficult to imagine a more interesting way to read about America's most colorful president than to open this delightful book. As a frail, asthmatic little boy, "Teedie" (his family nickname) lifted weights, hiked, rode horseback, swam, and rowed to build up his spindly body. In college he not only studied hard, made many friends, joined clubs, and kept a variety of creatures such as snakes and a tortoise in his room, but he also boxed and wrestled. Theodore Roosevelt continued to follow new and different paths. He lived what he termed "the strenuous life": He worked on cattle ranches in the West, overcame personal sorrow and adversity, became a national hero leading his Rough Riders regiment in Cuba during the Spanish-American War, and went into politics because he loved America and wanted it to be a strong, good nation. At forty-two he was the youngest man ever to be president.

The lively text of the book is surrounded by the author's wonderful illustrations. Every page teems with color, life, and fascinating detail—so appropriate to what the book jacket calls Theodore Roosevelt's "fierce and lovable spirit."

RUTH, GEORGE HERMAN "BABE"

Burleigh, Robert. *Home Run.* Illus. by Mike Wimmers. Harcourt Brace, 1998, 30 pp. (1-5).

George Herman Ruth (1895-1948) was only nineteen—with a round, childlike face and chubby hands—when he began his major league career in baseball. The other players called him "Babe," and the name stuck. Burleigh's lyrically written little book uses a prose form, but it has the condensed power of poetry—an ode not only to Ruth but to baseball itself. Before "The Bambino" (Italian for "babe" and another often-used nickname of Ruth's) began demonstrating his remarkable affinity with the bat, home runs didn't happen that often. Even the best hitters weren't expected to produce them. The writer explains that the old techniques of hitting were quite different from today's. Babe Ruth didn't simply set records with his batting; he changed forever the game itself by the way he used a bat. The reader is at the plate with him as he "swung 'through the ball.' Always 'through the ball.'" Ruth's innovative ways of handling the bat caused it to meet the ball with tremendous power and just-right direction, generating home run after home run. Ruth's success was highly influential in all of baseball. Today the home run is an often seen—but always exciting—highlight of what is widely regarded as America's national game.

SHACKLETON, ERNEST

Kimmel, Elizabeth Cody. *Ice Story: Shackleton's Lost Expedition.* Clarion Books, 1999, 120 pp. (6-up).

Primary listing under *History and Geography*

Although this suspenseful account of Ernest Shackleton's 1914 expedition focuses on just one part of his life, nothing could more clearly reveal the nature and character of this remarkable man than the disastrous yet magnificent ordeal in the bitter cold and imprisoning ice of the Antarctic. By the time Shackleton was sixteen, he had gained his doctor-father's permission to go to sea and for ten years had a successful career in the British merchant marine. Still greater challenges were calling, however. Shackleton, at twenty-six, was accepted as a member of an expedition to the Antarctic. For the rest of his too-short life, the lure of this frozen and implacable land drew him back again and again.

Shackleton was more than an explorer and adventurer, however. He was a born leader of men—strong, responsible, kind, and fair. The welfare of the men under him was always a high priority. Not just in times of crisis, but day in and day out he knew the importance of high morale, and he routinely planned ways to keep spirits up and banish boredom. In turn, Shackleton's men had absolute confidence in him. They knew he would never let them down; no matter what, he believed there was always a way out, and he was determined to find it. These qualities of character were crucial as the ship *Endurance,* with Shackleton and his twenty-seven men, was finally immobilized by the ice. In the extended time that followed, it was Shackleton's ability to deal wisely and courageously with incredible hardships that finally brought each one through the long trial. An inspiring record of an unusual man. Splendid photographs bring Shackleton and his men and their long battle with ice, bitter wind, and raging seas to life.

Kostyal, K. M. *Trial by Ice: A Photobiography of Sir Ernest Shackleton.* National Geographic Society, 1999, 64 pp. (3-8).

Ernest Shackleton (1874-1922) was among the men we think of as the last great explorers. Born into a family of ten children, he had no interest in following in his father's footsteps as a doctor. Ernest sought action and adventure, and yet he had a lifelong love of reading and a lively imagination. At sixteen he persuaded his father to let him go to sea. He fitted right into the strenuous, often hazardous life in the merchant marine. At twenty-four he had qualified to command any British ship anywhere in the world. But by then he had begun to dream of a special kind of voyage. A hundred years ago Antarctica, the fifth largest of our planet's continents, was still largely unknown. Two-thirds the size of all North America, Antarctica is one of the coldest areas on earth. Its barren expanses, bitter winds, and endless ice, with the South Pole at its heart, challenged some of the most intrepid explorers of the day. In 1901 Shackleton joined the National Antarctic Expedition let by Robert Scott.

The remaining twenty-one years of Shackleton's life were inextricably bound to Antarctica. He led several expeditions himself and wanted intensely to reach the South Pole (no one had yet, until Norwegian explorer Roald Amundsen achieved that in 1911), to cross the continent, to overcome the almost insurmountable difficulties encountered in this most forbidding and unwelcoming continent on the globe. Shackleton never reached those goals; over and over he endured unbelievable hardships and misfortune. Yet he was knighted by England's king, and history now considers him one of the preeminent figures among explorers. Shackleton will ever be remembered for his role in saving the lives of the twenty-seven men with him after the loss of the ship *Endurance.* His courage and gifted leadership not only became a legend, but they continue to inspire fortitude and endurance in others. Full of action and suspense, this well-written biography is lavishly illustrated with wonderful on-the-scene photographs.

SHAKESPEARE, WILLIAM

Aliki. *William Shakespeare & the Globe.* HarperCollins Publishers, 1999, 48 pp. (3-up).

Primary listing under *Dance, Drama, and Other Performances*

Very little is actually known about William Shakespeare, one of the most famous men in the world. Most of what we know relates to the plays he wrote 400 years ago, from 1588-1613. Years of scholarly digging through official records in the places where he lived and in historical accounts and looking for clues in his writings provide the meager total of our knowledge about the gifted man whose insight into human nature, genius with the pen, and high sense of both tragedy and comedy left the world a remarkable legacy. Author Aliki provides a clear, helpful overview of what *is* known of Shakespeare's origins, family, years in London, his writing, and connection with early theaters—especially the Globe—and finally his return to his home in Stratford-on-Avon and his death at fifty-two.

Aliki's book is an easy-to-follow account and a fine way to become acquainted with the man whose plays are still very much alive today. We learn that Shakespeare invented some 2,000 words and expressions in the English language. More than 100 of these are listed at the end of the book, words and expressions we hear all our lives: "lonely," "moonbeam," " excitement," and "shudder"; "a tower of strength," "the crack of doom," "to be or not to be," "eaten me out of house and home." Shakespeare gave us words that have helped to make our versatile English language more widely applicable and more fully expressive of the emotions and the doings of a broad spectrum of human beings.

SINGER, ISAAC BASHEVIS

Singer, Isaac Bashevis. *A Day of Pleasure: Stories of a Boy Growing Up in Warsaw.* Farrar, Straus and Giroux, 1969 (1963), 227 pp. (6-up).

The noted Jewish author has collected a number of stories of his childhood in Poland and grouped them in this volume. The stories are beautifully written, but more than that, they open a window into the lives of Hasidic Jews (Singer's father was a rabbi) in Poland preceding and during World War I. It is a world of which most Americans are completely ignorant, and the reader is jolted by its strangeness and appalled by its poverty—an extreme poverty that in the Western world seldom coexists with scholarly study and the discussion of intellectual ideas. We see that poverty in this splendid account and are humbled by the courage and strength of character of many of its people.

Note: As a boy, Singer had theological questions—the kind that most children either encounter as they grow up or ask for themselves. It is helpful for parents to read the book first so that they can knowledgeably use the opportunity to discuss the questions.

TALLCHIEF, MARIA

Tallchief, Maria with Rosemary Wells. *Tallchief: America's Prima Ballerina*. Illus. by Gary Kelley. Viking, 1999, 28 pp. (ps-4).

Primary listing under *Dance, Drama, and Other Performances*

In this brief, charmingly illustrated autobiography, Maria Tallchief herself looks back and reminisces about her early life and the significant choices involved in becoming a ballet legend. Born Elizabeth Marie, the daughter of an Osage Indian father and a Scots-Irish mother, Tallchief enjoyed a comfortable, even privileged childhood. She received early training in ballet and the piano and was gifted in both. As a teenager, however, she had to make the difficult choice between them, giving up the piano for ballet. Maria's parents had moved from Oklahoma to Los Angeles in order to give their daughter broader opportunities. Once the decision had been made as to her artistic goal, Maria committed herself fully to the years of intense focus and endless effort that brought her the tremendous success granted only to the few. Writing in her mid-seventies, Tallchief conveys both the soaring joy and the unrelenting rigor of her chosen career, insights helpful to aspiring young dancers.

TUDOR, TASHA

Tudor, Bethany. *Drawn from New England: Tasha Tudor*. Philomel, 1979, 96 pp. (5-up).

The daughter of artist Tasha Tudor has written a fascinating text-and-picture biography of her famous mother. Choosing a rural life in New England, the artist accomplished her work of writing and/or illustrating more than sixty children's books, while taking an active part in growing and preparing food, caring for animals, and rearing four children. Written with the intimate knowledge only a member of the family would possess and illustrated with family photographs and snapshots (and many of the artist's book illustrations, paintings, and drawings), the book is not only a delight to read, but presents an inspiring picture of a gifted artist who remained true to her deep convictions as to how her life should be lived.

TYNDALE, WILLIAM

O'Dell, Scott. *The Hawk That Dare Not Hunt by Day*. Bob Jones University, 1986 (1975), 182 pp. (6-up).

Primary listing under *Literature, Level III, Realistic Stories—Historical*

This is not primarily a biography of Tyndale, but he is a very significant figure in the story. His courage and dedication are clearly portrayed as he risks his life (which he ultimately sacrifices) to put the Bible into English and make God's Word available to the common man.

WASHINGTON, BOOKER T.

Amper, Thomas. *Booker T. Washington*. Illus. by Jeni Reeves. Carolrhoda Books, Inc., 1998, 48 pp. (1-3).

Simply but effectively written, this brief biography is a fine introduction for younger children to the life of Booker T. Washington, the early African-American leader. Born into slavery, Booker was nine at the end of the Civil War when the slaves were freed. Even before freedom he had longed to go to school. He wanted more than anything else to be able to read and to learn things from books. No longer a slave, Booker was still not free to go to school. His family was very poor, and he had to work long hours to contribute to their income. How Booker finally realized his dream of gaining an education completes the book's account, but the author outlines Booker's life in a brief afterword and chronology. The factual, quietly told narrative expressed concisely in short sentences has a surprisingly appealing story quality, further enhanced by the many fine illustrations that reach the reader's heart.

Washington, Booker T. *Up from Slavery*. Doubleday, 1998 (1901), 384 pp. (5-up).
   The classic autobiography of an outstanding American, Booker T. Washington. Born a slave just before the outbreak of the Civil War, Washington, though soon freed, struggled desperately to obtain an education and to help his people achieve a quality of life that would provide opportunity and personal dignity. He became an educator and a worker for civil rights. Washington was honored repeatedly for his achievements and was the founder of the outstanding black college, Tuskegee Institute.

WASHINGTON, GEORGE

d'Aulaire, Ingri and Edgar Parin. *George Washington*. Illus. by author. Beautiful Feet Books, 1996 (1936), 64 pp. (k-6).
   This is an excellent introductory biography of Washington, ideal for early readers or to read aloud. It has a large picture-book format with wonderful illustrations but also includes a substantial amount of text. George Washington was not simply a figurehead of history, but a remarkable man of unusual vision and strength of character. It is not "romanticized myth," as some contemporary educators speculate, to recognize that at crisis points in the Revolutionary struggle, it was the resolution and the faith in God of this committed leader that turned the tide of defeat and inspired the faltering American forces to endure—and ultimately to prevail. In peace it was Washington who guided the establishment of a just and free nation and who was loved and honored as the father of our country. Young children gain immeasurably when the stories of George Washington and other good and great leaders are shared with them.

Harness, Cheryl. *George Washington*. National Geographic Society, 2000, 48 pp. (k-5).
   Spirited narrative in a conversational tone and colorful, well-researched illustrations characterize this picture biography. Cheryl Harness brings George Washington vividly to life. At six-foot-two, he towered over most other men of his day and had the strength to match his height. Although his formal education was cut short after his father's early death, George continued to educate himself through reading and had a well-cultivated mind. His early youth, however, was more often spent in rugged wilderness surveying jobs—and later as a Virginia militiaman—than in the genteel world of his Virginia home. He became a "tough, ath-

letic frontiersman" and experienced soldier, a background that one day would prove indispensable.

Yet it was as a successful experimental farmer and family man at Mount Vernon that Washington found the life he loved best. But when tensions between England and the colonies reached the boiling point and his neighbors elected him to the Virginia legislature, as a committed patriot, he took on a responsibility that for years kept him away from home and his satisfying work. The writer follows Washington, soon to be in charge of the American war effort, through the years of harsh conflict—a very human man, yet an indomitable hero with a faith and a courage that simply would not give up. This fast-moving, readable account helps twenty-first-century youngsters know better the remarkable man so truly called the father of his country.

WILBERFORCE, WILLIAM

Everett, Betty Steele. *Freedom Fighter: The Story of William Wilberforce.* Christian Literature Crusade, 1994, 114 pp. (5-up).

In a day of increased consciousness about the tragic wrongs of the past, it is an irony that the name of William Wilberforce is virtually unknown in this country. In retrospect, he may well have done more than any other one man to end slavery internationally. Everett's concise and yet comprehensive biography offers a warm, vivid picture of the life of this remarkable man who spent forty-five years in the British Parliament. Gifted, wealthy, and blessed with an unusually gracious and likable personality, Wilberforce could have done as he pleased with his life. Instead, even as a very young man he felt drawn to public service. When he became a Christian in his mid-twenties, he was already in the House of Commons. Now his desire intensified to serve the people of his nation in practical ways and also to raise their moral awareness.

At the same time, he dedicated himself to work unceasingly to outlaw England's slave trade and to abolish slavery. During the many years of ceaseless efforts, Wilberforce never despaired and never gave up. Both anti-slavery goals were finally reached in the British Parliament—the latter part just two days before his death. What Wilberforce and his supporters accomplished in England had a great impact on public opinion in the United States and gave much-needed help to abolitionists there. It is a joy to read the story of this gentle man who fought to the end of his life for the freedom of the oppressed.

WILDER, LAURA INGALLS

Wilder, Laura Ingalls. *On the Way Home.* HarperCollins Children's Books, 1976 (1962), 112 pp. (6-up).

After the death in 1957 of the much-loved author of the Little House books, a diary she had kept in 1894 was discovered among her things. The entries record the journey of Almanzo and Laura as they left South Dakota and traveled to Mansfield, Missouri, where they were to spend the rest of their long lives. The Wilders' only child, Rose Wilder Lane, has framed the diary account with opening and closing chapters that put the journey in context and provide a setting for the glimpses of frontier life given in the journal.

Wilder, Laura Ingalls. *West from Home.* HarperCollins Children's Books, 1974, 144 pp. (4-up).

In 1915, Laura (who later wrote the Little House books) visited her daughter, Rose Wilder Lane, in San Francisco. Her letters home to her husband, Almanzo (whom she called Manly), during her two-month stay were found among Rose's things several years after the latter's death in 1968. Wanting to share her experiences with Manly, Laura writes of her trip west and of her impressions of San Francisco.

Zochert, Donald. *Laura.* Avon, 1976, 260 pp. (6-up).

A thoroughly researched account of the life of Laura Ingalls Wilder, author of the beloved Little House books. The book is well worth reading in relation to the quantity and variety of factual material presented, but as a biography it leaves something to be desired. In spite of the writer's dutifully sympathetic approach to Laura's life, there is an intangible lack, a kind of underlying remoteness. As a result, there is too often a strong sense that Zochert has simply tried to pass on as much as possible of the material he has researched (what items were being sold in the stores in the communities near where Laura and her family lived, what the names of some townspeople were, and other trivia) while never really quite understanding Laura or her family. Biographies, if they are to give the reader a sense of a life as it was lived, must have an essential empathy and a "story" quality, which Zochert's careful compilation of facts and almost stiffly respectful tone just don't convey.

Biographical Groupings

Allen, John Logan. *Jedediah Smith and the Mountain Men of the American West.* Chelsea House Publishers, 1991, 119 pp. (5-8).

Primary listing under *History* and *Geography*

One of the many things history preserves for us is the stories of various small groups of people who accomplished seemingly impossible feats (often without long-range goals). These achievements ultimately had lasting cultural, economic, or political effects. One such group was the mountain men of the American West in the early part of the 1800s. In his colorful account, Allen provides both the historical backgrounds and geographical settings of these men. He also focuses on the individual lives and exploits of a number of the stalwart adventurers. Jedediah Smith, Joseph Walker, Edward Rose, and Jim Bridger are some of the more famous names; many others are also profiled. Their exciting, often amazing stories are not only lively and colorful, but also offer a glimpse into the way a small, unique group of people have affected the destiny of millions.

Kaminsky, Marty. *Uncommon Champions.* Boyds Mills Press, 2000, 147 pp. (6-up).

As a teacher and parent, author Marty Kaminsky spends his life around children and has a special interest in helping them prepare to meet life's problems. In these fast-paced accounts of the lives of fifteen outstanding athletes, Kaminsky has brought together his concern for children and his lifelong passion for sports. All of the athletes profiled confronted conditions that threatened to crush all their hopes and defeat body or spirit—or, more often, both. In recounting their struggles and ultimate triumphs over serious misfortunes, the author seeks to inspire children—including all those not involved in athletics—to rise above hard circumstances or sudden disaster with the kind of courage, vision, and determination demonstrated by these remarkable people.

Kent, Deborah and Kathryn A. Quinlan. *Extraordinary People with Disabilities.* Children's Press, 1996, 288 pp. (4 or 5-up).

The central emphasis of this extensive biographical collection is the capacity for significant achievement by people with disabilities. Forty-eight people are profiled in some detail. Many of them are widely known—from Beethoven to Wilma Rudolph, Thomas Edison to Itzhak Perlman, for example. Many others are found in areas of endeavor less known by the public. The disabilities are varied—deafness, blindness, the aftermath of polio, amputation, paralysis, ALS (Lou Gehrig's disease), Down's syndrome, cerebral palsy, and others. The triumph of indomitable spirits, solid accomplishments, and hard-won goals can only be termed inspiring. A measure of the achievement of these remarkable people is that at the end of the book, it is what they have done and the strength of their characters and personalities that linger in the mind rather than the trying handicaps. The range of the biographical subjects offers an excellent opportunity for kids to learn of people they would like to know more about.

Note: Readers and their parents should be aware that not every person profiled is an ideal role model even though the courage and determination of all are admirable. Their overcoming of daunting disabilities can be recognized, whatever their chosen philosophy and lifestyle.

Leiner, Katherine. *First Children: Growing Up in the White House.* Portraits by Katie Keller. Tambourine Books, 1996, 157 pp. (4, 5-up).

Using often-amusing anecdotes and other relevant material about the children of the White House during seventeen different presidencies, the writer has created a pleasing and informative book. Seen against a background of White House life—which often reflects something of what is going on in the larger world outside—the children not only come to life as people, but the related presidents, first ladies, and others are also seen in new ways. From George Washington's adopted grandchildren through two centuries to the Clintons' only child, readers are introduced to a very lively—often mischievous—succession of youngsters. The book concludes with two supplemental sections: One follows up all the children included in the book and tells briefly what happened to each one, and a final chart lists all of the nation's presidents, first ladies, and the names and dates of each of their children.

The book is illustrated with a colorful scratchboard watercolor portrait of the most prominently featured child in each chapter and with many historical photographs.

Sanderson, Ruth. *Tapestries*. Little, Brown and Co., 1998, 32 pp. (3-6).
Primary listing under *Bible/Spiritual and Moral Teaching*
Sanderson, an artist, speaks in an "Author's Note" of her love for tapestries with their rich colors and intricate designs. As she retells, directly from the biblical accounts, the stories of twenty-three women of the Bible, the artist sees them as part of the tapestry of faith, with each one contributing the varied threads of her life to the overall design. The women are portrayed in softly glowing colors against beautifully detailed backgrounds, each story woven graphically and in the text into the whole. Each woman, unique in her background, her nature, and her special part in the design, stands out as an individual and yet blends with the others in the tapestry of faith. A beautiful and inspiring group.

Steele, William O. *Westward Adventure: The True Stories of Six Pioneers*. Harcourt, Brace, Jovanovich, 1962, 188 pp. (5-up).
Spanning the eighteenth century in chronological order, the writer has told of the adventurous treks in what was then the American West, of six widely different people (one of them a woman captured by Indians). Each person, none of whom is famous or remembered, emerges as a distinct individual, with his (or her) own reasons for making the hazardous journey. Certain qualities, however, of determination, ingenuity, and endurance seem common to all, and the ways in which each person pursued his or her particular goal makes fascinating, thought-provoking reading. Currently out of print, but still in some libraries or obtainable through interlibrary loan.

Stonaker, Frances Benson. *Famous Mathematicians*. Harper and Row, 1966, 118 pp. (4-9).
Primary listing under *Mathematics*
Brief, easy-reading accounts of the lives and work of eleven famous mathematicians, from ancient times onward. This is an excellent way to introduce stu-

dents to these men whose work contributed so significantly to major developments in the history of civilization, men about whom all students should have at least a general knowledge. Currently out of print, this excellent book is still in many libraries or available through interlibrary loan.

Yount, Lisa. *Asian-American Scientists*. Facts on File, 1998, 112 pp. (adv. 6-up).

   Primary listing under *Nature, Science, and Technology*

   Although the work of the twelve Asian-American scientists profiled is the chief focus of the book, the biographical details are of great interest in themselves. From China, Japan, and India, some came as children, some as adults. All had an intensity of purpose and a boundless capacity for study and work. A glimpse into their backgrounds and the cultural respect they all had for education and significant achievement help to explain the outstanding success of many of the Asian students around us today. Even facing the difficulties of trying to fit into a culture very different from their own didn't deter the students who became the book's distinguished scientists. Both informative and inspiring, their stories are well worth reading.

5

CELEBRATION
DAYS AND SEASONS

Brett, Jan, illus. *The Twelve Days of Christmas*. Dodd, Mead and Company, 1986, 28 pp. (all ages).

    Also listed under *Music*

    Another festive book to add to your family's Christmas celebration. This counting song is part of ancient tradition and focuses on the season's giving of gifts on the twelve days from Christmas on December 25 to the Epiphany on January 6. A full musical score with words and each day's verse shown separately on the two-page spreads are accompanied by outstandingly beautiful illustrations—a veritable feast for the eyes, full of appealing little details along with the central depiction of each day's gift.

Dalgliesh, Alice. *The Thanksgiving Story*. Illus. by Helen Sewell. Simon and Schuster, 1985 (1954), 32 pp. (k-3.)

    Primary listing under *History and Geography*

    This enjoyable and well-written little story is a fine way to share with children the story of the early New England colonists' struggles and their day of celebration and thanks to God when their needs were provided. It is told from the perspective of a fictional family involved in the celebration.

Drake, Jane and Ann Love. *The Kids' Winter Handbook*. Illus. by Heather Collins. Kids Can Press, 2001, 127 pp. (all ages).

    Also listed under *Crafts, Hobbies, and Domestic Arts* and *Outdoor Activities*

    A full-of-fun and useful book that not only includes a wide range of outdoor and indoor activities, but also has a concluding section, "Celebrate Winter," with directions for a treat tree, pinecone skier, gingerbread house, winter desserts, snacks and treats—and more. Other crafts and activities found in the handbook could also be a part of a winter celebration during the Christmas season or for the December birthday of a family member.

Edens, Cooper and Benjamin Darling. *The Glorious Christmas Songbook*. Blue Lantern Studio, 1999, 77 pp. (all ages).

    A delightful collection of more than fifty favorite Christmas songs that includes both a large selection of beloved traditional carols with their joyful proclamation of the Christmas story and also many secular Christmas songs full of nostalgia and good cheer. Lavishly illustrated with wonderfully colorful vintage illustrations. Musical scores of the melody lines of all songs are included. A splendid book to add to your family library.

Erlbach, Arlene. *Happy Birthday Everywhere!* Illus. by Sharon Lane Holm. The Millbrook Press, 1997, 48 pp. (2-5).
　　Also listed under *Crafts, Hobbies, and Domestic Arts*
　　Birthday greetings and celebration customs of nineteen different countries are described and illustrated in this full-of-fun book. Each country has a colorfully illustrated two-page spread. A little inset map shows where the country is in the world, and its traditional birthday customs are discussed in the text. Directions are given for one of these: making some object that is often a part of the celebration, making a recipe for a birthday party dessert, giving instructions for playing a special birthday game. Some children may want to include birthday customs of another country in one of their own celebrations. Clear directions and illustrations accompany each activity. Concluding the book is the music for our traditional "Happy Birthday" song, which is also sung in many other countries today. On the facing page are the words of the song in eight different languages—including how to pronounce the words!

French, Fiona. *Bethlehem: With Words from the Authorized Version of the King James Bible*. HarperCollins Publishers, 2001, 24 pp. (all ages).
　　This lovely book is indeed a joyful celebration of that which is truly Christmas—the Christmas story itself in the beautiful words of the King James Bible. Fiona French, inspired by England's cathedral windows, has illustrated each part of the biblical account with glorious simulations of the scenes in stained glass. Each Christmas Eve many families gather quietly during part of the evening, tree lights glowing softly, perhaps a log crackling in the fireplace, to read the Christmas story and think together about the wonder of Jesus' birth—God's gift to all the world. Next Christmas some of you may want to read the Bible's words from this special book that was created as a celebration of that wonderful coming to earth of Jesus, God's Son.

Turpin, Nicholas and Marie Greenwood, editors. *The First Noel: A Child's Book of Christmas Carols to Play and Sing*. DK Publishing, 1998, 31 pp. (all ages).
　　The music of Christmastime, with its beautiful carols proclaiming the wonders of Jesus' coming to earth and of the joy of the season, is a significant part of our celebration. This festive book has selected thirteen carols and combined them with fine reproductions of Christmas paintings. Each song is shown in a simplified musical score for piano (for both hands) and guitar. On the facing page for each carol is a lovely painting with the words of the song's additional verses below. Included are all the traditional favorites: "Hark! the Herald Angels Sing," "Away in a Manger," "O Little Town of Bethlehem," "The First Noel," "Silent Night," "It Came Upon a Midnight Clear," and seven more. This is a special book

for a shared family Christmas celebration and to include in your musical child's lesson repertoire.

Willard, Nancy. *Cracked Corn and Snow Ice Cream: A Family Almanac.* Illus. by Jane Dyer. Harcourt Brace and Company, 1997, 57 pp. (4-7).

This delightful book is reminiscent of an old *Farmer's Almanac,* and although it is classified as a children's book, it is, for many people, an all-ages collection. The book is organized on a through-the-year plan, with four large pages for each month, all illustrated with charming little colored pictures and decorations. A nature-related poem opens each month, followed by "Dates and Festivals," with holidays noted and special dates of famous people—births, discoveries, and so forth. The "Farmer's Calendar" has farm or gardening tips. A recipe is often included, as are a variety of informative tidbits and how-to's. A page each month is devoted to the "voices" of the writer's and illustrator's Midwestern farm fore-bears, as they speak of personal experiences, special days, farm lore, and school days. These pages are illustrated with "family album" pictures, as are two facing pages between each of the four seasonal divisions. A thoroughly enjoyable and lovable book.

Zalben, Jane Breskin. *To Every Season: A Family Holiday Cookbook.* Simon and Schuster Books for Young Readers, 1999, 111 pp. (all ages).

Do celebrate with this special book. More than a delightful cookbook of recipes for use on sixteen celebratory days throughout the year, *To Every Season* is one of those books that becomes part of the family tradition. Each section opens with a lovely description of the day being celebrated; its pages glow with exquisite drawings; its recipes are given in careful detail, with young cooks in mind—and the book is permeated with an atmosphere of warm family sharing and of everyone helping to give joy on a festive day.

6

CRAFTS, HOBBIES, AND DOMESTIC ARTS

Allison, Linda. *Trash Artists Workshop*. Fearon Teaching Aids, 1981 (all ages).

A collection of things to make from throwaway materials. On the whole, the objects made are actually either useful or truly creative, active fun rather than the sort of paper plate/doily things that seem to exist solely as projects for small children to carry home to fond parents. (An occasional such decoration may be welcomed, but it is nice to see the kinds of ideas in this more practical collection.) Directions are clear, drawings to illustrate abound, and a list of likely "trash" sources is included.

Bial, Raymond. *With Needle and Thread: A Book About Quilts*. Houghton Mifflin Co., 1996, 48 pp. (3-7).

It is with respect, appreciation, and love that the author writes of cherished traditions and cultural distinctives in American life. In this book about quilts, Bial conveys the deep relationship between the careful joining of the little pieces of fabric and the makers' perception of life and their own identity. The author talked to many present-day quilt-makers. A woman from West Virginia said, "This quilt's a piece of living history. It speaks to me in voices long passed away." Another commented, "I love to piece quilts. It's a joy. It's an art within." And as women through the generations found this lasting way of expressing themselves, they often joined together in groups, adding friendship and mutual support to this expression, which in turn became a part of the quilting tradition. Bial discusses the development of patterns that were shared, named, and replicated. He also speaks of the new patterns brought as precious memories of home by those who became new Americans. Both the informative narrative and the many photographs of wonderful quilts will add to children's love for the deeply rooted traditions that are part of the fabric of our lives.

Blanchette, Peg. *Kids' Easy Knitting Projects*. Illus. by Marc Nadel. Williamson Publishing Co., 2000, 64 pp. (2-7).

A handy book of seven simple knitting projects: a scarf, purse, hat, and four more. Basic how-to's with detailed drawings of stitches and step-by-step instructions are given for each object. With few exceptions, some initial guidance from an experienced knitter along with the written directions helps the beginner to a much faster start, but determined, persistent kids who don't expect to master a skill instantly can succeed on their own. Acquiring the ability to make something attractive and useful is not only enjoyable but a fine confidence-builder as well.

Brown, Osa. *Metropolitan Museum of Art Activity Book.* Abrams, 1990 (1983), 88 pp. (4-up).
  An attractive group of crafts, models, toys, games, and mazes to make and use, all inspired by treasures now in the museum's collection. A quite special book.

Chapman, Gillian. *The Egyptians.* Crafts from the Past Series. Morrow Avon, 2000, 40 pp. (4-7).
  Children as well as adults continue to find the culture of ancient Egypt intriguing. This pleasing and colorful book combines simple, well-written information about that culture with fourteen related craft projects and photographs of the Egyptian objects on which the projects are modeled. A list of materials needed and how-to instructions include clear, step-by-step illustrations, all in color. Among the projects are scarab seals, mural paintings, a model of a reed boat, and a decorated hand mirror and makeup box. The book concludes with a glossary of terms used in the text (highlighted in bold type).

Chorzempa, Rosemary A. *My Family Tree Workbook: Genealogy for Beginners.* Dover, 1982, 64 pp. (4-up).
  A practical workbook in which to record family data as to parentage and ancestry. For those with a developing interest in genealogy, the book provides a solid starting point—guidance on how to go about tracing ancestors and a short bibliography of related resource books. For those who don't care to pursue such a quest, the workbook simply gives the child a compact listing of family information that might readily be referred to in later years when needed for school assignments, passports, or even high-security jobs.

Cobb, Mary. *A Sampler View of Colonial Life with Projects Kids Can Make.* Illus. by Jan Davey Ellis. The Millbrook Press, 1999, 64 pp. (2-4).
  An unusual book that combines information about colonial home life with ten related projects—which are not difficult or complicated. The book starts by explaining just what a sampler is and its various functions in colonial life. The accompanying illustrations are delightful, and the various projects (which even include a sampler frame and a computer sampler along with the more usual stitchery) will entice readers to start their own samplers at once. *A Sampler View* is a charmingly different little book.

Cobb, Vicki. *The Secret Life of School Supplies.* Illus. by Bill Morris. HarperCollins Children's Books, 1981, 82 pp. (3-up).
  Fascinating facts behind the origins of everyday materials such as paper, ink, pens, chalk, paste, glue, erasers, and more. Children can make their own versions of these supplies. Clear instructions and explanations of how and why materials can be combined to produce the desired results help to ensure success in the projects.

Cole, Joanna and Stephanie Calmenson. *Rain or Shine Activity Book*. Illus. by Alan Tiegreen. Morrow Junior Books, 1997, 192 pp. (all ages).

This big, activity-filled book includes a variety of categories, many of which are not crafts. Sections that do involve crafts include a samurai helmet, dart glider, weaving, a bubble-blower, etchings, a spiral bracelet, and many others. Street rhymes, jump-rope rhymes, and street games chapters offer rhymes to use with outdoor activities and also a variety of games such as hopscotch, coin-tossing, Red Light-Green Light, and more. Other chapters include tongue-twisters, riddles, word games, brainteasers, paper-and-pencil games, card games, and magic tricks. There is something for everyone, a welcome guide that answers the question, "What can we *do*?" both indoors and outdoors.

Coyle, Rena. *My First Baking Book*. Illus. by Tedd Arnold. Workman Publishing Co., Inc., 1988, 144 pp. (1-up.)

This no-frills, tried-and-true book offers forty easy-to-follow baking recipes created especially for children. The book starts with a section of general information about baking and the utensils and materials (in addition to the recipe ingredients) the young cooks will be using. Appropriate cautions are included along the way. Breakfast baking, holiday specials, sweet tarts, and cookies are just some of the baked-goods groupings included. Step-by-step directions and illustrations make it easy for youngsters to follow along and soon learn how to bake things the whole family will enjoy.

Darling, Jennifer, editor. *Better Homes & Gardens New Junior Cook Book*. Meredith Books, 1997, 112 pp. (4-up).

One of the titles in the Better Homes & Garden's New Junior book series, this guide does a good job of combining colorful illustrations and general kid-appeal with loads of sensible kitchen advice and thoroughly explained recipes. Starting with basics on how to read recipes and food labels, measure correctly, plan menus, and set the table, the manual then proceeds with sections on breakfasts, lunches, dinners, and snacks—all presented appetizingly. The book concludes with a chapter for parents on cooking with kids and on getting them to eat well nutritionally. A useful and enjoyable guide. A sensible kid might do well to hang on to this book and take it along a few years later when he or she is ready for solo living.

Drake, Jane and Ann Love. *The Kids' Winter Handbook*. Illus. by Heather Collins. Kids Can Press, 2001, 127 pp. (3-up).

Also listed under *Celebration Days and Seasons* and *Outdoor Activities*

This well-put-together collection of fun things for kids to do in winter includes a number of projects to make: cool candles, fleece mitts, knitted scarf and hat, hooked rug, log carrier, winter blooms, and more. (One that caught my eye uses a leg from an old pair of panty hose, a light bulb, grass seed, potting soil, and a small dish or cup!) To top off the roster of things to do, look also for the simple winter-warmer recipes.

Drake, Jane and Ann Love. *The Kids' Summer Handbook*. Illus. by Heather Collins. Ticknor and Fields/Books for Young Readers, 1994, 208 pp. (3-up).

> Also listed under *Outdoor Activities*
>
> This book is much like its companion (next above), but with the activities geared to summer and some especially to vacation times at the beach, lake, meadow, or mountainside. Many of the projects and activities are also just as suited to a backyard or day trips. Making a raft, snorkel, crayfish trap, hammock, birdhouse, wildlife blind, plant prints, clay works, or rock art—and many more— are some of the possibilities. There are tips for camping and evenings around a campfire as well as rainy-day games and star-gazing.

Erlbach, Arlene. *Happy Birthday Everywhere!* Illus. by Sharon Lane Holm. The Millbrook Press, 1997, 48 pp. (2-5).

> Primary listing under *Celebration Days and Seasons*
>
> This birthday-activity book includes a number of craft projects and celebration recipes from nineteen different countries—fluffy paper flowers from Brazil, snowflake garlands from Egypt, the potato game from Israel, piñatas from Mexico, taartjes (tarts) from the Netherlands, and jelly (gelatin) and ice cream from Great Britain. Directions and recipes are clearly given and colorfully illustrated.

Granger, Neill. *Stamp Collecting*. The Millbrook Press, 1999, 93 pp. (5-up).

> In comparison with the time span of human history, the postage stamp has not existed for long. The first one, says Granger, was issued in Great Britain on May 6, 1840. Soon other countries adopted this practical system of paying for the delivery of mail. Many millions of the small, fragile bits of paper have been issued—in an endless variety of colors, designs, and even in varied shapes. It is not surprising that from the start these little "pictures," with their pleasing look, tiny details, and often the exotic aura of foreign lands, have appealed to the collecting instinct of many people. (The earliest known collector started his hobby on May 7, 1840, the day after the release of the first stamps.) *Stamp Collecting* is a readable and useful manual for the beginner, with its overview of the postage stamp's origins and colorful history, descriptions of areas of special interest the collector can pursue, and basic information about obtaining and handling stamps for a personal collection. The book is lavishly illustrated in full color, with pictures of fascinating stamps on

every page. It concludes with a helpful glossary (like every hobby, stamp collecting has its own specialized terms) and a comprehensive index.

Harris, Jack C. *Plastic Model Kits*. Crestwood House, Macmillan Publishing Co., 1993, 48 pp. (5, 6 up).

Making a realistic-looking replica from a plastic model kit is a tremendously satisfying activity. Whether it is a car, plane, ship, or other vehicle or object, few people can resist the appeal of a small-scale reproduction that they can put together themselves. The one hindrance is not knowing how to get started or how to carry out the planned model-making. This book helps the aspiring young model-maker understand better how to take hold and what problems to avoid. Starting with an introduction to plastic kits, the book discusses how to choose the first kit, what tools and materials will be needed, and how to proceed successfully. Many helpful suggestions are given. Chapters on assembling, customizing, and displaying models follow. Model-making clubs and plastic-model competitions are also discussed. A practical, helpful little manual to use for a good start—and to avoid the common problem of model kits that are either never finished or that look disappointingly unlike what the maker has visualized.

Hines, Anna Grossnickle. *Pieces: A Year in Poems & Quilts*. Greenwillow Books, 2001, 30 pp. (all ages).

Primary listing under *Literature: Poetry and Rhymes*

Not a "how-to" on quilting, this unusual little book of evocative seasonal poems and related quilt art could inspire almost anyone to long to create theme quilts. Illustrated with fourteen two-page spreads of exquisitely envisioned tiny quilts, each page vibrates with life in its riot of color, imaginative design, and enviable craftsmanship—simply irresistible. Crafters will find a concluding section, "The Story Behind the Quilts," of special interest.

Hogrogian, Nonny. *Handmade Secret Hiding Places*. Illus. by author. Overlook Press, 1990 (1975), 48 pp. (all ages).

Ideas for the youngster who longs for a little hideaway that can be constructed in a hurry. Clever, illustrative drawings accompany brief instructions for making a pole bean tepee, a dugout, a between-the-chairs hideout, and seven other secret hiding places.

Hopkinson, Deborah. *Fannie in the Kitchen*. Illus. by Nancy Carpenter. Atheneum Books for Young Readers, 2001, 32 pp. (ps-4).

Based on fact, this is the delightfully told story of how Fannie Farmer (1857-1915) became an American household name. As a young mother's helper in the Charles Shaw family, Fannie charms the Shaws with her delicious cooking and her patience with their little girl, Marcia. The youngster isn't happy to be replaced by a professional mother's helper and is determined herself to learn to cook. Fannie begins to help her, deciding to write out recipes she carries in her head so that Marcia can make them too. (Some people credit Fannie with inventing the modern recipe with its precise and tested measurements of ingredients and step-by-step directions on how to proceed.) Written in a humorous style, the story includes some of Marcia's cooking adventures. The lively narrative is enhanced by amusing illustrations that combine the artist's own drawings with researched nineteenth-century etchings and engravings. Fannie became a teacher, then principal, at the Boston Cooking School and wrote a comprehensive and enormously popular cookbook still known and loved after more than a century. The book concludes with a summary page on Fannie's life—and the recipe for her famous griddle cakes, which we now call pancakes.

Irwin, Margaret. *My Little House Sewing Book.* Illus. by Mary Collier. HarperCollins, 1997, 64 pp. (3-up).

Craft-inclined girls (and their mothers) will enjoy making some or all of the eight sewing projects based on Laura Ingalls Wilder's classic Little House stories. The attractive book includes information on sewing skills, lists of needed supplies, and six ready-to-cut full-size patterns. (Two of the projects don't need patterns.) Some of the things to be made include "Laura's Nine-Patch Pillows," "Mary's Braided Rug," "Alice's Embroidery Sampler," and "Laura's Prairie Sunbonnet." The book is generously illustrated, and detailed instructions are given for each item.

Kirkman, Will. *Nature Crafts Workshop.* Fearon Teaching Aids, 1981 (3-8).

A varied collection of craft and study projects using plants and animals. Hatching eggs in a homemade incubator and growing personalized pumpkins are just two of the more than forty projects.

Lasky, Kathryn. *The Weaver's Gift.* Frederick Warne, 1980, 64 pp. (all ages).

This is not a how-to book, but rather a wonderful birth-of-a-lamb-to-beautifully-woven-blanket account of the way wool is grown, sheared, spun, and woven. The sheep in this book are raised by a young Vermont couple, and the many accompanying pictures were taken by the author's husband, an outstanding photographer.

The book is more than a documentary on wool and weaving, for the writer captures the effort, the love, the satisfaction inherent in true craftsmanship. An added virtue of the book is its combination of clarity and simplicity with an effective vocabulary that doesn't talk down to the reader. Now out of print, this is one of those books that merits the extra effort to track it down.

Love, Ann and Jane Drake. *Kids and Grandparents: An Activity Book.* Illus. by Heather Collins. Kids Can Press, 2000, 160 pp. (1-up).

Also listed under *Growing Plants, Miscellaneous, and Outdoor Activities*

This book contains dozens of games, crafts, recipes, and varied activities kids and their grandparents can do together. More than ninety ideas and how-to's have been assembled in this attractive book with its many illustrations. There is something for everyone, and a number of the suggestions include aspects that are special fun to share with a grandparent and that will spark memories and family stories.

MacLeod, Elizabeth. *Bake and Make Amazing Cakes*. Illus. by Jane Bradford. Kids Can Press, 2001, 40 pp. (3-8).

Creating an unusual cake that evokes oohs and ahs and tastes good besides can be a very gratifying experience for a youngster with an interest in culinary arts. *Bake and Make* starts out with several pages of general instructions and tips for baking and then offers specific, well-illustrated directions for making nineteen delightful cakes: a lovable cat, cozy house, Christmas tree, dinosaur, and bus—to name only a few. Recipes for cake batters are included. A list is given of all items needed for decoration, along with drawings of how the cake should be cut, shaped, and put together to end up looking perhaps like a delicious hamburger or an appealing teddy bear. Even older kids—if they aren't experienced bakers—will need some initial guidance and supervision. The younger ones need much more. A little practice will yield thoroughly enjoyable creations that will bring a happy sense of skill and achievement to the young cake-makers.

MacLeod, Elizabeth. *Gifts to Make and Eat*. Illustrated by Jane Bradford. Kids Can Press, 2001, 40 pp. (3-up).

A handy book of inexpensive gifts to make that family and friends will love to eat. Also there are directions for making attractive containers or wraps to put the food items in. Chocolate clusters, fudge, granola, nut mixes, cookies, soup mixes, muffins, and herbed oil are just some of the goodies included. Complete directions are given for all the tasty treats and the decorative coverings, with a wealth of helpful illustrations. (Recipes give both U. S. and metric measurements.)

Merrill, Yvonne Y. *Hands On Rocky Mountains: Art Activities About Anasazi, American Indians, Settlers, Trappers and Cowboys*. Kits Publishing, 1996, 83 pp. (2-6).

A rather quirky but colorful combination of craft/art projects and brief historical and cultural information on the succession of people-groups of the "Rocky Mountain West," as the writer terms it. Each section pictures a number of artifacts related to the group under discussion, with instructions for making several of the objects. The history-culture information given is clear and factual, in the manner of the descriptive, detailed labels found with museum exhibits for children. The projects represent utensils, clothing, and miscellaneous accessories that reflect some of the group's distinctive art. Most definitely adult guidance is needed, as the instructions, though usually clear, are often too brief for most children to follow on their own. The book is generously illustrated with excellent color photographs and includes many small black-and-white drawings in the craft-instruction and history-culture sections.

The author's background is in organized group activities related to schools, libraries, and museum programs. These ideas for projects could be done at school or at home.

Paul, Ann Whitford. *The Seasons Sewn: A Year in Patchwork*. Illus. by Michael McCurdy. Harcourt, Inc., 2000, 36 pp. (3-6).

The introduction to this excellently written and illustrated little book discusses the patchwork tradition that developed in American culture. The writer researched more than 160 books and periodicals, finding the tradition's core: Seasonal patterns of life that related to people's activities were reflected in the patchwork designs that became traditional. The book follows the seasons and shows the resulting patterns—the Bear Paw, Turkey Tracks, the compass with its thirty-two directional points—to mention just a few of the patterns shown. By the mid-1800s the growing warm-weather sport of baseball was reflected in a pattern depicting its compact balls. The ways in which the patchwork was used in clothing, bedding, and other valued possessions is discussed and illustrated, with a variety of designs that can be copied by those who want to duplicate this traditional art.

Pawson, Des. *The Handbook of Knots.* Dorling Kindersley, 1998, 159 pp. (all ages).
    Not strictly a craft book and not a children's book, this delightful manual is just too good a book not to include. The author was given a book on knots when he was seven years old, and he has worked with knots and ropes ever since, becoming preeminent in his field. Many children who like to do things with their hands would find this book fascinating. Completely illustrated in color and very well organized, the book provides step-by-step instruction for each type of knot. Many of these are extremely useful—the kind you wish you knew how to tie when confronted by a particular need for a knot that won't slip or that can be used in some specific situation—stopper knots, binding knots, and bends (knots that tie two lengths of rope securely together); hitches, loops, splices, and whipping are some of those. In addition, the "Braids and Sennits" chapter shows knots that are not only useful but colorful and decorative. An attractive, sturdy, handy-sized, and eminently useful book.

Perl, Lila. *Hunter's Stew and Hangtown Fry: What Pioneer America Ate and Why.* Houghton Mifflin, 1977, 176 pp. (6-up).
    A fascinating glimpse into pioneer history in America from the perspective of the eating habits of various groups and regions. The writer not only relates food to the events of the time, but she traces the development of early kinds of cooking into contemporary eating styles. Twenty authentic pioneer recipes are included.

Perl, Lila. *Slumps, Grunts, and Snickerdoodles: What Colonial America Ate and Why.* Houghton Mifflin, 1975, 128 pp. (6-up).
    The writer offers thirteen authentic colonial recipes, but this is much more than a cookbook. In providing background information on corn oysters, shoo-fly pie, snickerdoodles and other foods, Perl also tells her readers much about the cultural history of the day.

Rhoades, Diane. *Garden Crafts for Kids.* Sterling Publishing Co., 1998, 144 pp. (3-7).
    A big, lavishly illustrated (splendid color photographs), full-of-fun book for kids to use in many ways. There are lots of plant-growing ideas and how-to's, along with make-it projects—woodworking for garden-related uses, watering can decoration, a seed caddy, beautiful garden markers, topiary (ornamentally shap-

ing individual plants), and a tool station. A great many kids have a natural interest in garden-related activities. Try turning them loose with this idea-filled book.

Ross, Kathy. *Crafts for All Seasons*. Illus. by Vicky Enright. The Millbrook Press, 2000, 175 pp. (3-up).

A big book of varied and attractive craft projects grouped seasonally—fall, winter, spring, summer. Fall offers a tree lapel pin, school bus picture frame, Thanksgiving cornucopia place cards, and more. Winter brings a baggy snowman (for indoors), a tiny Christmas tree ornament, and a George Washington hat among its projects. A giant shamrock for St. Patrick's Day, a vase for spring flowers, and a box photo album are some of spring's enticing ideas. The years' seasons move into summer with a plate-fan, a Fourth of July Uncle Sam mask, an earthworm puppet, and other vacation-days projects. Clear instructions for each of the appealing objects are enhanced by the many illustrations.

Roussel, Mike. *Clay*. Illus. by Malcolm S. Walker. Rourke Enterprises, Inc., 1990, 32 pp. (1-6).

Forming shapes with clay (or a clay substitute) is one of those enduringly popular activities that never seems to lose its appeal for children. In *Clay* (one of the Crafts Projects Series of books), young modelers will find ideas and how-to's for creating a variety of objects: birds, animals, faces, mosaic tiles, jewelry, and coil pots—just some of the projects offered. A list of tools and supplies needed and clear step-by-step instructions guide the reader through the process, accompanied by helpful illustrative drawings in color. A practical, enabling little manual. Other books in the series offer imaginative ideas for working with other materials: *Paper, Scrap Materials, Wood, Fabrics and Yarns,* and *Natural Materials*.

Rubenstone, Jessie. *Weaving for Beginners*. Harper Children's Books, 1975, 80 pp. (3, 4).

Clear, step-by-step instruction for beginners. Each procedure is illustrated by helpful photos, and directions are given for the kind of simple, uncomplicated articles the new weaver can handle successfully.

Note: Some libraries may still have Rubenstone's *Knitting for Beginners* and *Crochet for Beginners*, now out of print.

Sabbeth, Carol. *Kids' Computer Creations: Using Your Computer for Art and Craft Fun*. Williamson Publishing Co., 1999, 158 pp. (ps-5).

A fun-filled potpourri of computer-generated creativity. "Silly Squiggles" and "Mouse Gone Wild" are just two of the art activities; crafts include "Fingerprint Stationery," "Pop-Up Greeting Card," "Vincent's Seed Packets," and much more. Creative ideas abound for things to use for special celebrations and for gifts. Diverse as the possibilities for fun are, the book is also organized, practical, and very helpful for young computer users. Instructions are clearly and simply given, and words commonly used as symbols are defined: "Why is a Mouse called a Mouse?" "What is an Icon?" With many families choosing to help their children become familiar with the use of computers while in a home setting, this book can offer useful and enjoyable help.

Sadler, Judy Ann. *The Kids Can Press Jumbo Book of Crafts*. Illus. by Caroline Price. Kids Can Press, 1997, 208 pp. (5, 6-up).

This is a splendid book to turn over to your crafty kids. The projects are fun, practical, usable, and attractive. Best of all, the instructions are exceptionally clear and well stated, fully supported by the wealth of equally clear step-by-step drawings. All the finished projects and the instructional how-to's are in black-and-white drawings—no glossy pages, no color photos. But just leafing through the book brings something at once that the reader would like to get started on. (Yes, more girls than boys engage in this kind of activity, but there are a number of projects that handy and artistic boys would enjoy.) From a collage nameplate, decoupage magazine and book holder, papier-mâché bowl and picture cube to a button bracelet, pressed flowers, T-shirt pillow, painted clay pot, and charming twig basket, there is something for everyone—and 140 more projects.

Note: Children in the earlier grades may need some help, depending upon their individual skills.

Sato, Yoshio. *Animal Origami*. Kodansha Ltd., 1996, 48 pp. (4-up).

An attractive and clearly written manual on origami, the intriguing Japanese art of paper-folding. Each of the fifteen projects creates an animal or bird. Origami can be both whimsical and beautiful; it is an art, says the writer, to make people smile. Complete, step-by-step instructions with accompanying drawings are given in three categories based on degree of difficulty. The easily removed sheets of paper needed for all projects are included in the book. Designed for readily achieved success, the book provides an enjoyable introduction to this skill.

Walker, Barbara. *The Little House Cookbook*. Illus. by Garth Williams. HarperCollins, 1989 (1979), 240 pp. (adult/child projects).

A wonderful book of frontier foods from the Little House books. Walker has researched each one, adapted the recipes to contemporary measurements and equipment, and yet retained their authentic qualities. A rich variety of background information on cooking, eating, and kitchens is also included, along with specific references to the foods mentioned in the various stories.

Walker, Lester. *Carpentry for Children*. Overlook Press, 1985 (1982), 208 pp. (2-up).

A birdhouse, coaster car, puppet theater, raft, and doll cradle are just a few of the projects for which plans are included in this 200-page book. It is generously illustrated with photographs, drawings, and diagrams, along with the writer's step-by-step instructions.

Walker, Lester. *Housebuilding for Children*. Overlook Press, 1988 (1977), 176 pp. (2-up).

Here are plans, diagrams, and instructions for building six different child-sized houses: tree, wood-frame, junkyard, post and beam, factory-built, and glass. A crew of ten children ages seven to ten built all six of these one fall, and the writer photographed them in the process. More than ninety photographs and 150 line drawings are included.

Zalben, Jane Breskin. *To Every Season: A Family Holiday Cookbook.* Simon and Schuster Books for Young Readers, 1999, 111 pp. (3-up).

Primary listing under *Celebration Days and Seasons*

With its delightful recipes, outstandingly lovely illustrations, and cozy atmosphere, this is a very special cookbook for families to use together on their favorite celebratory days throughout the year. The recipes are given in careful detail so that children can be thoroughly involved in the shared joy of preparing special dishes for all to enjoy. Writer/artist Zalben's book is one to use and cherish with your family.

Ethnic Cookbooks—A Series of 25 Books. Easy Menu Ethnic Cookbooks. Lerner, 1982-96, 48-52 pp. (5-up).

Clear, colorfully illustrated recipes for each country are in separate volumes, from *Cooking the African Way* to (alphabetically) *Cooking the Vietnamese Way.* Preceding the recipes is information on the particular country, its food and customs, and comments on special ingredients. About eighteen appetizing recipes are given in each book. Your local bookstore can look up the complete list of titles if you are looking for a particular country's recipes. Or if your library has a set of *Books in Print* in its Reference section, simply look in the "Titles" volume under "Cooking the . . . Way."

In addition to the series are five other titles: *Desserts Around the World, Ethnic Cooking the Microwave Way, Holiday Cooking Around the World, How to Cook a Gooseberry Fool: Unusual Recipes from Around the World,* and *Vegetarian Cooking Around the World.* All have well-selected recipes and are attractive and fully illustrated in color.

7

DANCE, DRAMA, AND OTHER PERFORMANCES

Aliki. *William Shakespeare & the Globe.* HarperCollins Publishers, 1999, 48 pp. (3-up).

Aliki offers readers a veritable potpourri: quotations at the page corners from Shakespeare's plays; masses of delightful, colorful, and detailed illustrations accompanied by extensive captions—all tied together by the book's narrative text written in a lively, conversational style. Organized under headings of "Acts" and "Scenes" rather than chapters, the book provides a good deal of basic information about Shakespeare and his plays and about some of the prominent public figures and leading actors of the day.

Act Four of the book focuses on the Globe Theatre (the British spelling of *theater*) itself, starting with the original Globe, how it came into being, Shakespeare's relation to it, and its eventual demise.

Act Five fast-forwards to the twentieth century and Sam Wanamaker, an American actor and director who dreamed of building a new Globe as close to its seventeenth-century site in London and as identical to the original building as possible. Wanamaker envisioned it as a theater in which Shakespeare's plays would be performed as they had been four centuries ago. A series of illustrations shows how the builders went about fulfilling Wanamaker's dream. In 1997, two years before the 400th anniversary of the first Globe playhouse, the new Globe opened. The book's concluding pages offer a list of Shakespeare's plays and poems, a chronology of Shakespeare's life and of Wanamaker's Globe project, an illustrated list of 106 of the some 2,000 words and expressions invented by Shakespeare, and the names of Shakespearean sites to visit in London and Stratford-Upon-Avon.

Note: See also *Shakespeare's Theatre* by Andrew Langley, listed below. Reading both books is recommended.

Bentley, Nancy and Donna Guthrie. *Putting on a Play: The Young Playwright's Guide to Scripting, Directing, and Performing.* The Millbrook Press, Inc., 1996, 64 pp. (2-4).

This splendid volume plunges right into its theme, answering two initial questions: "What is a play?" and "What is a playwright?" The book then goes on to define and describe all that is involved in creating, producing, and performing a play. Types of plays, including improvisations and skits, are discussed. How to proceed is presented step-by-step, from scripting to performing. This is not a theoretical discussion but rather a hands-on instruction book. For youngsters (and their adult helpers) who want to take hold and *do* it, this book is a good place to start.

Berger, Melvin. *The World of Dance.* S. G. Phillips, 1978, 190 pp. (6-up).

A survey-style history of dance, ranging from the earliest known forms to those of the present, both as artistic expression and as social activity. Berger takes the position that dance forms reflect existing culture, springing "from people's basic beliefs and activities." Clear and concisely stated, the value of the book is in its information rather than its literary quality.

Bloom, Carol Ann. *Nifty, Thrifty, No-Sew Costumes and Props.* Good Year Books, 1998, 190 pp. (ps-up).

A practical and enjoyable book full of ideas and directions for children's costumes for every occasion: plays, skits, celebratory holidays, playing dress-up, or "let's pretend." Suggestions for building a collection of multi-use components focus on each type of garment and accessory, starting with the basic tunic. To that can be added collars, vests, hats, helmets, and crowns, for example. Foot-related items may be shoes, boots, paws, and claws. The whole range of possibilities is helpfully grouped in this manner. Well organized and easy to use, the book is true to its primary purpose—showing the reader how to make and find costumes and props with the least possible work and expense. Recycling is encouraged, and money-saving recipes are given for face paint, glue, clay, papier-mâché, and dyed pasta. Great for family fun, school, and church children's productions and activities.

Castle, Kate. *My Ballet Book: An Introduction to the Magical World of Ballet.* DK Publishing, Inc., 1998, 64 pp. (3-7).

An overview of ballet that offers an organized format of beautiful color photographs and informational captions. Not intended as an in-depth study, the book offers basic information on some of the many facets of the art of ballet, from what the student will be wearing in practice and also in performance, to a description of beginning instruction. Basic positions at the barre are shown, as well as other techniques. Readers are given a glimpse of life at a ballet school and behind the scenes at a performance. Also the varied kinds of ballet are discussed, with mention of some of the outstanding ballet artists. An exciting look at both the work and study and the beauty and glamour of this classical dance form.

Cole, Joanna and Stephanie Calmenson. *Rain or Shine Activity Book.* Illus. by Alan Tiegreen. Morrow Junior Books, 1997, 192 pp. (all ages).

Primary listing under *Crafts, Hobbies, and Domestic Arts*

Check the "Magic Tricks" chapter in this large book of activities for kids for some fun and easy tricks. See the primary entry for the book's contents.

Eldin, Peter. *Magic.* Larousse Kingfisher Chambers, Inc., 1997, 64 pp. (3-7).

The world of magic tricks with its clever illusions and surprise effects is appealing to many children. They enjoy knowing about the masters of the art and about some of the particular tricks and illusions for which they are famous. Eldin's book provides a lively account of magicians over the years, their showmanship and distinctive specialties, and the related organizations and trends that developed around them. Programs featuring magicians were very popular in nineteenth-century England, and the writer has included reproductions of the shows' flamboyant publicity posters. At the end of that century, Egyptian Hall, touted as the "House of Mystery," was the heart of English magicianship, with its elaborate programs and lavish illusions. By 1937 and the World War II era, these more extravagant shows had disappeared, and television soon became the chief venue for the trimmed-down but more sophisticated magic entertainments. Recently "spectaculars" have been returning, with Las Vegas now the magic capital of the world.

Eldin's book includes a discussion (and examples) of the classic illusions of magic shows: the beautiful girl being sawn in two, vanishing objects and people, levitation, "impossible" escapes, comedy magic, and mind-reading. A section on becoming a magician and an A-Z informational listing of the all-time magician greats rounds out the book's extensive coverage.

Elliott, Donald. *Frogs and the Ballet.* Illus. by Clinton Arrowood. Harvard Common Press, 1984 (1979), 57 pp. (all ages).

Using frogs (as they used alligators in the companion volume on the symphony orchestra, *Alligators and Music*), the writer and illustrator present clear directions and marvelous drawings on the basic ballet positions and movements. Preceding the main body of the book is a serious Foreword about ballet and a listing of the basic categorizations of ballet performance. There is both charm and humor in Elliott's method of presenting information, and this is a delightful book.

Feldman, Jane. *I Am a Dancer.* Random House, 1999, 35 pp. (ps-up).

Outstanding photography and a young ballet dancer's story told in her own words combine in this effectively created book. Thirteen-year-old Eva Lipman is the daughter of a Canadian diplomat and a Chinese mother who is herself a ballet dancer and choreographer. Eva, a student at the prestigious School of American Ballet in New York, has already lived in Hong Kong, Taiwan, and Canada. Her life now is focused on the demanding schedule of her ballet practice and regular academic classes at the Professional Children's School, but she also finds time to play the piano, enjoy nature in Central Park, and explore some of New York. Feldman has photographed the wide-ranging aspects of Eva's life—from the tiny apartment where she lives to the bare, serious practice rooms, the drama and glamour of the performance stage, and the family times with her parents—in a close-up, intimate way that takes the reader into her life. A picture with depth and credibility of a young girl with purpose and with a love for what she is doing clearly emerges. But though Eva wants to dance professionally (she is already among the children seen in such performances as *Sleeping Beauty* and *Swan Lake*), she also wants to complete her education. What lies ahead is in the still-unknown future.

Fonteyn, Margot. *A Dancer's World: An Introduction for Parents and Students.* Knopf, 1979, 128 pp. (6-up).

The great ballerina Margot Fonteyn offers advice based on her own extensive experience to children who want to study ballet and to their parents, who will be an important element in the endeavor. Clear, practical, and well-written, the book should be of value to all who are interested in dance training, whether ballet or other forms of dance. Fonteyn comments in the book on modern dance, folk, ethnic, jazz, and tap. Long out of print but still in some libraries, the book is worth the effort to track it down and make a special request for it if necessary.

Garfunkel, Trudy. *Letter to the World: The Life and Dances of Martha Graham.* Little, Brown and Co., 1995, 92 pp. (6-up).

Considered by many to be the predominant spirit and performer in pioneering modern dance, Martha Graham lived completely in and for her work. In this concise, yet surprisingly complete account of Graham's life and work, the writer has captured the intensity of her commitment, the capacity for almost superhuman physical endurance, and the tenacity of a spirit that kept an apparently unwavering focus on her chosen medium of expression for a phenomenal eighty years. She finished her last complete work when she was ninety-six and even accompanied her dancers for part of a Far Eastern tour during that same year. The writer follows the development of Graham as a performer, choreographer, and teacher from her early involvement and rigorous study through the growth and the changing forms and emphases of her most prolific years, and on into the later period of her role as an established icon of modern dance. Garfunkel illumines Graham's vision of dance and describes the ways she sought to convey emotion and reality through it.

Ladizinsky, Eric. *Magical Science.* Illus. by Dianne O'Quinn Burke. Lowell House, 1998, 80 pp. (3-6).

This unpretentious paperback offers a number of "magic tricks" that children can readily perform. The writer uses principles of chemistry and physics to create surprising and unexpected effects that appear magical. The well-organized, step-by-step instructions are illustrated with black-and-white drawings; all the needed materials are clearly listed, and at the end of each set of instructions Ladizinsky explains how the trick works from a scientific perspective. Some of the tricks require an adult presence at all times (as when matches are used, for example). This requirement is stated at the start of the instructions.

Langley, Andrew. *Shakespeare's Theatre.* Paintings by June Everett. Oxford University Press, 1999, 48 pp. (3-up).

As the title implies, Langley's book focuses throughout on Shakespeare's Globe Theatre (the British spelling), including related material on the other main theaters of the time. Shakespeare and his plays are, of course, an integral part of any discussions of theaters, but true to the author's central purpose, they are largely seen in the background. Starting his account with the opening of the new Globe Theatre in 1997, Langley summarizes its relation to the Globe Theatre of the past and briefly introduces Sam Wanamaker, the American actor and director responsible for building the new Globe. Today across the world Shakespeare's plays are presented in widely varying settings that reflect the ideas of their contemporary producers and directors. Wanamaker envisioned the new Globe as a theater in which the plays would be performed in the same kind of setting as they had been four centuries ago so that audiences could experience Shakespeare's art as its creator himself presented it.

The differences between today's theaters and those of Shakespeare's time are readily observed in the account of the painstaking building of the replicated theater. An outstanding feature of the book is the artistry of June Everett, whom Wanamaker met years before his dream became a reality. She was appointed Artist of the Record for the project, and for seventeen years she pictured the materials, craftspeople, and construction, accumulating a group of 150 wonderful pictures done from first to last, a number of which are reproduced in the book. Beautiful to see and filled with fascinating detail, the vivid representations are, like the project as a whole, a labor of love. It is heartwarming to know that although he died four years before the new Globe was completed, Sam Wanamaker's dream did come true. "This remarkable theater is now a thriving and extraordinary part of Britain's artistic life," concludes Langley.

Note: See above for *Shakespeare & the Globe,* by Aliki. The two books complement rather than duplicate each other.

Mara, Thalia. *First Steps in Ballet: Basic Exercises at the Barre.* Princeton Book Co., 1987 (1955), 64 pp. (3-up).

A much-used book for more than forty-five years, Mara details a wealth of basic barre exercises for home practice (not intended as a guide for self-instruction but as an aid in home practice for the ballet student). The book also includes a helpful Foreword for parents that emphasizes the importance of having only a bona fide teacher of ballet for a child and specifies ways by which a teacher's qualifications can be determined. Comments on what constitutes a well-structured class and program are also noted.

Martin, Judith. *Out of the Bag: The Paper Bag Players' Book of Plays.* Illus. by Seymour Chwast. Hyperion Books for Children, 1997, 48 pp. (4-up).

Find some big paper bags; round up a lot of big cardboard boxes, a few easy-to-find household items, and some poster paints. Dust off your sense of fun and imagination, and gather a little group of wannabe instant-actor kids. You're ready for *Out of the Bag,* seven hilarious little skits about everyday situations with a twist or two that keep everyone laughing. Think panache, think chutzpah—and have a ball! Kids will pick up right away on the paper-bag spirit.

Meyer, Charles R. *How to Be a Clown.* Amereon Ltd., 1976, 51 pp. (4-7).

Clowns have always appealed to a large number of children, and Meyer's book will appeal to clown fans. The writer traces the history of clowning, discusses the various types of clowns, clown makeup, costuming, and (briefly) clown acts and routines.

Moore, Jo Ellen, Ginny Hall, Leslie Tryon, and Betsy Franco. *How to Do Plays with Children*. Illus. by Joy Evans and Leslie Tryon. Evan-Moor Corp., 1994, 288 pp. (k-6).

 Primary listing under *Supplemental Teaching Resources*

 Written for adults, this book contains scripts and other helpful material for helping kids get started with plays and near-plays (readers' theater, for example). See the primary listing for more information.

Nolan, Paul T. *Folk Tale Plays Round the World*. Plays, Inc., 1982, 248 pp. (4-up).

 A fine collection of sixteen one-act, royalty-free plays adapted from folk tales of countries the world over. "Robin Hood and the Match at Nottingham," "A Leak in the Dike," "The Skill of Pericles," and "Johnny Appleseed" are just four of the plays included.

Presto, Fay. *Magic for Kids*. Larousse Kingfisher Chambers, Inc., 1999, 72 pp. (3-6).

 Many youngsters love the idea of putting on a magic show for their family and friends—and perhaps for a school program. The writer covers the subject in detail, from introductory material on how to use the book and an emphasis on the importance of well-practiced showmanship, on to a discussion of both general and specific helpful tips, and the variety of equipment needed. Thirty-one tricks are given in detail, each one accompanied by a "patter box" of suggested talk the young magician can use as he performs the trick. The book is generously illustrated and effectively written.

Streatfeild, Noel. *A Young Person's Guide to Ballet*. Frederick Warne, 1975, 120 pp. (3-up).

 Although focusing primarily on ballet (basic steps, history, famous ballet dancers, and schools), Streatfeild also discusses other forms of dancing. The writer approaches her topic by following the progress of two real children, Anna and

Peter, in their dance training. The text, though factual, has a pleasing literary quality, and there are fine drawings and photographs to illustrate the material. This is a particularly good book for all children to read, for it is not written exclusively for those with a strong involvement in dance. As Streatfeild says in her preface, "What this book tries to tell you is that, quite apart from a career, dancing is a lovely thing to be able to do and, because you have learnt something about it, watching dancing will give you pleasure all your life." Another excellent and helpful book now out of print but still available in some libraries and through special request.

Tallchief, Maria, with Rosemary Wells. *Tallchief: America's Prima Ballerina*. Illus. by Gary Kelley. Viking, 1999, 28 pp. (ps-4).

Now in her mid-seventies, Maria Tallchief looks back and remembers her early life and the key turning points that led to her career as a prima ballerina. From the start, music charmed and drew Maria, and she was given training in both ballet and the piano. Her parents soon realized, however, that the scope and quality of both general and artistic education available in their small community were greatly limited, and so the family moved to Los Angeles. A significant early decision Maria had to make was to give up the piano and give her undivided attention to ballet. It is here that Maria's future begins, and the lively account, enhanced by perceptive illustrations, moves through the events of Maria's developing artistic focus and the two remaining crucial decisions she faces. Maria Tallchief's own story of her formative years is not only enjoyable in itself, but it also offers authentic insights into the qualities that make possible a gifted artist's memorable work.

Yancey, Diane. *Life in the Elizabethan Theater*. Lucent Books, Inc., 1997, 112 pp. (4-12).

Whether a young reader has a special interest in the field of drama, or specifically in Shakespeare, or simply wants to be well-prepared for future literature classes, a familiarity with the setting of Elizabethan drama (Shakespeare's era) is helpful. Diane Yancey's book is one of a series, The Way People Live, that tries to provide a realistic background for cultural groups in history and in other parts of our world. In this particular book, the world of the theater is seen in relation to the life of people around it—especially to England's Queen Elizabeth I, a lover of plays and an enthusiastic supporter of dramatists and actors. The author tells how her long reign related to the growth and popularity of the theater in the sixteenth century. The account also observes the lives of the various groups of people that made up England. In the Elizabethan era, people from varied walks of life, from the wealthy and titled to the poor who went without some needed mundane things in order to pay for the cheapest space in a theater, shared the tragedy and comedy, the familiar twists of human nature, and the evocations of far-away places as they watched actors on a stage. Primarily, of course, the book's focus is on people who built the theaters, wrote the plays, and acted out the captivating scenes. An enjoyable and informative book, and a splendid one to read along with the books listed above by Aliki and Langley, which deal especially with Shakespeare.

8

GROWING PLANTS—
OUTDOORS AND INDOORS

Björk, Christina and Lena Anderson. *Linnea's Windowsill Garden.* Translated from Swedish by Joan Sandin. R & S Books, 1998, 59 pp. (4-up).

This informal, fun-filled indoor gardening book is just right for the youngster who wants to grow some houseplants but who might think a more serious book would make the project "too much like work." The information provided is all sound, but is presented in tidbit form—lots of practical hints and good instructions on planting, watering, and dealing with pests, interspersed with many clever black-and-white drawings. There are also instructions for creating a little tabletop mini-garden, ideas for using crates and boxes as plant stands, and even two brief recipes for using the reader's homegrown garden cress. A user-friendly and enjoyable little book.

Cole, Henry. *Jack's Garden.* Greenwillow Books, 1995, 23 pp. (ps-3).

This delightful book with its wonderful illustrations could inspire almost anyone to make a garden. Using a "This Is the House That Jack Built" form of cumulative verse, the writer begins with "This is the garden/that Jack planted." The first two-page spread shows the garden as yet unplanted; Jack stands with his shovel, and all around the borders are the simple gardening tools and equipment that will be used. Each one is labeled with its name. Continuing double-page illustrations and the lines of verse follow the same form, each picturing one stage of the garden-making process. As Jack plants seeds, labeled seed packets and a variety of seeds themselves are shown and identified. Then germinating seeds and seedling plants with their little root systems and small leaves are pictured. Garden spiders, bugs, slugs, butterflies, birds, and the colorful, easy-to-grow plants in full bloom (all identified) fill the continuing pages, concluding with brief "To Start Your Own Garden" suggestions.

Drake, Jane and Ann Love. *The Kids' Summer Handbook.* Ticknor and Fields Books for Young Readers, 1994, 208 pp. (3-up).

Also listed under *Crafts, Hobbies, and Domestic Arts* and *Outdoor Activities*

Along with many activities and make-it suggestions and directions, this handy book includes several on plant growing: a vegetable garden, wild garden, composting, and more. See the listings mentioned above for more on the book's contents.

Lerner, Carol. *My Backyard Garden.* Morrow Junior Books, 1998, 48 pp. (4-up).

Children who are ready to take vegetable gardening seriously will find this well-organized, clearly written, lovely book just what they need. (And adults who are also gardening beginners would find it equally helpful.) From planning and planting through harvesting, from soil preparation to fertilizing and insect control, the writer takes the gardener step by step, carefully describing each procedure—with dozens of detailed (and beautifully done) illustrations that leave the reader in no doubt as to exactly what each tool, plant, pest, or garden layout looks like. Two maps are provided showing the average time for the latest spring and earliest fall frosts in the various climate zones across the country. The last half of the book consists of a chapter for each month of the gardening year, and there is an excellent index at the end.

Lerner, Carol. *My Indoor Garden.* Morrow Junior Books, 1999, 48 pp. (4-up).

A companion volume to *My Backyard Garden,* this beautiful book offers everything a young houseplant enthusiast needs to know. Lerner's delightful illustrations could lure almost anyone into the joys of plant growing. Meticulously organized, the instructions guide the reader step-by-step through the basics of how to take hold of a project, what materials and equipment to use, how to plant and care for a wide variety of houseplants, and how to progress, if desired, to taking cuttings, dividing mature plants, and growing from seeds or layering. A chart of common houseplants indicates each plant's light and care needs and the method of propagation to use for that particular plant. Any adults who have never gotten into the growing of plants, but who would like to do so—in traditional style—might well start the adventure by sharing this book and perhaps also its companion, *My Backyard Garden,* with their child. A wonderful "do-it-together," shared-interest activity.

Love, Ann and Jane Drake. *Kids and Grandparents: An Activity Book.* Illus. by Heather Collins. Kids Can Press, 2000, 160 pp. (1-up).

Also listed under *Crafts, Miscellaneous,* and *Outdoor Activities*

Among the many ideas offered in this enjoyable book are some related to plants—a windowsill garden, drying petals for potpourri, and pressing and drying flowers, for example. See the other entries listed above for more about the book.

Lovejoy, Sharon. *Sunflower Houses: A Book for Children and Their Grownups.* Workman Publishing, 2001 (1991), 144 pp. (all ages).

The writer's emphasis on encouraging children and "their grownups" to share the joys of gardening struck a chord that continues to resonate. Lovejoy's later book, listed below, was not only warmly welcomed but generated so many requests for this earlier volume that a new printing resulted. *Sunflower Houses* focuses on a variety of gardening projects especially appealing to children—plants with which success can be expected and that kids can enjoy readily, as well as simple techniques and directions for planning different kinds of gardens. Intriguing ideas are given for creating little hideaways—something kids dearly love. How to use the "products" of gardening in special projects—making flower dolls, for example—is also included. Throughout the book, the author's delightful illustrations make the book a joy to see.

Lovejoy, Sharon. *Shoots, Buckets & Boots: Gardening Together with Children.* Workman Publishing, 1999, 159 pp. (all ages).

The author of this attractive book has "a special purpose and joy—connecting children to nature through gardening." In her attempt to do this, the writer has chosen a theme-project approach. The book contains twelve theme gardens that parents (or grandparents, aunts, uncles, cousins, or friends) and kids can grow together. One, for example, is the "Pizza Patch," a six-foot-wide circle with the planting arranged like giant triangular slices of pizza. The idea is to grow peppers, tomatoes, herbs, and whatever else in the way of veggies you want to try. When the garden is ready, pizza crusts are baked and then topped with the goodies the young gardener has grown. Other projects are container gardens, a "Sunflower House," a "Tub O' Spuds," and other innovations.

MacLeod, Elizabeth. *Grow It Again.* Illus. by Caroline Price. Kids Can Press, 1999, 40 pp. (ps-up).

A light-hearted book about "recycling" tops of vegetables or fruit you've eaten into newly growing plants—carrots and pineapples, for example. Or planting the seeds you have found in watermelons, oranges, beans, avocados, and papayas and planting garlic bulbs, potatoes, and yams. McLeod explains the how-to's. Easy, fast, and fun. (Just don't count on much in the way of food crops from some of your recycles.)

Raftery, Kevin and Kim Gilbert Raftery. *Kids Gardening: A Kids' Guide to Messing Around in the Dirt.* Illus. by Jim M'Guinness. Klutz, 1989, 85 pp. (ps-3).

A colorful kid-friendly guide to gardening. Spiral binding and very heavy stock pages make the book easy to use—and keep in usable shape. (The pages are the kind that wipe off easily.) Step-by-step instructions with accompanying illustrations start with overall plant needs and then go from soil preparation to planting, watering, and fertilizing, making compost, weeding, mulching, and transplanting seedlings. Additional sections deal with garden pests, several specific favorite garden veggies, and flowers and herbs, followed by a chapter on odds and ends for fun, such as sprouting from avocado seeds and sweet potatoes, growing garlic, and others. The book concludes with directions for a little worm farm and making a garden scarecrow. Attached to the book on the outside (removable, of course) are a sturdy little plastic trowel and six packets of seeds.

Rhoades, Diane. *Garden Crafts for Kids.* Sterling Publishing Co., 1998, 144 pp. (3-7).

A happy combination of gardening how-to's and crafts for the make-it-minded young gardener. Both activities are given a generous amount of attention. Planting and care instructions and ideas for a variety of plants are interspersed with directions for making handy garden accessories and decorative objects to complement a lovely plant. Illustrated with full-color photographs, the book is not only a helpful guide in the garden, but offers the plans and how-to's for crafting gifts for parents who are garden lovers.

Rosen, Michael J., editor. *Down to Earth*. Harcourt Brace and Co., 1998, 64 pp. (4-6).

Also listed under *Art*

Forty-one children's book authors and illustrators contributed the dozens of little stories and pictures about things that grow in the earth that comprise this beautiful and unusual book. Eve Bunting remembers the yellow primroses she gathered for her mother as a little girl in Ireland; Carole King planted marigolds beside her tomatoes; David Updike writes poignantly of lilacs and Nicholasa Mohr of the flame-red blooming trees of Borinquén, a Puerto Rican island. And so many more speak nostalgically—of damp, green moss, generations-old roses, and giant sunflowers. A feast of a book for reading aloud together or to treasure quietly and alone. Following the stories are how-to's for thirty-three different projects related to plants—an exciting variety of things to plant, make, and cook.

Michael Rosen, who put this book together, is himself the author of a number of children's books and supports animal welfare and anti-hunger causes. All the writers and illustrators represented in *Down to Earth* contributed their work so that the proceeds can go to Save Our Strength, an organization that, among other things, starts and supports community vegetable gardens in low-income areas.

9

HISTORY AND
GEOGRAPHY

Allan, Tony. *Pharaohs and Pyramids*. Time-Traveler Series. Usborne, 1977, 32 pp. (4-9).

See the entry below (author, Amery) for *Rome and Romans* in this same series for a description of the approach used. This is useful supplementary material, attractively presented and teeming with informative details.

Allen, John Logan. *Jedediah Smith and the Mountain Men of the American West*. Chelsea House Publishers, 1991, 119 pp. (5-8).

Less well known than the familiar sagas of pioneer wagons rumbling west on the Oregon Trail is the story of the West's trapper/explorer mountain men. Significantly active for about three decades beginning in 1806, these men were a key element in opening up the far West for the stream of pioneers that followed. It is difficult for people today to realize just how unknown the vast inland areas west of the Missouri River were at that time. There were few maps of the interior, and the existing ones were wildly inaccurate. No one yet knew a practical way to get across the country or what they would encounter on the way.

It was the information brought back by the Lewis and Clark Expedition of 1803-1806 that sent the mountain men on their quests. The often-incredible exploits and experiences of these men and the part they played in our nation's history comprise the focus of Allen's account—a fine combination of history, geography, and nonstop adventure. Readable, exciting, and splendidly informative.

Amery, Heather and Patricia Vanags. *Rome and Romans*. Time-Traveler Series. Usborne, rev. ed., 1998 (1976), 32 pp. (4-7).

A detailed survey of daily life and house and city layouts in first-century Rome. Full of clusters of information, the book is more suited to reference or browsing than to primary curriculum use. The work is lively and attractive and could be usefully coordinated with other in-depth material on ancient Rome.

Ammon, Richard. *Conestoga Wagons*. Illus. by Bill Farnsworth. Holiday House, Inc., 2000, 30 pp. (3-6).

Also listed under *Nature, Science, and Technology*

Perhaps no symbol of pioneering in America is better known than the large, slow-moving wagons with their rounded cloth tops and huge iron-rimmed oak wheels. It is easy for today's children to picture these wagons, as they have seen them in films and book illustrations—traversing the Oregon Trail, floating across a wide river, or circled as a defense against an Indian attack. These are all accurate pictures but just one part of the place such wagons held in American life between 1750 and 1850. Richard Ammon has written a clear and detailed account of the background, construction, and varied uses of the most famous of the storied wagons, the Conestoga. Bill Farnsworth's wonderful illustrations not only picture the wagon in the process of its construction and the functions of its work, but also include authentic settings of its era. Much more than a means of transporting the possessions of pioneer families across the continent, the Conestoga was the equivalent of today's "semi," traveling far and wide between cities, transporting the products of the nation's farms and factories. In the mid-nineteenth century the railroads ended the Conestoga's long-distance hauling, but until the arrival of trucks on the scene, wagons continued to haul goods from freight trains, farms, wholesale businesses, and small manufacturers to many destinations away from the railroad. *Conestoga Wagons* brings to life another significant part of America's history.

Appelt, Kathi and Jeanne Cannella Schmitzer. *Down Cut Shin Creek: The Pack Horse Librarians of Kentucky.* HarperCollins Children's Books, 2001, 58 pp. (3-7).
How splendid it is that little gems of history like this one are still published. In the dark days of the Great Depression, President Roosevelt's New Deal relief program included the Works Progress Administration, known as the WPA. (Later the word *Progress* was changed to *Project.*) Its goals were to provide jobs for the unemployed and to increase the cultural appreciation of art, theater, and literature. Many of the jobs created were tied to the construction of needed buildings, roads, and other projects requiring heavy physical labor. Many women, however, were in dire need of jobs, and Kentucky's Pack Horse Library Project met the WPA goals admirably. It employed women to bring reading material to poverty-stricken people who had no libraries and no other sources for books or magazines. With no roads at all going into some areas with difficult terrain, bookmobiles were not an answer, but packhorses, ridden by courageous, determined women, were. The authors have explained clearly just how the project was organized, with its central headquarters in each region and four to six carriers working from that library. The book gives full attention to both the "book ladies" as people and the isolated, struggling inhabitants. Generously illustrated with archival photographs of the period, this book preserves a wonderful little piece of our nation's history for today's children.

Benchley, Nathaniel. *Sam the Minuteman.* Illus. by Arnold Lobel. HarperCollins Children's Books, 1987 (1969), 64 pp. (k-3).
Primary listing under *Literature: Level I, Realistic Stories—Historical*
This enjoyable little story is a good introduction for early readers to the history of the American Revolution. One of the I Can Read History Series, the book has a controlled vocabulary and easy-to-follow sentence structure. Sam, with his

father, sees history in the making as they encounter British troops at Lexington, Massachusetts, when the Revolutionary War begins. Benchley has managed to inject a lively story quality in spite of the vocabulary and sentence limitations. (Such limitations often result in lifeless, boring reading matter that slows vocabulary acquisition; this book is better in that regard than many.)

Bennett, William J., editor. *The Children's Book of America.* Illus. by Michael Hague. Simon and Schuster, 1998, 111 pp. (all ages).

The editor has brought together a diverse collection of songs, poems, stories, and Michael Hague's outstanding illustrations. Each one is about some aspect of America's past. For example, the first Thanksgiving; the story behind "The Star-Spangled Banner"; a story of the bravery of Abigail Adams, wife of John Adams, America's second president—and many more. It is only by handing down these treasures of our American heritage from generation to generation and sharing the stories with the many new Americans in our nation that this legacy will live on. A fine book to add to the family library.

Bial, Raymond. *One-Room School.* Houghton Mifflin, 1999, 48 pp. (4-8).

An intriguing photo-essay on a significant part of America's past—the one-room school. Bial's photographs of wonderful old schools are outstanding, and the text is not only informative but conveys warmth and humor through quotations from students and teachers. These schools (210,000 of them) were educating half of America's children until the early 1900s. (Even as late as 1950 a substantial number were still functioning.) The education establishment as a whole and a good many powerful people advocating "progress" were very critical of these little one-teacher schools. Pressure increased nationwide for large, consolidated schools to which children were bused, often for many miles. By the end of World War II, many country people had moved to cities, which further hastened the end of local schools in rural areas.

Bial's enjoyable book is not focused on criticism of contemporary education, but is an informative and nostalgic view of a significant part of our past. A look back, however, at the schools that did so much for so many children is especially timely as our nation faces widespread failure and chaos in so many schools today.

Blackmore, Richard D. *Lorna Doone.* Buccaneer, 1981 (1869), 345 pp. (6-up).

Primary listing under *Literature, Level III, Realistic Stories—Historical*

Rural life in seventeenth-century England (with some events in London) form the background of this beloved old classic romance. Day-to-day living conditions and social patterns of the story illumine English history of the period, though the reader needs to remember that the author wrote it as a romance and included the requisite elements of suspense and imagination his readers would expect. Allowing for that, however, there is much in Blackmore's novel that provides a helpful context for all that was going on politically and economically during that period of England's colorful past.

Blos, Joan W. *A Gathering of Days*. Demco, 1990 (1979), 144 pp. (6-8).
    Primary listing under *Literature, Level III, Realistic Stories—Historical*
    This fictional journal of a young New England girl is set in about 1830. It captures effectively the speech and flavor of the time and could help to amplify a study of that period of American history.

Blumberg, Rhoda. *Shipwrecked!: The True Adventures of a Japanese Boy*. HarperCollins Children's Books, 2001, 80 pp. (3-7).
    Primary listing under *Biography*
    Based on years of painstaking research, Rhoda Blumberg's splendid biography of Manjiro, a poverty-stricken Japanese fisher-boy, offers significant historical information on Japan in the mid-nineteenth century and insights into some of the rest of the world as well. The shipwreck of Manjiro and the four men of their fishing enterprise is more than a disaster. They are stranded on a barren little heap of volcanic rock 300 wind-blown miles from Japan, but even an unlikely rescue wouldn't solve their problem. By one of Japan's laws, they could expect to be executed if taken home. Anyone leaving the country was not allowed to return, on pain of death—though the cause was a fierce storm over which they had no control. Even fishermen were restricted to coastal waters and could not be away for more than three days. Manjiro and the others had been marooned for months! The action- and suspense-filled odyssey that follows brings the castaways into the life of the world away from Japan, a life that reveals the boy's unusual intelligence and offers him the opportunity to learn extensively. It is Manjiro's knowledge of the world, and especially of the United States (which he greatly admires), that eventually makes him of significant help in behind-the-scenes negotiations that open Japan to trade and to some contacts with the Western world. This is an unusual and especially fine book.

Bober, Natalie S. *Abigail Adams*. Atheneum, 1995, 248 pp. (6-up).
    Primary listing under *Biography*
    This excellent biography draws extensively on the many surviving letters from Abigail Adams's lifelong correspondence with family and friends. Always keenly interested in national events, she frequently spoke of such matters in her letters, and her involvement became more personal with the onset of the Revolutionary War. Her husband, John, was an early delegate to the Continental Congress and some years later became the nation's second president. (Their son John Quincy would one day become the sixth president.) Much of Abigail's adult life was spent in close touch with the "inside" of national affairs, and many of her letters reflected her interest in the development and the politics of the struggling young nation.
    Abigail's lively narratives of family affairs and day-to-day living conditions offer an authentic picture of life in the mid-eastern seaboard states (and for several years in France and England) around the turn of the century. Both because money was in short supply all her life (notwithstanding her family's illustrious position and associates) and because Abigail was unusually conscious of the needs of people from all levels of society, her perspective on daily life was down to earth

and realistic. The story of this engaging and remarkable woman brings history vividly to life.

Bowyer, Carol. *Houses and Homes*. Usborne, 1978, 96 pp. (3-6).
An attractive captioned-picture survey of a wide variety of shelters across the world. Like all such books, the information is brief and specific, not in any way taking the place of an in-depth study. The value of such material is in opening up possibilities for further research and study and for giving students a broad view of the diversity that exists in the structures people call home

Brady, Esther Wood. *Toliver's Secret*. Random Books for Young Readers, 1993 (1976), 176 pp. (3-7).
Primary listing under *Literature: Level II, Realistic Stories—Historical*
Lively adventure at the time of the American Revolution. Under hazardous circumstances Ellen Toliver must carry a message destined for General Washington. An enjoyable story that is helpful to read as a supplement when studying American history of the Revolutionary period.

Brown, Marion Marsh. *Homeward the Arrow's Flight*. Field Mouse Productions, 1995 (1980), 185 pp. (5, 6-up).
Primary listing under *Biography*
A lively account of the life and work of Susan La Flesche (1856-1915), the first ever Native American woman doctor. Excellent supplemental reading in connection with American history from 1880-1915.

Bulla, Clyde Robert. *The Beast of Lor*. Illus. by Ruth Sanderson. Harper Children's Books, 1977, 54 pp. (1-4).
Primary listing under *Literature: Level I, Realistic Stories—Historical*
A brief, especially well-done story of a young Celtic boy in Roman Britain. Enjoyable simply as a story, it can be helpfully used with younger children as a good introduction to the concept of ancient history.

Burgess, Alan. *The Small Woman*. Buccaneer, 1996 (1957), 256 pp. (adv. 5, 6-up or parent/teacher read-aloud).
Primary listing under *Biography*
Outstandingly well written, this enthralling biography of missionary Gladys Aylward includes excellent historical and cultural material on China in the 1930s and 1940s.

Butwin, Frances. *The Jews of America: History and Sources*. Behrman, 1995 (1980), 120 pp. (5, 6).
This book gives a quite thorough treatment (within the limits of its modest length) of the place the Jews have had in the development and life of the United States. Excellent for a supplement to the study of American history or in connection with a focus on the broad range of ethnic and cultural backgrounds represented in our nation.

Chapman, Gillian. *The Egyptians.* Crafts from the Past Series. Morrow Avon, 2000 (1977), 40 pp. (4-7).

   Primary listing under *Crafts, Hobbies, and Domestic Arts*

   Parents and teachers will find this easy-to-use book an excellent supplemental resource as an early introduction to the culture of ancient Egypt. A surprising amount of relevant information is included with each of the book's fourteen craft projects, four of which are "Hieroglyphic Messages," "Board Games," "Pharaoh's Jewels," and "Canopic Jars." Photographs of the Egyptian artifacts on which the projects are based are included. The informative text is simple, clear, and well-written, and the step-by-step instructions for the craft projects are generously illustrated. Unfamiliar terms in the text are highlighted in bold type and are defined in the glossary at the book's conclusion.

Corbishley, Mike. *The World of Architectural Wonders.* Peter Bedrick Books, 1996, 45 pp. (4-8).

   Primary listing under *Art and Architecture*

   This is a particularly good book to use as a supplemental resource when studying the history of any of the cultures represented by these remarkable structures. A significant amount of information is included relevant to the civilizations of ancient Rome, Greece, and the rest of the fourteen sites discussed and pictured. The book is not only attractive but especially well written and well organized.

Curlee, Lynn. *Into the Ice.* Houghton Mifflin, 1998, 40 pp. (4-7).

   As long as human societies have existed, there have been explorers of one kind or another. They venture beyond the limits of the known, driven by a desire to expand their boundaries, to map new land and bodies of water, new mountains and flowing rivers—and sometimes to look for gold, to claim more territories for their distant rulers, to search for shorter trade routes, or to gain wealth and glory. Because of the forbidding cold and threatening masses of ice, however, the two extremities of Planet Earth, the top and the bottom of our world, were among the last areas to be explored.

   With the North Pole at its heart and its lower edges touching the far north of Asia, North America, and Greenland, the Arctic was virtually unknown until the latter part of the sixteenth century. Even then only a few ventured into its frozen expanse. From 1600 to 1900, whalers and fur traders pursued their commercial goals into the Arctic, at the same time gathering knowledge about the area, its resources, and the scattered groups of inhabitants, the Inuit. The author provides a well-written and clearly organized account of the long saga of northern polar exploration, starting with a brief overview of the earliest known ventures into the hazards and endless cold and highlighting the people and their experiences.

   Note: It is of special interest to compare the exploration of the Arctic with some of the expeditions to Antarctica, as recounted in *The Ice Story* by Elizabeth Kimmel and *Trial by Ice* by K. M. Kostyal, both listed below.

Curlee, Lynn. *Liberty.* Atheneum Books for Young Readers, 2000, 42 pp. (4-7).

   Known the world over and loved by all those for whom freedom has a special meaning, the Statue of Liberty has been a symbol for more than 100 years of America's unique history. Though Liberty is widely recognized as a magnificent sculpture, few people are aware of its full story, its relationship to our country's beginnings, and the ideals behind the often-desperate struggle for liberty and nationhood. A gift "from the people of France to the people of the United States," the statue was envisioned as a memorial to American independence and to the friendship between France and the United States. The inspiration of a French professor, Édouard de Laboulaye, the statue was first proposed in 1865 at a dinner party in his home. One of the dinner guests was a young sculptor, Frédéric-Auguste Bartoldi, a gifted man with a particular love for large monuments and memorials. From that evening on, Laboulaye's idea became virtually an obsession with Bartoldi. The author's account of the long and complicated process of turning the dream into reality is not only splendidly told, but reflects in spirit the vision, persistence, and purpose of those who sought liberty. Countless thousands of people seeking freedom and opportunity have been greeted by this beloved statue as they entered New York Harbor, and here is the fascinating story behind its creation.

Dalgliesh, Alice. *The Courage of Sarah Noble*. Illus. by Leonard Weisgard. Simon and Schuster Children's Books, 1987, (1954), 64 pp. (1-5).
>   Primary listing under *Literature: Level I, Realistic Stories—Historical*
>   Based on the true story of an eight-year-old girl who goes into the wilderness with her father to keep house for him until he can build their new home and send for the rest of the family (which includes a young baby). Not only good supplemental reading in connection with American history, but an interesting cultural reflection of the degree of responsibility sometimes entrusted to young children in that era.

Dalgliesh, Alice. *The Thanksgiving Story*. Illus. by Helen Sewell. Simon and Schuster Children's Books, 1985 (1954), 32 pp. (k-3).
>   A well-written story of the first Thanksgiving and the events leading up to it, told from the perspective of a fictional family, the Hopkinses. An especially timely supplement to American history, as fewer of our schools now emphasize the colonists' desire to thank God for His provision for their needs.

Daugherty, James. *The Landing of the Pilgrims*. Landmark Books Series. Random Books for Young Readers, 1981, 160 pp. (4-9).
>   Starting with the reasons for the devout Christian group known as Separatists to leave England and seek a new home across the sea, Daugherty has written a spirited account of the whole enterprise—the years in Holland, the weary weeks at sea in the *Mayflower*, the first near-starvation years in the Plymouth settlement, the friendly (and the hazardous) contacts with the Indians, and the gradual establishment of a stable community. Daugherty's account not only reads like a story, but it conveys the courage, vision, and faith of the diverse group of determined settlers. Books such as this are especially valuable today. Some schools are including less traditional American history in their curricula, and if children aren't given this kind of supplemental material at home, much of the nation's distinctive heritage will be lost.

d'Aulaire, Ingri and Edgar Parin. *Columbus*. Illus. by author. Doubleday, 1996 (1955), 57 pp. (ps-5).

Primary listing under *Biography*

The careful research that characterizes a d'Aulaire biography is reflected in the illuminating historical details woven naturally into the fabric of Columbus's story. The book provides splendid complementary material for use with related history curriculum.

d'Aulaire, Ingri and Edgar Parin. *Benjamin Franklin*. Doubleday, 1985 (1950), 48 pp. (1-4).

Primary listing under *Biography*

Groundbreakers in the development of the picture biography for children, the d'Aulaires have produced a fine introduction to one of the nation's founding fathers. A particularly interesting subject, Franklin was not only a staunch supporter of America's struggle for freedom, but a printer, writer, inventor, and innovator as well. Over the years he became a wise and experienced statesman, representing the United States abroad and at home helping to establish the young nation on a sound and lasting basis. The book may be used helpfully as a supplemental resource in the study of American history in its late colonial period and during and following the Revolutionary War.

de Angeli, Marguerite. *The Door in the Wall*. Doubleday, 1989 (1949), 111 pp. (3-up).

Primary listing under *Literature: Level II, Realistic Stories—Historical*

In late medieval England a boy crippled after an illness finds purpose in life. This well-researched and splendidly written book provides good details as to the customs of its time in the setting of an enjoyable story. There are castle and monastery scenes depicting everyday routines, a military attack on a castle, and social and family interaction. Excellent supplemental reading in connection with medieval English history.

Durbin, William. *The Journal of Sean Sullivan, a Transcontinental Railroad Worker*. Scholastic, Inc., 1999, 188 pp. (5-8).

Primary listing under *Literature: Level III, Realistic Stories—Historical*

Effectively researched and well written, this eventful account portrays a variety of colorful characters and provides a wealth of detailed information about the building of America's first transcontinental railroad. Though its characters are fictional, "Sean" writes about factual conditions and authentic happenings. Enjoyable simply as the story of a likable teenager who joins his father (a foreman for the Union Pacific Railroad) on the job, it also illumines a significant period and a landmark undertaking in the nation's history. Splendid supplemental reading for the study of American history in the post-Civil War years.

Ferris, Jeri Chase. *Thomas Jefferson: Father of Liberty.* Carolrhoda Books, 1998, 112 pp. (4-8).

Primary listing under *Biography*

History textbooks often make the great people of the past seem dull and uninteresting, when in reality their personalities and their lives are often as fascinating as a good novel. Any student exposed to American history will hear something about Thomas Jefferson, the nation's third president. Unfortunately, few of them will be given any idea of Jefferson as a person or be able to relate what he did as president to his individual character. But in this effective biography the writer brings the people of the past to life for young readers. In a well-researched account, Ferris offers a colorful, fast-moving narrative of Jefferson's life that is full of the personal descriptions, the focus on strengths and weaknesses, the revealing attitudes and opinions, the choices and decisions that show Jefferson as a unique individual, easy to remember and to associate with his place in history. Helpful supplemental reading relevant to the birth and early development of our nation.

Fisher, Leonard Everett. *Alexander Graham Bell.* Illus. by author. Atheneum Books for Young People, 1999, 28 pp. (4-7).

Primary listing under *Biography*

This brief but excellent biography will provide helpful supplemental reading related to a study of outstanding developments in nineteenth-century American history. Known the world over for his invention of the telephone, Alexander Graham Bell is not only one of the significant figures on the landscape of American technology and invention, but a humanitarian as well, with a deep concern for the welfare of others. Of special interest to Bell were the needs of the deaf. This aspect of his contribution to America—and the world—is covered effectively, along with a comprehensive discussion of Bell's scientific/technological work. Children will benefit from knowing more about Bell than that he invented the telephone, and from being able to relate what he did to a particular era of our history.

Foster, Genevieve and Joanna Foster. *George Washington's World.* Beautiful Feet Books, rev. ed. 1997 (1977), 357 pp. (5-8).

In a lively narrative style, the book recounts some of the events (both large and small) going on in the United States and other parts of the world at various stages of the life of its central character. The writers don't attempt to cover all of the world all of the time or to write a continuous biography of Washington. But the book helps to give a broader perspective than many students have previously been aware of. This work would be especially helpful as supplementary material during the study of either American or English history from 1732-1799 (Washington's lifetime).

Freedman, Russell. *Give Me Liberty: The Story of the Declaration of Independence.* Holiday House, 2000, 90 pp. (5, 6-9).

A stirring account of the events leading up to the Declaration of Independence and the American Revolution. The writer combines a clear and well-organized overview with the color and human interest of details often not included in comparatively brief books on the subject written for children. Freedman explains the issues and actions that caused the colonists to object to England's rule over them, vividly profiles the distinctive people that became American leaders and policy-makers, and follows the course of events that changed the future—first for America and ultimately for the world. It is the Declaration of Independence that proposes a philosophy of human rights based on the principle that God created people equal in their right to "Life, Liberty, and the pursuit of Happiness," a philosophy in rad-ical disagreement with any kind of oppressive and unjust rule imposed by those in power. And in spite of the human failings that mar even the most noble aspira-tions, the principles affirmed in this Declaration became a beacon of freedom and hope in the world from that time forward. *Give Me Liberty* presents the record of the birth of the United States in a splendidly written and effectively illustrated form.

Fritz, Jean. *Early Thunder*. Puffin Books, 1987 (1967), 255 pp. (5-up).
　　Primary listing under *Literature: Level III, Realistic Stories—Historical*
　　A young Tory boy living in Boston has to decide for himself where his loyalties lie. Daniel's story offers good historical background on the months immediately preceding the outbreak of the American Revolution.

Fritz, Jean. *Brady*. Puffin Books, 1987 (1960), 223 pp. (5-up).
　　Primary listing under *Literature: Level III, Realistic Stories—Historical*
　　This well-written story includes good historical background reading on antislav-ery sentiment and activity twenty-five years before the outbreak of the Civil War.

Fritz, Jean. *The Cabin Faced West*. Puffin Books, 1987 (1958), 124 pp. (3-up).
　　Primary listing under *Literature: Level II, Realistic Stories—Historical*
　　An easy-reading story of late eighteenth-century pioneering based on the lives of real people. The Hamilton family are part of a pioneer settlement in western Pennsylvania, and although the book does not include many specific historical events, one brief episode is based on an actual entry in George Washington's diary.

Gallagher, Jim. *Ferdinand Magellan and the First Voyage Around the World*. Explorers of the New World Series. Chelsea House Publishers, 2000, 63 pp. (4-up).
　　A fast-paced account of the life and achievements of the Portuguese explorer whose 1519-1522 expedition was the first to travel completely around the world,

though Magellan himself was killed near the end of the long odyssey. Magellan was among the number of strong, adventurous men of his era with an inner restlessness based on one or more desires—to make discoveries that would bring glory and financial gain to their nation, to expand knowledge of the as-yet unknown, and to gain personal fame and wealth. As the writer's account clearly shows, these intensely felt purposes brought nations and individuals into frequent bitter conflict. Some of the national enmities and rivalries that affected the course of world events in the fifteenth through the seventeenth centuries are still powerful elements at the beginning of the twenty-first century (though over different commercial assets!).

Of the individual men at the forefront of historic discovery, Magellan seems to have been one of the most courageous and determined and yet less indiscriminately ruthless than some of his contemporaries. The information on the world's physical geography and native peoples acquired by Magellan contributed substantially toward the almost universal global knowledge of today. His name is permanently commemorated in the Strait of Magellan, that dangerous southern waterway between the Atlantic and Pacific oceans that he discovered on his round-the-world journey.

Geisert, Bonnie and Arthur. *Prairie Town.* Houghton Mifflin, 1998, 32 pp. (ps-3).

With an increasing proportion of America's children growing up in large urban and suburban areas, few are aware of the small, rural communities that were founded long ago and that still exist. These small towns represent a long-established way of life and a reassuring sense of the things that endure. Rural communities have closer ties to the recurring rhythms of nature, to the sources of the food grown for the city-dwellers' tables, and to the interdependence of community members. As the railroads were built across the prairies, towns sprang up beside the rails. The Geiserts have portrayed a year in the life of such a community today. (The community pictured is fictional, but its character is based on reality.) Each page is filled with Arthur Geisert's wonderful little color-washed etchings of the details of daily life. Bonnie Geisert's brief narrative text illuminates the overall scene, leaving young readers to find each tiny building, animal, machine, and event. Children—and the adults fortunate enough to share the book with them—pore over the pages, each time finding something new. A sense of peace and permanence—and of the possibility of coping with life in spite of its difficulties—fills the atmosphere of these towns. In a closing page, the year is summed up, mentioning the small events that were pictured but not talked about throughout the book. Many children will enjoy trying to find each happening in one of the illustrations—a lovely way to spend a cozy, memory-making hour.

Geisert, Bonnie and Arthur. *River Town.* Houghton Mifflin, 1999, 32 pp. (ps-3).

During the widespread national expansion that took place in the eighteenth and nineteenth centuries, countless little towns were settled in favorable spots along America's many rivers. Some of these villages grew to be large cities; some shrank and died out. Others, however, just went on being little river towns. The Geiserts have created just such a place as it is today. Depicting the seasons of a year, the fascinating and wonderfully detailed etchings and accompanying account of the community's daily and seasonal activities evoke nostalgia for a simpler world and give children a glimpse of another way of life. Young readers will be charmed by the tiny details of the etchings and will pore over each page, identifying the remarkable number of buildings, boats, machines, bridges, businesses, churches, a school, homes, farms, trees, animals, people, the little islands in the river, and the freight train on the track. A wholly charming book, permeated with an atmosphere of order, activity, and community.

Note: *Mountain Town* and *Desert Town* are the two other books in this series.

Giblin, James Cross. *Chimney Sweeps*. Crowell, 1982, 64 pp. (3-up).

An award-winning account of the chimney-sweeping profession with an emphasis on the plight of the young "climbing boys" (sweeps' apprentices) who worked in England until the last quarter of the nineteenth century. The background material is interesting in itself and is especially helpful in relation to English literature of the eighteenth and nineteenth centuries, which often mentions chimney sweeps. Clever drawings of the sweeps of the past combine with photographs of contemporary chimney sweeps (the profession continues to flourish) to illustrate this unusual and informative little book. Now out of print, it remains on many library shelves or could usually be obtained through an interlibrary loan request.

Giblin, James Cross. *The Amazing Life of Benjamin Franklin*. Illus. by Michael Dooling. Scholastic Press, 2000, 48 pp. (3-7).

Primary listing under *Biography*

In this excellent picture biography the writer has maintained a fine balance between personal biography and the historical events in which Benjamin Franklin was so closely involved. A trip to England on business more than fifty years before the Revolutionary War was the beginning of a long friendship with many English people. As the years went by, no one regretted more deeply than Franklin the changes in what had been a familial kind of relationship between America and its "mother country." As a representative of some of the more powerful colonies, Franklin tried repeatedly to warn Parliament of the disastrous effects their actions would create, but his wise counsel was rejected. Grieved, but true to his convictions, Franklin never wavered in his support of the soon-to-come revolution and served the nation for years during his country's desperate struggle and beyond, after victory had finally come. Even at eighty-one, Franklin's service had not ended. He was asked to help with drafting the Constitution of the United States—the one still in effect today!

Gravett, Christopher. *The World of the Medieval Knight*. Illus. by Brett Breckon. Peter Bedrick Books, 1996, 64 pp. (4-up).

Knighthood—with its emphasis on honor, courage, and loyalty, its adventure, romance, and colorful panoply—has stirred the minds and imaginations of young readers for generations. Gravett and Breckon are not the first to write for children about knighthood's setting in the medieval world, but few write with such lavish detail. Well-written, accurate information and meticulously authentic drawings (all in color and on every page) make this setting come alive. Detailed descriptions, illustrations, and explanations cover every aspect of the knights' world, and the book concludes with a glossary and index.

Grun, Bernard. *The Timetables of History: A Horizontal Linkage of People and Events.* Simon and Schuster, 1991 (1982), 688 pp. (4-up).
  Primary listing under *Reference*
  An excellent source of a concurrent view of history. In a columnar form, the book lists, from 5000 B.C. through A.D. 1978, events and developments in world history under seven headings: History, Politics; Literature, Theatre; Religion, Philosophy, Learning; Visual Arts; Music; Science, Technology, Growth; Daily Life.

Harness, Cheryl. *The Amazing, Impossible Erie Canal.* Macmillan Books for Young Readers, 1995, 29 pp. (3-6).
  By the year 1815 America was eager to expand and to increase trade between the businesses and factories on the East Coast and the pioneer farmers and fur trappers west of the Appalachian Mountains. But this was easier talked about than done. Using wagons on the miserable roads that only recently had been Indian trails involved so much time, wear and tear, and expense that it was usually not worth the extreme effort. Ancient water routes did exist along parts of the way, but these were often widely separated, and a variety of other difficulties also existed. But some of the colonists from Europe were familiar with the canal systems of their homelands. People dreamed and people talked; could money be raised? Was it just a crazy idea?
  In a vivid account, bursting with color and action, the writer has brought alive the story of the amazing fulfillment of an impossible dream that became the Erie Canal. Wonderfully detailed drawings and information-laden maps surround the text on each double-page spread. A feast for the eyes and the inquiring mind, the book illumines a colorful and significant chapter in the history of America.

Harness, Cheryl. *Young Abe Lincoln: The Frontier Days, 1809-1837.* National Geographic, 1996, 32 pp. (3-6).
  Primary listing under *Biography*
  One of the author's attractive and well-written picture biographies, this account of Lincoln's early years not only portrays him effectively and credibly as a person, but it also gives an authentic sense of Midwestern American life during the early decades of the nineteenth century. The warmth and humor of Harness's text will appeal to young readers and encourage their grasp of its content. An appealing, colorful start in their understanding of the development of one of the most significant figures in all of American history.

Harness, Cheryl. *George Washington.* National Geographic Society, 2000, 48 pp. (3-6).
  Primary listing under *Biography*
  This very readable and well-researched picture biography is an excellent supplemental resource for use with American Revolutionary War history. The

writer/illustrator has done more than bring George Washington to life with her fast-paced, non-textbook style (a style, however, in which each word is well chosen and the clarity of thought admirable). Harness has also brought the related historical setting and events to life both in the narrative and in her colorful, content-filled illustrations. The youngster who has attentively read this biography *before* trying to grasp the overall picture of the American Revolution will already have a brief mental outline of the nation's birth.

Haskins, James and Kathleen Benson. *Building a New Land: African-Americans in Colonial America.* Illus. by James Ransome. HarperCollins Publishers, 2001, 44 pp. (2-5).

An enlightening and balanced account of the role of African-Americans during the colonial years (1607-1763). In the earlier years most of the people of black descent in America were not slaves but had come to this country from a variety of other places. Early colonists included people in voluntary limited servitude, and these were not all black by any means. Many British people, for example, came as indentured servants, paying for their boat passage to America with an agreed-upon number of years of servitude. During that period, African-Americans, along with others, were much less discriminated against than was the case later. It was after more colonists had settled in America, and agriculture, especially in the South, became economically powerful, that the demand for more and more laborers greatly increased the slave trade. While blacks and other unempowered people had had a variety of legal rights and some degree of self-determination in the earlier years, the position of African-Americans rapidly deteriorated after the large influx of slaves from Africa. The colonies in which England was most powerful were the least moderate where slavery was concerned, and for many years African-Americans were contributing labor and other efforts to building the new nation but had few (if any) rights or recognition. The book's summaries of conditions in various parts of colonial America provide good insights into African-American roles and circumstances up to the American Revolution.

Haugaard, Erik Christian. Two books: *A Messenger for Parliament; Cromwell's Boy* (Sequel). Houghton Mifflin, 1976, 218 pp. (6-up); 1990 (1978), 214 pp. (6-up).
Primary listing under *Literature: Level III, Realistic Stories—Historical*
Excellent historical material is an integral part of these fast-moving, adventure-filled stories of a young boy on his own. He becomes a messenger for Cromwell, the Puritan military leader who implemented the downfall of Charles I of England. There is a fine literary quality in the writing, and the books provide helpful supplemental reading relevant to the mid-seventeenth century. The first book above is out of print but is still available in many libraries, along with its in-print sequel.

Holling, Holling Clancy. *Paddle-to-the-Sea.* Illus. by author. Houghton Mifflin, 1980 (1941), 63 pp. (3-up).
Primary listing under *Literature, Level II, Realistic Stories—Modern*
This modern classic tells an intriguing story of a little carved Indian in a canoe that (with the kindly help of many people along the way) floats through the Great

Lakes water system and on to the sea. Much of the story involves geographical descriptions and also includes maps, diagrams of a sawmill, canal lock, lake freighter, etc. Every facing page is a beautiful full-color painting of scenes related to the voyage.

Holman, Felice. *The Wild Children.* Scribner's, 1983, 151 pp. (5-up).
    Primary Listing under *Literature: Level III, Realistic Stories—Historical*
    Conditions in Russia in the 1920s are graphically portrayed in this excellent story that focuses on one of the bands of wild, homeless children that roamed the country. Fine supplementary material to a study of post-World War I history—as well as being an extremely well-written, exciting, and very readable story with a satisfying ending.

Irwin, Constance. *Strange Footprints on the Land: Vikings in America.* Harper and Row, 1980, 192 pp. (5, 6-up).
    This fascinating, excellently written, and carefully researched study presents the evidence—some of it now universally accepted, other parts still controversial—of the exploration of North America by Norsemen from about A.D. 985 on. Irwin is careful to avoid jumping to conclusions or to sensationalize. But the sheer drama of the material and the narrative skill of the writer make the book read like a story. Quite apart from the light it sheds on early American history, it gives clear commentary on the larger movement of events in the whole history of man. So much rests on the readiness of a given period in civilization to use or understand new possibilities. When ships from Iceland and Greenland were repeatedly making landings in North America, some Europeans actually knew something of this, but there was no sense of need to investigate further; all the focus of world interest was in other directions. At the time of Columbus, however, the European vision had shifted, and the hour of expansion to the New World had come. An excellent, thought-provoking book for an advanced student. Currently out of print, this book is well worth looking for on library shelves and through an interlibrary loan request.

Jenkins, Steve. *Hottest Coldest Highest Deepest.* Houghton Mifflin, 1998, 30 pp. (3-6).
    One kind of information that many people never seem to tire of is about anything that is "the most." Writer Steve Jenkins has tuned in to that interest in compiling a group of geographical "mosts": the longest river in the world; the highest mountain, hottest spot, deepest lake, and a number of other record-holding sites on our planet. Jenkins's cut-paper collage illustrations are different, striking, and often very colorful, and his location and comparison-chart insets are excellent.
    Learning about these geographical extremes is enjoyable it itself, but perhaps the most lasting effect of reading such a book could be the curiosity generated, motivating the reader to try to find out more. For example, learning that Tutunendo, Colombia, has an average yearly rainfall of 463 inches and that the Atacama Desert in Chile has had no rainfall for the last 400 years will cause many readers to ask why and to consider what conditions would make such extremes occur, thus opening up expanded areas of research and learning.

Kimball, Violet T. *Stories of Young Pioneers: In Their Own Words.* Mountain Press Publishing Co., 2000, 225 pp. (5, 6-9).

Following the trail-breaking exploits of the trappers and explorers between about 1806 and 1840, a swelling tide of pioneers flowed west (chiefly by wagon and by foot) until the transcontinental railroad was completed in 1869. During those three decades, thousands of people gathered at starting points in Missouri and Kansas to follow the Oregon Trail. Many of the travelers were children and youths under the age of nineteen, members of family groups. The trek west was far from an extended picnic—often rather a grim ordeal. With few exceptions these youngsters were full participants in the long endeavor—usually at least six months in length.

What was it like for these young people, far from home comforts, friends, and extended family, usually walking—not riding—responsible for daily tasks, battling cold and heat, dust and downpours, illness and accident? Some of them wrote of their experiences as they traveled; others simply retained clear memories, which they recorded in later years. The author has brought together some accounts of these youthful pioneers' memorable journeys in their own words, weaving these into her vivid picture of life on the trail. At the end of each chapter Kimball includes a profile of one of the young travelers, some of whom lived long and active lives. Summing up her impression of the fortitude and good cheer reflected in the young people's records, Kimball writes in the book's introduction: "This book applauds the bravery of not only those we know of, but also of the nameless children who withstood the hunger, pain, and hardships of the trail, often without complaint." A number of archival photographs of people in the book are included, as well as many pictures of the terrain along the way.

Kimmel, Elizabeth Cody. *Ice Story: Shackleton's Lost Expedition.* Clarion Books, 1999, 120 pp. (6-up).

The story of discovery and exploration in Antarctica is somewhat more grim than that of its geographical opposite, the Arctic—which was difficult enough itself. Conditions in Antarctica, however, were far more severe and less understood than those in the polar north. Already known—and knighted for his previous intrepid expeditions—Ernest Shackleton led the 1914 expedition designed to cross for the first time the 1,800 miles from one side of the Antarctic continent to the other. Loaded with twenty-seven men, supplies, and equipment—including sleds and dogs—the three-masted ship *Endurance* sailed warily along the continent's western coast, through the endless masses of ice, looking for a suitable place to land. Shackleton had realized at once that the ice was heavier and greater in quantity than on his previous expeditions. One crashing encounter could tear a hole in the ship, sinking it as the *Titanic*—in the far less extreme climate area of the North Atlantic—had sunk only two years before. But the *Endurance* wasn't torn open. It was simply surrounded and immobilized by the ice. There was no radio contact; no one knew of their plight, and no one would come in time to rescue them. But Shackleton would not give up.

Hundreds of miles from anywhere and anyone, he had to get help, and he was going to fight to his last breath to save the men with him. A wonderful account of courage and endurance, with a triumphant ending. One of the most unforgettable sagas in the long line of risk-takers to whom we owe our knowledge of what was once unknown. The almost unbelievable story is brought alive by its splendid narrative and magnificent archival photographs of the men and their amazing ordeal.

Kostyal, K. M. *Trial by Ice: A Photobiography of Sir Ernest Shackleton.* National Geographic Society, 1999, 64 pp. (3-8).

Primary listing under *Biography*

The writer's action-and-suspense-filled biography of Ernest Shackleton provides a splendid introduction to a little-known part of our world. As the story unfolds of Shackleton's battles with the cold, the imprisoning ice, the bitter winds, the uncharted waters, and the ever-present dangers, the reader gains a vivid sense of the realities of Antarctica. Splendid photographs of the frozen world and of the men involved in the struggle just to survive give the reader a more-than-chilly feel of this remote continent.

Shackleton himself hoped to reach the Pole and cross the continent, but over and over he encountered extreme hardships that defeated his purpose. *Defeat*, however, was not a word in the vocabulary of the indomitable Shackleton. His story is one of bravery, tenacity, and selfless commitment to the needs of the men under him. The prolonged ordeal after the loss of the ship *Endurance* has become a classic legend of courage—of the human spirit against nature at its fiercest. Readers will not only gain an informed perspective on Antarctica—which even in our own technology-rich era remains a hazardous challenge to men and women— but they will also be inspired by Ernest Shackleton's remarkable story.

Note: Interested readers will find it worthwhile to read both of the above books.

Kroeber, Theodora. *Ishi: In Two Worlds.* University of Calif. Press, 1976 (1961), 255 pp. (adv. 6-up).

Strictly speaking, this is anthropology rather than history, and it is an adult book. But it is readable and interest-holding for an advanced eleven- or twelve-year-old with an interest in Native Americans. It is also valuable reading for parents or teachers. Ishi was the last North American Indian to live in the wild, the sole survivor of an Indian tribe that became extinct in the first quarter of the twentieth century. Befriended by San Francisco-based anthropologists, Ishi gradually revealed the tragic fate of his people. A unique and remarkable glimpse of a culture that no longer exists, and another reminder of the inhumanity with which most of our native people were treated—right up to early modern times.

Kroll, Steven. *By the Dawn's Early Light: The Story of the Star-Spangled Banner.* Illus. by Dan Andreasen. Scholastic, Inc., 1994, 40 pp. (4-7).

This suspenseful and often surprising account does more than tell the story behind the writing of our national anthem. It also shines a welcome light on an often-forgotten era in America's history. In 1814 the United States is at war with Great Britain, a war of intermittent battles on land and sea. Washington has just been attacked and burned, and the British are holed up at sea in their warships. Francis Scott Key, a successful Washington lawyer, has just learned that a close friend, Dr. Beanes, has been unjustly arrested by the British and imprisoned on one of their ships anchored offshore.

It is as Francis and Colonel Skinner (in charge of prisoner exchange) sail boldly out to the British ship holding Dr. Beanes and, climbing on board, state their case that the heart of the story begins to take shape. Though winning the prisoner's freedom and returning with him to their ship, they are not allowed to sail back to land but are forced to stay with the British warships, which launch a relentless night attack on the fort where the American flag defiantly flies. Shelling from their ships, the British have soldiers in large rowboats, ready to rush ashore and overrun the fort. The writer's thrilling account brings to life the fear and hope of that crucial time. As Key and his companions watch through the hours of the attack, constantly straining to see the flag, dawn finally spreads its faint light; the flag is still there. Pulling an old letter out of his pocket, Francis starts to write on its back the thrilling words that echo in our hearts.

Note: After reading Kroll's account, readers can find out more about this dramatic episode in American history in a splendid article in the July 2000 issue of *Smithsonian* magazine. Most libraries have this periodical on file.

Kurelek, William. *Lumberjack*. Tundra Books, 1996 (1974), 48 pp. (4-up).
　　Primary listings under *Art* and *Biography*
　　This prominent Canadian artist uses his painting and excellent text to detail a segment of modern history (1946 and 1951), showing lumbering as it used to be done, and revealing attitudes and customs of the time.

Kurelek, William. Two books: *A Prairie Boy's Winter*. Houghton Mifflin, 1984 (1973), 48 pp.; *A Prairie Boy's Summer*. Tundra Books, 1996 (1975), 47 pp. (4-up).
　　Primary listings under *Art* and *Biography*
　　These books offer excellent insights into social history of farm life in the 1930s on the Canadian prairie.

Kurelek, William: Paintings and comments; additional text by Margaret Engelhart. *They Sought a New World: The Story of European Immigration to North America*. Tundra Books, 1985, 48 pp. (4-up).
　　Noted Canadian artist William Kurelek referred to himself as a "historical painter." The son of Ukrainian immigrants, he wanted his art to preserve for future generations the experience of the Europeans who came to North America and struggled to build new lives and new homes. In this unusual book, twenty-eight of Kurelek's richly expressive paintings accompany a compact but wide-ranging chronicle of the immigrant experience. Writer Margaret Engelhart has woven together selections from Kurelek's writings on the subject, her own unifying background/historical research, and the related paintings—of the immigrants on their farms and in their workplaces; at church, school, and social gatherings—into a coherent and effective whole.

　　A large proportion of today's Americans and Canadians come directly from these earlier waves of European immigrants who sought new lives and, most of all, opportunities for their children. As presented in the book, Kurelek's vision of sharing the story of these courageous people not only brings a fresh understanding of their part in the development of life in North America, but can also increase young readers' understanding of what it means to be an immigrant today as people come—this time more from Asian and Latin American countries—with the same hopes: better lives for themselves, but most of all for their children.

Lasky, Kathryn. *The Librarian Who Measured the Earth*. Illus. by Kevin Hawkes. Little, Brown and Co., 1994, 48 pp. (3-up).

Primary listing under *Biography*

This excellent picture biography of Eratosthenes, who lived in Greece and in Egypt two millenniums ago, makes fine supplementary reading for study units on both the geography and history of the ancient world. His curiosity about the size of the earth led Eratosthenes to create a way of calculating its diameter, using some unique and surprising equipment—including camels. The answer he found was within just 200 miles of today's figure based on the use of modern technology.

The book's authentic background material on life in Greece and Egypt, complemented with informative illustrations, will encourage a fuller understanding of that long-ago world. For example, learning of the existence of the famous library in Alexandria where Eratosthenes spent much of his life is in itself a valuable piece of general knowledge for a young student. A lively, enjoyable, and useful book.

Latham, Jean Lee. *Carry on, Mr. Bowditch*. Houghton Mifflin, 1955, 251 pp. (5, 6).

Primary listing under *Biography*

This splendid biography provides much authentic background material on the eventful American history of the late eighteenth and early nineteenth centuries. It is full of well-researched details and reads like good fiction.

Latham, Jean Lee. *Anchors Aweigh: The Story of David Glasgow Farragut*. Harper and Row, 1968, 273 pp. (5-9).

Primary listing under *Biography*

Because virtually all of Farragut's life was spent in the navy, there is much historical material in his biography. Involved in the War of 1812, in extensive cruises at sea, in the War with Mexico, and a hero of naval combat in the Civil War, Farragut was frequently a part of events of national significance. This excellent source of historical material is also an account full of action and adventure. Currently out of print, this book is still in many libraries and available through interlibrary loan.

Lawlor, Laurie. *Window on the West: The Frontier Photography of William Henry Jackson*. Holiday House, 1999, 132 pp. (5-up)

Primary listing under *Biography*

When photographer William Henry Jackson began his portrayals of the American West in 1869, the first transcontinental railway had just been completed. Suddenly vast inland areas of the United States were at least potentially accessible. Interest in what was "out there" exploded. Although stories had been told about towering mountains, spectacular waterfalls, the geysers of Yellowstone, and other wonders, almost no one had actually seen them. There was a great desire to know about the intriguing, uncharted areas. Even more than that, corporations, manufacturers, and entrepreneurs of all kinds were impatient to find opportunities for money-making enterprises there.

It was at this restless, seeking time that William Jackson, already heading west to see and photograph out of personal interest, began to recognize the widespread demand for pictures of the West's spectacular mountain areas and fabled Indian tribes. He was in the right place at the right time, and his outstanding photography illumines for succeeding generations a significant era in American history and in geographic knowledge of American terrain.

Leedy, Loreen. *Celebrate the 50 States.* Holiday House, Inc., 1999, 32 pp. (ps-3).

A colorful look at America's fifty states (Washington, D.C., and the U.S. territories are also included). A map of each one offers information on its distinctives— its rank as to when it became a state in relation to the other states and the date when it happened; its capital, state bird, and flower, and a significant place or event. Other specific information is given, and in some cases a significant person is pictured and mentioned. Intended as a celebratory overview of our wonderful homeland rather than a detailed report, the pages are not cluttered but contain varied relevant pictures and caption-style notes. Each state display poses a question, such as the one related to Oregon: "How deep is Crater Lake?" (Answers are on the last page.) An atmosphere of warmth, humor, and enjoyment pervades each page, and the final picture reflects that spirit. It is a map of the United States as delightfully colorful as a patchwork quilt, and most readers will echo the words of the little girl on the facing page: "I want to visit every state!" A fine introduction to the geography and even a little of the history of our nation.

Leiner, Katherine. *First Children: Growing Up in the White House.* Portraits by Katie Keller. Tambourine Books, 1996, 157 pp. (4, 5-up).

Primary listing under *Biography*

This lively book about a number of the nation's First Children is a good choice for supplemental class reading for history or simply as entertaining but informative leisure reading. In addition to many personal anecdotes about the various children, the ample background material offers insights into significant ongoing events in the life of the nation and on the cultural and social changes through two centuries of American history.

Lewin, Ted. *Touch and Go: Travels of a Children's Book Illustrator.* Lothrop, Lee and Shepard Books, 1999, 67 pp. (5-up).

Ted Lewin writes and illustrates children's books, but when he isn't working on a book, he is likely to be found traveling in some of the less-known nooks and crannies of the world. Lewin has an endless interest in places and people, and this book consists of thirty-three little vignettes of individuals he has encountered in such places as Okavango Delta, Botswana; Floreano Island, Galapagos; Cooinda, Australia, and many more. Each sketch is usually one to one and a half pages long. Amusing, quirky, colorful, ironic, bizarre, poignant, baffling—the variety is exhilarating. A sixteen-page section in the center of the book has color photos of some of the stories' subjects. This is not only an unusual and enjoyable book, but it will broaden a child's concept of both the physical and cultural world while demonstrating an especially effective use of written language. (Children could try modeling some little stories of their own on the keen observation and the writing style of the book's well-told tales.)

Macaulay, David. *City*. Houghton Mifflin, 1974, 112 pp. (5-up).
    Primary listing under *Art* and *Architecture*
    Macaulay's minutely detailed description of the building of a Roman city offers a wealth of historical information along with its remarkable architectural coverage. Archaeology clearly demonstrates that the buildings used by any civilization reveal a great deal about the culture and daily life of its people. As the reader follows Macaulay's step-by-step description of the city's construction, much that was distinctively Roman is observed—and remembered.

Macaulay, David. Three books: *Castle; Cathedral; Pyramid*. Houghton Mifflin, 1977, 74 pp.; 1973, 77 pp.; 1975, 80 pp. (3-up).
    Primary listing under *Art* and *Architecture*
    See comments above on Macaulay's book *City* for ways in which these books are related to the history of their respective times.

Macaulay, David. *Mill*. Houghton Mifflin, 1983, 128 pp. (5, 6-up).
    Primary listing under *Art* and *Architecture*
    Using four imaginary but typical structures related to the textile industry (built at intervals of about twenty years), Macaulay not only shows technological change from 1810-1974, but he also focuses subtly on cultural patterns and labor-management relations over the years.

Macaulay, David. *Building Big*. Houghton Mifflin, 2000, 192 pp. (5-up).
  Primary listing under *Art and Architecture*
  The creator of a number of highly acclaimed books on buildings, Macaulay has focused this time on the very large—big both in size and in significance. The writer/artist looks closely at thirty-five notable structures—bridges, tunnels, dams, domes, and skyscrapers in a variety of locations across the world. In addition to the wealth of architectural detail, with many drawings and diagrams, Macaulay also provides background information, discussing why the structures were built. This text often includes references to prevailing circumstances and events in the area of the world and the time period in which the structure was being built. Such a book offers yet another opportunity for young readers to see "the big picture" and to relate what they are reading to the knowledge of history and geography they are (it is hoped) absorbing at school, through other reading, and in the news of the day.

Marrin, Albert. *Commander in Chief: Abraham Lincoln and the Civil War*. Dutton Children's Books, 1997, 246 pp. (5-up).
  Primary listing under *Biography*
  This excellent account of President Lincoln in relation to the Civil War is a splendid choice for supplemental reading when a history class is studying that period of history—or simply to read on its own merits. For more comments on the book's approach to its subject, see the listing under *Biography*.

Marrin, Albert. *Virginia's General: Robert E. Lee and the Civil War*. Atheneum, 1994, 218 pp. (5-up).
  Primary listing under *Biography*
  It would be impossible to see the life of Robert E. Lee apart from American history. This fine study of Lee as a historic figure and of the Confederate Army in the Civil War provides a valuable supplemental resource for students. Used with the author's matching volume on the Union Army's engagement in that war (*Unconditional Surrender: U. S. Grant and the Civil War*, Atheneum, 1994, 5-up), the reader will gain a comprehensive view of that tragic era of American history. For a fuller discussion of the content of *Virginia's General*, see the *Biography* listing.

Meadowcroft, Enid L. *By Wagon and Flatboat*. Harper and Row, 1938, 170 pp. (3-up).
  Primary listing under *Literature: Level II, Realistic Stories—Historical*
  In this story of pioneers on their way from Pennsylvania to Ohio in 1789, the writer has included a good proportion of historical detail, both as to the new American nation and as to day-to-day customs, items in use, and so forth. No attempt has been made to use anything approaching the authentic speech of the time, which somewhat detracts from the atmosphere of the book. The story does, however, provide worthwhile information in a pleasantly interesting form.

Meigs, Cornelia. *Invincible Louisa*. Little, Brown and Co., 1968 (1933), 260 pp. (6-up).
  Primary listing under *Biography*
  This fine biography of beloved author Louisa May Alcott provides excellent his-

torical sidelights on the New England of the last half of the nineteenth century. Insights on the slavery question and the Civil War are woven into the story of Alcott's life.

Mochizuki, Ken. *Passage to Freedom: The Sugihara Story.* Afterword by Hiroki Sugihara. Illus. by Dom Lee. Lee and Low Books, Inc., 1997, 32 pp. (1-up).

In 1940 five-year-old Hiroki Sugihara, this true story's narrator, is living with his family in Lithuania where his father is the Japanese consul. The family lives upstairs over the consulate offices, and, looking out the window one day, Hiroki sees a large group of people outside the consulate, pressed against the fence. World War II is in its second year, the Nazis have taken over Poland, and desperate Jewish refugees have fled to Lithuania. They have now come to the Japanese consulate to beg Hiroki's father to write visas for them so they can pass through other countries and escape the Nazis. Touched by the desperation of the hundreds of refugees, Hiroki's father cables to Japan (a wartime ally of Germany) for permission to write the visas. The response is no. Mr. Sugihara cables a second and a third time, but both answers are negative. Hiroki's father gathers his family around him, and they talk about the situation. They are all in agreement: The refugees must be given their chance; Mr. Sugihara must disobey his government at whatever risk to the Sugiharas and write the visas. This fascinating account tells the story of the brave and compassionate man whose courage saved perhaps as many as 10,000 Jewish refugees.

Moody, Ralph. *Little Britches.* W. W. Norton and Co., 1962 (1950), 250 pp. (5-up).

Primary listing under *Biography*

This remarkable biography of several eventful years in the life of a young boy in Colorado during the early part of the twentieth century is more than an account of one boy's experiences. It introduces the reader to an American world as remote from today as if it had existed hundreds of years ago. As at any point in our history, not all Americans faced the same conditions in a given time period, but the ways in which the Moody family had to cope, the part the children played in the life of the family, and the expectations and opportunities (or lack of them) that shaped people's lives are an integral part of American history. *Little Britches* reads like fiction in its exciting and event-filled narrative, but in reality it portrays significant aspects of our American past. For more details of the book's content see the *Biography* listing.

Morgan, Gwyneth. *Life in a Medieval Village.* Cambridge University Press, 1995 (1982), 52 pp. (5, 6-up).

One of the excellent series of Topic Books produced by Cambridge University Press. Scholarship and human interest are combined in this concise and yet detailed study of medieval village culture. The well-written text is generously illustrated.

Murphy, Jim. *A Young Patriot: The American Revolution as Experienced by One Boy.* Houghton Mifflin, 1996, 101 pp. (5-up).

At fifteen Joseph Plumb Martin (1760-1850) signed up for a six-month enlistment in the army. When he was released, Joseph spent a few months at home recovering from malnutrition and a serious illness (perhaps pneumonia) that followed what he called a "violent cold." With his health restored, he promptly reen-listed—this time for the duration of the war. In 1830 when Joseph was seventy, he wrote a detailed narrative of his wartime experiences. Largely unnoticed at the time, the book is now viewed by historians as one of the most detailed and impor-tant accounts of the War for Independence. Using Joseph Martin's book in the con-text of his own knowledge of Revolutionary history, Murphy does a fine job of highlighting the war's overall progress while keeping a central focus on the every-day experiences of that conflict's equivalent of G. I. Joe.

Well written and highly readable, Murphy's account is marred only by his apparent reluctance to fully acknowledge the heroic quality of General Washington's character and the indispensable part his spirit played in inspiring the ultimate victory of his hodgepodge "citizen's army" over Britain's trained, expe-rienced soldiers. Many contemporary historians have a bias against what they see as hero worship, and they fail to recognize the incalculable power of the human spirit in a person of heroic character and undaunted faith. Read Murphy's excel-lent book by all means, but for an inspiring view of Washington and the spirit that won America her independence, read also Louise Peacock's *Crossing the Delaware*, listed below.

Murphy, Jim. *Blizzard!* Scholastic Press, 2000, 136 pp. (5-up).

Full of vivid description, suspenseful events, and dozens of human interest sto-ries, *Blizzard!* is more than a gripping account of the disastrous East Coast storm of March 1888. The writer discusses the major long-term changes that resulted from the effects of that storm, with its mountainous deluges of snow, treacherous ice, and gale-force winds. Difficult as things were in areas away from urban cen-ters, it was in New York City, already the proud leader in national finance and the power base of many corporations, that the complete breakdown of coastal ship-ping, railroads, transportation of any kind, and the cutoff of communications occurred. This disaster put in motion much-needed and widely influential changes. Other large Eastern cities followed New York's lead, all of which eventually meant real change throughout America.

Illuminating the lively and well-written text are a wealth of archival photo-graphs from several historical societies and museums and many wonderful repro-ductions of vintage illustrations from the author's own collection. Last but not negligible is the book's effectiveness in conveying some of what city life (and more briefly rural life) was like in the late nineteenth century.

Neimark, Anne E. *Touch of Light: The Story of Louis Braille.* Harcourt, Brace, Jovanovich, 1970, 186 pp. (4-6).

Primary listing under *Biography*

Although this is primarily the story of Louis Braille and his invention of the raised dot symbols by which the blind can read, it also provides good supplemen-tary material on cultural and political history in France for the period of 1812-1852. The effect on Braille's family of the impoverishing war in which the French soldiers stripped the small farms and households of livestock, produce, anything at all of value; the hopeless condition of most of the blind of that day; the lack of concern of the French government for the needs of its people are all clearly part of Braille's story. Now out of print, this fine book is still in some libraries and should be obtainable through interlibrary loan.

O'Dell, Scott. *The Hawk That Dare Not Hunt by Day.* Bob Jones University, 1986, (1975) 182 pp. (6-up).
   Primary listing under *Literature: Level III, Realistic Stories—Historical*
   This exciting story of a young seaman who helped smuggle William Tyndale's Bibles into England has a fine, well-developed historical background. O'Dell brings out the way in which forces of intrigue from all over Europe had gathered to prevent Tyndale from carrying out his mission, and vividly pictures the religious and political turmoil on every hand.

O'Dell, Scott. *The King's Fifth.* Houghton Mifflin, 1966, 264 pp. (6-up).
   Primary listing under *Literature: Level III, Realistic Stories—Historical*
   O'Dell's story is written from an unusual perspective: The hero is a thoughtful and observant young Spanish map-maker with the conquistadors who ravaged the American southwest in their lust for gold. Good historical insights not often seen from this particular vantage point.

Olasky, Susan. *Annie Henry and the Birth of Liberty.* Adventures of the American Revolution Series. Crossway Books, 1995, 127 pp. (3-up).
   Primary listing under *Literature: Level II, Realistic Stories—Historical*
   A lively, appealing story of the young daughter of Patrick Henry, famous for all time for his stirring call to decisive action: "I know not what course others may take, but as for me, give me liberty or give me death!" Set in 1775 as the American Revolution is in its first tentative stages, the story blends historical events with the fictionalized adventures of Annie Henry. Good material on the social and cultural background of the period is woven into the story. There are three more Annie Henry books in this series.

Peacock, Louise. *Crossing the Delaware.* Illus. by Walter Lyon Krudop. Atheneum Books for Young Readers, 1998, 40 pp. (2-6).
   Without the American Revolution, fought two and a quarter centuries ago, there would have been no United States of America. And in the bitter cold of December 1776, that risk-all undertaking, that desperate bid for freedom, that unprecedented venture that would determine the future of us all, was within a hair's breadth of collapsing almost before it started. Still in the early months of the conflict, the Americans had suffered defeat after defeat, and the British were already sending word to their king that they had triumphed. Camped in the snow on the Pennsylvania side of the icy Delaware River, the Americans, many of them without shelter, felt hopeless and finished—except for General Washington. Across the river, he knew, were the comfortably housed and well-fed Hessian troops, mercenaries hired by the British. The Americans must win a battle immediately, and Washington thought of a desperate plan.
   This splendid book captures the spirit of purpose, courage, and commitment

that Washington inspired and that was needed to wage the long, hard war ahead. Washington's daring venture on that Christmas night proved to be a crucial turning point that well deserves this retelling.

Perl, Lila. *Slumps, Grunts, and Snickerdoodles: What Colonial America Ate and Why*. Houghton Mifflin, 1975, 128 pp. (6-up).
    Primary listing under *Crafts, Hobbies, and Domestic Arts*
    Revealing sidelights on the cultural history of the colonists are given in relation to what they ate and why. The specific origins of various regional foods are traced, and geographical and historical background as well as the settlers' domestic arrangements are interwoven in the account.

Perl, Lila. *Hunter's Stew and Hangtown Fry: What Pioneer America Ate and Why*. Houghton Mifflin, 1977, 176 pp. (6-up).
    Primary listing under *Crafts, Hobbies, and Domestic Arts*
    Through the foods eaten, the writer illumines the daily life of the westward-moving pioneers. One of the interesting aspects of the book is Perl's discussion of the distinctive culinary contributions made by specific immigrant groups who settled in various part of the United States.

Plotz, Helen, editor. *The Gift Outright: America to Her Poets*. Greenwillow Books, 1977, 204 pp. (all ages).
    Primary listing under *Literature: Anthologies*
    This excellent collection of poems about America offers a number of possibilities for tie-ins with historical events and personages. Now out of print, this fine book will still be found in some libraries and through interlibrary loan.

Porter, Jane. *Scottish Chiefs*. Simon and Schuster, 1991 (1809), 520 pp. (6-up).
    Primary listing under *Literature: Level III, Realistic Stories—Historical*
    A long, highly romanticized story of the Scottish hero William Wallace in the late thirteenth and early fourteenth-century period of English-Scottish conflict. Full of idealism, courage, hairbreadth escapes, and noble deaths, it also offers some general historical insights on the period and its events. For advanced readers.

Pyle, Howard. *Otto of the Silver Hand*. Dover, 1967 (1883), 136 pp. (4-9).
    Primary listing under *Literature: Level III, Realistic Stories—Historical*
    Set in Germany in the sixteenth-century, the story contrasts the harshness of the life under the iron-fisted feudal barons with the peace of the monastery where the story's central character is cared for. Excellent literary quality as well as an authentic historical setting.

Royce, Sarah. *Sarah Royce and the American West*. Ed. by Jane Shuter. Raintree Steck Vaughn Co., 1996, 48 pp. (4-8).
    Based on Sarah Royce's century-old memoir, *A Frontier Lady,* this excellently edited first-person account brings fresh perspectives on gold rush pioneering. Whether Sarah Royce is helping to find straying cattle, trudging through mud, cross-

ing rain-swollen rivers, encountering edgy Indians on the trail to California, or bearing and caring for four children during years of moving from one impermanent home to another, she keeps her balance—and her faith. Intelligent and keenly observant, Sarah records the realities of life in gold rush mining camps and offers glimpses also of Sacramento, San Francisco, and the as-yet-undeveloped Bay Area. Because Sarah, her husband, Josiah, and children are in California as a family, and because Josiah is seeking their fortune in storekeeping rather than mining, Sarah's perspective is broader than that of the thousands of miners digging and panning for gold.

In addition to Sarah's narration, the editor has included many sidebars and detailed picture captions that provide extensive background information. The book is generously illustrated throughout with photographs and reproductions of paintings. Enjoyable to read on its own, the book is also an excellent supplementary resource for the study of Western pioneering and the California gold rush.

Rushdoony, Haig A. *The Language of Maps*. Fearon Teaching Aids, 1982 (4-6).

This supplementary paperback includes teacher-directed lessons, student-directed activities, maps, and related graphics—all designed to teach and reinforce map-reading skills. Much of the information is practical and helpful, and some of the activities are interesting in themselves and would help to fix particular concepts in students' minds. Some of the questions and activities are contrived busywork, a failing that seems almost universal in workbooks. Overall, the book offers useful content for parents and teachers who prefer not to create their own supplementary map-reading activities.

Sauer, Carl. *Man in Nature: America Before the Days of the White Man—A First Book in Geography*. Turtle Island Foundation, 1975 (1939), 273 pp. (3-5).

As indicated in the introduction, we have not included textbooks in the book list. The unique nature of Sauer's geography text, however, mandated an exception. The writer believes that children will acquire a truer and more lasting view of the natural elements of the continent (land, water, weather, plants, and animals) that distinguished one area from another by first seeing and understanding North America as it was when only scattered Indian tribes populated its vast expanse, before the change brought by the white man's intervention. Sauer is not at all unmindful of the significance of modern social geography (differences in people and what they have made and used and changed in any given place). He simply wants to start by giving children a fundamental approach on which to build a lifetime of clear, ordered information about the world in which they live, an approach that could be applied to places other than North America.

It is impossible in a brief space to adequately describe the book's content, which not only offers factual knowledge but also draws its readers into a contemplation of the natural world and encourages creative thinking. At the same time, Sauer is not anti-civilization. While dealing fairly with the positive aspects of Indian life, he does not by any means see their lifestyle as idyllic.

It is important to remember that this book was written sixty-three years ago, so that the depiction of Eskimo life (spoken of in the book as continuing into the then present) must be seen to be now clearly past. The passage of time, however, does not diminish his description of pre-civilization geographical conditions in America. Numerous drawings, map-making, climate and weather observation, kinds of vegetation and animal life are integral parts of Sauer's discussion of each section of our continent. Not widely available in libraries, the book is well worth ordering through a local bookstore or directly from the publisher.

Note: Sauer's book was written long before the term "Native American" was popular.

Schmidt, Jeremy. *In the Village of the Elephants*. Walker and Co., 1994, 30 pp. (2-5).

Near the southern tip of India in the Nilgiri Hills, the Kurambas still live in tiny villages, following age-old patterns of life in the midst of changes that have come to them. Once part of a group of hill tribes who had been nomadic hunters for centuries, the Kurambas experienced a change in lifestyle about 100 years ago when the government decided that since they knew so much about the forest and the wild elephants, they would make good mahouts (elephant drivers). So the Kuramba men became mahouts and began to drive the elephants owned by the government and used in the country's logging industry. Today still each man is responsible for "his" elephant's care, and the sons in the family start at about twelve to learn how to become mahouts.

Traveler and writer Jeremy Schmidt takes the reader into the tiny village where Bomman and his family live and both tells and shows (in photographer Ted Wood's splendid pictures) what life is like for a boy of India who lives among elephants and whose first responsibility each morning is to take the elephant Mudumalai down to the river and give him a scrub-all-over bath! A wonderful window on a very different place and a very different way of life that still goes on today.

Sootin, Harry. *Robert Boyle: Founder of Modern Chemistry*. Franklin Watts, 1962, 133 pp. (6-up).

See also *Biography* and *Science* listings.

Boyle's father was the wealthy Earl of Cork, one of the powerful English landowners in Ireland in the seventeenth century. The family was intimately involved in major political events of the period. As well as recounting Boyle's contributions to scientific development, the book sheds light on the English role in Ireland, the Royalist-Puritan confrontations, the relatively brief rule of Cromwell, and the Restoration. Boyle's family had connections with both sides of the conflict, and the way the family interests were affected makes enlightening reading. Brief mentions of cultural patterns and the "advantageous" marriages arranged by the Earl for some of his sons and daughters (at least two of which were disastrously unhappy) show quite clearly the very real situations on which many historical novels have been based. A wonderful older book, especially helpful for advanced readers. Long out of print, this book might be found through interlibrary loan.

Speare, Elizabeth George. *The Bronze Bow*. Houghton Mifflin, 1961, 272 pp. (5, 6).
  Primary listing under *Literature: Level III, Realistic Stories—Historical*
  A well-written, suspenseful story set in Palestine at the time of Christ. Good historical background and details of daily life under Roman rule.

Steele, William O. *The Buffalo Knife*. Harbrace, 1990 (1952), 192 pp. (4-up).
  Primary listing under *Literature: Level II, Realistic Stories—Historical*
  In the framework of an adventure-filled story of two young boys and their families moving west, the writer provides information on early pioneering. While the American Revolution was still being fought in the far eastern part of the country, inland settlers were continuing their local conflicts with Indians, extending farmlands, and ever pressing on to new frontiers. Young Andy and Isaac float more than 1,000 miles down (and up) the Tennessee River on a flatboat, encountering a variety of hazards and new experiences on the way, arriving finally at their destination at what would someday become Nashville, Tennessee. Good supplemental material on the history of the westward movement in America, this would also be an interesting book to read while focusing on the Revolutionary War. Much was going on away from the eastern states while the struggle for independence was at its height—a good exercise in broadening students' perceptions.

Steele, William O. *The Perilous Road*. Harbrace, 1990 (1958), 192 pp. (4-up).
  Primary listing under *Literature: Level III, Realistic Stories—Historical*
  Steele's well-written Civil War story focuses on a Tennessee mountain farm family who feel sympathy for both sides of the conflict. The exception to this family feeling is eleven-year-old Chris, who is enraged at the Yankee soldiers for taking his family's winter food supplies and their only horse. When Chris's older brother joins the Union Army, Chris's sense of betrayal is complete. The story offers clear insights on the impact of the Civil War on a family and on the position occupied by people who had no immediate large gain in view no matter which side won or lost.

Steele, William O. *Westward Adventure: The True Stories of Six Pioneers*. Harcourt, Brace, Jovanovich, 1962, 188 pp. (5-up).
  Primary listing under *Biography*
  Steele has drawn upon a variety of sources, including firsthand journals and reports, in recounting the true experiences of six very different eighteenth-century people who struggled through or around the Appalachian Mountains into

the "lands of western waters." These were areas crossed by some of the main inland rivers in territory that would someday be within Tennessee, Kentucky, and other nearby states. Arranging the stories chronologically, Steele virtually spans the century and gives an almost "you are there" feeling to the reader. There is a sense of the movement of history—the interaction with various Indian groups, the mixed motives that drew people to the wilderness, the realities of pioneer life. Currently out of print but still in some libraries or available through interlibrary loan.

Stevens, Byrna. *Ben Franklin's Glass Armonica*. Illus. by Priscilla Kiedrowski. Dell, 1992 (1983), 48 pp. (k-3).
> Primary listing under *Music*
> The story of yet another ingenious invention of the amazing Mr. Franklin. This could be used as an "extra interest" tie-in with American history of Franklin's time.

Stevenson, Robert Louis. *The Black Arrow*. Simon and Schuster, 1987 (1888), 336 pp. (5-up).
> Primary listing under *Literature: Level III, Realistic Stories—Historical*
> Stevenson's exciting story should effectively help to illumine the period of the Wars of the Roses, for the history that is absorbed in the process of reading a gripping story is often retained more fully than when it is read in a textbook.

Stevenson, Robert Louis. *Kidnapped; or the Lad with the Silver Button*. Huntington Library Press, 1999 (1886) 4-7; Sequels: *David Balfour: Being Memoirs of the Further Adventures of David Balfour at Home and Abroad*. Atheneum, 1994, 356 pp. (4-7); *Catriona*. Koenemann, 1998, 240 pp. (5-up).
> Primary listings under *Literature: Level III, Realistic Stories—Historical*
> In Stevenson's classic adventure tale and its suspenseful sequels, the main focus is on the lives of the central characters, but a good deal of historical material is an integral part of the background of the stories. (David's friend Alan, for example, is a former Jacobite leader.) Also, see the primary listing entry describing the Huntington Library edition of *Kidnapped*, which uses the original text and has an extensive introduction that includes material on the historical context of the story.

Sutcliff, Rosemary. *Blood Feud*. Dutton, 1977, 144 pp. (6-up).
> Primary listing under *Literature: Level III, Realistic Stories—Historical*
> A broad sweep of action and adventure based on an actual historical event during the era of the Viking raids. Scenes in England, Ireland, Denmark, and an extended stay in Constantinople. Splendidly written, with the fine literary quality one expects in a work of Sutcliff's.

Tunis, Edwin.
> SPECIAL NOTE: A number of books by this author (written chiefly in the 1970s) included in the original edition of *Books Children Love* are now out of print and not widely available. Some of the titles are *Colonial Living, Frontier Living, Indians, The Tavern at the Ferry*, and *The Young United States*. These

books are filled with attractive illustrations of the objects, buildings, and people of the subject areas and places. Some of the books will perhaps remain on the shelves in libraries where older books are not readily discarded. Tunis's books provided good supplementary material related to American history, were also good reading in themselves, and are worth looking for.

Twain, Mark. *The Prince and the Pauper*. Harper and Row, 1909 (1882), 296 pp. (5-up).
  Primary listing under *Literature: Level III, Realistic Stories—Historical*
  Twain's famous story about the young prince and the beggar boy who exchange roles has a strong appeal simply on the story level. But the portrayal of mid-sixteenth century life in England offers enlightening background for study of the period's history. Twain's strong consciousness of social injustices is reflected throughout.

Urdang, Laurence, editor. *The Timetables of American History*. Simon and Schuster, 1981, 470 pp. (4-up).
  Primary listing under *Reference*
  This is a splendid approach to a broadening of students' grasp of history. In a columnar form, *Timetables* shows, year by year, what was occurring at the same time in the United States and elsewhere under four categories: History and Politics; The Arts; Science and Technology; Miscellaneous.

Verne, Jules. *Michael Strogoff: A Courier of the Czar*. Airmont, 1964 (1876), 340 pp. (6-up).
  Primary listing under *Literature: Level III, Realistic Stories—Historical*
  Few children's stories of pre-Revolution Russia are available, and while the imaginary adventures of the story's hero are the dominant theme, insights into some aspects of Czarist Russia and into the politics of the era are a part of the background of Strogoff's exploits.

Walsh, Jill Paton. *Children of the Fox*. Farrar, Straus and Giroux, 1978, 114 pp. (5, 6-up).
  Primary listing under *Literature: Level III, Realistic Stories—Historical*
  Three stories of courage and adventure in the Grecian world of the fifth century B.C. The stories are fictional, but the historical events involved are factual, as are the Athenian general, the Spartan leader, and so forth. Now out of print, the book is still available in many libraries.

Warren, Andrea. *Orphan Train Rider: One Boy's True Story*. Houghton Mifflin Co., 1996, 80 pp. (4-7).
  Over a period of seventy-six years from 1854 to 1930, more than 200,000 children without parents, or whose parents could not (or would not) care for them, were sent from large Eastern cities to other parts of the country to be placed in new homes. They were transported in groups by train. The intention of the Children's Aid Society and other such agencies behind these mass uprootings was benevolent,

an effort to place children in homes where they would be loved and cared for, rather than having to grow up in orphanages or become homeless street children. In practice, the results were mixed. "Many children found parents who loved them and took care of them; others never felt at home with their new families. Some were mistreated," the author points out.

The last of the people who rode the "orphan trains" are now quite old. Some of them feel that their stories are part of our history and should be known by today's generations. Lee Nailling is one of these. He tells his own touching story, along with discussing the orphan-relocation program as a whole. Many archival and personal photographs are included. As young readers follow the events in Lee's life, they are not only learning about another part of history, but their compassion for children around them today who may be in foster care or who lack love and support in their own homes may be broadened, giving them a kind and understanding perspective that will remain in their hearts.

Washington, Booker T. *Up from Slavery*. Doubleday, 1998 (1901), 384 pp. (5-up).
   Primary listing under *Biography*
   This autobiography (written in 1901) of the courageous life of Booker T. Washington offers valuable historical material on the realities of life for African-Americans during the post-Civil War years, and on the related cultural and political conditions. Parents or teachers can effectively use excerpts and facts from this book, which is longer than many children are ready to read through for themselves.

Wells, Rosemary. *Streets of Gold*. Illus. by Dan Andreasen. Dial Books for Young Readers, 1999, 39 pp. (3-6).
   Primary listing under *Biography*
   This well-written and beautifully illustrated picture biography tells the story of Mary Antin who, with her family, emigrates to America from Russia in the late nineteenth century. Several of its themes make it excellent supplemental reading for history segments focusing on people's search for freedom from oppression, on immigration, or on ethnic or religious persecution. Based on Mary Antin's own autobiography, *Promised Land,* which she wrote in the early twentieth century, the account has an appealing story quality as it tells of the persecution this Jewish family suffers in Czarist Russia and of Mary's joy in the freedom and opportunity for education in America.

Wilder, Laura Ingalls. *On the Way Home*. HarperCollins Children's Books, 1976 (1962), 112 pp. (6-up).
   Primary listing under *Biography*
   This firsthand account of the Wilders' 650-mile journey from South Dakota to Missouri reflects a variety of historically interesting facts. In her diary, Laura mentions small, simple matters that help to give a vivid picture of life in 1894. The reader is struck forcibly by the almost unbelievable changes that have occurred in virtually every aspect of life since the Wilders made their journey.

Wilder, Laura Ingalls. *West from Home*. HarperCollins Children's Books, 1974, 144 pp. (4-up).

Primary listing under *Biography*

A collection of letters to her husband by Laura Ingalls Wilder (author of the *Little House* books) during a 1915 visit she made to her daughter in San Francisco. Laura's keen observations take the reader back to the time about which she writes, and, as always, such comments lend life and reality to the historical facts.

Wilkes, Angela. *A Farm Through Time*. Illus. by Eric Thomas. DK Publishing, Inc., 2001, 32 pp. (3-up).

A beautiful book offering an informative overview of an English farm's development and changes over 1,200 years, from the year 800 to the present. Each two-page spread pictures a part of the farm with its buildings, equipment, and animals of the period being discussed. The text, in a pleasing type style—easily read but blending with the background—runs across the top of the pages, providing information and pointing out the distinctive features of the particular era, the ways in which the land was used, and the changes time and technological, political, and social developments have made. Some of the two-page spreads have a half-page foldout that shows an additional perspective (the inside of a house, for example). Children will enjoy the cheery atmosphere and wealth of detail in the many colorful illustrations.

Note: Realists will certainly recognize that the level of sparkling cleanliness, attractive clothing, and the appearance of prosperity seen in the book's lovely pages are surely closer to the ideal than to reality for the vast majority of farmers, even the successful ones. But that fact doesn't keep the book from being useful and enjoyable—just something to keep in mind.

Woolridge, Connie Nordhielm. *When Esther Morris Headed West: Women, Wyoming, and the Right to Vote*. Illus. by Jacqueline Rogers. Holiday House, 2001, 29 pp. (3-5).

Told in a rollicking, amusingly illustrated style, this is the account of an interesting and significant bit of American history. Half a century before the United States Congress in 1920 finally recognized the right of women to vote, the Territory of Wyoming had granted that right to women in 1869. How a large, middle-aged woman, Esther Morris, brought this about makes a lively and often very funny story—which also makes its valid point about voting rights for all adults.

10

HUMOR

NOTE: Humorous stories and poems are not listed here, but are included with the *Literature* listings. The comments on each such book mention its humorous quality.

Archbold, Tim, Mik Brown, and Tania Hart-Newton. *Ha! Ha! Ha! Over 400 Very Funny Jokes.* Kingfisher, 1999, (not paginated) (4-up).
> A collection of kid-appeal jokes including a section of "Classic Knock, Knocks"; one of "Crack-Ups: Very Silly Jokes," and the concluding section: "Elephantastics: A Trunkful of Unforgettable Jokes." Oodles of cartoon-style drawings accompany the jokes.

Cerf, Bennett. *Riddles and More Riddles.* (Formerly in two volumes.) Beginner Books, 1999 (1960, 1961), 48 pp. (k-3).
> Kid-style humor with the benefit of Cerf's taste and style. Children need a goodly portion of this sort of fun—something they love.

Gounaud, Karen Jo. *A Very Mice Joke Book.* Houghton Mifflin, 1981, 47 pp. (2-5).
> A lighthearted collection of jokes and riddles all about well-known mice (such as the best-known mouse of all, Fay Mouse; the historic dictator Mouseolini; and the writer of the Declaration of Independence, Tom Mouse Jefferson). Clever, humorous illustrations on almost every page.

Hills, Tad. *Knock, Knock! Who's There?* Little Simon, 2000, 20 pp. (k-3).
> Knock, knock jokes still offer the younger set the kind of hilarity they love. Hills's little book is for the very young: easy-read, brightly colored, and amusingly illustrated. Each joke is on a two-page spread (heavy card stock) with the first question and answer on the left page—"Knock, knock. Who's there?" "Liz." On the right page is the second question: "Liz who?" The right half of the page then opens out with the punch line: "Liz-en to my song." Enjoyable reading practice and squeaky-clean humor.

Keller, Charles, compiler. *Ballpoint Bananas and Other Jokes for Kids.* Simon and Schuster Children's Books, 1976 (1973), 96 pp. (3-7).
> Wacky riddles, ridiculous rhymes, and taunts and teases. (If junior-high-type insult humor isn't for you, just avoid this book.)

Keller, Charles. *The Little Giant Book of School Jokes.* Illus. by Jeff Sinclair. Sterling Publishing Co., Inc., 2000, 359 pp. (3-7).

Children often especially enjoy jokes related to something that has an important place in their lives—school. Some of the jokes are short and snappy: "Why were students able to study underwater?" "Because they had a sub." Others are a little longer and a little more subtle: "Teacher to young man running in the hall: 'I'm going to have to report you to the principal. What's your name?' Student: 'Ignatius Cornelius Fogenheimer.' Teacher: 'Well, don't let me catch you doing it again.'"

Silly, of course. But in an era in which the jokes many children hear from classmates at school are often objectionable, a fat book of decent jokes could be well worth having!

Walker, Barbara K., compiler. *Laughing Together: Giggles and Grins from Around the World.* Free Spirit Pub., 1992 (1977), 132 pp. (3-up).

Jokes, cartoons, riddles, rhymes, and short tales gathered from almost 100 countries and political or ethnic groups. In some cases, the item is shown in both its native language and English, while the rest are simply in English translations. Observing the similarities (and the differences) in humor from one country or ethnic group to the next expands students' world awareness as well as their literary sense. But most of all, these are kid-type jokes to laugh and have fun with.

Watson, Clyde. *Quips and Quirks.* HarperCollins Children's Books, 1975, 64 pp. (3-7).

For hundreds, perhaps thousands, of years, people have called each other names designed to reveal some peculiarity, quirk, or flaw. The writer diligently researched old books and dictionaries and came up with a choice collection of terms for such trying people as boors ("clunch" and "lumpkin" are just two of the synonyms); chatterboxes ("flapjaw," "windjammer," and others put that message across), and so on. This is a book for word fans who have the good sense not to use their new-found, fun-to-say words in inappropriate situations!

11

LANGUAGE
ALPHABETS, WORD USE, WRITING,
BOOKS, AND MORE

Agee, Jon. *Elvis Lives! And Other Anagrams*. Farrar, Straus and Giroux, 2000, 72 pp. (4-up).

Anyone who enjoys word-play will enjoy this combination of anagrams, clever drawings, and humor. For example, a sketch of a very messy room is labeled "DORMITORY." A pig is coming through the door saying, "DIRTY ROOM," which, of course, uses the same letters as the word *dormitory*. On another page, a boa constrictor, wrapped completely around a hefty lady, is asking, "ONE HUG?" To which the woman replies, "ENOUGH!" More than simply entertaining, this kind of word-play increases a youngster's awareness of word formation and sharpens his or her perception of the importance of using letters correctly and with purpose to convey meaning.

Borden, Louise. *The Day Eddie Met the Author*. Illus. by Adam Gustavson. Simon and Schuster Children's Books, 2001, 29 pp. (2-5).

Eddie loves to read, and he wants to know more about how to write well. So he is very excited that a real author is coming to his school. All the children have been reading the author's books, and they know there will be a question-and-answer time when the author finishes speaking. Eddie has thought and thought and then written out his question on a piece of yellow paper. His teacher tells him it is a great question: "How do you write books that have parts just for me?" Everyone seems to have a question, the time runs out, and the author hasn't heard Eddie's question. But standing downheartedly in the third-grade line to go back to class, Eddie feels a hand on his shoulder. The author has noticed his raised hand with the piece of yellow paper and wants to hear his question. Her answer is food for thought to the aspiring young writer, as are several aspects of the story, including a quote from the author's talk to the students: "Some of you may be wondering how to become a writer. The best way to become a writer is to be a reader."

Brookfield, Karen. *Book*. Eyewitness Books Series. Alfred A. Knopf, Inc., 2000 (1993), 63 pp. (4-7).

This organized potpourri of wonderful illustrations and paragraph-length captions offers a wealth of fascinating information about the development of the written word: how some alphabets evolved from pictures; the inventions of paper-making, handwritten books, printing, binding, the typewriter, and many other related developments. More than 300 specific items are grouped in loosely chrono-logical order in line with discoveries and inventions across the years.

Charlip, Remy, et al. *Handtalk: An ABC of Finger Spelling and Sign Language.* Simon and Schuster Children's Books, 1984 (1974), 48 pp. (ps-up).

    Basic how-to's of talking with hand signals: finger spelling and signing. This book offers just a start, but it does follow the same methods used by the deaf. As a game, it is enjoyable; as a means of communicating with the hearing-impaired, it has a deeper and much more significant dimension.

Cole, Joanne and Stephanie Calmenson. *Rain or Shine Activity Book.* Illus. by Alan Tiegreen. Morrow Junior Books, 1997, 192 pp. (all ages).

    Primary listing under *Crafts, Hobbies, and Domestic Arts*

    This omnibus of things to keep kids happily occupied offers a number of lan-guage-related activities: tongue twisters, riddles, word games, and others. See the primary listing for more information on the book's contents.

Cummins, Julie. *The Inside-Outside Book of Libraries.* Illus. by Roxie Munro. Dutton Children's Books, 1996, 45 pp. (4-up).

    Libraries are favorite places of kids who love to read, and author and illus-trator Julie Cummins and Roxie Munro have portrayed more than a dozen widely differing libraries. From two immense and prestigious ones—the Library of Congress and the New York Public Library—to the tiny, one-room Ocracoke Library and the compact library tucked below the flight deck on a U. S. Navy nuclear-powered aircraft carrier, a variety of rooms-for-books are described. The possibilities and attractions of specialized as well as general-use collections offer young readers new views of the wonderful world of books—and one look at a "library" that lends tools. (As useful and even lovable as tools are, that entry could have been omitted!) Munro's illustrations are delightfully warm and col-orful, capturing that special atmosphere unlike any other—created only by books.

Feder, Jane. *Table, Chair, Bear: A Book in Many Languages.* Ticknor and Fields Books for Young People, 1995, 27 pp. (ps-2).

    A colorful, intriguing little book that encourages an early interest in languages. Pictured centrally on each page is a familiar object often found in a child's own room. The object is identified (in English) in large type above the object, with the word's phonetic pronunciation in small type beneath it. Vertically, in the page mar-gin, the word is shown in twelve other languages, with the phonetic pronunciation beneath each one. A phonetic symbol guide is provided on the first page, and a list of the order in which the languages are shown (in the same order on each page) follows that guide. Many children find it fascinating to see, for example, the word *lamp* in Portuguese (Brazilian), *um abajur,* and its pronunciation, *oom ah-bah-zhoor.* This is one of those books that encourages the curiosity—a wonderful gift of childhood and one of the priceless elements of learning. Some adult (or older sibling) guidance and participation is helpful with the younger children. For all ages, before starting the book, do make a copy of the order in which the languages appear on each margin. Then (initially) move it along, page by page, rather than having to constantly turn back to the front of the book to be sure which language you are looking at! An especially interested reader will soon memorize the order in which each language appears.

Fisher, Leonard Everett. *Alphabet Art*. Simon and Schuster Children's Books, 1984 (1978), 64 pp. (5-up).

Also listed under *Art*

This elegant book shows the development of written language by means of excellent graphics. An opening chart shows the nearest equivalents for our alphabet of today in Sinai, Phoenician, Greek, and Roman. The body of the book is made up of the alphabets of thirteen languages still in use today. A brief introduction outlines the development of written language, and a page accompanying each alphabet sketches the history of that language. Splendid enrichment material, encouraging an interest in the written forms of other languages.

Gwynne, Fred. *The King Who Rained*. Illus. by author. Prentice Hall, 1970, 48 pp. (1-5).

The writer of this long-lasting book contrasts literal and figurative speech and plays with homonym confusion. Deadpan humor and zany illustrations abound. A wonderful introduction to games with language.

Joyce, Susan. *Alphabet Riddles*. Illus. by Doug DuBosque. Peel Productions, Inc., 1998, 30 pp. (ps-2).

With bright poster-color pictures, clever rhyming riddles, and intriguing blanks to fill in,* this book is an entertaining way to encourage kids' word skills in reading and printing words out. Each page has its word with missing letters to be determined and its riddle-rhyme: "e_ _o / I start with an e and end with an o. /I'm a sound that repeats. / I bounce back and grow./ When you say, 'Hello.' / I say, 'Hel-lo-lo-lo.'/ What can I possibly be? Do you know?" Four- and five-letter words are in the majority, with three of only three letters and six of six to ten letters. On the next to the last page are "Ideas for Parents and Teachers" on how to maximize the use of word riddles—some very helpful suggestions.

*Writing the mystery word—with its blanks—on a piece of paper and filling that in rather than writing on the book page will extend the usefulness of the book.

Leedy, Loreen. *The Furry News: How to Make a Newspaper*. Holiday House, Inc., 1990, 29 pp. (ps-3).

Using a story format, the author has written a clear, practical guide kids can use to produce a little newspaper. In the story, Big Bear is aggravated because his city paper doesn't cover events in his neighborhood. He and his friends are inspired to start a paper of their own. Then the author (in the guise of Big Bear) lays out the organization, division of duties, and how-to's. Whether for a club or other organization or a school project, the framework is put in place, and with appropriate guidance along the way, kids can produce their own newspaper. Aspiring young newspaper publishers, editors, reporters, and feature writers will find excellent help and advice in this amusingly illustrated and very well-written book.

Leedy, Loreen. *Messages in the Mailbox: How to Write a Letter.* Holiday House, Inc., 1991, 28 pp. (ps-3).

Mrs. Gator is teaching her class at school how to write letters, first a friendly letter and then a business letter. A student asks, "What will we write about?" The teacher has lots of suggestions: your pets, your hobbies, your family, good news, and bad news. Suggestions follow as to whom they could write. Then the details of a general form to use, of addressing the envelope, ideas for creating novelty paper, turning a letter into a puzzle, using postcards and more are discussed. Special purpose letters (thank-you's, invitations, letters of sympathy or of apology, and others) are modeled. Finally, business letters—inquiries, requests, complaints, protests—and letters to the editor round out the kinds of letters people need to know how to write. On the last page is a list of all the state and territory postal abbreviations. Full of amusing and relevant illustrations throughout. A useful book to have in your family library for kids' reference.

Lewin, Ted. *Touch and Go: Travels of a Children's Book Illustrator.* Lothrop, Lee, and Shepard Books, 1999, 67 pp. (5-up).

Primary listing under *History and Geography*

The vignettes that comprise this book are ideally suited for use as fresh and different material in a writing class. The little encounters with people along the writer's way as he traveled are brief and usually quite simple. What does the writer do (typically in less than two short pages) to create a vivid, interest-holding picture of a person, his or her setting, and what he does? After adequate discussion, readers could try writing about some brief encounter of their own with a person that interested them, using one of Lewin's little stories as a model. For further comments on the book, see the *History and Geography* listing.

Moncure, Jane Belk. *My "i" Sound Box.* Illus. by Colin King. Sound Box Library Series. The Child's World, 2001, 31 pp. (k-2).

Designed to help early readers sound out words beginning with "i," the main focus of the book is on the short "i" sound. A little girl, wearing a top labeled "i" and referred to as Little i, is the device used to provide a story line. Little i has a carton that she calls her sound box, and she looks for things that begin with an "i" sound to put in the box. She finds a crowd of inchworms, some rather aggressive-looking iguanas, and when they don't stay in the box, Little i goes looking for them. All of this gives many opportunities for the reader to sound out the names using the short "i." Further activities and words beginning with the short "i" follow, and the two concluding pages have several words beginning with the long "i." A child who is reading well could read the book alone, but its full usefulness would require adult help.

Pfeffer, Susan Beth. *Who Were They Really?* Millbrook Press, 1999, 72 pp. (3-up).

The characters in most stories for children are the product of the writers' imaginations. An author's characters may reflect a variety of things observed in real-life children, but the story-person as a whole is not a replica of any one child. In some famous stories, however, one or more of the characters is based closely on a real person. Susan Pfeffer discusses twelve well-known stories of that sort. Charles Dodgson (who used the pen name Lewis Carroll) was a family friend of four young sisters, one of whom was named Alice. Alice was especially interested in Dodgson's storytelling. When she asked him to write down the stories he had been inventing verbally, he decided to make a book of them, basing the central character on the real Alice Liddell—*Alice in Wonderland* (1865). Meanwhile, across the Atlantic, Louisa May Alcott was writing of her own family, the Alcotts, with only minor changes in the characters, in her most famous book, *Little Women* (1868). Writing about these and ten other famous stories with real-life characters, Pfeffer provides interesting biographical information about the authors and the characters, along with the circumstances that led to the use of real people in these fictional stories.

Samoyault, Tiphaine. *Alphabetical Order: How the Alphabet Began.* Translated by Kathryn M. Pulver. Penguin Books, 1998, 30 pp. (4-7).

A great deal of information has been packed into this slim, colorful book. No words are wasted, and the approach is direct, taking it for granted that the reader wants answers about where alphabets came from and how the sounds their symbols represent were captured in written form to open up new worlds of communication. The writer goes to the roots of the earliest known attempts people made to express facts and ideas in a written form—not at first in letters, but in little pictures. She touches briefly but effectively on various pre-alphabet systems, moving then to the development of alphabets.

Every part of the text is accompanied by relevant illustrations, graphically presenting the change from pictogram to abstract symbol. Alphabets from which our own (A, B, C and so forth) system developed are traced, and other world alphabets are also described. Additional sections provide information on some of the handwritten styles of pre-printing-press writing (calligraphy) and of the later printed typefaces used (typography). Other types of alphabets are also noted and illustrated: semaphore, Morse code, sign language, and Braille. An intelligent and lively treatment of a subject well worth exploring.

Schnur, Steven. *Spring—An Alphabet Acrostic.* Illus. by Leslie Evans. Clarion Books, 1999, 26 pp. (ps-3).

This delightful book provides both beauty, with its lovely linoleum-cut art, and an exercise in the playful use of words. Each page focuses on a sentence that starts with a letter of the alphabet and is arranged in an acrostic form so that vertically the first letters of each line spell out a relevant word. The first page highlights the month of April:

> *After days of*
> *Pouring*
> *Rain, the last*
> *Ice and snow finally*
> *Leave the earth.*

As a child reads the sentence and discovers the vertically formed word, he or she has a sense of solving a puzzle. Finding the meaning of the sentence—which is not in the usual form—and identifying the vertical word demonstrate a new relationship with the use of words. Words have been chosen, controlled, moved around for a purpose. For the child, of course, on the conscious level this is simply a beautiful book to be enjoyed—but on a deeper level, the child has become aware that *he or she also* could choose and control words for a specific purpose.

Wegman, William. *ABC.* Hyperion, 1994, 56 pp. (ps-up).

The author's clever text and entertaining photographs of dogs combine to create an unusual and often hilarious alphabet book. Few children can resist the appeal of dogs, and when each letter is formed by artfully posed Weimaraners—with still other dogs on the facing pages—what more could one ask? Below each letter is a playful sentence that reinforces the use and sound of the letter. An effective laugh-and-learn combination.

12

LITERATURE: LEVEL I

Fables, Folk Tales, and Fairy Tales

Aesop. *Aesop's Fables*. Illus. by Fritz Kredel. Grossett and Dunlap, 1947, 234 pp. (all ages).

A fine collection of dozens of Aesop's wise and pithy little tales. These ancient stories with a moral are as timely today as they were centuries ago. They are valuable for children not only for their charm and the timeless lessons they teach, but also for the literary background they offer. Many of the fables are woven firmly into the fabric of our culture and are frequently alluded to in a variety of contexts— for example, the fox and the "sour grapes" he couldn't reach. When a child who is familiar with these fables hears someone refer to an attitude as "sour grapes," the child has the satisfaction of knowing just what is meant.

Andersen, Hans Christian. *Hans Andersen: His Classic Fairy Tales*. Illus. by Michael Foreman. Harper and Row, 1978, 185 pp. (1-up).

A fine selection of the classic Andersen tales most appreciated by children. Beautifully illustrated.

Brown, Marcia. *Stone Soup*. Illus. by author. Atheneum, 1989 (1947), 48 pp. (ps-3).

A lively retelling of the old tale. In this version, villagers refuse to help some very hungry soldiers. The soldiers arouse the villagers' interest by saying they're going to make soup with stones. They always *flavor* their delicious soup with . . . And the intrigued villagers proceed to furnish the soup ingredients (added to the elegant stones already simmering in the big pot of water). A Caldecott Honor Book in 1955.

Grimm. *The Complete Brothers Grimm Fairy Tales*. Ed. by Lily Owens. Gramercy Books, 1996, 680 pp. (1-up).

A collection of all the Grimm brothers' fairy tales (more than 200), including the classic favorites: "Cinderella," "The Frog Prince," "Sleeping Beauty," and "Hansel and Grethel." With a wide variety to choose from, careful selections can be made, avoiding the fiercer or more violent stories when parents prefer to do so.

The many illustrations have been selected from various earlier editions of the Grimms' collections.

Lang, Andrew. *The Red Fairy Book*. Dover, 1966 (1890), 367 pp. (3-up).
    For more than a century children have enjoyed Lang's excellent collections of lovely, classic fairy tales from various cultures. *The Red Fairy Book* is just one of the series, which includes *The Blue Fairy Book*, *The Yellow Fairy Book*, and a number of other color-titled volumes.

Lucado, Max. *Just the Way You Are*. Illus. by Sergio Martinez. Crossway Books, 1994 (1992), 31 pp. (ps-5).
    Primary listing under *Bible/Spiritual and Moral Teaching*
    An appealing story of a kindly king who wanted to help an orphaned family of five children living in one of his villages. When he sent word to the children that he was going to adopt them and be their father—and that he would soon be coming for them, they were wildly excited and happy. But then something happened that seemed to change everything. All the village people told the children they must think of ways they could impress the king with their talents and gifts. Only then, they said, would the king take them to live with him. Four of the children knew they had talents, and they began spending all of their time preparing gifts for the king. Only the youngest child felt she had no gift. So she just kept doing what she always did at the city gate, earning a little money for her family's food with small chores and cheering tired travelers with her friendly ways—for she was kind and caring. What happens when the king, alone and simply dressed, comes to look for the children is the heart of this lovely allegory. Captivating illustrations with their gentle touches of humor match perfectly the heartwarming narrative.

Pinkney, Jerry, and Aesop. *Aesop's Fables*. Illus. by Jerry Pinkney. SeaStar Books, 2000, 87 pp. (all ages).
    Nearly sixty of Aesop's best-loved fables make up this enjoyable collection. Pinkney's lively and humorous retelling and illustrations are especially appropriate and entertaining. Each fable is told with wit and clarity, and at the end a pithy sentence sums up the fable's essence. It has been almost 2,600 years since the fables were written, and their truth and applicability are still a fresh pleasure to share with today's children.

Fantasies, Talking Animal Stories

Alexander, Lloyd. *The Truthful Harp*. Illus. by Evaline Ness. Holt, Rinehart, Winston, 1967, 26 pp. (k-2).
    A story for younger children set in the same mythical kingdom of Prydain that Alexander used in one of his fine series for older children. An inept, weak king ven-

tures out as a bard into his world of castles and knights. The king's little handheld harp plays an important part in teaching him the value of being truthful. Other significant values are also brought out in this clever story. Excellent use of language. Out of print, this is one of those books worth looking for in libraries.

Anderson, Lena. Translated by Elisabeth Kallick Dyssegaard. *Tea for Ten*. R&S Books, 2000, 24 pp. (ps-k).

Hedgehog sits in her kitchen feeling lonely. Hoping wistfully that some friends would come over ("Then she wouldn't be just ONE"), she is delighted to hear a knock at the door. "Here comes Uncle Will. Hurrah! Now we are TWO." A "counting" story involving ten different kinds of creatures. Appealingly illustrated, the cozy details and soft, delicate colors perfectly fit the atmosphere of affection and hominess that pervades the story.

Barrett, Judi. *Animals Should Definitely Not Wear Clothing*. Illus. by Ron Barrett. Simon and Schuster Children's Books, 1988 (1970), 32 pp. (k-3).

Children will love the hilarious pictures and brief text (all in very large lowercase letters) in this amusing book. Its theme is what would happen if animals (already so appropriately garbed in their own skins) were put into human clothes. Great for fun and for good vocabulary-expanding reading.

Berenstain, Stan and Jan. *The Berenstain Bears Go to School*. Illus. by author. Random House, 1978, 32 pp. (ps-2).

This lively picture book is one of a widely popular series designed to provide early readers with stories that teach everyday-life lessons in a format they will enjoy. The delightful Bear family are entertainingly pictured (the clever characterizations and very human facial expressions are great fun) in a wide variety of situations. In . . . *Go to School*, some of the fears and potential problems about school that worry kids are confronted and solved, with much of the tension of such situations defused for readers by the book's irresistible humor.

Best, Cari. *Montezuma's Revenge*. Illus. by Diane Palmisciano. Orchard Press, 1999, 30 pp. (ps-3).

A warm, rollicking, delightfully illustrated tale with a sagacious and articulate dog as its central character. Montezuma, nicknamed Monty, is a wonderfully well-behaved dog, and he dearly loves his family—Sally, Steve, and his best buddy Sam. There is just one big problem: They don't take him along when they go on vacation, leaving him with Darryl, the "detestable dog-sitter." Determined that things must change, Monty still doesn't know how he can make that happen, until he meets up with Wild Bill, a scruffy, smelly, ill-natured tramp of a dog. Monty's plan, which he puts into effect the day his family comes home, is the hilarious climax of the story—and one with lasting results that please Monty and his whole family.

Brooke, L. Leslie. *Johnny Crow's Garden*. Illus. by author. Warne, 1903, 48 pp. (ps-up).

This is a picture book with its own special flavor. The illustrations are unique, often hilarious. The brief, rhymed text throws in words not often found in early-childhood books (children love the sound of them) in lines like these: "Then the Stork/Gave a Philosophic Talk/Till the Hippopotami/Said: 'Ask no further, "What am I?"'/While the Elephant/Said something quite irrelevant/In Johnny Crow's Garden." This book has been treasured for years by those fortunate enough to have encountered it. Two other Johnny Crow titles are equally enjoyable: *Johnny Crow's Party* and *Johnny Crow's New Garden.* Out of print but still in many libraries.

Brown, Alan. *The Windhover.* Illus. by Christian Birmingham. Harcourt Brace and Company, 1997, 32 pp. (k-3).
      In an opening high on the side of a school building, a pair of small falcons* have built a nest, and it is through the eyes and the imagined consciousness of the first of their little hatchlings that the story is told. The writer supplies some of the narrative's information through the artist's wonderful illustrations alone, in order to keep the baby bird's first-person account more credible. Thus, the reader sees one of the schoolboys climbing stairs to the old building's attic while the following text speaks of "a dark shape" whose "two hands easily grab me." Three brief sentences and several pictures reveal a lonely boy longing for a creature he can be close to. But the little falcon, caged in the boy's room, can't eat the food the boy brings. He becomes weak and thin. A happy solution for both the falcon and the solitary boy develops, and the reader gives a sigh of relief. Perceptively written, with outstanding portrayals of the little falcon.
      *Such falcons are called kestrels in the United States—often referred to as wind-hovers in Britain.

Brown, Margaret Wise. *The Little Fur Family.* Illus. by Garth Williams. Harper and Row, 1968 (1951), 32 pp. (ps-3).
      A wonderful little book about simple natural joys, family love, the pleasure of venturing forth into the outdoors—and of returning to the total security of home and parents. Fur symbolizes perfectly the soft, deep, infinitely warm atmosphere of love and assurance created in the book. All of Margaret Wise Brown's books have been loved by children for decades, with this book, *Goodnight Moon,* and *The Runaway Bunny* as special favorites.

Bunting, Eve. *I Like the Way You Are.* Illus. by John O'Brien. Clarion Books, 2000, 40 pp. (k-4).
      Turtle and Spotted Turtle (Spottie) are friends. Some differences in the way they like to do everyday things and in their skills and talents could easily lead to conflict between them. But instead of either friend insisting on doing something all his way, they work out comfortable compromises. Spottie, for example, doesn't eat breakfast, while Turtle doesn't eat lunch. They decide that when they are spending a day together, they can have brunch. When they go to the gym together, Turtle is very good at exercising, while Spottie is not. On the way home, however, it is Spottie who excels as they sing together. His voice is beautiful, while Turtle's voice is like a harsh bark. Neither wants to hurt the other's feelings, so nothing unkind

is said about Spottie's workout or Turtle's singing. Each appreciates the other's strengths and is kind about his weaknesses. Bunting's gentle, humorous narrative and illustrator O'Brien's lively, amusing drawings combine to create an enjoyable story that makes a helpful point.

Burgess, Thornton W. *Old Mother West Wind.* Illus. by Harrison Cady. Little, Brown and Co., 1985 (1910), 140 pp. (k-3).

Entertaining stories of animals that behave entirely like human beings. These are favorites of a bygone day, but many people still enjoy them in spite of their seeming more dated than the usual timeless classic. There is an emphasis on "mother wit" and a strong moral tone as to the folly of pride, boasting, and other such faults.

Carle, Eric. *Rooster's Off to See the World.* Illus. by author. Simon and Schuster Children's Books, rev. ed. 1998 (1972), 25 pp. (ps-3).

A rooster, then two cats, three frogs, four turtles, and five fish set off to see the world, but when night comes, home begins to seem better than adventure. Group by group, the travelers turn back, and finally the rooster himself goes home, enjoys his dinner, and, happily asleep on his perch, dreams of a wonderful trip around the world. Carle's bold, brilliantly colored illustrations have long appealed to young readers.

Note: This book was originally titled *The Rooster Who Set Out to See the World.*

Clement, Gary. *The Great Poochini.* Groundwood Books, 1999, 28 pp. (ps-3).

The matter-of-fact way in which realistic patterns of everyday life and far-out fantasy are joined is one of the charms of this entertaining story. A quiet, mannerly dog of medium size—called Jack by his master, Hersh—is in reality Signor Poochini, the renowned opera-singing tenor, idolized by fans of dog opera. During the day he lives in Hersh's big old house in a large city. When Hersh is at home, they take walks, share mealtimes, and listen to the opera. Hersh, of course, has no idea that Jack, who does ordinary things like chasing cats and fetching sticks, is really a great dog opera star. Every night Signor Poochini waits until Hersh is asleep; then he leaps out through the window, which Hersh always has open, and hurries to a secret location known only to canine opera buffs. His double life works perfectly until one awful night when Hersh is going to be away until the next day—and hasn't left the window open. The surprising solution to Signor Poochini's plight forms the entertaining climax of the story.

Complemented by the author's colorful, detailed, and often hilarious illustrations, this very funny book is made even more entertaining by the punning jokes that run through both the text and the pictures—as when Signor Poochini plans an evening snack at a quiet bistro. Perhaps, he thinks, he will have "a small plate of Fettuccine Arfedo and a glass of Dog Perignon, or maybe just a nice piece of hound cake." Kids will love looking for the puns as they read.

Cole, Brock. *The King at the Door*. Illus. by author. Farrar, Straus and Giroux, 1979, 32 pp. (1-up).

A clever story of a little boy who befriends an old man who is claiming to be the king. The innkeeper is skeptical—and unhelpful. The little boy is kind and generous and ultimately goes to live with the king. A classic theme that underscores good values.

de Brunhoff, Jean. *The Story of Babar*. Illus. by author. Random Books for Young Readers, 1966 (1933), 47 pp. (ps-up).

Children continue to enjoy this fanciful story (and the others in the Babar series) of the mild and gracious elephant Babar, his wife, Celeste, their children, and special friends. In *The Story of Babar*, the orphaned Babar is befriended by a rich, kindly old lady and given his opportunity for a new life in which he shares his good fortune and becomes a wise and benevolent leader. Translated from the French, the Babar stories have an interestingly different flavor.

Erickson, Russell E. *A Toad for Tuesday*. Illus. by Lawrence Di Fiori. Lothrop, 1998 (1974), 64 pp. (k-2).

When Warton, a lovable little toad, ignores his brother Morton's advice and sets out on skis to take some beetle brittle to their Aunt Toolia, he doesn't realize that he is going to fall into the clutches of an owl who is looking for a special little tidbit to save for his birthday dinner the next Tuesday. Ingeniously imagined encounters with eccentric animal characters, warmth, humor, and good underlying values characterize this and the other stories of the series. There is considerably more text (and a much more extensive vocabulary) in these books than in beginning-reader series, and they would usually need to be read aloud to children at the early level. Other titles include *Warton and Morton*, *Warton and the Castaways*, and others.

Ets, Marie Hall. *In the Forest*. Illus. by author. Puffin Books, 1974 (1944), 45 pp. (ps-2).

A world of adventure takes place in a little boy's imagination as he plays in the woods. Young children can identify with the vividness of the boy's make-believe activities.

Ets, Marie Hall. *Play with Me*. Illus. by author. Puffin Books, 1976 (1944), 45 pp. (ps-1).

This lovable story involves a succession of little wild creatures so dear to the hearts of children. A small girl finds that if instead of pursuing the animals and insects she longs to play with, she sits very quietly, they will come to her.

Flack, Marjorie and Kurt Wiese. *The Story About Ping*. Illus. by Kurt Wiese. Puffin Books, 1993 (1933), 32 pp. (ps-2).

A modern classic, this simple story of a young duck who lives on a boat on the Yangtze River of China has been loved by children for more than sixty-five years. When Ping, through his own doing, is left behind one evening, he sets out in search of the "home" boat. He is briefly caged as a prospective meal, but he escapes and finally hears the familiar "La, la" (Come, come) call of his owner. Even though he knows he'll receive a swat for being the last to respond, he joyfully swims home.

Gág, Wanda. *Millions of Cats*. Illus. by author. Putnam, 1996 (1928), 32 pp. (ps-1).

As its longevity attests, this wildly impossible story continues to be loved by children, generation after generation. They enjoy every minute of the old man's bewilderment as he realizes that instead of coming home with one cat, he has somehow involved himself with millions and billions and trillions of them.

Galdone, Paul. *The Little Red Hen*. Illus. by author. Houghton Mifflin, 1985 (1973), 48 pp. (ps-3).

This is just one edition of the timeless classic that has been enjoyed by children for generations. The moral rightness of taking responsibility, working, and then reaping the reward is underscored. Galdone's clever and humorous illustrations are especially effective as he captures the laziness and indifference of the animals who refuse to help the Little Red Hen work.

Gammell, Stephen. *Once Upon MacDonald's Farm*. Simon and Schuster Books for Young Readers, 2000, 28 pp. (k-3).

Everyone knows that Old MacDonald had a farm—but the MacDonald and his farm of this entertaining book are a bit on the different side. Stephen Gammell's wonderful pencil drawings and awkward hand-lettered text perfectly represent the dilapidated farmstead—and the equally down-at-the-heel farmer himself. One day MacDonald decides that he really *must* have some animals on his farm, and he goes out and buys several. It would be like telling readers the end of a suspense story ahead of time to reveal what happens next. This is one of those completely zany stories kids love. Read it with them and share the fun.

Godden, Rumer. *A Kindle of Kittens*. Illus. by Lynne Barnes. Viking, 1979, 32 pp. (k-3).

An enchanting story by a gifted writer. She-Cat, a stray tabby, must find homes for her four lovely kittens. How she goes about it makes fine reading. Warmth and humor permeate each page, and illustrator Lynne Barnes, using the town of Rye, England, as a setting, has captured the writer's tone perfectly in her delightful pictures. Out of print but still in many libraries. Definitely worth looking for.

Grahame, Kenneth. *The Reluctant Dragon*. Illus. by Ernest H. Shepard. Holiday, 1953 (1938), 58 pp. (2-up).

This is the original story, later adapted and popularized by Disney, of a dragon who didn't want to breathe fire or engage in combat. A durably entertaining tale, its pleasing literary style includes the use of an above-average vocabulary and an enriching literary style.

Karon, Jan. *Jeremy: The Tale of an Honest Bunny*. Illus. by Teri Weidner. Viking, 2000, 80 pp. (ps-1).

Jeremy, a very special handmade English bunny, doesn't want to be sent to his new home in North Carolina in a box; he wants to deliver himself. As he finds, it is a long way from England to America. Jeremy needs help from many people along the way— and in turn often finds himself helping and encouraging others. Throughout his adventurous journey, disasters are averted at the last moment, and he is often cheered by hospitable warmth and cozy times of comforting food and homey chat. Jeremy is often reminded of the words of blessing his dear English maker, Lydia, has sent him off with: "For He shall give His angels charge over thee, to keep thee in all thy ways." Wonderful, reassuring words for any child as they go in imagination with Jeremy, whose long journey finally leads him home. Full of Jan Karon's irresistible humor and endearing detail, *Jeremy* is one to read aloud and share.

Keats, Ezra Jack. *Jennie's Hat*. Illus. by author. HarperCollins Children's Books, 1985 (1966), (k-2).

A visual confection is created as Jennie's friends, the birds, transform the plain hat in which she is so disappointed into a mass of color and beauty. A longtime favorite story.

Kipling, Rudyard. *Just-So Stories*. Black-and-white illustrations by author; color illustrations by J. McGleeson. Doubleday, 1912 (1902), 247 pp. (1, 2-up).

Kipling's way with language adds to the charm of "How the Leopard Got His Spots" and other familiar tales. Some stories in the collection are more appealing than others; select these and read them aloud, getting into the spirit of Kipling's fascinating use of words. These stories are a unique part of our English-language heritage of classic works.

Kraus, Robert. *Leo the Late Bloomer*. Illus. by Jose Arvego. HarperCollins Children's Books, 1994 (1971), 30 pp. (ps-3).

A picture book with a short, easy text that effectively makes a very good point for children whose pacing is different from some of their friends. Leo's father worries because his little son can't yet read or write—but Leo is simply a late bloomer, and in his own good time he happily acquires all the needed skills.

Kuskin, Karla. *James and the Rain*. Illus. by author. Simon and Schuster, 1995 (1957), 32 pp. (ps-1).

James goes out to play in the rain and asks a series of animals if they "know any excellent rainy-day games." The text rhymes and has a counting build-up as well. Loved by small children for more than forty years.

Lasky, Kathryn. *Lucille's Snowsuit*. Illus. by Marylin Hafner. Crown Publishers, 2000, 26 pp. (ps-1).

It's a snow day; no school for Lucille's older brother and sister. While they quickly don their parkas, ski pants, and knit caps, shouting, "Get your snowsuit on," and dash out to revel in the snow, Lucille is heading for difficulties. Putting on her boots first, she can't pull the suit's legs over them. Starting over, struggling, beginning to sweat in the warmth of the house, Lucille is roaring with rage when her mother comes to her rescue. Soon completely dressed for the outdoors, Lucille lies sulking on the floor. "Snowsuits are for babies," she snarls. What happens next makes for both a satisfying conclusion and a happy change of mind for Lucille. The moral of the story is surrounded by laughter—but it is unmistakably there. Using an "animals behaving as people" setting makes the action and illustrations especially amusing. (All the characters are chubby pigs.)

Lionni, Leo. *The Biggest House in the World.* Illus. by author. Knopf, 1968, 30 pp. (ps-up).

When a little snail tells his father he wants to have the biggest house in the world, his father tells him the story of a snail who had the same wish and who learned how to make his little snail house bigger and bigger and more and more elaborate, with dire consequences. The little snail learns from the story and as a result lives a happier life. An emphasis on lasting values is subtly made in this colorfully illustrated book.

Lionni, Leo. *Inch by Inch.* Illus. by author. Astor-Honor, 1960, 30 pp. (ps-1).

A little inchworm talks a robin out of eating him by offering to measure her tail. He then measures a succession of birds: the flamingo's neck, the toucan's beak, and others. When the mockingbird says he must measure her song or be eaten, he has to think of a way to escape. Colorful, imaginative illustrations.

Lobel, Arnold. *Frog and Toad Are Friends.* Illus. by author. HarperCollins Children's Books, 1970, 64 pp. (ps-2).

The quiet, endearing atmosphere and recounting of the small details children love (in this and the other stories in the series) set a much-imitated standard for easy early-reading books. Frog and Toad demonstrate the qualities of true friendship—as well as make mistakes and worry over trifles. Lobel's stories do more than laud friendship, however. The writer has an unerring ear for just the right turn of phrase and a wry, subtle wit that focuses on the frailties and foibles of human nature in the guise of his little Frog and Toad friends. Not only children, but their parents as well, thoroughly enjoy these appealing stories. Other titles include *Days with Frog and Toad, Frog and Toad Together,* and *Frog and Toad All Year.*

Lobel, Arnold. *Mouse Soup.* Illus. by author. HarperCollins Children's Books, 1977, 64 pp. (k-2).

This continuingly popular I Can Read book is comprised of stories within a story. A clever mouse talks himself out of being eaten by a weasel by telling his captor stories and then sending him on a wild goose chase while he makes his own escape.

MacDonald, Betty. *Mrs. Piggle-Wiggle.* Illus. by Hilary Knight. Lippincott, 1947, 118 pp. (k-3).

First graders seem to especially enjoy *Mrs. Piggle-Wiggle.* A fantasy version of the somewhat rare adult who isn't at all bothered by the wide-ranging activities of children, she loves childlike fun herself. In fact, she goes along with their fantasies. At the same time, she is reassuringly firm and confident, correcting their attitudes and behavior by providing highly imaginative ways of dealing with responsibility. Full of hilarity, the story (and the others in the series) make effective, practical points in a way children not only accept but enjoy. Other series titles are *Hello, Mrs. Piggle-Wiggle*, *Mrs. Piggle-Wiggle's Farm*, and *Mrs. Piggle-Wiggle's Magic*.

Note: Some libraries may still have original versions of the Mrs. Piggle-Wiggle books. The one currently in print is a HarperCollins edition revised in 1957.

McCloskey, Robert. *Make Way for Ducklings*. Illus. by author. Viking, 1941, 67 pp. (k-2).

Children have enjoyed this modern classic for more than sixty years. When a mother mallard and her eight little ducklings brave the dangers of city streets, it takes the expertise of a New York policeman to insure that Mother Mallard and her flock safely keep their appointment with Father Mallard at the Public Garden Park. (Winner of the Caldecott Medal in 1942.)

Meddaugh, Susan. *Martha Speaks*. Houghton Mifflin, 1992, 30 pp. (ps-up).

Since this irresistibly funny picture book was written ten years ago, it has become a perennial favorite of all ages, including the adults who are fortunate enough to share the fun. When Martha dog is given a bowl of alphabet soup, a strange thing happens. Instead of going down to her stomach, all the letters of the alphabet go up to her brain, and Martha starts to talk.

The writer's choice of just the right words is perfectly complemented by also just-right illustrations, catching all the laughable expressions of people—and of Martha dog herself. Martha becomes quite carried away with her new ability, and her family is soon very, very tired of her endless chatter. But in the dramatic climax of the story, Martha is uproariously vindicated, and family harmony is restored. A wonderful all-family read. (Many middle-school kids particularly love this story.)

Milne, A. A. *Winnie the Pooh* and *The House at Pooh Corner*. Both illus. by Ernest H. Shepard. Dutton, 1926, 161 pp.; 1928, 180 pp. (1-3).

Milne's incomparable stories of Pooh and his friends (the real thing, not the Disney adaptation) have been taken to children's hearts for several generations. It is not the story line but the subtleties—conversations, the little eccentricities and habits of the books' characters, the marvelous qualities of Milne's use of language—that live on in the hearts of those whose childhood is long behind them. Pooh's little "hums," his fondness for honey and condensed milk—and his related plumpness; Owl and his atrocious spelling; Christopher Robin's loving and indulgent, "Silly old bear." The Pooh stories reflect a great understanding of the way children think and play, the way they like to experiment with sounds. Like so many books, however, that are loved with a passion by devoted readers, the Pooh stories aren't every child's favorites. But by all means give each child the opportunity to find out whether he has a special place for Pooh and his friends in his heart. (The way parents relate to the stories makes a significant difference in children's reaction to them.)

Minarik, Else Holmelund. *Little Bear's Friend.* Illus. by Maurice Sendak. HarperCollins Children's Books, 1960, 64 pp. (ps-2).

Little Bear radiates an infectious joy that spreads to those around him. In the four episodes of this book, he takes a little girl who has lost her way back to her parents, watches over a straying duckling, fixes the broken arm of his friend's doll, and bravely overcomes his sadness when his friend must return home at summer's end. This book is one of a series in which a warm, wise mother and benevolent, strong father play traditional parental roles. Other titles in the series include *A Kiss for Little Bear*, *Father Bear Comes Home*, and *Little Bear's Visit*. (A Harper I Can Read book.)

Oakley, Graham. *The Church Mouse.* Illus. by author. Atheneum, 1972, 36 pp. (ps-3).

This completely delightful story is representative of a particular kind of children's book in which a graphic artist combines his art with a story line and turns author. Oakley's drawings of the clever little mice that have taken shelter in an old English church and their sturdy ally, the cat Sampson, are full of fascinating details. The humor is clever, and the basic theme of a whole group of helpless mice uniting to thwart (with Sampson's help) their enemies has an unfailing appeal. Titles in the series include *The Church Mice Adrift*, *The Church Mice and the Moon*, and others. A later title, *The Church Mice and the Ring*, is the only one currently in print, but do look for these in your library.

Peet, Bill. *The Luckiest One of All.* Illus. by author. Houghton Mifflin, 1982, 30 pp. (1, 2).

Rhymed and delightfully illustrated, the story starts with a little boy wishing he could be a bird. The bird wishes it were a fish, and so it goes, through all sorts of creatures and contraptions. Finally, the cat wishes it were a little boy—who can do so many things! Good fun—and good encouragement to appreciate whatever one's lot may be.

Peters, Lisa Westberg. *Cold Little Duck, Duck, Duck.* Illus. by Sam Williams. Greenwillow Books, 2000, 29 pp. (ps-2).

This book has a rich vocabulary and an appealing use of the words that will encourage little listeners or early readers to *say* the words, love their sounds, and add them effortlessly to their own stock of language. "One miserable and frozen spring brisk brisk brisk," the story begins. *Miserable* is one of those many words that kids, when given the chance, love to say, to savor it as they mumble it to themselves, "misable, misable." And what fun to give a shiver on a nippy morning and say, "Brisk brisk brisk." The story and lovable pictures are enough to make the book worth reading, and when the joys of vivid language are added—"of crocuses and apple buds pink pink pink and blades of grass in squishy mud snack snack snack"—it makes one want to sit right down and read it aloud to an eager bunch of kids. So many of today's children are language-starved; nourishing vocabulary tastily served is most welcome.

Piper, Watty (retold by). *The Little Engine That Could*. Illus. by Ruth Sanderson. Putnam, 1930, 48 pp. (ps-1).
   This is an authentic edition of the timeless classic that encourages stick-to-it-iveness. Children love the repetition, sound effects, and triumphant "I thought I could!" ending.

Potter, Beatrix. *The Tale of Peter Rabbit*. Illus. by author. Warne, 1901, 58 pp. (ps-2).
   This is no doubt the best known among a long list of timeless classics created by Beatrix Potter that children continue to take to their hearts and from which they learn valuable lessons. Like all the famous "animal character" stories of early childhood, her books aren't really about animals at all. They are about life and people. Who can forget the clearly drawn character of the naughty, debonair Peter Rabbit—and the consequences of his ill-advised venture into Mr. MacGregor's garden? After almost a century, Potter's combination of stories true to the realities of human nature with her wonderful little drawings are deservedly more popular than ever.

Potter, Beatrix. *The Complete Tales*. The Penguin Group, 1997, 400 pp. (ps-2).
   This large, beautiful book contains all the wonderful classic Beatrix Potter tales, with the addition of four other stories of hers. All the beloved illustrations are included—new color reproductions of the Frederick Warne originals. A biographical profile of the author is also given. A lovely book to treasure and read to succeeding generations of children. They will love Potter's engaging tales as dearly as their grandparents and parents did—and still do!

Seuss, Dr. *The 500 Hats of Bartholomew Cubbins*. Random Books for Young Readers, 1990 (1938), 45 pp. (k-3).
   This entertaining story, one of the author's early books, continues to be enjoyed today. Young Bartholomew, who lived in the Kingdom of Didd, set off early one morning carrying a basket of cranberries to sell at the market. On his head is his old red hat with its feather sticking straight up in the air. As he reaches the town, everyone is dashing to the sidewalks to make way for King Derwin, whose carriage is coming at a fast pace up the street. "Hats off to the king," a Guardsman shouts, and everyone, including Bartholomew, obeys. As the procession rumbles past, Bartholomew is astonished to see the king staring angrily right at him. From that point on, the bewildered boy finds himself in serious difficulties with the ill-tempered monarch. The king demands that Bartholomew take his hat off in the king's presence—and Bartholomew keeps taking his hat off, only to have another appear on his head in its place. Purple with rage, the king persists, threatening the boy with ever more ferocious consequences. How Bartholomew ultimately triumphs makes a lively, humorous story, full of Seuss's flair for intriguing language and for an unexpected turn of events.

Seuss, Dr. *Bartholomew and the Oobleck*. Random Books for Young Readers, 1949, 45 pp. (k-3).

This is the second of two stories about Bartholomew Cubbins, and we now find him serving as a page boy for the same self-centered and ill-tempered King Derwin of Didd. The king decides that he is tired of having the same old things come down out of the sky—the rain, sunshine, fog, and snow. To Bartholomew's dismay, the king sends for his ancient, scruffy magicians and orders them to get something new and different coming down from the sky. The result of their spell is even more dismaying to Bartholomew. Blobs of a gooey green substance (which the magicians call oobleck) begin falling, in ever-increasing size and quantity. The consequences seem at first to be negligible, but it is soon evident that oobleck is a serious disaster. The narrative and accompanying illustrations are hilarious, but needless to say, Bartholomew is not amused. In desperation he confronts the king about his responsibility for this smothering substance that threatens to suffocate and bury the entire kingdom and all its people. What the king finally says that breaks the spell and saves the land of Didd adds a satisfying moral to the story—one to which everyone can relate.

Steig, William. *Sylvester and the Magic Pebble*. Illus. by author. Simon and Schuster, 1988 (1969), 32 pp. (ps-1).

There is a subtle emphasis throughout this story on the value of family, love, the supremely important things that are often taken for granted. Sylvester finds a magic "wishing" pebble, thoughtlessly wishes himself a rock, and then can't touch the pebble and wish to be himself again. His grieving parents finally happen across the "rock," and his father casually picks up the pebble lying nearby, lays it on the rock . . . bringing a happy ending. (Winner of the Caldecott Medal in 1970.)

Steig, William. *Toby, What Are You?* Illus. by Teryl Euvremer. HarperCollins Children's Books, 2001, 29 pp. (ps-1).

Toby is having great fun pretending to turn himself into a doormat, a coffee table, a bridge . . . He assumes his chosen guise and then asks his parents, "What am I?" They guess—sometimes right and sometimes not, but with attention and focus. Steig's whimsical words and Euvremer's equally whimsical, softly colored illustrations are a perfect match. Everyone has fun, including the young readers who will usually decide that they, too, want to get in on the game. But there is more than a game going on. Toby and his parents (a tastefully dressed family of benign-looking ferrets) live in a cozily decorated house that is the essence of hominess. And underlying the games and the laughter is a pervasive atmosphere of warm, parental love, of parents taking time to play with their child, of an ordered and cheerful life. Imaginative fun, happy mealtime, more play, and then off to bed, with father and mother tucking Toby in. Wonderfully reassuring to little persons growing up in a hurried and often anxiety-ridden world.

Stevens, Janet and Susan Stevens Crummel. *And the Dish Ran Away with the Spoon*. Illus. by Janet Stevens. Harcourt, Inc., 2001, 47 pp. (k-3).

Two sisters have collaborated on this farcical frolic inspired by nursery rhymes, starting with "Hey diddle diddle, the cat and the fiddle,/The cow jumped over the moon;/The little dog laughed to see such sport,/And the dish ran away with the spoon." The cat, the cow, and the dog have a big problem: Every night everyone in the rhyme goes through their parts; last night Dish and Spoon ran away as usual—but they didn't come back. "Without Dish and Spoon," worries Cat, "there's no rhyme. No more diddle diddle. It's over." With a lot of very funny bickering and complaining, the three set off in search of the missing pair. They encounter a fork in the road (table fork, that is). He has no idea where Dish and Spoon are, but draws a map of the area for their worried friends. The fun-to-see map is full of nursery rhyme locations: Humpty Dumpty's Wall, Little Boy Blue, Wolf's House, and so on. Young readers will catch the drift at once and rollick on, enjoying the hilarious illustrations and the dialogue dripping with snappy allusions to nursery rhyme characters and situations. Adventures ensue, including some narrow escapes, before the happy ending. Great fun.

Wahl, Jan. *The Six Voyages of Pleasant Fieldmouse.* Illus. by Peter Parnall. Delacorte Press, 1971, 94 pp. (k-3).

Delightfully expressed adventures with a unique flavor of their own. The humor is subtle, the vocabulary outstanding, and the imagery enriched—a book that has maintained its appeal for decades. Pleasant Fieldmouse had always lived in the forest, but he decided to build a raft with a sail, travel along the stream that reaches the huge lake he has never explored, and venture into unknown territory. He believed that "everybody, sometime, ought to be going someplace." Illustrated with whimsical black-and-white drawings.

White, E. B. *Charlotte's Web.* Illus. by Garth Williams. HarperChildren's Books, 1952 (1922), 184 pp. (k-3).

The beloved modern classic in which Fern, a little girl who loves animals; Wilbur, a pig who needs a friend; Charlotte, a wise and beautiful spider; and a rather self-centered rat, Templeton, share each other's lives, experience joy and pain, and have the opportunity to grow in understanding. Children have been charmed for decades by this thoroughly enjoyable story. The use of language and overall literary quality is outstanding.

Wild, Margaret. *The Pocket Dogs.* Illus. by Stephen Michael King. Scholastic Press, 2000, 29 pp. (ps-2).

Mr. Pockets is a kindly but rather absent-minded person who wears every day, in all seasons, his very big old coat with its two big pockets. The pockets are just the right size for his two small dogs—Biff in the right pocket and Buff in the left. While on their daily walk to town, Biff's foot makes a little hole in the pocket, which keeps growing bigger. He barks, "Ruuuuuf! Ruuuuuf!" but Mr. Pockets doesn't know Biff is trying to tell him about the hole. When, on the next day's walk, Biff falls completely out of the pocket, it's a scary adventure for Biff and a worrisome time for Buff and Mr. Pockets. With a perfect blend of words, rhythm, and entertaining illustrations, this is a story young children will want to hear over and over—right through to its happy ending.

Williams, Margery. *The Velveteen Rabbit*. Doubleday, 1922, 44 pp. (k-up).

This modern classic is a lovely fantasy about a stuffed toy rabbit that becomes real through a little boy's love. Effective simply as a story, it also conveys a valid sense of the lasting significance a special love for a childhood toy can have. Love as a life-giving force is satisfyingly affirmed.

Zion, Gene. *Harry the Dirty Dog*. Illus. by Margaret B. Graham. HarperCollins Children's Books, 1956, 32 pp. (ps-1).

Harry, a beloved pet dog, hates baths and runs off briefly to avoid one. He then gets so dirty that he changes color, and when he tries to return home, his family doesn't recognize him anymore. Harry's subsequent adventures and the happy ending keep young listeners chuckling. Popular for more than forty-five years, all of the stories in the Harry series are full of delightful humor and are excellent for reading aloud.

Realistic Stories—Modern

Barasch, Lynne. *The Reluctant Flower Girl*. HarperCollins Children's Books, 2001, 31 pp. (k-3).

April is upset and unhappy. For all of her life, her big sister has been her best friend. They have skated, ridden bikes, and shared sweet bedtime treats. And now Annabel is going to marry her boyfriend, Harold. April is going to be the flower girl; she has even helped Annabel choose her wedding dress, but she is still very unhappy and even angry about losing her best friend. April has tried to discourage Harold from marrying her sister, but nothing seems to work—and now the wedding is taking place. Barasch manages to combine humor with sensitive perception in both the narrative and the delightful illustrations. Children will thoroughly enjoy the moments of suspense at the wedding when April has to decide whether she will let something happen that will delay the ceremony. A warm, lovable story.

Bemelmans, Ludwig. *Madeline*. Illus. by author. Viking Children's Books, 1993 (1939), 64 pp. (k-3).

Clever, humorous drawings and a brief, sprightly story in rhyme characterize this and the other books in the Madeline series of stories that have become modern classics. Little Madeline and eleven other small girls live in a vine-covered house in Paris under the tender care of the devoted Miss Clavel. Madeline is the one to whom things always seem to happen. In this book she awakens in the night with appendicitis. In others of the series, Madeline launches into various endeavors, and somehow whatever she undertakes turns into more than was expected. The stories are full of warmth and kindness, as well as madcap adventures.

Best, Cari. *Red Light, Green Light, Mama and Me.* Illus. by Niki Daly. Orchard Books, 1995, 29 pp. (ps-1).

Lizzie is doing something very different today; her grandma has the flu, and so for the first time, Lizzie is going to work with her mother. All through the day—hurrying to the subway, riding the train, meeting Mama's "work family" in the children's department of the big Downtown Public Library—there is an underlying sense of closeness and stability in the relationship between Lizzie and her mother. Young readers will enjoy the warmth and joyousness of the day, and some will find a special sense of reassurance—even if Mama is usually away at work each day, they can share that part of life as well. Whatever the circumstances, it's "Mama and me" with love and understanding. The lovable illustrations perfectly complement this sensitively written story.

Blades, Ann. *Mary of Mile 18.* Illus. by author. Tundra Books, 1996 (1971), 38 pp. (1-4).

This simply written, beautifully illustrated story is set in a homesteaders' small farming community in northern British Columbia. Life there is almost as rugged as it was for the pioneers of past centuries: no indoor plumbing, no electricity, no phones or television—and winters that last for seven months of the year. Mary, one of the Fehr family's five children, finds a part-wolf pup and longs to keep him in spite of the strictly enforced rule, "Our animals must work for us or give us food." How Mary finally is granted her wish forms the story's satisfying conclusion. The author/illustrator taught the little school at Mile 18, and her detailed "primitive" illustrations (a full-page color painting faces each page of text) convey the reality of this remote corner of the wilderness. (Mile 18 is a Mennonite community according to a note at the end of the book, and this fact answers some questions that might arise as to lifestyle.)

Brett, Jan. *Daisy Comes Home.* Putnam, 2002, 30 pp. (k-3).

A trip to the Li River area of Guang Xi Province, China, provided the author with the inspiration for this engaging story. Mei Mei is sure she has the six happiest hens in China. But Daisy, the smallest of the hens, isn't as happy as Mei Mei thinks she is. Picked on by the other hens (when no one is looking), Daisy leaves the henhouse one night to sleep in a basket at the river's edge. The water rises, and in the morning she finds herself adrift on the river. The story of Daisy's adventures and perils—and her triumphant return home—is especially interest-holding with its fresh and intriguing setting. But it is the accompanying full-page illustrations that make the book truly outstanding. Jan Brett has captured the look of the landscape, with its oddly shaped mountains, and of the buildings, the artifacts of daily living, the clothing, and the animals. There is an authentic Chinese flavor to all that meets the eye, and each page is fascinating to see.

Bunting, Eve. *Jin Woo*. Illus. by Chris Soentpiet. Clarion Books, 2001, 30 pp. (ps-2).
     Both writer and artist have captured in a relaxed and natural way the deep emotions of Mom, Dad, and David as they prepare to welcome the new member of the family, five-month-old Jin Woo from Korea. The reader not only feels the joy and excitement of the parents in adopting another son, but also understands David's fears and anxieties. "Were they this excited when they adopted me?" David wonders. Throughout the story, as the wise parents freely express their happiness and anticipation over their new son, they also express their love and commitment to David. They warmly include him in preparations, the immediate "togetherness" at the baby's welcome, the ride home from the airport, and the settling in. An appealing and attractive book, with the extra benefit of instilling wise and loving values in the minds and hearts of young readers.

Carle, Eric. *Pancakes, Pancakes*. Illus. by author. Simon and Schuster Children's Books, 1991 (1970), 32 pp. (ps-1).
     An entertaining story that, in a playful way, gives a young child some idea of the processes behind a simple article of food—a pancake. Jack is very hungry, but before he can have a huge pancake for breakfast, he must obtain (from raw materials and primary sources) all the needed ingredients. The story is accompanied by Carle's patchwork-of-color illustrations with their fine underlying textural detail.

Chorao, Kay. *Shadow Night: A Picture Book with Shadow Play*. Dutton Children's Books, 2001, 29 pp. (ps-1).
     After James goes to bed, the shadows on his bedroom wall frighten him, and he calls for Mama and Daddy. They show him how they can make shadow shapes with their hands and demonstrate that the shadows can be part of a funny story. Before James settles down to sleep, he tries a little shadow play himself. The author's illustrations throughout the book are delightful, and the story is just right for allaying nighttime fears—and starting an enjoyable family activity of shadow-making.

Creech, Sharon. *Fishing in the Air*. Illus. by Chris Raschka. HarperCollins Publishers, 2000, 28 pp. (k-3).
     Early in the morning a father and son open the car trunk and put in "two poles and the can of worms and a sack of sandwiches and a thermos of water." A fishing trip—but much more. A beautiful story of the bond between father and son—a bond that reflects the earlier one between this father and his father. What the fishermen see is shared, described, cherished, and enriched with imagination and understanding; and what they see calls up memories of when the father himself was a boy. These memories are also shared and linked to this time of closeness and joy. Raschka's flowing, swirling drawings with their warm and lovely colors that evoke the "clear, cool river, rolling along over sandy-colored stones," "the rolling green fields with bright red flowers here and there like floating rubies," "the tall green trees" are the perfect background for the companionship of father and son, the time together that they share of the past and the future.

de Paola, Tomie. *Now One Foot, Now the Other*. Illus. by author. Putnam, 1981, 48 pp. (all ages).

Also listed under *Special Needs*

Grandpa has a stroke, and his family members think he can't hear or understand them. Young Bobby, however, senses this isn't true and is able to help his grandfather on the road to recovery. Bobby assumes the protecting, helping role his grandpa used to play with him. Excellent.

Edwards, Michelle. *Zero Grandparents*. Harcourt, Inc., 2001, 58 pp. (1-2).

Everyone in Mrs. Fennessey's class at Jackson Magnet School is excited about planning for Grandparents' Day. Everyone, that is, except Calliope James, who has no living grandparents. "Why does everyone else have a grandma but me?" she wonders unhappily. The day before all the other children will bring at least one grandparent to school with them, Calliope looks through the big photo album her father had given her. When she finds an old picture of Grandma Flory Sophia Turnipseed who died before Calliope was born, she notices that Flory Sophia looks like her and wishes more than ever that her grandma were alive. She thinks about the things she knows about her grandma, and she finds the lacy shawl and pair of mittens Flory Sophia had knitted that have been given to her. Then she has a wonderful idea. Calliope's plan, and how it changed her day from "Zero Grandparents" to "Grandparents' Day," brings a warm and happy ending to this simply told story. Children will not only enjoy this book, but it can help them to understand the needs of others.

Ehlert, Lois. *Waiting for Wings*. Harcourt, Inc., 2001, 34 pp. (ps-2).

Primary listing under *Nature, Science, and Technology*

This book is not a "story" but is being included among the stories so that it won't be overlooked for young children. With its gorgeous riot of color—flowers and butterflies—the text tells briefly in rhyme of the process by which a tiny egg becomes a butterfly, and also includes several additional pages about butterflies. Kids will love its brilliant hues and simply-told account—and for a weary parent or harried teacher on a gray day, its pages are a burst of sunshine.

Fowler, Susi Gregg. *Beautiful*. Illus. by Jim Fowler. Greenwillow Books, 1998, 30 pp. (ps-2).

Uncle George is a gardener, and on his young nephew's birthday George gives him the tools and seeds he needs to make his own garden. The beloved uncle is ill and has to go away for a while for special care. " 'That's why I want you to have your own garden this year,' said Uncle George. 'Maybe you won't feel I'm so far away.' " When Uncle George finally comes home, his nephew's plants are almost in bloom, but the boy is sad; his uncle is very frail, and Momma has said, quietly, that Uncle George isn't going to get well, and he just wants to be with them. When the boy tells his uncle that the plants are going to bloom, Uncle George whispers, "Ready for glory. Beautiful." This brief, gently told story deals lovingly with one of life's most painful times. Throughout the story, the soft colors of the poignant illustrations glow with love and hope and beauty in the midst of deep sadness.

Gundersheimer, Karen. *Happy Winter*. Illus. by author. HarperCollins Children's Books, 1982, 40 pp. (ps-3).

This is a story of children at home doing simple, homey things—playing in the snow, dressing up, baking a cake (the recipe is included). The text is pleasant if not outstanding, but the wonderfully detailed illustrations are absolutely delightful. The whole atmosphere of the book is warm, cozy, and appealing.

Herriot, James. *James Herriot's Treasury for Children*. Illus. by Ruth Brown and Peter Barrett. St. Martin's Press, 1992, 246 pp. (ps-up).

Primary listing under *Animals*

This large and beautiful volume contains all eight of beloved Yorkshire veterinarian James Herriot's books of animal stories for children. Complete with warm and wonderful illustrations, each story reflects Herriot's endless love for "all creatures great and small" and his irresistible sense of humor. A book for the family to enjoy together and to keep and cherish.

Hoban, Russell. *A Birthday for Frances*. Illus. by Lillian Hoban. HarperCollins Children's Books, 1968, 32 pp. (k-3).

Hoban captures children's ways of thinking and speaking in this perceptively done story involving sibling jealousy. Sisterly love triumphs in the end. This is one in the series of Frances books; all are good.

Karon, Jan. *Miss Fannie's Hat*. Illus. by Toni Goffe. Augsburg, 1998, 32 pp. (1-4).

Miss Fannie, tiny, sprightly, and ninety-nine years old, has a closetful of hats and loves each one—straw, felt, suede, plush—adorned with flowers, feathers, ribbons, and scarves. But she loves her beautiful pink straw with the silk roses best, the one she has worn each Easter Sunday for thirty-five years. When Miss Fannie's church (which she loves even more than her hats) decides to have an auction to raise money for some needed repairs, she is asked to give one of her hats for the sale. The difficult decision as to which hat to part with and the outcome of Miss Fannie's choice go right to the heart of loving, giving, and delighting in special blessings. Jan Karon, author of the best-selling Mitford novels, has given us a lovable, meaningful, and charmingly illustrated story—with plenty of her delightful humor along the way.

King-Smith, Dick. *Sophie's Tom*. Illus. by David Parkins. Candlewick Press, 1991, 111 pp. (ps-3).

In his several Sophie stories, the author has given children another entertainingly portrayed character to enjoy. Determined, not reluctant to push her own agenda in ingenious ways, Sophie is an interesting, likable—and sometimes outrageous—little person with an appealing family. As the story opens, it is Christmas morning and Sophie's fifth birthday. She enjoys having her birthday on Christmas and especially appreciates her great-great-aunt's gift of five dollars for Sophie's Farm Money fund. (She plans to be a "lady-farmer" when she grows up and has already started saving for her farm.) Meanwhile, she has decided that she wants a pet, and when she finds a black cat with orange eyes in the yard, she is ready to adopt it. Full of hilarious conversations and activity, the story is a delight for young readers (or listeners) and for anyone reading it aloud.

Lasky, Kathryn. *My Island Grandma*. Illus. by Emily McCully. Smithmark, 1979, 32 pp. (1, 2).

A brief, delightful story of the special times a little girl has with her grandmother. Abbey, her parents, and her grandmother spend every summer on a little island off the coast of Maine. Abbey can run over to her grandmother's cabin whenever she likes, and together they explore, sail, pick berries, stargaze, and share a close, loving relationship. An especially welcome aspect of the story is the portrayal of the grandmother as an active, resourceful, and interesting person.

Lowry, Lois. *Zooman Sam*. Illus. by Diane de Groat. Houghton Mifflin, 1999, 155 pp. (1-4).

When Sam has to get ready for Future Job Day at his preschool, it's time once again for the Krupniks, his lovable family, to go into action. (Some readers will remember Sam and his older sister Anastasia from Lois Lowry's earlier stories.) Sam and his schoolmates must dress the part of their chosen career. Sam knows that most of the boys want to be firemen, but he wants to be somebody more unusual. Both parents and children will find themselves laughing all the way through this entertaining story from its joint family effort to outfit Sam appropriately for his role as a zookeeper, through various crises that occur at home and at school, and into the hilarious sessions in class when Sam (with a marked flair for the dramatic) talks about his chosen career. Author Lowry's awareness of how children think and speak is a special quality of her writing, as is her gift for portraying a warm, close, loving family with a pair of wise parents who thoroughly enjoy *their* roles.

McCloskey, Robert. *Time of Wonder*. Illus. by author. Viking Children's Books, 1957, 63 pp. (2-up).

Beautifully illustrated by the author, the book is in a picture-book format but with a substantial amount of text. Evocative descriptions of the natural world, of two children's experiences during summer on an offshore New England island, provide the quiet story line. This is an excellent book to use in encouraging children to observe their surroundings, the weather, and other natural phenomena. Good to read aloud, suggesting that the children try to picture in their minds what is being described in the story.

McCully, Emily Arnold. *The Mixed-Up Grandmas Treasury*. An I Can Read book. HarperCollins Publishers, 1993, 190 pp. (ps-2).

This treasury combines three hilarious Grandma stories: *The Grandma Mix-Up*, *Grandmas at the Lake*, and *Grandmas at Bat*. Grandma Nan and Grandma Sal love their grandchild Pip dearly, and she loves them. Nan and Sal, however, are very different from each other. Grandma Nan is on top of everything, but too much so; Grandma Sal is too easy-going and careless, but both are good sports and care about Pip. Each one wants Pip to do things her way. Pip, on the other hand, wants to do things the way she and her mom and dad do them—which includes letting Pip make some of her own choices. Pip and her grandmas work the problems out in the varying circumstances of three different settings. It is not hard to guess what kind of complications may arise in each situation before all works out well. Full of fun—and everybody learns something.

McGinley, Phyllis. *The Most Wonderful Doll in the World.* Illus. by author. Scholastic, 1992 (1950), 61 pp. (2-up).

A little girl has an active imagination that makes a doll she doesn't have "the most wonderful doll in the world," with an ever-growing list of marvelous attributes and clothes. By the end of the story she has learned the difference between wishful thinking and reality.

Millman, Isaac. *Moses Goes to School.* Farrar, Straus, and Giroux, 2000, 30 pp. (k-3).
Primary listing under *Special Needs*

This lively and colorfully illustrated story of a day at school with Moses tells its readers how many deaf and hard-of-hearing children are educated. Moses and his school friends communicate using American Sign Language, often referred to by its initials, ASL. The writer has included drawings showing hand positions and movements used in ASL. It is helpful for children with normal hearing to know what it is like to be unable to hear and how hearing-impaired children are equipped to communicate, learn, and prepare for their future. This cheerful story provides a good introduction to the subject. Refer to the primary listing shown above for more information on the book's contents.

Scott, Ann Herbert. *On Mother's Lap.* Illus. by Glo Coalson. Houghton Mifflin, 1972, 39 pp. (ps-1).

Warmly pictured and with minimal text, the story's theme is simple: There is always room for one more on Mother's lap. By using an Eskimo mother and children in the illustrations, the theme's universality is emphasized.

Spier, Peter. *Crash! Bang! Boom!* Illus. by author. Doubleday, 1972, 44 pp. (ps-2).

Here is a wonderful collection of sounds. The book includes many, many of Spier's small, detailed pictures (each two-page spread shows related activities going on, with accompanying sounds named under each picture). There is a tremendous sense of action throughout, and the book would lend itself creatively to one-on-one or small-group activity, with children identifying and imitating sounds, or for reading practice in decoding the written names of the sounds accurately.

Spier, Peter. *Peter Spier's Christmas* and *Peter Spier's Rain.* Both illus. by author. Doubleday, 1983, 38 pp.; 1982, 36 pp. (all ages).

Spier is in a class by himself with his softly colored, incredibly detailed pictures in these two irresistible wordless books. In *Christmas* the reader follows an obviously warm, close family of two parents and three children through the beloved season: preparation and anticipation of every kind; deeds of kindness to others; the crèche and the Christmas Eve church service; the gifts and the arrival of fond grandparents; the bountiful dinner (with heads bowed first in thanks), the piled-up kitchen counters and wall-to-wall clutter—and, to end the day, the tired but warmly content husband and wife companionably cleaning up the mess, bringing order out of chaos, finally sharing a quiet moment by the fire. Even right after Christmas, Spier's book makes you want to do it all over again—and with even more of the serene love that simply spills out of its pages.

In *Rain*, a young brother and sister—boots, raincoats, and rain hats on, an umbrella to share between them—go walking in the rain. In the course of their wanderings, they engage in every wonderful in-the-rain activity imaginable. As always, Spier's pictures have a life of their own, creating images of innocent childhood play, loving parents, and warm, sheltering homes.

Waybill, Marjorie. *Chinese Eyes*. Herald, 1974, 32 pp. (k-2).
Primary listing under *Special Needs*
A Korean adoptee is teased by other children and called "Chinese eyes." Her confidence is restored by a wise mother's words. The story deals in a subtle way with prejudice, helping children to understand a new way of seeing those who are "different."

Yashima, Taro. *Crow Boy*. Illus. by author. Viking, 1955, 38 pp. (ps-3).
Primary listing under *Special Needs*
An unusual picture-book story of a shy little Japanese schoolboy nicknamed Chibi, who is unlike his schoolmates. Shunned throughout his years at school, a new teacher finally makes contact with the boy no one knows and helps others to see his unique nature and abilities.

Realistic Stories—Historical

Amper, Thomas. *Booker T. Washington*. Illus. by Jeni Reeves. Carolrhoda Books, Inc., 1998, 48 pp. (1-3).
Primary listing under *Biography*
A brief, factual biography rather than fiction, this fine little book nevertheless has an excellent story quality. The writer has the gift of reaching the reader's heart with his account of Booker, born into slavery and when freed at the end of the Civil War, too poor to be able to go to school. Even before his freedom he had longed for an education. How his dream came true completes that part of the story of Booker's life. The many accompanying illustrations capture the underlying emotion of the perceptive narrative. The young reader is happy to learn in a brief Afterword that Booker T. Washington went on to become one of the early African-American leaders who did great things for his people.

Avi. *Prairie School.* An I Can Read Chapter Book. Illus. by Bill Farnsworth. HarperCollins Publishers Inc., 2001, 48 pp. (2-3).

In 1880 many people were still pioneering in the western part of the United States. The Bidson family—Ma, Pa, and nine-year-old Noah—left Maine and settled in a part of Colorado on the rolling prairie. Noah led an active life, helping with many chores, enjoying the freedom of his happy, outdoor days, and soon growing to love the prairie. But Noah's parents wanted more for their son. They themselves could barely read and write, and they knew how much better Noah's life could be as he grew up if he learned more than they did. Mrs. Bidson's sister Dora, a teacher back East, was coming to visit, and Ma and Pa asked her to teach Noah. The angry little boy saw no need for reading and writing on the prairie. He stubbornly refused to learn. How the perceptive and gifted teacher found a way to change Noah's mind, and how he came to understand that an ability to read could help him know much more about the prairie he loved, is effectively told. Especially well written and beautifully illustrated, *Prairie School* is not only an enjoyable story, but makes a strong case for the tremendous value of reading—in an attractive and appealing form.

Bailey, Linda. *When Addie Was Scared.* Illus. by Wendy Bailey. Kids Can Press, Ltd., 1999, 29 pp. (ps-3).

Based on a real-life Addie, this lovingly told and beautifully illustrated story speaks with understanding of a little girl who jumped at every sudden or strange sound and imagined dangers on every hand. But one day, at her beloved grandmother's, Addie faced a threat that really existed—and found a deep-down strength and courage she didn't know she had. Enjoyable for all as a story and especially helpful for little people with many fears.

Benchley, Nathaniel. *Sam the Minuteman.* Illus. by Arnold Lobel. HarperCollins Children's Books, 1987 (1969), 64 pp. (k-3).

This enjoyable story provides a good introduction to historical fiction for early readers. Sam, with his father, sees history in the making as they encounter the British troops at Lexington, Massachusetts—the start of the Revolutionary War. Allowing for its "early reader" limitations, Benchley has done a good job of including some drama and characterization in the story.

Beskow, Elsa. *Pelle's New Suit.* Gryphon House, 1989 (1929), 32 pp. (ps-1).

In this long-lasting and much-loved tale, the little Swedish boy Pelle seeks help, step by step, in transforming the wool from his lamb into a new wool suit. The quaint, colorful illustrations are especially appealing. Long a classic, this book has entranced generations of children.

Note: Moved, in this revised edition, from the "modern" to the "historical" category. See "Notes on the Book's Organization." The dividing line has been moved from 1920 to 1930 due to the passage of time since the story's original publication date.

Bulla, Clyde Robert. *The Beast of Lor.* Illus. by Ruth Sanderson. HarperCollins Children's Books, 1977, 54 pp. (1-4).

An imaginative story of a Celtic boy in England and of his friendship with a gentle elephant brought to Britain by an invading Roman army. An excellent possibility for use in connection with an early-grade introduction to ancient history. Well-written and interest-holding.

Bulla, Clyde Robert. *The Sword in the Tree*. Illus. by Paul Galdone. HarperCollins Children's Books, 1962, 128 pp. (2-up).
    Shan, the son of Lord Weldon, has exciting adventures in the days of King Arthur. Robbers in the woods, brave knights, and fabled Camelot are all a part of this well-written story. Courage, determination, and honesty are some of the implicit underlying values.

Bulla, Clyde Robert. *A Lion to Guard Us*. Illus. by Michele Chessare. HarperCollins Children's Books, 1989 (1981), 128 pp. (2-up).
    Jemmy and Meg (eight and five) depend on their eleven-year-old sister to find a way to get them all from England to the Jamestown Colony in Virginia. Their father has gone ahead to make a home for them, but now their mother has died, and the callous Mistress Trippett, for whom she worked, has turned them out. Exciting adventure and a happy ending in this easy-to-read story.

Bulla, Clyde Robert. *Pirate's Promise*. Illus. by Peter Burchard. HarperCollins Children's Books, 1994 (1958), 96 pp. (2-up).
    Sold by his uncle as an indentured servant, Tom is forced onto a ship sailing for America. On the voyage the ship is attacked, and Tom finds himself among the motley crew of the piratical *Sea Bird*. Through it all, Tom's spirit and courage remain strong. How he survives many dangers and makes a fresh start in the New World makes exciting, suspenseful reading.

Dalgliesh, Alice. *The Courage of Sarah Noble*. Illus. by Leonard Weisgard. Simon and Schuster Children's Books, 1987 (1954), 64 pp. (1-5).
    A charming story of eight-year-old Sarah, who goes with her father into the wilderness where he has bought land for a new home. All the rest of the family (including a young baby) stay at their old home until Sarah's father can build the new house. Sarah keeps house for him, and friendly Indians become Sarah's second family. (Based on a true story of the eighteenth century.)

Hall, Donald. *Ox-Cart Man*. Illus. by Barbara Cooney. Viking Penguin, 1979, 37 pp. (k-3).
    This beautifully written and illustrated story resonates with the peaceful, productive life of a long-ago era. On their hilly New England farm the ox-cart man and his family make and grow a variety of food and useful things: a shawl woven from the wool of their sheep, mittens knitted from the wool, candles, shingles, brooms, maple sugar, honey and honey combs, potatoes, apples, turnips, and cabbages. At the end of the busy seasons of spring and summer, and after the harvesting of fall, the ox-cart man filled up his cart with all the things that were left over after he and his family had stored away what they needed to keep. He harnessed up his ox and walked for ten days through the wonderful countryside, past

farms and villages, to the busy Portsmouth Market. There he sold everything he had brought with him, even his ox and cart. Then he bought a few small things to carry back and set out for home. What will he do though without his ox and his cart *next* October? Young readers/listeners will enjoy finding out the answer to that question. A lovely sense of timeless peace and order pervades the book, enhanced by the artist's illustrations—which won her the Caldecott Medal for that year. A very special book.

Larcombe, Jennifer Rees. *The Baby in the Basket.* Illus. by Steve Björkman. Crossway Books, 1999, 19 pp. (ps-3).
   Primary listing under *Bible/Spiritual and Moral Teaching*
   This true story of baby Moses has all the elements of a suspenseful, surprise-ending story. In order to save the baby's life, his mother puts him in a watertight basket and then puts the basket in the reeds at the edge of the river! Moses' big sister Miriam keeps out of sight but watches to see what will happen to her baby brother. Vivid, colorful illustrations in the Egyptian setting and the writer's lively style make the familiar story especially enjoyable.

13

LITERATURE: LEVEL II

Fables, Folk Tales, and Fairy Tales

Andersen, Hans Christian. *The Snow Queen*. Translated by Naomi Lewis. Illus. by Angela Barrett. Candlewick Press, 1996 (1991), 46 pp. (3-6).

Under a dark spell, little Kay has been abducted by the beautiful but icy Snow Queen. His dear friend Gerda sets out on a quest to find him and bring him home. This is the longest of any of Andersen's many stories and one that he especially enjoyed writing. In spite of trials and dangers, there is help along the way from animals and birds, a variety of people, and a legion of angels. Vivid descriptions are enhanced by beautiful and imaginative illustrations, and children will share the joy of the faithful friendship of Gerda and Kay.

Brumbeau, Jeff. *The Quiltmaker's Gift*. Illus. by Gail de Marcken. Pfeifer Hamilton Publications, 2000, 44 pp. (ps-4).

This brilliantly illustrated, engaging story tells of an aged woman known as the Quiltmaker whose life is imperiled by a greedy king. Miserably unhappy in spite of all his possessions, the king, whose subjects are forced to lavish gifts upon him, still seeks for more, demanding the gift of a quilt. The Quiltmaker explains to the king that each of the many quilts she makes is given only to a needy person—and she refuses to give one to the king. What follows this confrontation not only provides the story's colorful and suspenseful action, but also develops the moral of the story, as the king finally learns that happiness is found in giving, not grabbing.

The book is enhanced by its quilt-block designs that include an extensive sampling on the double-page spread of both the front and back endpapers, with each block also showing up on a page of the story.

Colum, Padraic. *The Boy Apprenticed to an Enchanter*. Illus. by Edward Leigh. Peter Smith, 1991 (1966), 150 pp. (4-up).

An imaginative, colorful fairy tale. Its imagery, settings, and vocabulary are all above average, and, as in any good fairy tale, right ultimately triumphs over wrong.

Craft, K. Y. (adapted by). *Cinderella*. Illus. by K. Y. Craft. SeaStar Books, 2000, 29 pp. (3-up).

For moments of sheer dreaming, this recent retelling of a story loved for centuries meets the criteria for a romantic and beautiful fairy tale. Poor, oppressed, humble, and gracious, Cinderella is touched by the wand of a youthful and beau-

tiful fairy godmother and makes appearances at the palace balls in dresses designed
to charm readers with their minutely detailed magnificence—based on seventeenth-
and eighteenth-century gowns of the French aristocracy. (Even the attire of
Cinderella's prince is noteworthy.) The story takes its expected course, enhanced
not only by the primary illustrations, but by captivating illuminated borders on the
pages of text, each with its own exquisite details. The story is gently told, with less
than the usual emphasis on the comeuppance of the horrid stepsisters. When
Cinderella and her prince inherit the kingdom, they become "known far and wide
as the fairest and kindest rulers the people had ever known."

Craik, Dinah Maria Mulock. *The Little Lame Prince*. Troll Communications, 1997
(1875), 107 pp. (3-up).
    A delightful fairy tale that lauds goodness and kindness in a most appealing
manner. The magic flying cloak that unfolds itself from a dark, shabby-looking little wad of cloth into a marvelous means of escape for the lonely little prince is
something a child will never forget. For some unknown reason, this wonderful
story has been largely forgotten in recent years. Now that it is back in print, more
children will be able to enjoy its exciting story and its account of the triumph of
good over evil!

Farjeon, Eleanor. *The Little Bookroom*. Illus. by Edward Ardizzone. Henry Z.
Walck, 1956, 302 pp. (3-up).
    The writer herself selected for this book her favorites among the stories she had
written for children. Imagination, humor, warmth, and understanding infuse these
tales, whose characters range from kings, peasants, animals, and birds to everyday
children. It is unfortunate that this book, like so many of Farjeon's titles, is now
out of print, but it is still widely available in libraries and through interlibrary loan.

Lang, Andrew (collected and edited by). *Arabian Nights*. Dover, 1969, 424 pp. (k-6).
    This popular old favorite, a version read by children for 100 years, contains all
the well-known Arabian Nights tales and can be enjoyed by all ages.

Lucado, Max. *The Song of the King*. Illus. by Toni Goffe. Crossway Books, 1995,
29 pp. (1-4).
    In a familiar fairy tale pattern, a king has set a test for the three most renowned
knights in his kingdom. Each knight wants to marry the lovely princess, and her
brother gives them a message sent by his father the king. The knight who successfully traverses Hemlock, the dark and dangerous home of the sinister Hopenots,
and reaches the king's castle first will be given his daughter's hand in marriage. As
in all good fairy tales, there is action, suspense, and the triumph of right. Enjoyable
simply as a story and enhanced by lively, often humorous illustrations, this allegory reveals a profound spiritual truth.

MacDonald, George. *The Princess and Curdie*. Penguin, 1966 (1883), 224 pp. (3-up).
    When a lovely fairy commissions Curdie, the little miner boy, to save the king
and the princess, his life changes forever. To help him in his task, Curdie is given

the magic power of discerning the true character of anyone he encounters. How Curdie carries out the fairy's wishes and the part played by the use of his special gift makes a fairy story that children have loved for many decades. As in all of MacDonald's work, spiritual truth is clearly woven into this tale, and qualities of courage, loyalty, and compassion are underscored.

Perrault, Charles. *Perrault's Complete Fairy Tales*. Dodd, Mead, 1982 (1697), 184 pp. (3-up).

In this fine collection are some of the best-known fairy tales of Western literature—such stories, for example, as "Puss in Boots," "Little Red Riding Hood," and "Cinderella." In addition to the unfailing charm of the imaginative tales, Perrault's stories are full of witty comments on human nature, which are a part of the subtle teaching elements of such literature.

Pyle, Howard. *The Wonder Clock*. Dover, 1915 (1888), 318 pp. (3-up).

Twenty-four stories of adventure and wonder in the world of princes, princesses, talking animals, and ogres. A long-lasting classic with the extensive vocabulary and elaborate writing style so characteristic of Pyle.

Ruskin, John. *The King of the Golden River*. Dover, 1974 (1851), 96 pp. (3-up).

Another timeless classic. Ruskin's tale of two brutal bothers and a kind and noble younger brother is beautifully written with especially fine descriptions and an outstanding use of language.

Wiggin, Kate Douglas and Nora A. Smith, editors. *The Arabian Nights: Their Best-Known Tales*. Illus. by Maxfield Parrish. Simon and Schuster, 1937 (1909), 368 pp. (all ages).

This collection of twelve favorite tales, including "Ali Baba and the Forty Thieves," "Aladdin and His Wonderful Lamp," and "Sinbad the Voyager," has recently been reissued, reset in the original typeface. The famous Maxfield Parrish illustrations are printed from new color plates of the originals.

Myths and Legends

Climo, Shirley (retold by). *Stolen Thunder*. Illus. by Alexander Koshkin. Clarion Books, 1994, 40 pp. (1-5).

In this old Norse myth, King Thrym of the frost giants steals the hammer of Thor, the biggest and strongest of the mythical Norse gods. Strong as he is, Thor can't count on winning all encounters unless he has Mjolnir, his magic hammer, with him. Thor is enraged by the theft and accepts the offer of Loki, the troublemaking trickster, to negotiate with Thrym to get the hammer back. The frost king sends Loki back with the message that he will accept only one price for the return of the hammer: Freya, the goddess of love and beauty, must become his bride. This is unthinkable to both Thor and Freya, and Loki thinks of a way to trick Thrym and get the hammer back without involving Freya. His plan is highly implausible, which means there is lots of room for a ridiculous encounter—which ultimately becomes fatal for Thrym. Climo's lively retelling and Koshkin's lavish and colorful illustrations perfectly match the myth's entertaining exaggerations.

Hawthorne, Nathaniel. *A Wonder Book and Tanglewood Tales*. Ohio State University Press, 1972 (1852-53), 476 pp. (4-up).

This combined volume comprises Hawthorne's adaptations of classical myths. The events of the stories follow the originals except in cases where the writer thought it best, in a children's book, to make changes or deletions. The tone is quite different from that of versions nearer the original form, and some people object to Hawthorne's tales on that ground. The tales are, however, American classics in their own right. From one viewpoint, they provide a helpful way to introduce children to some of the rather complicated characters and events that they may later encounter in a more advanced study of mythology. Traditional values are strongly underscored in Hawthorne's versions of the stories.

Pyle, Howard. *The Merry Adventures of Robin Hood*. Dover, 1968 (1883), 325 pp. (4-6).

A fine collection of the always-enthralling, yet familiar tales—and many not so well-known. Pyle's language retains the flavor of an earlier time, making the prose especially rich and valuable as a literary experience. As to the story elements, courage, idealism, and heroic adventure are still important ingredients in good reading for children, and they are amply found in this favorite classic.

Fantasies, Talking Animal Stories

Bond, Michael. *A Bear Called Paddington*. Houghton Mifflin, 1960, 128 pp. (3-7).

A little bear, Paddington, who has emigrated from "Darkest Peru," is adopted by a British family and becomes involved in a variety of humorous adventures. This is a reading-for-fun book with a good atmosphere of kindness and family warmth but not much depth. Other Paddington stories in the series also make enjoyable reading.

Carroll, Lewis (pen name of Charles L. Dodgson). *Alice in Wonderland* and *Through the Looking Glass*. Putnam Pub. Group, 1986 (1865), 307 pp. (3-up).

No works of children's literature have become more thoroughly absorbed into the English-speaking cultures than Lewis Carroll's classic fantasies about the little girl who enters a most confusing dream world, first by way of a rabbit hole and later through a mirror. References to the characters and events of the stories are found everywhere, and even people who have never read the books have heard of the White Rabbit, the Mad Hatter, the Cheshire Cat, the White Queen, the Walrus and the Carpenter, and the rest of the cleverly drawn creations encountered by Alice.

Children are able to appreciate the Alice stories at widely varying ages. Some simply plunge into their topsy-turvy atmosphere and enjoy the sound of the language and the ridiculous scenes long before they are able to understand much of the subtle humor that adults so thoroughly enjoy. Other children, particularly if they are reading the books for themselves, may find the illogical, dreamlike sequences of events and the challenging language of the dialogue confusing. In the latter case, the children may enjoy the stories more when they are considerably older and more sophisticated in their reading. If the stories are first read aloud by an adult who knows and appreciates them, often children will thoroughly enjoy them.

Collodi, Carlo. *The Pinocchio of C. Collodi*, translated and annotated by James Teahan. Schocken, 1985 (1883), 206 pp. (3-up).

This excellent translation is based on the premise that earlier translations have often lost the flavor of speech that Collodi (whose name was actually Carlo Lorenzini) intended the characters of his story to use. Teahan's version uses very natural, colloquial language in its dialogue, and the plentiful notations explain references to the original nineteenth-century Italian setting and culture. The classic tale of Gepetto and Pinocchio, the little wooden boy who comes to life, is the same as in earlier translations, but quite different from the shallow Disney version. Collodi's story is rich in its portrayal of human nature and the inner battle between good and evil. The folly of bad companions, the dire results of lying, and a number of other basic values are graphically illustrated, along with the adventure and humor for which the story is so well known.

Note: This fine edition is not currently in print, but do try to find it if possible. In any case try to avoid editions that are abridged or condensed.

Ford, Paul F. *Companion to Narnia*. HarperSF, 1994 (1980), 512 pp. (4-up).

Primary listing under *Reference*

A detailed guide to the themes, characters, and events of the seven Narnia books.

Godden, Rumer. *The Doll's House*. Puffin Books, 1976 (1947), 125 pp. (3-up).

An endearing story about a doll's house and its inhabitants, with a wooden farthing doll (an old-fashioned, inexpensive doll) as its heroine. In addition to its fine literary quality, the book underscores important values in contrasting responsibility and true worth with outward show and disloyalty.

Grahame, Kenneth. *The Wind in the Willows*. Illus. by Michael Hague. Holt, Rinehart and Winston, 1980 (1907), 205 pp.

Grahame's classic story charms with its lovable characters and its long-vacation atmosphere. Mole has a sudden case of spring fever, gives up on his house-cleaning, and wanders in the fields and meadows. He finds himself by a river (he has been such a stay-at-home that he has never seen it before) and meets the Water

Rat, who invites Mole into his boat, something else he has never seen before. "Believe me, my young friend," Rat says dreamily, "there is *nothing*—absolutely nothing—half so much worth doing as simply messing about in boats." A world of friendships, new and exciting experiences, the joy of carefree wandering, of picnicking, and playing has opened for Mole—to say nothing of the adventures ahead with Mr. Toad of Toad Hall. And under the surface is subtle encouragement in kindness, patience, industry, and loyalty. Richness of language and a deep appreciation of nature add to the book's depth.

Heide, Florence Parry. *The Problem with Pulcifer*. HarperCollins Children's Books, 1983, 64 pp. (3-up).

A brief, clever satire on TV addiction. Pulcifer's parents are terribly worried because he simply isn't interested in watching television. All he wants to do is read. But in his society, TV-watching has taken over to such an extent that classes in school all watch TV, and libraries have many more audiovisual items than books. Pulcifer's parents try everything to induce him to switch from reading to TV, even taking him to a psychiatrist. Children will enjoy the fun as the situation-reversal humor is developed—and perhaps will be encouraged to take a more critical view of TV as well.

Holman, Felice. *The Cricket Winter*. Norton, 1967, 107 pp. (3-4).

A whimsical, well-written story of a boy who feels no one is listening to him, and a cricket that understands Morse code. Together the boy and the cricket are able to improve the lives of a varied group of small animals living under the boy's sun porch, and in the process to develop some qualities of understanding and self-restraint of their own. An excellent book, unfortunately out of print, but still available in many libraries and through interlibrary loan.

Juster, Norton. *The Phantom Toll Booth*. Knopf Books for Young Readers, 1961, 255 pp. (3-6).

A light-hearted allegory full of humor that reinforces a number of important values. Milo is a young boy who finds life boring. When he's in school, he wishes he were out, but when he's at home, he wishes he were at school. Finding a huge package in his room (it turns out to be a small-scale toll booth), he follows the enclosed directions and finds himself on a suspenseful journey through a strange and different world. The adventures of Milo and the two companions he encounters make lively reading—and will keep the reader on his or her toes to catch the point of the clever humor, much of which is based on wordplay.

King-Smith, Dick. *Babe: The Gallant Pig*. Illus. by Mary Rayner. Crown Publishers, 1983, 118 pp. (all ages).

The lovable story of Babe, the piglet who is foster-parented by Fly, farmer Hogget's sheep dog. When the young piglet is purchased and brought to the Hogget sheep farm one day, the plan is to feed him well, and when he reaches the right size, turn him into bacon, ham, and all the other tasty pork products. But Babe is no ordinary piglet. Lonely for his mother, he senses Fly's strong maternal nature and is soon like one of her own puppies to her. Even the kindly Hoggets soon feel there is something special about Babe and begin to give up any thought of turning him into bacon. Meanwhile, Babe becomes very interested in Fly's work of herding the sheep, and Fly is delighted to mentor him. Of course, the fact that the animals can talk makes many entertaining conversations possible. What comes of all this is the triumphant climax to the irresistible and endearing story. It is exceptionally well written, and even those who have seen the movie version of the book will enjoy reading it.

Kipling, Rudyard. *The Jungle Book*. Grossett and Dunlap, 1950 (1894), 280 pp. (3-up).

The timeless stories loved by generation after generation of children—stories of Mowgli and the wolves, Tomai of the elephants, Rikki Tikki Tavi, and others. The charm of the tales is enhanced by the rhythmic, bardic flavor of Kipling's prose. Especially good for reading aloud.

Lawson, Robert. *Rabbit Hill*. Viking Children's Books, 1944, 127 pp. (3-up).

A modern classic with a fine literary quality. Children took this book to their hearts when it was first written more than fifty years ago, and it continues to be popular with succeeding generations. Lively, humorous, and warm, the story of Little Georgie, Uncle Analdas, Porkey, and all the other Little Animals is enhanced by Lawson's irresistible drawings. (Its sequel is *The Tough Winter*.)

Lewis, C. S. *The Lion, the Witch, and the Wardrobe*. Macmillan, 1950, 154 pp. (3-up).

In this opening book of the outstanding series known as The Chronicles of Narnia, Peter, Edmund, Susan, and Lucy (brothers and sisters) enter the land of Narnia through the back of a huge, old wardrobe. The children are charmed by the fauns, dwarfs, and animals they meet, but soon they find that Narnia is a land under a curse: It is winter the year round, and the forces of evil reign.

Impelled by a desire to help the faun who has been imprisoned for helping Lucy on her first venture into Narnia, the children are caught up in a stirring adventure in which the great golden lion, Aslan, leads the forces of good in the struggle to free Narnia from the evil queen and lift the chilling curse. There is not only excitement and suspense in this and the other six books that comprise the Chronicles, but a wealth of fascinating characters, a pervasive, witty humor, and a keen insight into human nature. The latter is reflected in the unaffected naturalness of the children's dialogue. The Chronicles are not only splendid creative literature, but Christian truth is symbolized throughout as an integral part of the Narnia experience. Other

Chronicles titles are: *Prince Caspian, The Voyage of the* Dawn Treader, *The Silver Chair, The Horse and His Boy, The Magician's Nephew,* and *The Last Battle.*

Lewis, C. S. *The Complete Chronicles of Narnia.* Illus. by Pauline Baynes. HarperCollins Publishers, 1998, 524 pp. (3-up).

    A big, beautiful book that includes all of the beloved Narnia stories (see the listing above). The lively original illustrations that harmonize so effectively with the text are newly in color, and an appealing introduction by Lewis's stepson, Douglas Gresham, offers a touching insight on Lewis and what he meant in Gresham's life as a young boy. A wonderful book to add to the family library or to a child's personal collection of favorite stories.

MacDonald, George. *At the Back of the North Wind* (adapted). Zondervan, 1981, 128 pp. (3-up).

    MacDonald, the minister/writer so much respected by C. S. Lewis, wrote a number of stories for children. In this one, Diamond, an unusual little boy with great sensitivity to the needs of others, is encouraged by the North Wind, who becomes his special friend. The poverty and illness so common at the time in which the story is set are vividly depicted, and there is a good deal of sadness throughout. For this reason, it should be used carefully, possibly in connection with British history of the last half of the nineteenth century. (This edition has been edited to delete some of the writer's discursive passages and to increase ease of reading. Many people may wish to read MacDonald's original text, first published in 1871. Unabridged versions are always preferable in many ways, but if the material is too difficult for children to understand, an edition like this can be worth trying.)

Nesbit, Edith. *Five Children and It.* Viking Penguin, 1996 (1902), 256 pp. (4-up).

    A lively family of English children of an earlier era become involved in a succession of suspenseful, imaginative adventures. In this book, for example, the children unearth a rather temperamental sand fairy that bears no resemblance whatever to conventional fairies. Written with wit and charm, Nesbit's books have been popular with children for decades. They include *The Phoenix and the Carpet, The Enchanted Castle, The Railway Children,* and the Bastable children stories.

Norton, Mary. *The Borrowers.* Harbrace, 1953, 180 pp. (3-up).

    Norton's books have that special magic that make them a delight to read. In this (and the other *Borrowers* titles), tiny Lilliputian-sized people survive by "borrowing" things secretly from the people of the full-sized world and ingeniously adapting them to their daily use. The stories are well-written, humorous, suspenseful, subtly conveying universal truths about human nature.

O'Brien, Robert C. *Mrs. Frisby and the Rats of NIMH.* Atheneum, 1971, 233 pp. (3-up).

    A suspenseful fantasy about the widowed Mrs. Frisby (a mouse) and her little family; about a community of rats very unlike other rats; and also about parental devotion, neighborly kindness, friendship, self-respect, sacrifice, and the thinking through of moral values. Exceptionally well done, delightful to read, and full of keen, subtle commentaries on human nature as portrayed by the little animals of the story.

Paterson, Katherine. *The Field of Dogs*. Illus. by Emily Arnold McCully. HarperCollins Children's Books, 2001, 89 pp. (4-up).

Everything has gone wrong for Josh. His father's death was hard to take, but he still had his mom, his friends, and Manch, his loved dog. Then his world falls apart. His mother marries again, has a new baby, and they all move to his stepfather's home in Vermont. Now, mixed up and miserable, out following his dog's trail across the snow, Josh reaches the edge of the woods. In an open field Manch is playing with several other dogs—and they are all laughing and talking together! Then the laughter stops, and Josh overhears that they are all being threatened by a bullying pack of big dogs looking for trouble. He decides they need help, even though they won't talk to *him* and shun his help. In growing suspense the hazards increase, and Josh has to act, as Manch's life is at stake. An exciting climax and some surprising developments involving help when Josh least expects it bring the story to a satisfying conclusion—and provide him with a happier, less self-pitying perspective on his life.

Sewell, Anna. *Black Beauty: The Autobiography of a Horse*. Grossett and Dunlap, 1945 (1877), 301 pp. (4-up).

The reason for classifying as fantasy this story that deals with an issue (cruelty to animals) that was widespread and acute at the time the book was written is that the story is told as though by the horse, Black Beauty. Throughout the book the animals talk to each other and think in a human manner. Apart from that, however, the book is realistic as it tells about the lovely black horse that went from comfort and happiness to great misery before finally being restored to a loving home. Use with caution for younger children, as the very tenderhearted among them may react intensely to the cruelty shown to Black Beauty.

Sharp, Margery. *The Rescuers*. Little, Brown, 1959, 149 pp. (3-up).

The perilous adventures of Miss Bianca offer excitement and suspense in a delightful form. A beautiful white mouse of impeccable taste, indomitable courage, and infinite resourcefulness, Miss Bianca is an appealingly drawn central figure. In *The Rescuers*, Miss Bianca—aided by a faithful helper, Bernard—and Nils—a mouse brought especially from Norway for the task—go to the rescue of a

Norwegian poet imprisoned in the fearsome Black Castle. The overall literary quality, language, and settings are outstanding, the pace of the events fast-moving. Subtle humor and clever insights on human nature abound, and sound values are demonstrated. Other titles in the series include *Miss Bianca*, *Miss Bianca in the Orient*, and *Miss Bianca in the Salt Mines*. Currently out of print, many of these delightful stories are still widely available in libraries.

Tolkien, J. R. R. *The Hobbit*. Houghton Mifflin, 1937, 317 pp. (3-up).
    The exciting adventures of Bilbo Baggins, the hobbit who didn't know he had the courage, curiosity, and ability to lead. However, the wizard Gandalf was sure he possessed these qualities. Bilbo's encounters with the formidable dragon Smaug, the loathsome subterranean creature Gollum, and the many other hazards of the quest he shares with the treasure-hungry dwarves bring out the strengths that had been lying dormant as he lived his former quiet, comfortable life.
    The Hobbit can be read alone as an enthralling story in itself, but it is also the important prelude to Tolkien's immensely popular Lord of the Rings trilogy and its tales of Middle Earth. Widely-read modern classics, Tolkien's fantasies are appreciated for their superb story quality, keen insight, and literary excellence. Christian readers also welcome Tolkien's deeply Christian philosophy, which is reflected throughout his work.

Realistic Stories—Modern

Bartlett, Susan. *Seal Island School*. Illus. by Tricia Tusa. Viking, 1999, 69 pp. (2-5).
    Every year Seal Island's little one-room school has a different teacher. "So far away and so few people," they say. Pru thinks Miss Sparling is the best ever teacher. What can they do to keep her from leaving? Pru and Nicolas come up with a plan. This cozy story, full of simple, happy doings, might just make its readers all wish they could go and live on a Maine island. Or it might help them to bring some of the island's spirit into their own everyday lives. A happy, satisfying book that recognizes the joys of small things.

Bunting, Eve. *The In-Between Days*. Illus. by Alexander Pertzoff. HarperCollins Pub., 1994, 119 pp. (3-6).
    With an understanding of complex human emotions and an excellent ear for kid-speak, Eve Bunting has created a warm and surprisingly suspenseful story. George Bowser (the narrator of this first-person account), his gentle, patient father, David, and lively, talkative little brother, James, have painfully weathered the death of the family's wife and mother following James's birth five years earlier. One of only forty-three families living year-round on Dove Island, their life follows the flow of recurring seasonal patterns and close neighborly relationships. Summers mean tourists and a busy time for David's bike rental shop. But there is one difference this

summer; a young woman with a sunny smile and a quiet friendliness comes in to rent a bike—and into the Bowsers' lives. They all like their new friend, but when George realizes that his father and Caroline are beginning to care for each other, George thinks of a very unpleasant plan to get Caroline out of their lives. Only when it is almost too late does George realize the pain he has caused and make a last-minute effort to right the wrong. Against the warm, homey background of island life, the author has written of two appealing boys and two kind, perceptive adults who all find a way to move beyond the "in-between" days of their lives.

Cleary, Beverly. *Henry Huggins*. Morrow Avon, 1950, 160 pp. (1-4).

Easy to read, this book chronicles the hilarious events in the life of Henry Huggins, a most well-meaning young boy. Somehow Henry's projects always seem to end up rather differently from what he had planned. The story is full of the kind of humor most kids strongly relate to, a good choice for reluctant readers. There are a number of additional titles in the series, and Cleary is also the author of other popular series.

De Jong, Meindert. *The House of Sixty Fathers*. HarperCollins Children's Books, 1956, 192 pp. (4-up).

The dramatic and suspenseful story of a Chinese boy separated from his parents during the Japanese occupation of World War II. The writer not only understands children, but he is aware of the high level of courage, determination, and devotedness that children can reach. Authentic in its detail, warm and inspiring in its spirit, this is a splendid modern classic.

De Jong, Meindert. *Hurry Home, Candy*. HarperCollins Children's Books, 1972 (1953), 256 pp. (4-7).

The appealing story of Candy, a little dog whose early life is made up of one disaster after another. During the difficult times when he is homeless, uncared for, and barely surviving, people along the way show him kindness and understanding just when he needs it most. Several would have given him a home, but another mishap or old fears from previous unkindnesses terrify him into flight before he learns to trust. When an ideal master and a home he loves come into his life, there is still one more fear from the past to overcome. The writer has perceptively described the effect that human callousness can have on a living creature wholly dependent on human kindness—a kindness that Candy can finally trust for the devotion and care his lonely heart has always longed for.

De Jong, Meindert. *The Wheel on the School*. HarperCollins Children's Books, 1954, 256 pp. (3-up).

More than a wonderfully well-written story, De Jong's book puts readers in the heart of another time, another culture. It is, however, a world to which children of any time or place can relate, because the writer knows so well the universal qualities of childhood. The six children of a small Dutch school and their fine schoolteacher dream a dream—to bring the storks back to their little town. Within the framework of this simple plot, a wide range of suspenseful events and personal crises take place, all seen in the light of strong traditional values. Humor, insight, models of restored or improved human relationships, and growth in understanding are all offered in this fine story.

Denton, Judy. *Angel Bites the Bullet*. Illus. by Jill Weber. Houghton Mifflin, 2000, 130 pp. (3-6).
　　Everything seems to go wrong when Angel's kindhearted parents let her mom's friend Alyce move in while her apartment is being redone after a fire. Angel has two beds in her room, so she has to share the room with Alyce—and Alyce's sheepdog, cat, canary, and clutter. Angel and her friend Edna decide that something has to be done; maybe the answer would be to find a husband for Alyce. But things don't seem to be working out quite as they planned, and Angel, worrywart that she is, imagines quite a list of possible disasters lurking just ahead. A hilarious little romp with Angel, her lovable family, and an assortment of friends and acquaintances. Young readers who haven't yet encountered Angel will laugh their way through her adventures and be looking for the rest of the stories in writer Judy Denton's popular series.

Enright, Elizabeth. *Thimble Summer*. Holt and Co., 1995 (1938), 124 pp. (3-6).
　　One of those wonderfully written stories of children and everyday life that makes the reader feel he or she can see and taste the things being written about. In this case, readers can join Garnet, Jay, Eric, and the others as they play, work, seek adventure, and dream during a long, hot summer on a farm in the 1930s. Although the distinctive flavor of a specific period is present in the story, its appeal is timeless, and today's children will enjoy it just as children have been doing for more than sixty years.

Enright, Elizabeth. *Gone-Away Lake; Return to Gone-Away*. Harbrace, 1990 (1957), 192 pp.; 1990 (1961), 191 pp. (3-6).
　　Adventure, imagination, and delightful characters make this pair of books memorable. Julian and his cousin Portia explore the area around their summer home and make some surprising discoveries. The stories stay just (barely) this side of fantasy, and reading about the almost-abandoned little summer community of the past that the children find, of the fascinating old houses, and remarkable people they encounter will inspire many a daydream. Written in the 1950s, the stories will remind some adults of those peaceful—and far safer—childhood days that can no longer be taken for granted. Along with the liveliness and interest of the stories, excellent values of kindness, fairness, and helpfulness are subtly emphasized. Other enjoyable books by Elizabeth Enright are still available in libraries.

Estes, Eleanor. *Ginger Pye*. Harcourt Children's Books, 2000 (1951), 306 pp. (3-up).
　　Winner of the 1952 Newbery Award, this warm, often hilarious story of life with the Pye family is as fresh and appealing as it was fifty years ago. A cluster of lovable family and extended-family members are background for the experiences of Rachel and Jerry Pye and their reactions and ideas about what occurs. Although they both have friends of their own, the brother and sister, only a year apart in age, often cope with life's surprises and complications as a team. When Jerry is

given permission to get the puppy he longs for, everyone welcomes Ginger, who soon makes a place for himself as an amazingly intelligent and devoted pet. But with Ginger's coming, a mysterious and malign stranger enters the fringes of their lives. When Ginger disappears while the whole family gathers for Thanksgiving, Jerry and Rachel feel sure the stranger has snatched their beloved dog. How they find out who the villain is and how Ginger comes home are the happy climax of this delightful account.

Gates, Doris. *Blue Willow*. Viking Children's Books, 1940, 176 pp. (3-5).

Before the disastrous "dust bowl" years turned thousands of farms into dry fields blowing in the wind, the Larkins had a farm in Texas. But with the farm gone, Janey and her parents have to take to the road, along with thousands of migrant workers during the 1930s, going wherever there is farm work. Now they have settled briefly in the San Joaquin Valley of California while Janey's father works in the cotton fields. Janey has found a friend, Lupe Romero, and even a place by the river with hanging willows like the ones in Janey's precious blue willow plate, all that is left of the settled, more secure life of the past. In spite of the almost-too-good-to-be-true ending, there is enough reality in this well-written story to have given it a lasting readership over the more than sixty years since it was written.

Henry, Marguerite. *Misty of Chincoteague*. Rand, McNally, 1990 (1947), 176 pp. (2-9).

The exciting story of a brother and sister, Paul and Maureen, who tame two island ponies—a mare and her colt—from Assateague, a wild island off the coast of Virginia. For decades the horse stories of Marguerite Henry have been avidly read by children. With few exceptions, new readers will universally enjoy this suspenseful tale—and be ready to start in on all the rest of the writer's lastingly popular books.

Holling, Holling Clancy. *Paddle-to-the-Sea*. Illus. by author. Houghton Mifflin, 1980 (1941), 63 pp. (4-up).

In a Canadian wilderness cabin north of Lake Superior, an Indian boy carves a foot-long canoe with the figure of an Indian seated in it. Equipped with a tin rudder and a lump of lead for ballast, the little canoe, when put in the water, will keep heading forward and will return to an upright position if upset. Dreaming of the long water-path that leads to the sea, the Indian boy takes the canoe to the place where melted snow will flow to the first of the Great Lakes. On its bottom, the boy has carved these words: "PLEASE PUT ME BACK IN WATER. I AM PADDLE TO THE SEA." In a beautifully illustrated story that has charmed readers for sixty years, Holling tells of the little carved Indian's journey, of the places encountered, and of the people who help the canoe on its way. Many geographic details and drawings are included.

King-Smith, Dick. *Mysterious Miss Slade*. Crown Publishers, 1999, 123 pp. (3-5).

When the Reader family move from the city to a home in the country, Patsy and Jim are anxious to explore their surroundings. As they walk through fields near their new home, they turn down a steep lane that leads to a wooded hollow. There, stepping out of a large, dilapidated old caravan, is a very tall, thin, rather grimy elderly woman dressed in worn-out, grubby clothes. A black patch covers one eye. Surrounded at once by an assortment of well-cared-for animals, she greets the children with a lovely smile and speaks cordially to them in a gracious manner. The children are charmed by Miss Slade's kindly warmth—and her many pets. Soon the whole Reader family become her friends and want to help her to have a more comfortable and happy life. They know that the villagers' idea that she is a witch is completely mistaken—but there *is* a mystery in her life. After some unexpected near disasters (from which the Readers rescue her), the mystery is solved, and Miss Slade's new friends have their hopes for her fulfilled. A lively story full of warmth, kindness, laughter, and a happy ending.

Kjelgaard, Jim. *Big Red*. Holiday, 1956 (1945), 254 pp. (4-7).
    This outdoor action story with its central theme of the devotion between a young man and a magnificent dog has retained its popularity since it was written more than fifty years ago and is a good example of its type. Danny and his father farm and trap on a small scale in the mountains of northern New England. How Danny is given the care of his wealthy neighbor's champion Irish setter show dog, Big Red, how the dog reacts to his encounter with a marauding bear, and a variety of other suspenseful events make up the story. Courage, loyalty, and integrity of purpose are some of the values that underlie its development.

Little, Jean. *From Anna*. HarperCollins Children's Books, 1973, 203 pp. (3-7).
    Also listed under *Special Needs*
    Anna Solden, the youngest of five children, wonders why all the things that seem to come so easily to her brothers and sisters are so hard for her. Awkward, uncoordinated, struggling unsuccessfully to read, she increasingly isolates herself. When her family emigrates to Canada from Germany, a doctor there discovers that she has acute vision problems. Appropriate treatment is undertaken, and a new world slowly opens to Anna. This is a most perceptively written story by a writer who herself has had lifelong vision impairment. Little is particularly good at depicting the interaction between family members, and along with an interest-holding story line, she has provided a thought-provoking background to Anna's metamorphosis.

Little, Jean. *Mine for Keeps*. Viking Children's Books, 1995 (1962), 208 pp. (3-7).
    Also listed under *Special Needs*
    Sally has spent several years at a special boarding school for handicapped girls, learning skills that will help her to be independent someday in spite of her cerebral palsy. Now she is going back home to live. Wonderful though her family is, even that change seems scary; but worst of all is knowing she must go to a regular school and walk into a class full of strangers with her leg braces, her crutches, and her overwhelming fear. What happens in Sally's life—and in the lives of her family and friends—makes a warm, lively story that is not simply enjoyable to read but that

increases the reader's understanding of the problems and fears of those with special needs.

McCloskey, Robert. *Homer Price.* Puffin Books, 1998 (1943), 208 pp. (3-7).
    Small-town life in the Midwest of the early 1940s provides the setting for
Homer Price and his friends, family, and neighbors. The stories themselves are very
funny, written with a kind of casual nonchalance about their outrageous improb-
ability. Whether it's "The Case of the Sensational Scent," "The Doughnuts," or
any of the other four stories, kids will find the combination of the hilarious happenings and the laid-back way they are told very entertaining.

McDonough, Alison. *Do the Hokey Pokey.* Illus. by Jackie Urbanovic. Cricket
Books, 2001, 112 pp. (3-7).
    Brendan Breen and his family have recently moved, which means changing
schools. Brendan, who is quite shy, is anxious to be accepted in a low-key way.
He is horrified when his cheery and likable mother—who is not at all shy—takes
a weekend job playing the recorded music and leading party guests in lively dances
such as the bunny hop, the hokey pokey, the Macarena, and others at wedding and
birthday parties—and sometimes at school functions. He is sure his classmates will
soon find out that the energetic and ebullient Jean Breen is his mother. Brendan
cringes with embarrassment at even the thought, and he begins trying to plan ways
to keep this from happening. There is an appealing cast of characters and a little
mystery on the side. Enjoyable and laughter-filled, the book also reflects sound perceptions and positive values.

Morpurgo, Michael. *The Silver Swan.* Illus. by Christian Birmingham. Penguin
Putnam Books for Young Readers, 2000, 28 pp. (2-5).
    An especially beautiful book—visually and in spirit—about a boy and his
intense love for a wonderful swan. The artist's outstanding drawings in chalk pastels are poignantly lovely, and the writer's sensitive and perceptive telling of the
story has found a strong, yet gentle balance point between nature's endearing wonders and its sometimes painful realities.
    Note: Mute swans (the kind of swans in this story) are found mainly in parks
in the United States, with a smaller number living wild on the Atlantic coast. Many
of these swans are wild in England, where the story is set.

Ransome, Arthur. *Swallows and Amazons.* Buccaneer Books, 1995 (1930), 352 pp.
(4-8).
    This is the first in a much-loved and timeless series of books begun by Ransome
seventy years ago. The "on holiday" world of the four Walker children—John,
Susan, Titty, and Roger (baby Vicky is much too young to be included)—is created quite simply in a realistic setting of the English Lake Country. A little sailboat, an island in the lake (not far from shore and the farmhouse in which Mrs.
Walker and Vicky are comfortably installed), and permission from their naval officer father to camp on the island—these are the down-to-earth elements from which
the story is fashioned. But for the Walkers (and their many devoted readers) a

world of imagination, adventure, unexpected events—and some practice in carrying responsibility and functioning as a team—is opened up in a way that makes irresistible reading. Although each book is a separate story, it is especially enjoyable to read them in sequence. *Swallowdale* follows the opening book, then in order: *Peter Duck, Winter Holiday, Coot Club, Pigeon Post, We Didn't Mean to Go to Sea, Secret Water, The Big Six, Missee Lee, The Picts and the Martyrs,* and *Great Northern.*

Rylant, Cynthia. *The Cobble Street Cousins: In Aunt Lucy's Kitchen.* Illus. by Wendy Anderson Halperin. Simon and Schuster Books for Young Readers, 1998, 55 pp. (2-5).

Tess and her twin cousins Lily and Rosie have just moved in to Aunt Lucy's big attic room. All their parents are dancers doing a world ballet tour, and the girls had decided they would much rather spend the year in the big, old house on Cobble Street with Aunt Lucy than go to boarding school or move from hotel to hotel with their parents. Summer has just started, and the three cousins are thinking of things to do. Lily suggests a cookie company, and they plunge right in. Lily (who wants to be a poet) writes an ad in rhyme that Tess and Rosie print out by hand and post in the local market, on the library bulletin board, and in Aunt Lucy's flower shop. Soon orders are called in by neighbors, and the three enterprising cousins bake and deliver Cinnamon Crinkles hither and yon. Readers will enjoy every moment of this lively, funny, enchantingly illustrated story as they follow the outgoing trio around town—meeting friendly people, trying to matchmake for their young aunt, dreaming of their own futures, and thinking of another project when they tire of making cookies. A warm, sunny story full of joy, kindness, and the wonderfully amusing conversations of Rosie, Tess, and Lily.

Say, Allen. *Tea with Milk.* Houghton Mifflin Co., 1999, 32 pp. (3-up).

Artist/writer Allen Say has based this appealing story on a significant time in his parents' early lives. His father and mother, Asian by parentage, are each reared away from their own cultures. Then, before they have met, they are placed by circumstances in Japan. Through most of the book the focus is on May, as she is known in San Francisco where her father has worked since before her birth. The family's return to a small town in Japan when May finishes high school makes her feel like a stranger to herself. Worst of all is not being able to converse with anyone in English—the language she always used in America, except with her parents. The last straw is when her parents try to arrange a marriage for her with a young man they have selected. May knows she could never make such a marriage and decides on a desperate plan.

How she works out her plunge into independence, and her joy in meeting Joseph from Hong Kong (who is starving for a conversation in English) are part of her new future. May and Joseph make some discoveries about what really creates "home" and are even able to feel less alienated in the culture that had seemed so foreign to them. Say's beautiful illustrations are outstanding and sensitively reflect and complement the captivating narrative.

Seredy, Kate. *The Good Master.* Viking, 1935, 196 pp. (3, 4-up).

Another modern classic that has stood the test of time, this warm, perceptive story has been pleasing children for more than sixty years. Hungarian farm life is the setting for the story of Jancsi and Kate, his headstrong visiting cousin. Lively events and some important growth in maturity and understanding blend to form a satisfying whole in this well-written tale. Several other books by Seredy should be available in libraries, but the only one other than *The Good Master* now in print is *The White Stag.*

Sobol, Donald J. *Encyclopedia Brown: Boy Detective.* BDD Books for Young Readers, 1998 (1963), 96 pp. (3-6).

Light, easy reading, full of humor, and particularly popular with boys, this initial volume and the many others of this series are a good choice for encouraging reluctant readers. Encyclopedia Brown (no one calls him by his real name, Leroy) is a ten-year-old boy who has read so much that he is a walking reference source. Encyclopedia's father is the unbelievably successful chief of police of Idaville, and much of his success depends on the quick, infallibly right solutions discovered by his clever son to any crime in the community. Each chapter of the books is a "case," and the solution to each is in a section at the back of the book. A recent addition to this series (#22) is *Encyclopedia Brown and the Case of the Slippery Salamander.*

Stewart, Sarah. *The Gardener.* Illus. by David Small. Farrar, Straus and Giroux, 1997, 32 pp. (2-5).

It is 1935, and the Great Depression has brought misfortune to many people. Hard times have come to the Fitch family, and Lydia Grace is being sent to the big city to live with her kind but unsmiling Uncle Jim until her family's situation improves. Wanting to bring joy and beauty with her, she packs a lot of seeds and is overjoyed to find unused window boxes on the old building that has Uncle Jim's bakery on the first floor, with living quarters above. No one could have a greener thumb than Lydia Grace, and the flowers she soon has blooming everywhere bring smiles to all—except Uncle Jim. But Lydia doesn't give up and finds a "secret place" in which to prepare a floral display she hopes even her uncle won't be able to resist. Lydia Grace's warm, generous spirit and her courage in the face of adversity make her an inspiring heroine of this charming and often amusing story. Delightful illustrations capture completely the book's bright spirit.

Tada, Joni Eareckson. *You've Got a Friend.* Illus. by Jeff Meyer. Crossway Books, 1999, 31 pp. (1-5).

Also listed under *Special Needs*

Fresh and original, Meyer's vivid, full-page illustrations bring the reader at once into the spirit of this appealing story. Permanently injured in an accident, Ben feels hopelessly sidelined and alone as he watches life from his wheelchair. How can he ever again be part of things the other kids are doing, kids whose legs still work, who can walk and run and ride their bikes? Ben and Tony used to be best friends, but they aren't part of each other's lives now. Tony wishes he could still be a friend to Ben, but how can you do fun stuff with someone in a wheelchair? Besides, Tony is so down about the hard things in his own life that he can't picture being able to reach out to Ben. How Ben and Tony (with some special help they aren't even aware of) find their lost companionship is the heart of the story. Reaching out to others from her own wheelchair, author Joni illumines Ben's and Tony's unspoken discovery that *being* a friend is the way to *have* a friend.

Wiles, Deborah. *Love, Ruby Lavender*. Harcourt, Inc., 2001, 188 pp. (3-7).

Loving, articulate, feisty, vulnerable, and often very funny, Ruby herself makes this story, set in little Hallelulia, Mississippi, enjoyable. Ruby doesn't hesitate to express her feelings, and when Miss Eula, her grandma and best friend in joy or woe, flies to Hawaii to see her new baby granddaughter, Ruby wonders how she will get through the summer. Who will have time to listen and to tell her just what to do about her frequent tormentor, that "*tip-tap*ping Melba Jones"? Who else will care about her three hens rescued from certain death and the three eggs that will soon be hatching out? And she *must* tell Miss Eula about the new teacher she will have in the fall. Letters fly back and forth to Hawaii as many events take place, some of them very unexpected. Readers will enjoy getting to know the appealing Ruby and her Hallelulia family and neighbors.

Realistic Stories—Historical

Barasch, Lynne. *Radio Rescue*. Farrar, Straus and Giroux, 2000, 31 pp. (3-6).

Almost eighty years ago, the author's father was a ten-year-old boy living in New York City, who was longing to become a ham radio operator. The story, based on some of his experiences, is told as though he were the one recounting it. In those days, instant communication across distances was often impossible; at best it was difficult. Overseas long-distance phone lines didn't exist, and even within the United States long-distance phoning was very limited. But a new invention, "wireless radio," broadcasting in Morse code, reached not only across the continent but across the world. Young Robert longed to be part of this exciting activity. It was not easy, however, to break into it. No one was allowed to send Morse code via radio without an amateur (ham) license. This meant learning the dot-dash system so thoroughly that one could pass an exam based on decoding test material tapped out in code.

As author Barasch tells the appealing story, she includes details of the material her father worked hard and long to learn, proudly earning his license. The story is climaxed as the young broadcaster reacts to a frantic and fading message from a heavily flooded area in Florida. Written and illustrated with nostalgia, humor, and suspense, *Radio Rescue* is a delightfully different story.

Brady, Esther Wood. *Toliver's Secret*. Random Books for Young Readers, 1993 (1976), 176 pp. (3-7).

In this story of adventure and suspense during the American Revolution, Grandfather sprains his ankle, and ten-year-old Ellen Toliver must disguise herself as a boy and carry a secret message for Washington. Things don't work out quite as planned, and Ellen must react quickly to dangers and mishaps. In the process of carrying through her mission, a fearful Ellen learns that she has more courage and sense than she realized.

Brink, Carol Ryrie. *Caddie Woodlawn*. Simon and Schuster Children's Books, 1973 (1935), 288 pp. (4-up).

A Newbery Award-winning book when it was written, Caddie Woodlawn has long been a modern classic. Its story of the red-haired tomboy who runs and climbs with her brothers in the Wisconsin woods and farmland of the 1860s is still enjoyed by today's young readers. Impulsive, independent, and sometimes mischievous, Caddie's warmth and kindness of heart help her finally to accept with grace the responsibility of becoming a young woman and taking her part in serving the needs of others as part of wholesome growing up.

Buff, Mary and Conrad. *The Apple and the Arrow*. Houghton Mifflin, 2001 (1951), 75 pp. (3-6).

The story of the young Swiss boy who stood bravely as his father, under duress, shot an apple off his head with an arrow is part of the Western world's folklore. Although the exact dates and details are legend rather than documented history, the account has its roots in fact and represents the reality of the early struggle for freedom from Austria by the people who formed the nation of Switzerland. The writers have brought William and Walter Tell's heroic roles to life. Near the end of the thirteenth century the people of three cantons (a canton is loosely equivalent to an American state) in what became Switzerland had agreed to rebel against the unjust and oppressive rule of Austria. As the account has it, the famous incident involving the apple and the arrow was the dramatic crisis that led to the rebels' decisive victory. More than that one incident was, of course, involved. This exciting, suspenseful, and well-told story makes the historic legend live and contributes effectively to the ongoing cause of freedom.

Bunting, Eve. *Dandelions*. Illus. by Greg Shed. Harcourt Brace, 1995, 44 pp. (3-5).

The Boltons—Papa, Mama, Zoe, Rebecca, and the yet-unborn baby Mama carries—leave the settled familiarity of the Illinois home they shared with Mama's parents for an unknown future of homesteading in the Nebraska Territory. Home is now the little "soddie" Papa built with sod cut like bricks from the ground; it has one window and one door. Neighbors are the Svensons, three hours away; the nearest town, a day's ride. Zoe knows that Mama is lonely, homesick, and fearful. She feels Papa's self-doubt: Has he done right to bring her mother to so many hardships? But Zoe's heart also lifts with the joy and hope Papa feels in having land of their own. Returning from a trip to town with Papa, Zoe sees a large patch of brilliant yellow dandelions beside the road. "Dandelions for Mama," she exclaims, and Papa digs up a large clump for her, roots and all. How Zoe uses the dandelions and the significance they have for Mama and all the Boltons form the satisfying conclusion of this fine story. The book is not simply about pioneering, but about love, hope, and caring; about working and enduring together; about what every family, in every era and setting, needs to share.

Burnett, Frances Hodgson. *The Secret Garden.* Harper and Row, 1987 (1911), 256 pp. (4-up).

One of the best beloved of the classic children's stories. Mary Lennox had been orphaned in India. Her father, a British officer, and her young, beautiful mother had died suddenly of cholera. Mary's world crumbled around her, and the opening sentence of the book reads: "When Mary Lennox was sent to Misselthwaite Manor to live with her uncle, everybody said she was the most disagreeable-looking child ever seen." A kind, sensible young servant-girl and her brother who knows and loves the natural world, a mysterious invalid boy hidden away in a wing of the huge house—all have their part in the story. Most important, however, is the secret garden Mary finds, which eventually brings remarkable changes into all their lives. Wonderful to read aloud—or alone. (Be sure to look for an edition like this one that has not been abridged, condensed, or had the wording changed.)

Two more stories by Burnett: *Little Lord Fauntleroy* and *The Little Princess.* Throughout all her books, the writer emphasized kindness, fairness, courage, and a whole roster of values parents want to see developed in their children's lives.

Canfield, Dorothy. *Understood Betsy.* Buccaneer, 1981 (1916), 219 pp. (3-6).

An enduring story (written more than eighty years ago) of an overprotected little girl whose life and self-awareness take on new dimensions when she goes to live with Vermont farm relatives. Enjoyable as a story, the book also has a good emphasis on overcoming self-pity and needless fears and on developing mature, compassionate ways of seeing.

Colver, Anne. *Bread and Butter Indian.* Holt, Rinehart and Winston, 1964, 96 pp. (3, 4).

A warmly satisfying story of little Barbara Baum who lived inland from the coastal area of Pennsylvania in 1793. At that time such settlements were pioneer villages, part of the movement that kept pushing the frontier farther and farther west as the years went by. When Barbara, playing down by the creek, gave her piece of sugared bread to a hungry old Indian, she didn't know that someday he would befriend her in an important way. Family and community activities that reflect the culture of the time and place form an authentic background for the story, the main events of which are based on the true experience of the real Barbara Baum, great-great-grandmother of the writer's husband. Also based on actual family records is the adventure-filled sequel, *Bread and Butter Journey.*

de Angeli, Marguerite. *The Door in the Wall.* Doubleday, 1989 (1949), 111 pp. (3-up).

A beautifully written story set in late medieval England. A ten-year-old boy is left crippled by illness and learns to find purpose in life. His eventful story is told against a setting of local conflict and changing scenes. There is a splendid use of historical background, rich vocabulary, and emphasis on important values.

Dodge, Mary Mapes. *Hans Brinker or The Silver Skates.* Random House, 1989 (1865), 352 pp. (3–6).

Still as enthralling as ever is this classic story of the Brinker family in nineteenth-century Holland. A wonderfully interest-holding story, beautifully told, and strong in areas of Christian values—honor, compassion, patience, faith, diligence, loyalty. A head injury has reduced the once-strong, loving father of the family to a mentally afflicted invalid subject to sudden, uncontrollable rages. Without the father's provision, the wife, son, and daughter struggle against acute poverty, each doing what he or she can to aid their survival and to care for the father and for each other. Both the Brinker children excel at ice skating, and some of the most exciting scenes of the book are built around events related to their skill on the ice. As they have for more than 130 years, children will thrill to the courage and drama of the story and rejoice in the final resolution of the tragic circumstances the Brinkers have met with such patience and faith.

Estes, Eleanor. *The Moffats.* Harcourt Children's Books, 1941, 290 pp. (3–7).

Fun-filled horse-and-buggy-days adventures occur frequently in the lively Moffat family. There are Sylvie, Joey, Jane, and Rufus (ranging from fifteen to five) and Mamma, struggling to make ends meet as a dressmaker because Papa died right after Rufus was born. Still in print after sixty years, the book's depiction of a close, caring family and a simpler age, in this book and others in the series, continues to appeal to today's children, as does its timeless humor.

Fleischman, Sid. *The Whipping Boy.* Illus. by Peter Sis. Greenwillow Books, 1986, 88 pp. (4–up).

A rollicking story full of adventure, suspense, and humor. A thoroughly bratty young prince and his goodhearted, street-smart whipping boy find themselves struggling together for survival. Taking a wry look at some of the unjustifiable practices of the past, popular writer Sid Fleischman includes the learning of some solid values and behaviors at the heart of his entertaining story told in a colloquial style.

Fritz, Jean. *The Cabin Faced West.* Puffin Books, 1987 (1958), 124 pp. (3–up).

When Ann Hamilton and her family move from Gettysburg to the western frontier of the 1780s (over the Allegheny Mountains in western Pennsylvania), Ann feels that she will never be at home away from her old friends and comfortable city ways. How Hamilton Hill becomes the place Ann would rather be than anywhere else in the world is a significant part of this easy-reading story. Warm family life, a troubled, on-the-defensive neighbor boy, and a surprise visit from a famous American contribute to the eventful tale. The main characters are real people (Ann was the writer's great-great-grandmother), and some events in the story really happened.

Guarnieri, Paolo. Translated by Jonathan Galassi. *A Boy Named Giotto*. Illus. by Bimba Landmann. Farrar, Straus and Giroux, 1998, 24 pp. (2-5).

Primary listing under *Art*

Art critic Paolo Guarnieri has created a charming story about a real person, the famed artist Giotto (Jôt´tō), c.1266-c.1337. Out in the countryside, tending his father's sheep, the young boy has no wish to raise farm animals. He is already longing for just one thing—to be an artist. Drawing with charcoal on any pale substance he can find, or even just using a stick in the sand to portray animals and people, Giotto becomes so absorbed in what he is doing that he forgets to start home with the sheep when he should and then forgets to check to be sure they are all there! When the famous artist Cimabue (also a real historical person) makes a (fictional) visit to Giotto's little town, the boy sees a beautiful painting the artist has done and decides he would like to be Cimabue's student. In real life Giotto did become the older artist's student, and Guarnieri obviously enjoyed thinking of a way they might have met. The marvelous illustrations—warm, imaginative, radiating with rich, deep color—reflect the spirit that imbued Giotto, a young boy destined for lasting greatness.

Hale, Lucretia P. *The Peterkin Papers: The Return of the Lady from Philadelphia*. St. Martin's Press, 1994 (1880s), 256 pp. (3, 4).

The zany Peterkins know how to make the simplest project impossibly complicated. For more than 100 years children have chuckled over the mixed-up activities of this fuddle-headed family: the parents, the three children whose names we are told—Agamemnon, Elizabeth Eliza, and Solomon John—and the two youngest who are referred to only as "the little boys." Lots of fun to read aloud.

Hall, Donald. *Old Home Day*. Illus. by Emily Arnold McCully. Browndeer Press, 1996, 43 pp. (3-up).

Like picture biography, picture history has become an increasingly popular genre of children's books. In these books, the content is factual, but with such a perfect bonding of enthralling text and wonderful illustration that they read like fiction. In a delightful turnaround, distinguished writer Donald Hall has given children a book of just this sort: the lively "history" of a purported New Hampshire village from its prehistory wilderness through to the bicentennial celebration of its existence as a community—held in 1999 (a date three years later than that of the book's publication). In other words, instead of a picture history that reads like a story, *Old Home Day* is fiction that is so appealing we wish it were true. Rich in human interest and often warmly humorous, this is a book that rewards reading—and rereading.

Hunt, Irene. *Trail of Apple Blossoms*. Silver Burdett Press, 1968, 64 pp. (3-6).

A well-written story of Johnny Appleseed, the quiet, kindly man who spent almost fifty years during the first half of the nineteenth century walking the trails and roads of western Pennsylvania, Ohio, and Indiana. The friend of whites and Indians, of animals and birds, Johnny (John Chapman) had a unique mission in addition to the unofficial doctoring he practiced along his way. Everywhere

Johnny went, he carried and planted apple seeds, leaving a legacy of beauty and fruitfulness behind. In this particular story, Hunt emphasizes Johnny's loving, peaceable ways and his knack for soothing spirits and calming troubled waters. (Because almost all that is known about John Chapman is legendary, this story has been included with the fiction rather than being listed primarily in *Biography*.)

Karr, Kathleen. *Man of the Family*. Farrar, Straus and Giroux, 1999, 172 pp. (4-up).

Based on her own family history, Karr's warm, often amusing story covers an eventful year in the life of her father István (Stephen) Csere. It is 1924; a decade earlier, István's parents fled Hungary just ahead of the outbreak of World War I. A teacher in his homeland, Michael Csere knows little English and in America becomes a subsistence farmer. On the little twenty-five-acre farm he and his wife Louisa raise small crops for their personal needs, hundreds of egg-laying chickens, and five children. At ten, eldest son István finds he now has a dual role—helping his father with the work of the farm and keeping an eye on the younger children for his mother. Not an exciting prospect, and yet the year ahead brings much that is unexpected: a tragic explosion at the neighbors'; threats from the "mortgage man"; a marauding weasel in the henhouse; a special family picnic in the woods to cheer Anya (Mama), homesick for family, friends, and the mountains of Hungary; and Apa (Papa) coming home from the city with a showy crystal chandelier for their modest little parlor. The writer's portrayal of this lovable family and the details of their daily lives resonates with authenticity. She is writing about real people and real happenings with sympathy, honesty, humor, and love. A brief, easy-to-use glossary of the family's Hungarian names and frequently used terms is found at the beginning of the book.

Kimmel, Elizabeth Cody. *Balto and the Great Race*. Illus. by Nora Koerber. Random House, 1999, 99 pp. (3-6).

Although a true account of actual events, the story quality of this book has placed it here with the fiction. In January 1925, a health crisis had developed in Nome, Alaska. A dreaded and potentially fatal disease, diphtheria, had struck Nome and quickly become an epidemic. Many of the infected were children. (At that time, immunization was just a hope for the future.) An antitoxin serum had been developed that could save many lives, but Nome had only enough of the serum to treat a very few people. Word of the crisis had been communicated across America by telegraph, but with winter snow and ice in control, no connecting highways, and the nearest railroad 650 miles away, Nome was cut off from the rest of the world. This is the story of the dog-sled relay that was quickly organized to bring serum from the railroad, and of Balto, the Siberian husky whose remarkable instincts and leadership kept the serum safe as he made the successful last lap delivery to Nome. An exciting and suspenseful story from the past.

Lowell, Susan. *I Am Lavina Cumming*. Milkwood Editions, 1993, 200 pp. (3-7).

An exceptionally well-written story with a flavor of authenticity and originality that makes it especially enjoyable to read. It is based on the real-life experiences of the writer's grandmother in the early part of the 1900s. Lavina Cumming is born on Bosque Ranch in Arizona Territory and lives there happily with her parents and five brothers, outdoors much of the time. When her mother dies, however, her father regretfully decides that the only way ten-year-old Lavina can have the kind of upbringing and education he wants for her is to send her to his much older sister in California. In spite of the distress and anxiety she feels, Lavina knows that she must obey and go. The character of this interesting young girl is wonderfully portrayed as she finds herself in an elegant and affluent home with a decisive and particular aunt, a widowed cousin, and the cousin's badly spoilt little daughter. Lavina must deal with her own homesickness and the challenges of her radically changed life. But it is the disastrous earthquake centered in nearby San Francisco that turns things upside down and creates a new perspective for Lavina.

MacDonald, George. *The Christmas Stories of George MacDonald*. Chariot Victor, 1981, 94 pp. (3, 4).

The drama and often pathos of these stories of nineteenth-century children offer a glimpse of the past in a Christian context. The lovely, colorful illustrations provide an authentic background. One story in particular, about the death of a baby, may understandably seem too emotional or too depressing for some children. Wise selection and reading the stories aloud will make the best use of this seasonally oriented book.

MacLachlan, Patricia. *Sarah, Plain and Tall*. HarperCollins Children's Books, 1985, 58 pp. (3-7).

Based on a true event in the author's family history, this Newbery Medal book is the story behind the Hallmark Hall of Fame production of the same name. But even those who have seen the film—perhaps more than once—will find the book rewarding reading. At the end of the story, Anna and Caleb and Papa have felt real fear that Sarah misses the sea and her old life so much that when her trial visit is over, she will decide not to stay and marry Papa, but will leave them and go back to Maine. When Anna tells her this, Sarah smiles. " 'No,' she said. 'I will always miss my old home, but the truth of it is I would miss you more.' " Words to read over, words to think about. And for those who may not yet have seen (or read) the story, here is another special book to enjoy for the first time.

Meadowcroft, Enid L. *By Wagon and Flatboat*. HarperCollins Children's Books, 1944 (1938), 170 pp. (3-up).

The year is 1789, and George Washington has just been elected president of the United States. The Burd family have decided to leave Pennsylvania and make a new start in Ohio where land is cheap and opportunity beckons. Joining forces with another family, the Burds' long journey by wagon and flatboat commences. Sickness, danger from Indian attacks, and the privations of their pioneer existence often bring fear and discouragement, but faith and courage prevail, and they finally reach the little settlement of Losantiville (later named Cincinnati). Not as strongly written as William O. Steele's stories and without the distinctive, highly authentic atmosphere he is able to create, this is still a readable and informative story of the early westward movement in America. Good values are emphasized throughout.

Moss, Marissa. *Rachel's Journal.* Harcourt Brace, 1998, 43 pp. (3-5).

This lively travel journal of a fictional pioneer girl takes ten-year-old Rachel and her family from Illinois to Sacramento, California, in 1850. Based on the writer's research into diaries, letters, pioneer guidebooks, and histories, the account offers, as through a child's eyes, a wealth of authentic detail and a degree of insight into the pioneers' thoughts and emotions. Although the story's people are fictional, readers are assured that every one of its incidents—suspenseful, painful, exciting, hopeful, humorous—actually happened to someone traveling that same pioneer trail. The book is particularly attractive in format. The pale buff pages are lightly ruled and margined, with the text itself simulating hand printing in black ink. The margins are filled with informative or humorous little notes and sprightly colored drawings. The overall level of creative writing and drawing skills is, of course, somewhat precocious for most ten-year-olds, but in such an appealing book, this literary license can be cheerfully overlooked.

Olasky, Susan. *Annie Henry and the Birth of Liberty.* Crossway Books, 1995, 127 pp. (3-up).

High-spirited, impulsive, and interested in all that goes on around her, Annie Henry thrives on adventure. It is 1775, and the tensions between the American colonies and their "mother country," England, are intensifying. The daughter of lawyer/landowner Patrick Henry, the patriot who is still remembered for his stirring words, "give me liberty or give me death," Annie is more interested in the affairs of the colonies than either of her brothers. Her father has often found himself talking seriously about such matters to his young daughter. Annie's mother has died recently, and as the story opens, her father is away leading Virginia militiamen. Annie, her newly married sister, and two teenaged brothers encounter unexpected crises, and the lively, courageous girl finds herself involved in more adventures than she could have imagined. The writer's imagination offers an eventful account of what it might have been like for the spunky youngest child of an American leader as the momentous struggle for freedom began. Excellent values and plenty of humor characterize the story.

Paterson, Katherine. *Jip: His Story.* Lodestar Books, 1996, 181 pp. (4-up).

"My life began the afternoon of June 7, 1847, when I tumbled off the back of a wagon on the West Hill Road, and no one came to look for me." So begins the warm, humorous, and suspenseful story of Jip, an appealing boy with an unknown past and a love for people (and animals) that is enhanced, rather than quenched, by his difficult life. Often-honored writer Katherine Paterson has created an unusual setting for this heartwarming story—a hard-scrabble "poor farm" in the hills of Vermont. Jip has been content with his days of varied chores and care of the farm animals, but disturbing changes are on the way. A sinister stranger tries to convince Jip that he has been sent to find a long-lost son who may be Jip; the town fathers decide to send an old man wrongly labeled a lunatic to live at the poor farm, and soon after, an unhappy widow and her three children become the newest inhabitants. Jip's generous kindness brings hope and help to the troubled people around him, and Jip in turn is helped toward a hopeful future by Teacher and her

Quaker sweetheart as Jip faces terrible danger created by the past. The story is pervaded by a spirit of loving compassion and the steadfast faith embodied in an old hymn that repeatedly brings encouragement.

Rand, Gloria. *Sailing Home: A Story of a Childhood at Sea.* Illus. by Ted Rand. North-South Books, 2001, 29 pp. (3-6).

A lively account based on a real family's life on a beautiful four-masted ship, the *John Ena.* The ship was forty-eight feet wide and just under 313 feet long, with spacious living quarters, plush furnishings, and all the comfortable amenities. The ship was not, however, a pleasure-cruise yacht but, in the late 1880s, an equivalent in its function to the steamship freighters of later times. Cargo was shipped around the world, and instead of being separated for months at a time from a land-based family, Captain Madsen brought them along. Matilda, Albert, and Dagmar led active, interesting lives. (Ena, the youngest, was a baby during the period covered in the book.) Combining relevant research with the Madsen family journal loaned to the author, Rand is able to recount many details of the children's activities and their family celebrations and festivities. The book has picture-book-sized pages and wonderful color illustrations throughout, along with a substantial and enjoyable text. Three pages at the end include photographs of the family and their breathtaking "tall ship" and an informative Afterword telling something about the Madsens in the years beyond the book.

Spyri, Johanna. *Heidi.* Grossett and Dunlap, 1945 (1880), 325 pp. (4-up).

The beloved story of the vibrant Swiss girl who brings change and new life to those around her. It has lost none of its unique charm over the years. Not the least of the joys of Heidi's story is the atmosphere created by the descriptions of mountain life—the goats on the steep slopes, the sparkling air, the meals of milk, bread, and cheese. A lovely, timeless classic. This is another of those wonderful old books that has been altered in some editions, made into movies, and otherwise changed from the original text in its presentation. To gain its true atmosphere and value, be sure to obtain one with the original text.

Steele, William O. *The Buffalo Knife.* Harbrace, 1990 (1952), 192 pp. (3-up).

Nine-year-old Andrew Clark and his friend Isaac Brown float with their families down the Tennessee River to a new home in what would years later become Nashville, Tennessee. Their fathers have built a big flatboat, complete with a cabin to live in and pens for pigs and chickens. A thousand miles of river, some of it full of treacherous shoals, have to be traversed, while hostile Indians lurk nearby. Authentic details of late eighteenth-century pioneer life and a high level of writing skill provide a colorful background for this well-told, often humorous tale.

Wilder, Laura Ingalls. *The Little House in the Big Woods.* HarperCollins Children's Books, 1953 (1932), 237 pp. (3, 4).

Set in the time before the Ingalls family moved to the prairie, this is the "how it all began" book of the warm, homey Little House series based on the lives of the writer, her husband, and other family members. The time period of the whole series covers a number of years, beginning about 1872. Pioneering, farming, and family life provide the background for these appealing, authentic stories. Fine values, faith in God, and a concern for the needs of others are demonstrated throughout. The other titles in the series are *The Little House on the Prairie, Farmer Boy, On the Banks of Plum Creek, By the Shores of Silver Lake, The Long Winter, The Little Town on the Prairie, These Happy Golden Years.* Some years after these stories were published, a final volume, *The First Four Years*, was added. It covers events during the first years of Laura and Almanzo's marriage.

Wilkes, Maria D. *Little House in Brookfield.* Illus. by Dan Andreasen. HarperCollins Publishers, 1996, 298 pp. (3-up).

Young readers—and their parents and teachers who have wished there were more books in Laura Ingalls Wilder's beloved Little House series—will take to their hearts this family-centered story of Laura's mother, Caroline Quiner, who became the outspoken, much-loved Ma Ingalls of the Little House books. In 1845 Brookfield, Wisconsin, is a growing frontier village, and a mile from town Grandma Quiner, Mother, and the five young Quiners are making a valiant effort to survive on their small family farm. It has been almost a year since the ship Father was on was lost at sea in a terrible storm. Without his presence and strength, everyone except three-year-old Eliza and baby Tom must do their share of the work. But however difficult their lives and no matter what material things they must do without, there is always faith, love, laughter, and hope. Wilkes, like Wilder, writes with a good-sense balance of realism and idealism. Whether the whole family is out in the rain and mud trying to salvage their winter supply of vegetables or excitedly celebrating a birthday or Christmas, the Quiner family come alive in all their human failings, their determined courage, and love of fun. Wilkes's prequel is a welcome addition to the Little House tradition.

14

LITERATURE: LEVEL III

Fables, Folk Tales, and Fairy Tales

Irving, Washington. *Rip Van Winkle, The Legend of Sleepy Hollow and Other Tales.* Smith Pub., 1980 (1819), 232 pp. (6-up).

Famous tales from the pen of one of the most noted figures of nineteenth-century American literature. As with so many other stories that have long been woven into our culture, few children today read the stories as Irving wrote them. The idea of the man, Rip Van Winkle, who slept in the woods for twenty years, awoke, and went back to his village to find everything changed may be vaguely familiar, but the delightful humor and shrewd characterizations have been missed in watered-down versions of the tale. The same is true, perhaps to an even greater extent, of the headless horseman and the whole story of Sleepy Hollow. Cartoon versions are sometimes seen at Halloween, but again such treatments bear little resemblance to the fine literature of the originals. This specific edition is still available in some libraries or can be requested through interlibrary loan. Or check in large bookstores for other editions of these stories that use the original material.

Manniche, Lise (translated and illustrated by). *How Djadja-Em-Ankh Saved the Day.* HarperCollins Children's Books, 1977 (1942), 19 pp. (4-6).

The special interest of this brief tale is its background and the form in which it has been reproduced. Translated from the original hieratic script by Egyptologist Manniche, it is printed on paper made to resemble papyrus and is in a scroll form, although the sheets fold flat in sections rather than being rolled. By unfolding the sheets in one direction, the reader finds information about the Egypt of 4,500 years ago and fascinating material on Egyptian writing—they used both hieroglyphics and hieratic script. By turning the sheets the other way, the reader can follow the little folk tale that comes to us from the ancient world.

McKinley, Robin. *Rose Daughter.* Greenwillow Books, 1997, 306 pp. (5-9).

A gentle, magical story of love, devotion, inner beauty, and the overcoming power of goodness. The old fairy story "Beauty and the Beast" is at its core, but McKinley has taken the tale to new heights in the development of characters, their energetic overcoming of hardships, and the story's rich appreciation of the loveliness of the natural world, with roses and their enchanting fragrance a central and pervasive symbol. The deeply happy ending reflects unchanging values affirmed in a final irrevocable choice.

Tales from the Arabian Nights. Illus. by Brian Wildsmith. Henry Z. Walck, Inc., 1962, 281 pp. (5-up).

First published by the Oxford University Press, this version uses sophisticated language in a traditional "wonder tales" style. This in itself lends a special atmosphere to the stories, giving the diction an exotic flavor that suits the descriptions of jewels, luxurious fabrics, and magical events with which the tales abound, and which Wildsmith's illustrations so effectively depict. Now out of print, but in many libraries and well worth trying to find.

Myths and Legends

Climo, Shirley (retold by). *Atalanta's Race: A Greek Myth*. Illus. by Alexander Koshkin. Clarion Books, 1995, 32 pp. (5-up).

A lively and excellently written retelling of an ancient Greek myth that captures the perspectives of a world in which the mythical Greek deities are powerful yet flawed with human failings. A kingdom in which a king who wanted a son but got a daughter could simply order one of his soldiers to take his baby and abandon her on a high mountainside. The child is rescued by a bear and then cared for by a woodsman. She becomes a skilled hunter and peerless athlete. Reclaimed by her father, Atalanta, a proud and willful girl, refuses all her many suitors, scorns the idea of love, and when ordered by the king to marry, gains his consent to choose her husband in her own heartless way. When the handsome Melanion becomes a suitor, the gods decide to take a hand, and the stage is set for the story's climax and its surprising end. Alexander Koshkin's glowing paintings complement and enhance the text.

Gottlieb, Gerald (retold by). *The Adventures of Ulysses*. Shoe String Press, Inc. 1988 (1959), 170 pp. (5-up).

Originally one of the excellent old Landmark Books, this version of *The Odyssey* offers an exciting story in contemporary language. Fine as a story that will be enjoyed simply for its adventure, it also acquaints the reader with famous literary characters and events.

Hamilton, Edith. *Mythology*. Little, Brown and Co., 1942, 497 pp. (7-up).

A splendid collection of Greek, Roman, and Norse mythology. The distinctive flavor of the different original writers has been preserved by Hamilton, a widely known classicist. The book is excellent in its story quality and valuable in providing in one volume a broad introduction to the mythology of that part of the ancient world in which Western civilization has its roots.

Kingsley, Charles. *The Heroes*. Macmillan, 1954 (1856), 193 pp. (5-up).

Stirringly retold stories from Greek mythology, exciting hero tales of Perseus,

Theseus, and Jason. Aside from the important literary background provided in studying the mythology of the ancient world, such reading offers much in its color, imagery, and food for imagination. Though currently out of print, this book is still in many libraries.

Lang, Andrew. *Tales of Troy and Greece.* Faber and Faber, 1978 (1907) 302 pp. (5-up).

Lang's classic retelling of the Homeric Greek epic of Odysseus and other important Greek myths. The writer has adapted the stories and included background information on setting and ancient Greek and Trojan culture. The adventures are heroic, and the language is in harmony with the content, embodying some of the flavor of Homer's work and of other early mythologists. Still available in many libraries, but now out of print.

Picard, Barbara Leonie (retold by). *The Iliad of Homer; The Odyssey of Homer.* Oxford University Press, 2001 (1960), 216 pp.; 1991 (1952), 284 pp. (5-12).

Picard recounts the stories of *The Iliad* and *The Odyssey* in a lively, dramatic style. Opening new worlds of the imagination to readers, the accounts also provide background on the world of ancient Greece that is invaluable for students in later secondary and college studies.

Note: A single combined volume, *The Iliad and The Odyssey of Homer*, retold by Picard, is available: Simon and Schuster, 1991.

Pyle, Howard. *The Story of King Arthur and His Knights.* Simon and Schuster Children's Books, 1984 (1903), 320 pp. (5-up).

The famous saga of the legendary King Arthur, with all its romance, idealism, knightly valor, pomp, and ceremony. Pyle uses an enriched vocabulary and a phrasing similar to the language of the King James Version of the Bible—with the addition of vivid descriptions of appearance, color, and texture. The language suits the imagery and drama of the story, which is full of action and events. Competent readers who enjoy the stories will broaden their language abilities painlessly; advanced readers particularly enjoy the wonderful phrasing.

Sutcliff, Rosemary. *The Light Beyond the Forest; The Sword and the Circle.* Puffin Books, 1994 (1980), 144 pp.; 1994 (1981), 264 pp. (5, 6-up).

Retellings in Sutcliff's gifted prose of some of the Arthurian legends. The first book is the story of the quest for the Holy Grail. Written later, but with events that precede those of the Grail quest, *The Sword* deals with the coming to power of Arthur and with adventures of the storied knights of the Round Table. With their glowing idealism, their gallant heroes who fight for right and honor—and often for the deliverance of fair maidens—the stories are a fresh delight to read, even for those already somewhat familiar with the legends.

Westwood, Jennifer. *Stories of Charlemagne.* S. G. Phillips, 1976, 153 pp. (5, 6).

Legends about the great Charlemagne retold from the old French epics, the *chansons de geste* (songs of deeds). As with the stories of the great English hero

King Arthur, these are literature rather than history, but they accurately reflect the way in which the people of the twelfth and thirteenth centuries thought about the eighth-century heroes whose exploits they celebrated.

Fantasies, Talking Animal Stories

Alexander, Lloyd. *The Book of Three*. Holt, 1995 (1964), 224 pp. (5, 6-up).

Alexander has written, with a Welsh flavor, a tale of high adventure in a mythical kingdom in the days of enchanters, armored warriors, and perilous quests. Taran, Assistant Pig-Keeper to a very special ceremonial pig, longs to become a hero. When the kingdom of Prydain is threatened by evil forces, he takes up the challenge on the side of right. Alexander combines humor and exciting action with a fine literary style in all of his work, including the other books that comprise The Prydain Chronicles: *The Black Cauldron, The Castle of Llyr, Taran Wanderer, The High King*.

Avi. *Perloo the Bold*. Scholastic Press, 1998, 225 pp. (4-7).

Mild-mannered, peace-loving Perloo, one of the furry underground Montmers, is astounded when he learns that just before she died, their leader, Jolaine, has chosen him to succeed her. All he really wants to do is ski hastily back to his cozy burrow and let someone else take over. Unfortunately, Jolaine's son Berwig, who is determined to take the office himself, has plans to curtail freedoms, intimidate the citizenry, and start a war with the nearby Felbarts. Perloo soon finds himself involved in a suspenseful conflict with Berwig and his malicious aide Senyous. Fast-moving and very funny throughout, an entertaining story with sound underlying values.

Bond, Nancy. *A String in the Harp*. Puffin Books, 1987 (1976), 370 pp. (6-up).

A long, engrossing story that combines several important elements: the individual growth and positive adjustments that keep the Morgan family from disintegrating after the sudden death of Mrs. Morgan; the vivid sense of a particular part of Wales, both as it is in its natural setting and in its mythic past; and the use of fantasy to make reality more understandable.

Cooper, Susan. *Over Sea, Under Stone*. Harcourt Children's Books, 1966, 252 pp. (4-7).

Three bright, likable, and adventurous kids; their much-loved but rather mysterious great-uncle Merry; the tall, three-storied Grey House where they are staying; a very old map found in the attic; the churning sea and Cornish cliffs—and several menacing characters lurking about—combine to start this story off without delay. Jane, Simon, and Barney soon realize that the old map is a key to something far more important than treasure, and they find themselves caught up in a quest for a grail that will empower them in a deadly serious struggle of good against evil. The first in a five-book sequence, The Dark Is Rising, Cooper's splendidly written blend of reality and fantasy offers an exciting story on a foundation of sound values.

Cooper, Susan. *The Boggart*. Macmillan Publishing Co., 1993, 196 pp. (4-7).

Out of the blue, Emily and Jessup's father inherits an old, partly ruined castle in the Western Highlands of Scotland, and the family are soon on their way from Canada to visit Castle Keep. Charmed by the atmosphere of the ancestral home, no one has any idea that the Boggart, an ancient magical spirit, is a long-time resident there. Boggarts are invisible; small, sly, and mischievous, they take great delight in playing tricks, and the Castle Keep Boggart is no exception. As the children find, this can be baffling—and they have no idea what lies ahead when, unaware, they take the Boggart with them when they return to Toronto. Confronted with modern technology, the Boggart's pranks take on new dimensions, and the fast-paced story alternates between hilarity and crisis. As problems increase, the Boggart becomes very homesick, and it takes an ingenious combination of Jessup's computer know-how and some ancient magic to bring a happy solution. Very well written, with likable, perceptively portrayed characters.

Goudge, Elizabeth. *The Little White Horse*. Penguin Putnam Books for Young Readers, 2001 (1946), 238 pp. (4-6).

This is the kind of fantasy/reality combination that Goudge did so well. Orphaned Maria Merryweather is sent to live with her father's elderly cousin on his estate, Moonacre Manor. Strange, unexplained things start to occur as soon as she arrives, and Maria's unusual adventures in her new home are beautifully and suspensefully told. One of the lovely things about any book of Goudge's is the warmth and coziness, the intriguing details she describes so appealingly. Underlying all of Goudge's writing is her sound sense of values.

Jones, Diana Wynne. *Cart and Cwidder*. Book One, The Dalemark Quartet. HarperCollins Publishers, 1995 (1975), 214 pp. (6-up).

When Clennen, a traveling minstrel, is killed, his three children aren't yet aware that he has for years been a secret agent for the northern freedom-loving part of the land of Dalemark. The North and the rigidly ruled South are in bitter conflict of purpose, though not yet engaged in outright war. Clennen and his family have been traveling in their cart through the South, giving musical shows in the villages. They are on their way north, and the children, beginning to realize that a web of danger they don't understand threatens them, are trying to keep moving on, anxious to return to their home. Adventure, puzzling events, and grave peril become part of their daily lives as they continue making music along the way. Clennen has bequeathed to his youngest son, Moril, his legendary ancient cwidder, the largest of the lute-like instruments they possess. As they find themselves in serious jeopardy, Moril realizes that his cwidder has powers that go beyond music—if he can just use the instrument for right, and in the right way. A colorful and suspenseful saga.

Lawhead, Stephen R. *Dream Thief*. Zondervan, 1996 (1983), 256 pp. (6-up).

From the space station Gotham to a deserted subterranean city on Mars, to a sinister control center in a remote corner of India, dream research scientist Dr. Spencer Reston races against time to find the evil force threatening to control the minds of all mankind. Rich in imagination and suspenseful action, this complex science-fiction novel with its underlying Christian worldview is not a children's book but will be appreciated by advanced young readers who find the realm of science-fiction fantasy especially appealing.

L'Engle, Madeleine. A trilogy: *A Wrinkle in Time; A Wind in the Door; A Swiftly Tilting Planet*. Dell, 1976 (1962), 192 pp.; 1974 (1973), 208 pp.; 1978, 278 pp. (5-up).

These imaginative stories are sometimes spoken of as science fiction, but they actually have little in common with much of that genre. They may be more accurately classified as fantasy in which events (and the people involved) transcend the usual limits of time and space. In the framework of well-crafted story plots, subtle forces that are larger than any single set of events are consistently felt. In the first book of the three, Meg, her little brother, and her friend Calvin embark on a perilous quest to free her father from his captivity in another world. The conflict between good and evil is implicit, not only in this opening book, but throughout the trilogy. L'Engle writes excellent prose on a level of complexity that demands some mind-and-imagination stretching, always a rewarding experience in reading.

Seidler, Tor. *The Revenge of Randal Reese-Rat*. Illus. by Brett Helquist. Farrar, Straus and Giroux, 2001, 233 pp. (5-9).

Randal Reese-Rat, a member of the upper crust of New York's wharf rat society, makes no secret of his anger at losing Isabel Moberly-Rat to the heroic Montague Mad-Rat. When a mysterious fire breaks out at the newlyweds' home, Randal, though innocent, is sought as an arson suspect. The writer masterfully controls a complex variety of characters, locations, and twists of plot in this especially well-written and highly entertaining story. An outline of events cannot convey the amusing details of the imaginatively crafted tale.

Siegel, Robert. *Whalesong*. Peter Smith, 1995 (1981), 143 pp. (5-up).

Siegel's lyrical fantasy of the young whale Hruna combines beauty of language and setting with interest-holding action in an allegorical form. To say that *Whalesong* is the story of Hruna's coming of age and of his Lonely Cruise—an obligatory rite of passage—gives little idea of the book's scope. The ocean environment, the close bonds among the pod (group) of humpbacked whales, the threat to the continued existence of their species by high-tech commercial whale-killing, the fascinating patterns of the whales' lives and journeyings—all are part of this fine book. Recommended for older children, the book would also make a very special read-aloud choice for many third and fourth graders as well.

Spires, Elizabeth. *The Mouse of Amherst*. Illus. by Claire A. Nivola. Farrar, Straus and Giroux, 1999, 64 pp. (5-7).

The whimsical story of Emmaline, a white mouse who lives for a time behind the wainscot of the bedroom in which poet Emily Dickinson (1830-1886) writes. Emmaline has various entertaining experiences while in the Dickinson home, but needless to say, poetry and the nature and spirit of the poet herself are the book's subject. Eight of Dickinson's best-loved poems appear in the book, along with seven poems of Emmaline's. Nivola's delicate, sprightly drawings match the book's atmosphere. This is a special book to read and enjoy, rather than weightily analyze—though that could, of course, be done.

Swift, Jonathan. *Gulliver's Travels*. Putnam Pub. Group, 1947 (1726), 352 pp. (5, 6-up).

Swift's story of the seafaring Lemuel Gulliver is a masterpiece of adult satire, but the wonderfully and playfully imagined worlds of the tiny Lilliputians, the immense Brobdingnagians, the eccentric Laputans, and the dignified Houyhnhnms so captured the imaginations of children that *Gulliver's Travels* has been a children's classic for generations. At the same time it continues to be studied in college literature classes. Some children will especially enjoy hearing the stories read aloud; other advanced readers will want to delve into its fascinating pages for themselves. (Look for an edition that uses Swift's text.)

Tolkien, J. R. R. *Farmer Giles of Ham*. Houghton Mifflin, 1978 (1949), 63 pp. (5-up).

In this insightful, somewhat satiric story, a reluctant hero eventually becomes wealthy and powerful and is finally made king. The story includes hilarious encounters with a devious and calculating dragon and a pompous king. Giles is not quite the alienated antihero of modern fiction, but certainly an antihero nonetheless. Look for splendid settings, outstanding humor, and *challenging* vocabulary.

Tolkien, J. R. R. The Lord of the Rings trilogy: *The Fellowship of the Ring; The Two Towers; The Return of the King*. Houghton Mifflin, 1967 (1954-55), 423 pp.; 352 pp.; 440 pp. (5-up).

Some children may be ready to follow their reading of *The Hobbit* with the trilogy, but just at the time when some book-oriented children seem capable of going on to these beautifully written fantasies with their strong Christian underlayment, a real division of interest arises among children. Some of them simply do not continue to enjoy fantasy as much, particularly when it is written in the challenging vocabulary and demanding sentence structure of The Lord of the Rings. Since some of these children will later be ready for the trilogy (and others will never care for it), it is wiser simply to make the books available but not to press the issue. A trial family read-aloud start of the first book should reveal listener interest.

Note: The release of the movie *The Fellowship of the Ring* and the projected screen appearance in two successive years of the remaining books of the trilogy may encourage a number of kids to read the books. Seeing the movie as a fam-

ily and then moving to the read-aloud trial start suggested above could be a
worthwhile approach.

Verne, Jules. *From the Earth to the Moon*. Bantam, 1993 (1874) 208 pp.
(6-up).

    An exciting and suspenseful story of space travel—written more than a century
and a quarter ago. Youngsters interested in today's space shuttles and interplane-
tary travel will be especially intrigued by Verne's detailed descriptions of his fictional spaceship, how it works, and the trip to the moon. There is no way to
explain the amazing foresight Verne showed, for although technical details differ,
he clearly had an almost prophetic vision of coming breakthroughs in space travel.
For example, in this particular story, it is the United States that is launching the
moon-flight—and from southern Florida!

Verne, Jules. *Twenty Thousand Leagues Under the Sea*. Scribner's, 1960 (1874),
403 pp. (5-up)

    The ever-fascinating story of the submarine *Nautilus*, Professor Aronnax, and
his two companions as they roam the undersea world while held in the power of
the mysterious Captain Nemo. The book is suspenseful, imaginative, and prophetic
of the powerful submarines that did not exist at the time the story was written.
Readers will also want to continue the story in its sequel, *The Mysterious Island*.
Other Verne titles to look for: *Journey to the Center of the Earth, Master of the
World, Voyage to the Moon*.

Realistic Stories—Modern

Bauer, Joan. *Backwater*. Putnam, 1999, 185 pp. (6-up).

    Ivy Breedlove, a quiet, history-loving girl in a family teeming with successful,
hard-edged lawyers, determined that she must follow the pattern; a mysterious
Aunt Jo, whom Ivy is resolved to find and interview for the family history she is
trying to finish in time for Great-aunt Tib's eightieth birthday; a solitary cabin two
days away on a snow-covered mountainside in a roadless wilderness—Aunt Jo's
home. These are significant components of this thoroughly enjoyable, thought-provoking story. Ivy is an articulate, often very funny, first-person narrator of what
follows. Fearful and without any rugged outdoor experience, she manages with
Aunt Tib's backing to get her father's reluctant consent to hire wilderness guide
"Mountain Mama" to make a trip to the cabin. Adventure, suspense, overcoming
fear, and struggling through the wrenching physical challenges prove to have more
than temporary value as Ivy learns to know Aunt Jo. The book is splendidly written, with a fine blend of effective characters, exciting action, humor, and a serious
emphasis on the importance of accepting family members for who each one truly
is, rather than expecting all to fit the same mold.

Bauer, Joan. *Hope Was Here.* Putnam, 2000, 186 pp. (6-up).

Warm, poignant, fast-paced, and very funny—this is an irresistible story. When Hope is born, premature and fatherless, struggling just to survive, her feckless mother abandons her to the care of her Aunt Addie—the only other family member. Sturdy, responsible Aunt Addie is there for Hope through the years, an unfailing rock in their precarious world, but the hurt of the past still weighs on Hope's heart. When Addie, an inspired professional comfort-food cook, accepts an offer to take charge of a successful diner in rural Wisconsin, Hope is despondent at the thought of leaving good friends and the bustle and excitement of New York. As they leave for Wisconsin in the old Buick, pulling a U-Haul trailer, Hope has no idea of the unexpected and colorful adventures—and the fulfillment of a lifetime dream—that lie ahead. Already a proficient waitress in her out-of-school time and with a gift for reading character, Hope has a significant role to play in the new setting as they confront local politics and corruption. The ultimate importance of honor, trust, courage, and love underlies the whole of this fine, often hilarious story.

Bodett, Tom. *Williwaw!* Alfred A. Knopf, 1999, 192 pp. (5-up).

When their fisherman father radios to say he is delayed at sea, Ivan and September Crane are sure they can handle things alone until his return in two weeks. Living in a remote part of Alaska, they have both learned a lot about self-reliance. Listening to their fervent pleas, their dad decides to trust them. With an emphatic prohibition to Ivan *not* to wire into the radio connection to hook up his computer game—and a promise from Ivan—he signs off. Later that night, with his sister asleep, a restless Ivan rebelliously breaks his promise, and, working hastily in a dim light, he effectively "fries" the radio so crucial to their safety. Without it, they are completely cut off from emergency help in case of need. Realizing her anger won't mend the radio, September—and Ivan—try to make plans to remedy the situation. Any plan involves trips to town across sometimes-hazardous Bag Bay; each plan simply leads to more complications, and before the crisis is over, the two find themselves on the bay in the midst of a williwaw, a fierce and unpredictable storm like the one that took their mother's life years before. A fast-moving, suspenseful, and well-told story—and a practical and realistic lesson about wrong choices and formidable consequences.

Bonners, Susan. *Above and Beyond.* Farrar, Straus and Giroux, 2001, 151 pp. (4-7).

Jerry's class is assigned to do oral reports on local history. When he decides to do his on a favorite older cousin who years before used his rock-climbing abilities to rescue a little girl, he has no idea what his research will be setting in motion—or that it will even involve a new boy at school whom he is befriending. The story will have readers thinking about broadening horizons, about friendship, kindness, life-changing decisions—and drawing mistaken conclusions. Not in the least heavy, this splendidly written story is very readable, often amusing, and definitely worthwhile.

Bunting, Eve. *Blackwater*. HarperCollins Children's Books, 1999, 146 pp. (5-up).

His summer plans ruined by the unwelcome visit of an unfortunate (and obnoxious) cousin, thirteen-year-old Brodie is angry and upset. It's the last straw when he sees schoolmate Pauline (his golden-haired dream girl) flirting with an older boy. Brodie suddenly recognizes an opportunity to play a harmless prank on them without being seen, and he seizes the chance. A stunning disaster follows, and due to his cousin's unsolicited lies and his own genuine though unsuccessful rescue efforts, Brodie finds himself hailed as a hero. Unable to summon the courage to reveal what actually happened, and not even aware himself of the final momentary steps from the prank itself to tragedy, Brodie lives in torment, his inner guilt shredding his well-being and hammering on his conscience. The moral issues are complex, but the reality of right and wrong and the healing power of honesty and truth are clearly demonstrated.

Burnford, Sheila. *The Incredible Journey*. Yearling Books, 1996 (1960), 148 pp. (4-up).

A warm and wonderful story of a family's pets (two dogs and a Siamese cat) as they try to make their way home. On their suspenseful trek they cross wild forestland, escape hazards of many kinds but fall victim to others, become temporarily separated from each other, narrowly miss death—but never lose the inner compulsion to reach home and the people who love them. A beautiful, perceptively written story.

Calvert, Patricia. *Picking Up the Pieces*. Simon and Schuster Children's Books, 1999, 176 pp. (6-up).

Eight months ago Megan had known who she was: a happy and loved daughter and big sister; popular at school, active, attractive, a star on the basketball team; a fortunate teenager with hopes and dreams just waiting to be fulfilled. But that was before Dex Cooper, a twelfth-grade transfer student from California with a bronze sunburn and streaky blond hair, wheels up on his Yamaha 450 and offers her a ride home from school one afternoon. On a fast detour through the park, the paved road suddenly becomes gravel; the bike slides and flips. Megan flies into the air; a second later she is permanently immobilized from the waist down—which just about cancels out everything about the old Megan, it seems. Now as she sits in her wheelchair watching her family dash around doing the last-minute things before they all leave for the cabin they've rented every summer for years, Megan thinks of all she won't be able to do this time, of how much extra work and expense she causes her caring parents, of how helpless she feels. Life lies ahead without new dreams to take the place of the old.

What Megan learns that summer starts her on at least a few steps toward a future for her new self. A perceptive and honest look at what sudden loss and irrevocable change are like—and what it means to accept, let go, and be willing to look ahead with hope.

Creech, Sharon. *The Wanderer*. HarperCollins Publishers, 2000, 305 pp. (5-8).

Splendidly written, highly readable, and unquestionably quirky, Creech's captivating story leaves readers with worthwhile discoveries to think about. Thirteen-year-old Sophie doesn't really know why she wants so desperately to be included in the somewhat risky voyage planned by her three uncles to visit their father. But she does know that she wants to be at sea, breathing the moisture-laden air, feeling the restless wind, gazing out at the far horizon, and watching for whales, dolphins, and sea birds. Two of the uncles have brought their sons (Sophie's age) but had no intention of including a girl. Sophie's determination and her demonstration of ship and sailing know-how finally prevail, however, and the six adventurers board the *Wanderer,* a forty-five-foot sailboat, head up the coast from Virginia to Nova Scotia, and then start across the Atlantic to England. A problem Sophie has with her past and a time of serious peril at sea provide mystery and suspense. But it is the interaction among the family members, the changed perceptions each one has of the others by the time the voyage is over, along with the story's appealing and unique atmosphere that linger in the reader's mind.

DiCamillo, Kate. *Because of Winn Dixie.* Candlewick Press, 2000, 182 pp. (4-7).
     Opal has no idea when she adopts a big, lovable, homeless dog that he will be only the first of the new friends entering her life. Just arrived in a little Florida town and with some worries on her mind, Opal is feeling very much alone. There are just the two of them, and her kind, gentle father, the new pastor of the Open Arms Baptist Church, is so busy helping the needy and working on sermons that Opal has many long, summer hours to fill. Winn Dixie (Opal has named the dog after the supermarket where they met) runs headlong into one encounter after another, becoming the unplanned element that brings together Opal and Miss Franny, and Otis, and Sweetie Pie, and Gloria, and Amanda—even Opal and the exasperating Dewberry boys, Dunlap and Stevie. Kindness, caring, understanding, and the ability to realize that things are often not what they seem at first glance illumine the warm, captivating, eventful, humor-filled story.

Farley, Walter. *The Black Stallion.* Random Books for Young Readers, 1944, 192 pp. (5-up).
     The first in the series of fast-action boy-and-horse Black Stallion stories that have been so popular for almost sixty years. A shipwreck at sea, a half-drowned boy clinging to the rope of a magnificent black stallion as it swims toward a small, uninhabited island—these are some of the ingredients of Farley's suspenseful tale. It is far from being great literature, but its simple, fast-moving style holds the interest of reluctant readers and provides easy just-for-fun reading even for youngsters who also enjoy more challenging material.

Haugaard, Erik Christian. *The Little Fishes.* Peter Smith, 1990 (1967), 214 pp. (5-up).
     This is a moving story about twelve-year-old Guido (and the two other children he helps), orphaned by war and poverty, surviving on his own in the Naples, Italy, of 1943. It is, in another sense, the story of all the children everywhere who must try to live on the streets, children for whom the adult world is simply not making provision. Guido sometimes has to steal to eat, but he knows it is stealing and neither steals nor begs if there is any alternative. In spite of the wretchedness of his life, Guido remains strong in spirit, caring, and giving. A fine, deeply real book that will enlarge children's understanding and compassion.

Hergé. A series: The Tintin books. Little, Brown and Co. (4-7).

Published in many countries and languages, this series of picture-story books has a large following of devoted readers. The format is similar to that of a comic book, but the dialogue involves more reading. Tintin, the intrepid boy reporter, his companion Captain Haddock, and their friend Professor Calculus become embroiled in one hair-raising adventure after another in every corner of the globe. In one story they may be in Egypt, in another Peru, for example. The colorful drawings reflect the meticulous research of the writer/cartoonist as they show authentic details of places, objects, and activities in the stories' divergent settings. In addition to nonstop action, the dialogue and events are full of the sort of humor that particularly appeals to children (and to a good many adults as well). Especially helpful in providing palatable reading practice (and fun) for reluctant readers. A variety of Tintin titles are readily available in bookstores.

Holm, Anne. *North to Freedom*. Harcourt, 1990 (1965), 192 pp. (4-7).

First published in Denmark more than thirty-five years ago, the English translation of Holm's moving and suspenseful story was warmly received. David, whose only memories are of his miserable existence in a Communist prison camp, is suddenly allowed to escape, with only a few cryptic directions and the advice to make his way to Denmark. David's experiences hold the reader's attention from start to finish, but the most notable aspect of the book is the delineation of David's character. Molded by circumstances in which deprivation and fear were completely dominant, David has also been powerfully influenced by a fellow prisoner, a remarkable man who has died before the story opens. The writer has imagined what the responses of a boy with such a background, combined with the guidance of his former mentor, might be, and the result is unusual and thought-provoking. (The reason given for David's release and the crucial encounter that reveals to him his identity tend to strain the reader's credulity, but do not at all outweigh the lively interest and thoughtful value of the story.)

Holman, Felice. *Slake's Limbo*. Simon and Schuster Children's Books, 1974, 126 pp. (5-up).

At thirteen, Aremis Slake has become accustomed to neglect of every kind and to ridicule, oppression, and fear. One of today's rootless children without nurturing care, he considers himself unbelievably fortunate to find a small underground refuge behind the wall of a subway tunnel. There is reality, pathos, and a good deal of humor in this unusual story. The writer expects sensitivity and perception from her readers—who are rewarded with a sense of having gained an awareness of another aspect of the human condition and enjoyed a fast-moving, thoroughly interesting story in the process.

Honey, Elizabeth. *Fiddleback*. Alfred A. Knopf, 2001, 202 pp. (5-9).

This fast-moving, hilarious romp is not only entertaining but has the added interest of a foreign setting, the Melbourne area of Australia. The "Stella Street Tribe," as a group of neighboring friends call themselves, decide to go camping between Christmas and New Year's. (It's summer there.) Seven adults, five children, and a dog head out of town for a secluded, tree-shaded spot on the river where they settle in happily. Of course, this is before Cass thinks she has glimpsed someone slipping behind a tree, and a few food supplies go missing. While this turns into an unexpected but not sinister development, Mad Mattock, the bullying, chainsaw-toting manager of a nearby timber mill, is another matter. He is furious at the presence of the campers because he has some illegal personal plans for the wood of a very old and valuable tree nearby. Adventures and "characters" abound, but twelve-year-old Hanni's lively and funny first-person narration and the warmth, caring, and friendship among the whole group of campers leave the most lasting impression.

Jiménez, Francisco. *The Circuit*. Houghton Mifflin, 1997, 116 pp. (5-9).

Based on experiences of the writer's childhood, the stories of *The Circuit* convey an authentic sense of the life of a Mexican migrant-worker family in California more than half a century ago. Without sentimentality, the narrative reflects the grinding poverty, the lack of adequate housing, the repeated disappointments, and the scant weeks of school for the children between harvesting strawberries, grapes, cotton, and other crops. Perhaps the most devastating to the family is the frequent moving, the lack of any place that can be called home. The courage, endurance, faith, and care for each other—and the unquenchable sense of fun—of people with seemingly so little to cling to or build on is remarkable, as is the life-changing effect of compassion and a willingness to offer help and opportunity. (Francisco himself is a college professor in Santa Clara, California.) An effectively-told account of a segment of life largely unknown to many.

Johnson, Emily Rhodes. *Write Me If You Dare!* Front Street/Cricket Books, 2000, 195 pp. (4-6).

Still mourning in her heart for her mother, killed in a car accident three years before, eleven-year-old Maddie tries to find reassurance in random occurrences she interprets as signs of encouragement from her mother. Outwardly, however, Maddie is a capable, endearing, take-charge person, helping her father with his beekeeping and farmers' market Saturdays, enjoying her cats and dog, living the country life she loves with her dad and grandfather. When she finds a tattered balloon in the woods with a plastic-encased note attached daring the finder to write, Maddie sees it as another sign. Her dad is dubious about her making any contact with the sender, but Maddie finds fourteen-year-old Pearl Paradise a welcome pen pal—even though she becomes convinced that Pearl is withholding some big secret about herself from Maddie. The correspondence is an outlet for the storm of emotions Maddie experiences when her beloved dad begins seeing a friendly librarian—who isn't at all like her mother. A developing friendship with a new girl at school and an unexpected revelation about Pearl help Maddie to see the people in her life in new and more understanding ways and to overcome the fears that have been with her since her mother's death.

Morpurgo, Michael. *Waiting for Anya*. Viking, 1991, 172 pp. (5-9).

For young Jo Lalande the war hasn't seemed real. The German occupation appears to have bypassed the little French village near the Spanish border where he has always lived. But all this is about to change as a company of German soldiers is being garrisoned right in the heart of the village. Their purpose is to patrol constantly, looking for anyone trying to cross the border. Secretly Jo has recently become part of a rescue operation for Jewish children, based at an elderly widow's remote farm. As the widow's Jewish son-in-law, Benjamin, smuggles each little group of children across the border under cover of darkness, he continues to hope that among the next group of children will be his daughter Anya. Suddenly, with the arrival of the soldiers, rescuing the latest group of children, the largest they have yet had, becomes infinitely more dangerous.

More than simply a suspenseful, interest-holding story, the author's handling of character development and complex issues of inner conflict over choices that must be made is perceptive and balanced. Young readers can grow along with Jo as he risks his own freedom, perhaps even his life, in the successful rescue—and also as he learns to endure ambiguities and hard realities without bitterness.

O'Hara, Mary. *My Friend Flicka.* HarperCollins Children's Books, 1973 (1941), 272 pp. (6-up.)

A modern classic since it was written sixty years ago, O'Hara's story of a boy and his horse has considerably more depth and fully developed characterization than many such stories. Ten-year-old Ken, dreamy and absent-minded, is constantly at odds with his strong, competent rancher-father. Ken longs for a colt of his own; his father insists he must first demonstrate more efficiency and maturity. Ken's mother finally convinces her husband that perhaps a reversal of the process might work. Having his own colt might be just the incentive Ken needs to keep his daydreaming under control. The story of how Ken responds to being given his colt, Flicka, is the central theme of the book, but there is much more than that involved. The relationships within the family—Ken and his brother, the husband and wife, the parents and sons—and the changing cycle of activities on the ranch are all explored perceptively. Finally, the book's setting in the wildness and beauty of Wyoming is an ever-present element throughout this appealing story.

St. John, Patricia M. *Where the River Begins.* Moody Press, 1980, 127 pp. (4-7).

Francis is a very troubled boy. His family has disintegrated, and the rough gang he has recently joined won't let him end his association with them, even though he very badly wants out. In his desperation he turns to the Glennys, a kindly farm family who had befriended him in an earlier misadventure. The Glennys are not only kind, but they have a living faith in God. As Francis temporarily shares their home, he comes to know the source of the love and goodness in their lives. St. John does a splendid job of writing a thoroughly realistic contemporary story with a Christian message that has nothing forced or preachy about it.

St. John, Patricia M. *Star of Light.* Moody Press, 1953, 256 pp. (5-8).

Hamid lives in a tiny mountain village in the valley below the Riff Mountains of Morocco. His widowed mother, with no source of income, has no choice but to marry the harsh Si Mohamed. When it becomes evident that Hamid's little sister Kinza is blind, his stepfather first rents and then plans to sell her to a callous old beggar—a little blind child appeals to the pity of passersby and increases their giving. Desperate to save her child, Hamid's mother entrusts Kinza to Hamid and sends him on a risky quest. This is the story of what happens as Hamid carries out his mission. The writer spent some years in Morocco and brings great authenticity to the depiction of people, places, and events.

St. John, Patricia M. Three books: *Rainbow Garden, The Secret at Pheasant Cottage, The Tanglewood's Secret.* Moody Press, 1960, 255 pp.; 1978, 160 pp.; 1948, 147 pp. (4-8).

Three stories of preteens who mature in their relationships with others and who learn and grow spiritually as they struggle through family crises. As in St. John's other books, there is a refreshing appreciation of the beauties of the natural world, along with lively plot developments. The specifically Christian emphasis is well integrated with the development of the stories.

Serraillier, Ian. *The Silver Sword.* S. G. Phillips, 1959, 187 pp. (6-9).

Three children—Ruth, Edeb, and Bronia—are on their own in the turmoil of Warsaw, Poland, during World War II. Fearful that they may never again see their parents (snatched away by the Germans), the children learn after several years of hazardous survival that their father escaped the Germans and was going to try to reach Switzerland. Sustained by a moving faith and courage, the little family (the two older ones are now in their mid-teens) and Jan, a streetwise, light-fingered casualty of the tragic times, set out for Switzerland. They are in danger from Russian as well as German troops, and both their faith and courage are taxed to the limit before they win through to a satisfying reunion and a new life.

Stolz, Mary. *A Dog on Barkham Street.* Harper Children's Books, 1960, 184 pp. (4, 5).

A keen understanding of children and the way they think underlies this lively, humorous story of young Edward Frost as he struggles with his own irresponsibility, his fear of a neighborhood bully, and his longing for a dog of his own. The writer manages to suggest valuable ways of dealing with the struggles of preteen life, all in the framework of an interest-holding, enjoyable story.

Streatfeild, Noel. *When the Sirens Wailed.* Random House, 1976, 176 pp. (4-6).

Three London children from an impoverished working-class family are sent to the country during World War II to escape the bombing. Holding out against being separated, they are taken in by a crusty but kindly retired colonel and the comfortable country couple who work for him. The colonel is determined to help the children as to their manners and speech, but after some difficulties in adjustment, the children's lives are going quite smoothly when the old colonel dies. The ensuing crisis and its resolution are an important part of the story's development. Lively action, well-handled humor, and a strong element of family devotion all play prominent parts in the appealing story. This fine book focuses on war-time experiences of English children that are well worth knowing about. It is no longer in print but will reward a persistent search.

Realistic Stories—Historical

Aiken, Joan. *The Wolves of Willoughby Chase*. Doubleday, 1987 (1962), 176 pp. (5-up).

Hungry wolves ranging the countryside and a sinister, cold-hearted governess left in charge of Bonnie and her cousin Sylvia provide Victorian melodrama in this straight-faced but tongue-in-cheek tale. When Bonnie's father, Sir Willoughby, must take her mother on a sea cruise in the hope of restoring her health, he has no idea of the true character of his distant cousin, Miss Slighcarp, in whose hands he has placed not only the two girls but all the business of his estate as well. After a short time with the cruel governess, Bonnie and Sylvia are planning to run away when she forcibly sends them into captivity with her dreadful sister, the bullying Mrs. Brisket. Perils and suspense abound, but with the aid of their faithful friend Simon, the girls make new plans for escape. Whether readers simply thrill to the lively action or laugh out loud at the hilariously portrayed villains they love to hate, children today continue to take this book to their hearts just as they have for forty years. A splendid family read-aloud full of adventure, impeccable values, irresistible humor—and the triumph of good over evil.

Note: Don't take the "historical" categorization too seriously. Aiken loved to mix a not-quite-identifiable era of the past with public figures and circumstances that never existed. The books, however, *are* set in a vaguely historical past—certainly not in modernity.

Aiken, Joan. *Black Hearts in Battersea*. Houghton Mifflin, 1999 (1964), 233 pp. (5-up).

Enterprising and delightful young people once again cope with evil schemes and despicable plotters in this artful combination of humor and fast-paced adventure. Simon, the faithful friend of the heroines of *The Wolves of Willoughby Chase*, is the tale's central figure. Leaving Yorkshire, he travels to London where he expects to stay with the kindly Dr. Field and study art. But at the lodging house to which the doctor's letter has directed him, Dr. Field is nowhere to be found. All the residents insist that they have never seen nor heard of him. The reader is plunged at once into a captivating mélange of intrigue and unexpected events. Kidnapping, a political plot, peril at sea, and mistaken identities are all handled deftly—and almost plausibly! Aiken not only writes wonderfully well, but the central figures of the story demonstrate kindness, loyalty, courage, and determination in ways that inspire. Here are suspense, hilarity, and drama on a sound and steady foundation. (But see previous listing's note as to the "historical" designation.)

Alcott, Louisa M. *Little Women*. Little, Brown and Co., 1968 (1868), 444 pp. (5-up).

It is quite probable that no other children's novel has been as dearly loved as has this wonderful old classic. The elements of the story are simple enough—a gentle, scholarly, minister-father (away serving as a chaplain in the Civil War during the first half of the book); a warm, strong mother dedicated to her family but also concerned about the needs of others; four teenaged daughters; a wealthy, crotchety neighbor and his handsome, fun-loving grandson. Each girl is very different from the others, with their individual personalities and resultant interaction an important part of the story development. The reader immediately becomes involved with this lively, very human family, and the lessons in character, the compassionate but firm view of life and human failings so clearly expressed by the writer, are just as applicable today as they were more than 100 years ago. (Movie versions, unfortunately, fail to capture the true atmosphere of the story and the nature of its characters, giving viewers a poor idea of what the book has to offer.)

Of the eight children's novels Alcott wrote, the three most outstanding are *Little Women, Eight Cousins,* and *An Old-Fashioned Girl.* But thoroughly enjoyable to read are the others: *Little Men* and *Jo's Boys,* which follow *Little Women; Rose in Bloom,* the sequel to *Eight Cousins;* and two unrelated stories, *Jack and Jill* and *Under the Lilacs.* We are listing Alcott's books in the grade 5-up section (where technically they belong), but many of them should be read aloud to younger children. As is the case of most of the classics written some time ago, it is important to introduce children to the language and atmosphere of these books at as early an age as possible—but never in a way that creates in the listener a dislike of the story. The parent or teacher should feel his or her way and be guided by the child's particular preferences.

Avi. *Night Journeys.* Morrow, 1994 (1979), 160 pp. (4-8).

Orphaned at twelve, young Peter York is taken into the Quaker home of Justice of the Peace Everett Shinn and his family. Shinn is against violence; yet when a hunt is on for two escaped indentured children, he feels it is his responsibility to take part in the effort to find and return the children to what amounts to a life of slavery. The suspenseful events of the story confront Peter with a reality quite different from his earlier views; he had thought he would like to have a part in collecting some of the reward money. Peter's foster father also faces a moral crisis in this unusual, excellently written book. The setting is Pennsylvania in the late 1760s.

Avi. *The Secret School.* Harcourt Children's Books, 2001, 160 pp. (4-8).

In the spring of 1925, Ida Bidson is looking forward to finishing eighth grade in the little one-room school in a remote spot in Colorado. She has been studying hard all year, and if her final grades are good, she can start high school in the fall. But when the teacher is called away by family illness, the school board decides to simply close the school for the year. Ida is almost in despair, and her classmate Tom is just as anxious as she to graduate and go on to high school. They come up with a plan, and all the students vote on it—deciding to keep classes going, with Ida in charge. But they have to keep it a secret from the school board, as the board would never agree to a student substituting for the teacher, no matter how mature, responsible, and knowledgeable Ida is. Resourceful, determined, and with the parents' permission, Ida pins up her hair and takes charge. The secret plan succeeds—until disaster threatens due to a parent Ida must deal with. The story throughout is interesting, well written, often funny—and saturated with excellent values.

Blackmore, Richard D. *Lorna Doone*. Buccaneer Books, 1981 (1869), 345 pp.
(6-up).

A favorite old classic, the romantic and suspenseful story of the beautiful Lorna,
a ward of the fierce and sinister Doones, and of John Ridd, the strong, gentle man
who loves her. John and Lorna's dramatic story is told against a background of
seventeenth-century rural England. Vivid descriptions, appealing characterizations,
mystery, humor, and stirring action have kept this story popular for more than 130
years. (With its great length and challenging language level, this is a book for
advanced readers.)

Blackwood, Gary. *The Shakespeare Stealer*. Dutton Children's Books, 1998, 216 pp.
(5-up).

Orphaned soon after his birth in 1587, the story's first-person narrator writes
briefly of surviving the meager care of the small local orphanage. Widge (a persistent nickname given him on his arrival) is apprenticed at seven to a learned but
self-seeking man. Dr. Bright wants to train Widge as an eventual assistant in his
scientific pursuits, and he teaches him to read and write in both English and
Latin—and also in an invention of Bright's own, a form of shorthand. Dr. Bright
has written a little book telling of his shorthand system, and when Widge is fourteen, a dark and sinister stranger appears—with a copy of Bright's book in hand.
The stranger demands a demonstration of Widge's shorthand skill and pays Bright
to transfer the boy's apprenticeship to him.

Widge soon learns that his new master is a man to fear greatly, and the latter
wastes no time in telling the boy what he wants. They are going to London, near
Shakespeare's Globe Theatre. Widge is to attend performances of *Hamlet* and,
without getting caught, write the play down in shorthand. The purpose is to pirate
the text of the play and transcribe it for a disreputable producer and his group of
touring actors. (Pirating plays was frequently done by a variety of means in real
life at that time.) Adventure, danger, and suspense not only ensue, but the fast-
paced and well-written tale perceptively develops the character of Widge as he finds
camaraderie and kindness, learning values no one has previously taught him, realizing the worth of "honesty and trust, loyalty and friendship. And family. And
home."

Blos, Joan W. *A Gathering of Days*. Demco, 1990 (1979), 144 pp. (6-8).

An unusual and beautifully done fictional journal of a New England girl in her
thirteenth and fourteenth years. The writer has set the time in about 1830, and
although she has simply imagined her material in its specific details, she has captured the speech and thought of the time.

Bly, Stephen. *The Dog Who Would Not Smile*. Crossway Books, 1992, 127 pp.
(5-7).

Nathan encounters one disaster after another as he tries to find his misplaced
parents. Afraid that their trek to Nevada to look for gold might be too unsettling
and strenuous for Nathan, his parents have temporarily left him in Indiana with
his grandparents. When both grandparents succumb to a sudden smallpox epi-

demic, Nathan takes a stagecoach for the long ride to Nevada. He thinks his parents will have received the letter he wrote telling them he was coming—but nothing works out as he expects. Encounters (some quite strenuous and painful) with Indians, gold-obsessed miners, rattlesnakes, a spunky girl, and a murderous outlaw sparkle with the writer's irrepressible humor. Accompanied by the lonely wolflike dog that appears to have adopted him, Nathan persists in his search. Light, funny, fast-paced, and suspenseful, with a wealth of fine values smoothly integrated into the story.

Bronte, Charlotte. *Jane Eyre.* Grossett and Dunlap, 1983 (1847), 552 pp. (6-up).

Orphaned, penniless, and friendless, Charlotte Bronte's famous heroine Jane Eyre endures enough childhood misfortune to thoroughly crush a weaker spirit. Jane, however, weathers the difficult early years, quite unaware of the drama, tragedy—and great joy—that will come to her as the result of a change in the direction of her life. At eighteen the shy, intense, far-from-beautiful Jane comes to Thornfield Hall as governess to the ward of the abrupt, darkly brooding Mr. Rochester. Suspense builds as Jane becomes aware of mystery and danger. But many twists and turns of the plot are yet to come before the final resolution. This enthralling literary classic will be best appreciated by advanced readers.

Defoe, Daniel. *Robinson Crusoe.* Simon and Schuster Children's Books, 1983 (1719), 368 pp. (5-up).

This is another of the famous old classics that everyone knows about, but that is not really known because it is not being read in its original form. After running away to sea, Crusoe is wrecked and spends the next twenty-four years on an uninhabited island near South America. One of the charms of island survival stories is the amazing ingenuity demonstrated by the individual or group trying to stay alive, and Crusoe is no exception. But even inventiveness and hard work can't entirely prevent loneliness. Reading the Bible brings encouragement and fresh determination, and later Crusoe rescues a young native who becomes his helper and companion. They continue to have a variety of adventures and are finally rescued from their isolation. A wonderful reading experience both for its enthralling story and its capacity-stretching language. (For advanced readers or read aloud.)

de Treviño, Elizabeth Borton. *I, Juan de Pareja.* Farrar, Straus and Giroux, 1987 (1965), 192 pp. (4-7).

A fascinating account of the life of Juan de Pareja, born into slavery in Seville, Spain, during the early part of the seventeenth century. As the reader learns in the author's Afterword, Pareja does indeed appear in history and was closely associated with the life and work of the great Spanish artist Velázquez for most of Pareja's life. As the writer indicates, there are no detailed records to turn to, but even the sparse facts created an atmosphere in which her fiction fits with great naturalness. Juan's first-person narrative is beautifully written, and the generous and caring nature reflected establishes the tone of the story. The settings and customs are different enough from readers' experience—even apart from the artist's world Juan inhabits—to provide a multilayered background for the life of the boy who was first a conventional slave but who became a trusted companion, was given his freedom, but chose to stay with Velázquez as a friend and assistant through the artist's life. An enriching, eventful, and enlightening story.

Dickens, Charles. *Oliver Twist*. Buccaneer Books, 1982 (1838), 541 pp. (6-up).
   The famous classic story of Oliver, a foundling, who arouses the wrath of those in charge of the orphanage by asking for more gruel. Apprenticed to a miserly and harsh undertaker, Oliver soon runs away, only to come under the power of Fagin, the devious criminal who trains children in thievery and profits from their loot. As always, the story as written by the author is an infinitely more enriching experience than film versions, watered-down condensations, or selected excerpts. Skilled, advanced readers with a love for language, setting, and characterization are ready for Dickens by or before sixth grade, but such reading should be a joy, not a hated task. Parents and teachers need to feel their way on this. Other works of Dickens that advanced readers may particularly enjoy are *David Copperfield, Great Expectations, A Tale of Two Cities,* and *Our Mutual Friend.*

Donaldson, Joan. *A Pebble and a Pen*. Holiday House, 2000, 157 pp. (5-9).
   Matty Harris has just completed eighth grade. It is 1853, and she has a dream of becoming a skilled penman, but her widowed mother has no understanding of her daughter's hopes. When Matty learns that her mother is determined to marry her off to a prosperous but domineering widower with seven children, she decides her only recourse is to leave home secretly. With the help of her older brother and a letter of recommendation from her teacher (who has no idea she plans to run away), Matty takes the train to Ashtabula, Ohio. Platt Rogers Spencer, the famous penman (a historical person), has a small summer school where he teaches Spencerian writing and related clerical skills to selected students. (It would be more than twenty-five years before typewriters were produced, and all business records were handwritten.)
   Permitted to enter on a trial basis, Matty, the only female student, struggles with more than her studies. By the end of the eventful summer, however, her hopes are encouraged, and an opportunity for work and further study lies ahead. Then a letter from her brother regretfully asking for her help puts an end to her plans. Matty realizes it is right for her to return home. With the confidence and maturity she has gained, she knows that life still beckons and that her time will come. An enjoyable story that opens a window on a seldom-explored aspect of mid-eighteenth-century American life.

Doucet, Sharon Arms. *Fiddle Fever*. Clarion Books, 2000, 166 pp. (5-8).
   Fourteen years old and with an inner restlessness building that only needs one spark to set it off, Félix LeBlanc hears the piercingly sweet notes of a fiddle in the hands of Nonc Adolphe, and life for him will never be the same. Part of a close-knit farming family in the Cajun bayous of Louisiana, Félix is surprised and elated to have the family black sheep, his mother's brother Adolphe, turn up without warning. It is 1914, and something has actually happened to break the endless monotony, to bring in a little of that world beyond their fields and levees. But to Félix's mother,

the event is a disaster. Permanently angry at Adolphe for simply walking away with-out a word years before to become a traveling musician, Maman knows that music is a recurring gift in her family, and she fears any influence Adolphe will have on her son. But it isn't simply Nonc Adolphe; it is the passion to play the fiddle that has gripped Félix. Conflict, rebellion, a complexity of interactions in all their intensity finally bring Félix to a crisis that threatens all he holds dear. A beautifully written and perceptive story (with its share of humor) that has a deeply satisfying resolution.

Durbin, William. *The Journal of Sean Sullivan, a Transcontinental Railroad Worker.* Scholastic, Inc., 1999, 188 pp. (5-8).

Fifteen-year-old Sean joins his father, a foreman for the Union Pacific Railroad—and keeps a journal of his experiences. Though fictional, the account is a very realistic look at one of the significant developments in our nation's history. It is 1867, right after the Civil War, and two railroad companies (the Central Pacific and the Union Pacific) are in the midst of a huge undertaking. One is lay-ing track toward the east, the other toward the west; when they meet in north-eastern Utah, a continuous railway line will be established for the first time across the entire continent. Full of the colorful details of Sean's day-to-day life, the account balances factual background with human interest. Outgoing and percep-tive, Sean's likable personality and eventful experiences move the story at a lively pace. Very well written, the book also reflects many fine values just as relevant today as they were 135 years ago.

Forbes, Esther. *Johnny Tremain.* Buccaneer, 1981 (1943), 305 pp. (6-up).

When Johnny's hand is badly burned, he realizes he can no longer continue training to be a silversmith. With courage and determination he puts the past behind him and involves himself in the fight for the freedom of the American colonies. Popular for sixty years, Forbes's book has long been a modern classic.

Fritz, Jean. *Early Thunder.* Puffin Books, 1987 (1967), 255 pp. (5-up).

Fourteen-year-old Daniel West, living in Salem, Massachusetts, is from a Tory family and considers himself a staunch Tory as well. But all around him the unrest and the resentment over arbitrary English sanctions against the colony grow stronger. Dan finally has to face the issues as he sees them and make a choice. The way the characters speak and some of the attitudes expressed have been somewhat shaped to modern readers' abilities and tastes, but on the whole the book is worth reading—not only as an interesting tale, but also for the historical material and the account of the personal decision-making through which Daniel struggles.

Fritz, Jean. *Brady.* Puffin Books, 1987 (1960), 223 pp. (5-up).

Young Brady Minton hasn't really given any thought to the issue of slavery. But even in 1836 it has become a serious and bitterly controversial topic for many. When Brady accidentally sees some runaway slaves being hidden near his home, his habit of talking without thinking causes him to blurt out what he has seen. Fortunately he is talking to his family and some visiting relatives who are sympa-thetic to the work of the Underground Railway. But Brady soon realizes that his habitual inability to keep a secret has caused his father to distrust him. How Brady comes to his own conclusions about slavery and demonstrates a new maturity are the underlying theme of this suspenseful and well-thought-through story.

Gray, Elizabeth Janet. *Adam of the Road*. Illus. by Robert Lawson. Viking Children's Books, 1942, 370 pp. (4-7).

There have always been people for whom the road—any road—is not simply a cleared strip of terrain that makes travel easier. For them it is a central part of their way of life. Adam's father, Roger, a minstrel in thirteenth-century England, talks to him about the road: "It brings all kinds of people and all parts of England together. And it's home to a minstrel, even though he may happen to be sleeping in a castle." Adam has often shared the road with his father since his mother's death, and being able to feel at home there keeps him from despair when everything seems to be going wrong. Accidentally separated from his father as he tries to catch up with the man who has stolen Nick, his beloved dog, he has one adventure after another. Outgoing and cheerful, Adam manages to keep his head, learn from his misfortunes, and depend on the road to finally bring a happy reunion. Full of humor, colorful characters, action, suspense, and solid values.

Haas, Jessie. *Unbroken*. Greenwillow Books, 1999, 185 pp. (6-up).

An especially well-written story set in the Vermont of 1910. Shattered by the sudden death of her mother, Harriet Gibson's world has fragmented around her. It had been just the two of them in a close, loving companionship. Harry's father had died before she could even remember, and the only family she knows of is her father's sister Sarah, who has never had anything to do with them. But now her mother's will directs that Harry is to live with Sarah and her husband on their mountain farm—a horse-and-buggy hour from town—a responsibility Sarah accepts in spite of her obvious hostility toward the memory of Harry's mother. As the stunned, grieving girl tries to put her life together, she is encouraged by supportive friends and finds an inner strength and resolution she had never before had to summon. Ready to enter high school in the coming fall, Harry thinks of her mother's concern for her continued education, and against Aunt Sarah's opposition determines to go somehow. If she can only train her colt in time, he could provide the needed ride to school every day. Orphaned like herself in the accident that killed not only Harry's mother but the colt's mother as well, the nervous young horse resists. It takes another accident to bring a surprising new perspective into Harry's life and changes she had never dreamed of.

Haugaard, Erik Christian. *A Messenger for Parliament; Cromwell's Boy*. Houghton Mifflin, 1976, 218 pp.; 1978, 214 pp. (6-up).

This pair of stories can be read separately or in sequence. Oliver's mother dies when he is eleven, leaving him to the dubious mercies of his weak-willed, drunken father. In a desperate effort to survive, Oliver joins a ragged group of children camped in a war-ravaged cathedral. Set against the background of the English civil wars, the stories follow Oliver as he becomes a part of the people surrounding

Cromwell, first as a messenger boy, later with even greater responsibilities. The historical background is excellent, the writing is perceptive and enthralling, and the author has used solid realism without wallowing in depravity or sordidness. The first of the above books is out of print, the second still in print. Both are in many libraries.

Hawse, Alberta. *Vinegar Boy*. Moody Press, 1970 (5-up).

The writer has created an appealing and credible set of fictional characters and events and related them to the crucifixion of Christ. Abandoned as a baby and known simply as "Boy" or "Vinegar Boy," the child with the large, disfiguring red birthmark on his face has been raised in the Roman garrison. For three years (since he was eight) one of his duties has been to take the sponge and the bags of vinegar and wine to Golgotha's hill when there is a crucifixion scheduled. For some time the boy has been planning to seek Jesus out and ask him to miraculously remove the birthmark that has brought him so much scorn and distaste. The day comes; the boy joyfully prepares to set forth, only to be stopped at the last minute. He must carry vinegar to Golgotha, and Jesus of Nazareth is one of the three being executed. Hawse has written a dramatic, well-crafted story that focuses on both the tragedy and triumph of the cross, as it touches the lives of Vinegar Boy and those around him.

Henry, Marguerite. *Justin Morgan Had a Horse*. Simon and Schuster Children's Books, 1991 (1954), 176 pp. (4-6).

This well-written story of the first Morgan horse has become a modern classic. Set near the end of the eighteenth century in Vermont, it is not at all romanticized, and a majority of the story's characters seem markedly lacking in sentiment or idealism—which could, of course, be true to historical fact! The hero, however, has a deep devotion to the plucky little horse and demonstrates the worthwhileness of other important values. The cultural patterns of the time have an authentic ring as portrayed in the story, and their hard realities may be a good balance to the high adventure and drama of many stories of the late eighteenth century.

Holman, Felice. *The Wild Children*. Scribner's, 1983, 151 pp. (5-up).

It is the early 1920s in Russia (not long after the revolution), and everywhere is an awareness that people are disappearing. The secret police come without warning, usually at night, and people vanish without a trace. When twelve-year-old Alex, accustomed to a comfortable, secure life, awakens to find his parents, sister, and grandmother gone, he finally realizes that it is only because he was asleep in the large hidden storage closet that could only be reached through his parents' room that he wasn't taken with his family. Slipping out of town, he makes a hazardous trip to Moscow, seeking his uncle—only to learn that the uncle, too, has recently vanished. Alone and desperate, he is befriended by one of the bands of displaced children that are everywhere, eluding the authorities, surviving on their own, shunning the unbearable misery of the government's prisonlike "children's homes," into which thousands are locked away. Freezing, starving, dying of illnesses, they at least have a degree of freedom on their own. This splendidly written story follows Alex and his new friends as they struggle to survive and finally make a high-risk bid for real, permanent freedom. This fine book is now back in print after being out of print for several years.

Lawrence, Iain. *The Wreckers*. Delacorte Press, 1998, 196 pp. (6-up).

As a boy, author Iain Lawrence was enthralled by stories of sea adventures, a favorite being *Treasure Island*. In this, his first book, he captures the action-filled and perilous atmosphere he had admired as a young reader. It is 1799, and four-teen-year-old John Spencer, the story's first-person narrator, has gone to sea for the first time with his landlubber-shipowner father. As they near the coast of Cornwall on their return, Mr. Spencer's stubborn and unwise order to the protest-ing captain to stay close to land in the midst of the stormy night brings not simply disaster but horror and tragedy. Lured toward land by false beacon lights, the ship crashes on the rocks, and the ghoulish wreckers of a small Cornish village move in like vultures. Suspenseful and sometimes grim, the tale moves at a breathtaking pace. Courage, caring, moral conviction, and determination are pitted against evil greed and brutality. The cast of vividly portrayed characters, some of whom are a mystery in themselves, lend depth and substance to the exciting action. A rousing tale of adventure and the ultimate triumph of good over evil.

Little, Jean. *The Belonging Place*. Viking Penguin, 1997, 121 pp. (4-7).

Her family is emigrating to Canada, and Elspet Mary doesn't want to leave Glen Buchan, the small Scottish village where she has finally started to feel she belongs. Her mother's sudden death three years before in a tragic accident has been just the first in a succession of losses and changes almost too much to bear. Now, though she is dearly loved by her adoptive family (Uncle Will and Aunt Ailsa and their two young sons), fears and insecurities still run deep in Elspet's inmost being. The thought of another uprooting, another big change, fills her with distress. In this warm, often humorous, family-centered story full of lively happenings, Elspet Mary finds the answer to her doubts and fears and finally knows with complete certainty where she belongs.

Montgomery, Lucy Maud. *Anne of Green Gables*. Grossett and Dunlap, 1970 (1908), 299 pp. (5-up).

One of the most widely known and best-loved children's stories of all time, *Anne of Green Gables* is set on Canada's beautiful Prince Edward Island. It is there that orphaned, red-haired Anne Shirley comes to live with an elderly brother and sister, Matthew and Marilla Cuthbert. By turns a bookish dreamer and an impul-sive spitfire, Anne is essentially an appealing child with a desperate need to love and be loved. How she not only finds a place in more than one heart, but learns to know herself better, is the underlying theme of Montgomery's eventful, often humorous story. Five more Anne stories comprise the *series: Anne of Avonlea, Anne of the Island, Anne of Windy Poplars, Anne's House of Dreams, Anne of Ingleside.* A briefer series starting with *Emily of New Moon* is not as widely known and goes in and out of print, but is worth looking for. The other two titles are *Emily Climbs* and *Emily's Quest.*

Note: For readers with a special interest in *Anne of Green Gables*, there is an annotated edition, published by the Oxford University Press; 396 pages comprise the story itself with masses of informative notes included. This is followed by 100 pages of appendices with chapters on the geography of Prince Edward Island, its early settlers, its gardens and plants, and a number of other sections on matters related to the story's era and its subject matter.

Montgomery, Lucy Maud. Two books: *Pat of Silver Bush; Mistress Pat.* McClelland-Bantam, Inc., 1988 (1933), 278 pp.; 1988 (1935), 277 pp. (5-up).

On Prince Edward Island, life at the old Gardiner Farm, Silver Bush, is rich in beauty, family, friends, and the humor that is part of all Montgomery's stories. Little Pat Gardiner loves everyone and everything at Silver Bush—her parents, four brothers and sisters, and the sometimes-quirky Judy Plum, who combines the functions of a devoted nanny and a general factotum. Beyond that, Pat loves with an overwhelming intensity the farm's every tree, flower, shrub, field, and pond—but most of all, the welcoming old white house. The two books move through twenty-four eventful years of Pat's life, and it is doubtful if anything in children's literature more sensitively and appealingly combines a heartfelt joy in simple, natural beauties and the poignant essence of the love of home than is reflected in this family-centered chronicle.

Overshadowed by the widely popular Green Gables stories, this pair of books was out of print for some time, often disappearing from library shelves. Now they are readily available in paperback, either on the shelf in a local bookstore or by special order.

Note: The first book is a little slow to get into the flow of the story; don't give up on it because of the start—and miss two very special books.

Morpurgo, Michael. *The Wreck of the Zanzibar.* Illus. by François Place. Viking, 1995, 69 pp. (4-9).

Just off the far southwest corner of England lie the Scilly Isles. Often battered by fierce storms, many of these windswept dots of rocky earth have nevertheless long been home to independent, hardy inhabitants. As the story opens, family members have come from the mainland to one such island for the funeral of Michael's Great-aunt Laura, who had lived to be 100. Aunt Laura has left each one a gift, and Michael's is a diary she kept of the most eventful months of her life in long-ago 1907. In Laura's account, which comprises the book, the author has created a wonderful and unusual story of a family—of faithful parents, a strong, courageous girl, and her adventure-seeking twin brother who runs away to sea; of life on the edge of loss and starvation and of hopeful life regained; a story of shipwreck and of a giant sea turtle washed up almost—but not quite—dead on the shore. Beautifully written, this is a special book, one to savor and long remember.

O'Dell, Scott. *Island of the Blue Dolphins*. Houghton Mifflin, 1960, 184 pp. (5-up).

This is the widely-praised modern classic that tells the story of a courageous Indian girl, Karana, who spent eighteen years alone on an island off the coast of California. Frequently in danger, dependent on her own efforts for physical survival, and without the comfort of even one other human being's presence, Karana not only lives but grows in strength and serenity. A lovely story, enhanced by its close relationship to the natural world of plants, animals, sea, and sky.

O'Dell, Scott. *The Hawk That Dare Not Hunt by Day*. Bob Jones University, rev. 1986 (1975), 182 pp. (6-up).

A gripping story of Tom Barton, a young seaman who helped smuggle William Tyndale's Bibles into England. Forces of intrigue from all over Europe gather to prevent Tyndale from accomplishing his mission of putting God's Word into English and getting it into the hands of anyone who wants to read it. Religious and political turmoil are on every hand, and Tom's involvement with Tyndale becomes acutely dangerous. A well-written story with excellent historical background material.

O'Dell, Scott. *The King's Fifth*. Houghton Mifflin, 1966, 264 pp. (6-up).

A story of the Spanish conquistadors and the lust for gold that distorted their values and bred disaster. Esteban Sandoval, a young map-maker, loses his joy of adventure as he, too, falls under the spell of the shining metal. But as he experiences great hardship and suffers at the hands of ruthless men, he finds a new perspective and better, newly ordered values. An unusual setting and group of characters enhance the story's valid assessment of greed and its consequences. Excellently written.

Porter, Jane. *Scottish Chiefs*. Simon and Schuster Children's Books, 1991 (1809), 520 pp. (6-up).

This romantic tale of William Wallace, Scottish hero during the ten years that spanned the end of the thirteenth century and the start of the fourteenth, was a favorite children's classic for more than 100 years. Generations of children thrilled to the story's idealism, patriotism, and drama, to "escapes through mysterious underground passages, movable pillars, secret doors . . . wardrobes replete with disguises." Like the stories of her literary superior, Sir Walter Scott, Porter's melodramatic and highly romanticized tale is long, the vocabulary and sentence structure challenging. But advanced readers with a taste for historical novels will still find much to enjoy and learn in the stirring adventures of Wallace and his friends.

Pyle, Howard. *Men of Iron*. Harper and Row, 1981, 330 pp. (6-up).

Adventure, conflict, and romance in early fifteenth-century England. Myles Falworth's family have lost home and fortune with the dethroning of Richard II and accession of Henry IV. As he grows into manhood, it is Myles's responsibility to make his own way and to try to restore the fortunes of his family. A longtime classic that is still well worth reading.

Pyle, Howard. *Otto of the Silver Hand.* Dover, 1967 (1883), 136 pp. (4-9).

    A story set in the Germany of feudal barons. The time period covers several years preceding and just following the accession in 1593 of Count Rudolph of Hapsburg as German emperor. In the context of an eventful story, the reader becomes aware of the harshness of life (both in castle and cottage) in feudal times. The contrasting life in the monastery where Otto is cared for after receiving a cruel injury may perhaps be idealized, but the point is well made as to violence and harshness, in contrast to love and justice.

Rawlings, Marjorie Kinnan. *The Yearling.* Scribner's, 1985 (1938), 416 pp. (5-up).

    Rawlings's justly-praised classic about Jody, a twelve-year-old farm boy, and his love for a pet deer is, of course, about a great deal more than that. Its portrayals of the 1860s back-country of northern Florida, of the people who lived there and wrested a living from its untamed land, reflect a clear-eyed realism without cynicism. Jody's childhood ends with the death of the deer, but as he has endured heartbreak and what seems briefly to be betrayal, has faced the basic issues of hunger and survival, he has also grown up and is ready to deal responsibly with his life. The descriptions of the natural world and the penetrating insights into human nature add to the pleasure and value of reading this Pulitzer Prize-winning book.

Rawls, Wilson. *Where the Red Fern Grows.* Bantam, 1974 (1961), 256 pp. (6-up).

    An authentic story of a boy in the Oklahoma Ozarks in the early part of this century. Billy wanted a pair of coon hounds more than anything on earth, but there was simply no money to buy them. How Billy's dream became reality, and what his dogs meant in his life are the thrust of this well-written book. A thought-provoking background element is the way that the trapping of wildlife and related activities are viewed by the kind, God-fearing people of the area. Excellent to spark some serious discussions, not just about the treatment of wildlife, but about the process of "raised consciousness" in relation to such issues.

Scott, Sir Walter. *Ivanhoe.* Dodd, Mead, 1979 (1820), 499 pp. (6-up).

    One of the most lastingly popular of Scott's classic novels, *Ivanhoe* is set in the period following the Norman Conquest. Full of drama, intrigue, romance, and pageantry, the story follows the fortunes of Wilfred, Knight of Ivanhoe. Leading female characters are the lovely Rowena and the vivid, charming Rebecca. Like all of Scott's work, *Ivanhoe* is long, written in an era when short sentences and brief books were exclusively related to beginning readers—when they existed at all. The language is challenging, and it is important for children to be able to read such books with pleasure. Advanced readers with a taste for the wonderful atmosphere of the romantic classics will find great enjoyment in *Ivanhoe* and in some of Scott's other novels: *Rob Roy, Quentin Durward, Kenilworth,* and *The Black Dwarf.*

Speare, Elizabeth George. *The Bronze Bow.* Houghton Mifflin, 1961, 272 pp. (5-up).

    The story is set in Palestine at the time of Christ. In the context of a suspenseful plot, the need to learn to love rather than hate is emphasized (the hatred of the

Jews for the Romans, the scorn of many Romans for the Jews, for example). The characters are especially well-drawn; historical and cultural background details are effectively used.

Speare, Elizabeth George. *The Sign of the Beaver*. Bantam Doubleday Dell, 1983, 135 pp. (5-up).

When Matt's father leaves him to care for their new homestead in the Maine woods, they didn't expect Matt's solitude to last for more than seven weeks at most. The two of them have just built a cabin and planted corn and pumpkins. Now Pa must go back to Massachusetts and bring home the rest of the family. From the start, Matt is plunged into unexpected events, some with lingering consequences. After he is rescued from a dangerous swarm of bees by an Indian chief and his grandson Attean, Matt soon finds himself chosen by the grandfather to teach the Indian boy to read. The weeks turn into months with no sign of Matt's family. As Attean's grandfather prepares to move his tribe's encampment permanently and seek land to the west, he is reluctant to leave Matt alone with the deep snows of winter coming soon. Due to the dangers of travel, anything could have happened to Matt's family; perhaps they will never return, and Matt is invited to make his home with the Beaver tribe. The decision is surprisingly difficult, but one Matt is finally glad he made as he did. A well-written account of the sudden growing up of a pioneer boy and his friendship with the land's native people.

Steele, William O. *The Perilous Road*. Harbrace, 1990 (1958), 191 pp. (4-up).

Young Chris Brabson is sure he has about as fine a life as a boy can have. But the Civil War is underway, and when Yankee soldiers take all the Brabsons' store of winter food, their only horse, and Chris's treasured deerskin shirt, hatred fills the boy's heart. But even worse, his parents don't share his rage. They are sorry to lose the things they badly need, but they also realize the need that has prompted the soldiers' raids. They feel sympathy for both sides in the conflict. How Chris tries to take matters into his own hands and harm the Union cause, and what he learns about the realities of war, make up the central theme of this effectively written story.

Stevenson, Robert Louis. *The Black Arrow*. 1888. Atheneum. A reissue of the 1916 edition. Illus. by N. C. Wyeth, 328 pp. (5-up).

An enthralling classic full of peril and suspense. In the turmoil of one of the Wars of the Roses (in fifteenth-century England), young Dick Shelton finds himself pursued first by one side and then the other. He finds refuge with an outlaw band who, with their dreaded black arrows, are avenging wrongs done to them. His subsequent adventures and final attainment of knighthood make thrilling reading. The wonderful old N. C. Wyeth illustrations first appeared in the early edition referred to above.

Stevenson, Robert Louis. *Kidnapped; or the Lad with the Silver Button*. Huntington Library Press, 1999 (1886), 334 pp. (5-up).

Another of Stevenson's classic adventure stories, this one about David Balfour and his friend Alan Breck, a fleeing Jacobite leader, set in the mid-eighteenth century. Planning to cheat David of his rightful inheritance, David's uncle has him kidnapped and taken to sea by a dishonest ship's captain. At sea David and Alan meet and become comrades. Sea battles, perilous chases across the Scottish hills, and a mysterious murder are some of the suspenseful events that follow. In the exciting sequels (*David Balfour*. Atheneum Books for Young Readers, 356 pp.; *Catriona*. Koenemann, 240 pp.), David and Alan continue to have hazardous adventures. David also meets the lovely Catriona, whose scoundrel father does not look kindly on the young Scotsman. All is eventually well, but not before the overcoming of many seemingly insurmountable difficulties.

Note: *Kidnapped* can be found in many satisfactory current editions. This Huntington Library Press edition, however, is a special one, using the original text exactly as written by Stevenson, including Scottish dialect words. The story is preceded by an introduction and notes by Barry Menikoff, a leading authority on Stevenson. The book concludes with explanatory notes on matters mentioned in the text with which general readers are not familiar, a glossary of the Scottish dialect words used, and a gazetteer identifying the location of places mentioned.

Stevenson, Robert Louis. *Treasure Island*. 1881. Atheneum. A reissue of the 1911 edition. Illus. by N. C. Wyeth. 273 pp. (5-up).

One of the world's best-known books for children, Stevenson's story of pirates and high adventure continues to be a favorite. Many of today's young people, however, are familiar only with movie, TV, or abridged versions of the original story. The original text creates its own wonderful atmosphere of colorful characters, sinister meetings, faraway places, and suspense-filled moments. (See mention of the N. C. Wyeth illustrations in the above entry for *The Black Arrow*.)

Stockton, Frank R. *The Lady or the Tiger and Other Stories*. Scribner's, 1914 (1884), 201 pp. (5-up).

Stockton's classic short stories are a bit hard to classify today. They are clearly dated; yet they are still highly readable, with their mild satiric commentary on human nature, sophisticated (in the manner of another era) humor, and occasional excursions from the realistic to the fantastic. Included in this collection is the writer's most lastingly famous work, "The Lady or the Tiger," a story that, once read, is never quite forgotten. For advanced readers.

Sutcliff, Rosemary. *Blood Feud*. Dutton, 1977, 144 pp. (6-up).

During the ninth to eleventh centuries the Vikings, seagoing Scandinavian warriors, frequently raided coastal Europe and the British Isles. Less known is the Vikings' southeastward thrust extending to and beyond Constantinople. Kidnapped from England, the orphaned seventeen-year-old Jestyn is taken to the slave market in Dublin. There he is bought by a young Viking, Thurmond, who becomes Jestyn's friend. Later Thurmond gives Jestyn his freedom, but they stay together on an adventurous trek that ranges from Denmark, through a wild area (later a part of Russia), and on to Constantinople in the heart of the Byzantine

Empire. What occurs on this strange journey and how Jestyn finally realizes his own destiny—which is quite different from the restless warrior life into which he has been drawn—makes exciting and thought-provoking reading and offers new insights on a little-known part of history. This splendid book is currently out of print but is still in libraries.

Sutcliff, Rosemary. *Sword Song.* Farrar, Straus and Giroux, 1997, 272 pp. (7-up).

This last book of the late Rosemary Sutcliff, distinguished writer of historical fiction for young people, combines swashbuckling adventure with the perceptively developed character of Bjorni Sigurdson, a Viking swordsman. Exiled for five years from his home village for an unintentional killing, Bjorni is on his own at sixteen in the rigorous world of Viking raids, warring Scottish chieftains, and the unrelenting need to earn the food, clothing, and minimal shelter that mean survival. Accompanied by his great black hound, the only living creature with a place in his heart, Bjorni becomes a soldier of fortune. The Christian message of love and forgiveness is known by some, but its followers are far outnumbered by those committed to the fierce Viking philosophy of battle and conquest or to the clan violence of the Scottish and others. But Bjorni meets people from whom he learns and begins to see with a maturing perception the effects of life based on ceaseless conflict. Adventures, misfortunes, and in-the-nick-of-time respite characterize the five years in which he grows to manhood. When near the end of his exile he encounters a courageous girl who has, through an enemy's greed and violence, lost all left to her by her slain family, he finds he has a new perspective on the future and his choice of a way of life.

Terhune, Albert Payson. *Lad: A Dog.* Buccaneer, 1981 (1919), 286 pp. (5-up).

This and a number of other Terhune titles comprise the stories of the wonderful collies of Sunnybank. The tales are exciting and eventful, but they are written in a dated and sometimes highly sentimentalized manner. They are, however, enjoyable and cheerful reading for lovers of dog stories.

Twain, Mark. *The Adventures of Tom Sawyer.* Dodd, Mead, 1958 (1876), 307 pp. (6-up).

A perennial classic, the story of boyhood in a small nineteenth-century Missouri town. Tom and the fence-painting episode, his embarrassed fondness for Becky Thatcher, and a number of the other story elements are firmly interwoven into the fabric of traditional American culture. Tom Sawyer provides a good introduction to the work of one of the prominent figures in American literature. Reading the book aloud encourages discussion and analysis of Twain's humor and insight, as well as his attitudes toward the cultural patterns of his day and toward the church and Christianity.

Twain, Mark. *The Prince and the Pauper.* Harper and Row, 1909 (1882), 296 pp. (5-up).

Twain's famous classic about young Prince Edward and Tom Canty, his beggar-boy look-alike. In writing this exciting and imaginative story of the two boys' exchange of roles, Twain was not only weaving an entertaining tale, but also show-ing how cruel and inhumane some of the laws and customs of mid-sixteenth-cen-tury England were. A challenging level of language is maintained, and the historical material incorporated into the background relates effectively to the study of English history.

Verne, Jules. *Michael Strogoff: A Courier of the Czar*. Airmont, 1964 (1876), 397 pp. (6-up).

An exciting adventure story set in nineteenth-century Russia, in which a heroic young man, Michael Strogoff, journeys through thousands of dangerous miles to save western Siberia from disaster at the hands of the savage Tartars.

Walsh, Jill Paton. *Children of the Fox*. Farrar, Straus and Giroux, 1978, 114 pp. (5, 6).

Three stories of courage and adventure set in the fifth-century Grecian world. Although the young people of the stories are fictional, the historical events are not, and of course the Athenian general Themistokles, the Spartan leader Pausanias, and others mentioned are people from history. Well-written and entertaining as well as offering excellent ancient-world historical background. Currently out of print, the book is still in libraries and is worth looking for.

Wiggin, Kate Douglas. *Rebecca of Sunnybrook Farm*. Houghton Mifflin, 1925 (1903), 355 pp. (5, 6-up).

Written almost a century ago, this lively story of a young girl's passage from childhood to early womanhood holds up despite its age. Excellent values of patience, sacrifice, and aspiration are underscored, but in a fresh and far from stuffy manner. Humor and happy solutions offer a good balance to the more serious side of this story that has been a favorite with girls since its first appearance.

Willis, Patricia. *Danger Along the Ohio*. Clarion Books, 1997, 181 pp. (4-7).

It is 1793; one of the many families moving west—Amos, Clara, Jonathan, and their widowed father—have left eastern Pennsylvania for land in the Ohio coun-try. Floating down the Ohio River on a flatboat, the youngsters are separated from their father when Indians attack. Hiding from the Indians, the children decide to try to follow the river to Marietta, their planned destination, hoping their father will be there when they arrive. Alone, without food, tools, or weapons, the trio's problems multiply when, only a day into their trek, Amos insists on rescuing an injured and drowning Indian boy from the river.

Suspenseful, fast-paced, and spiced with humor, the story carries the reader along with the struggles of the three likable young pioneers. The specific details of their searches for food, the efforts to avoid being seen by Indians who are not far away, the discussions and decisions among the three, and the ways in which they deal with fears and setbacks provide consistent credibility as they win through with courage, ingenuity, and risky kindness to an enemy in need.

Wyss, Johann David. *The Swiss Family Robinson*. Sharon Publications, 1981 (1814), 432 pp. (5, 6-up).

The much-loved classic story of a Swiss family shipwrecked at sea who find refuge on an island and create for themselves a home and way of life. Difficulties, adventures, ingenious inventions, and surprising discoveries abound. This is another of the wonderful classics that has been trivialized in mass media forms. As originally written, the language and attitudes of the past are clearly reflected, and there is an explicitly godly tone. This is a splendid book to read aloud over a period of weeks.

15

LITERATURE: ANTHOLOGIES
Stories, Poems, and Rhymes

Bennett, William J., editor. *The Children's Book of Heroes*. Illus. by Michael Hague. Simon and Schuster, 1997, 111 pp. (2-6).

> Primary listing under *Bible/Spiritual and Moral Teaching*
>
> This splendid, beautifully illustrated collection of twenty-one poems, stories, and biographical accounts ranges from suspenseful adventure to compassionate service, from faraway lands to American ballparks. Some of its heroes are famous historical figures; others are largely unknown. Some are found in myth and legend; others are fictional characters of the contemporary scene. One and all, they demonstrate the "worthy actions" of true heroes that Bennett mentions in the book's introduction.

Bennett, William J., editor. *The Children's Book of Virtues*. Illus. by Michael Hague. Simon and Schuster, 1995, 111 pp. (ps-up).

> Primary listing under *Bible/Spiritual and Moral Teaching*
>
> A treasure for the family library. Wonderful little poems, fables, and stories that have long been a part of our literary tradition are grouped under headings such as "Courage," "Honesty," "Friendship," "Perseverance," and others. Parents, you may have wished you could read your child the poem that encourages, "If at first you don't succeed, try, try, again"—but what are the rest of the poem's words, and where can you find the poem? Or you may know that your children would love the story of the little Dutch boy who put his finger in the leaking dike and saved his town—but you only remember the bare bones of the story. And what about "The Lion and the Mouse," and "The Boy Who Cried Wolf?" All stories you want your children to know. These and many more are found in this beautifully illustrated book—one you will want to preserve for your grandchildren.

Bennett, William J., editor. *The Book of Virtues for Young People*. Silver Burdett Press, 1996, 378 pp. (5-up).

> Primary listing under *Bible/Spiritual and Moral Teaching*
>
> Like Bennett's *Children's Book of Virtues* (listed above), this collection combines pleasurable reading with challenging moral emphases. The 116 stories, folk tales, and poems are grouped in categories: "Self-Discipline," "Courage," "Responsibility," "Honesty," and six other equally important qualities of character. Bennett has written short introductions to each of these sections, explaining

clearly just what each quality involves. Whether a particular reading selection is one of Aesop's timeless fables, an exciting story from the life of a historical figure, a rousing poem, a tale of quiet heroism or keen wisdom, each one powerfully demonstrates in an appealing form a particular characteristic a young person should appreciate and want to work at developing. A fine collection and a wonderful resource for reading aloud.

Brewton, Sara and John E. and J. B. Blackburn (compiled by). *Of Quarks, Quasars and Other Quirks: Quizzical Poems for the Supersonic Age.* Crowell, 1990 (1977), 128 pp. (5-up).

A collection of short poems by a variety of poets, focusing on topics particularly related to space-age phenomena/technology. Many of the poems are humorous, some ironic, and some designed to question or criticize.

Cole, William (selected by). *Poem Stew.* Lippincott-Raven, 1981, 96 pp. (all ages).

A wonderful collection of rhymes about food—clever, funny, great to listen to and learn.

Ferris, Helen (selected by). *Favorite Poems Old and New.* Doubleday, 1957, 640 pp. (all ages).

More than 700 poems for children attractively presented in a pleasingly chunky anthology. This is a well-selected collection and a delight to browse through.

Note: The "new" poems of the book's title were, of course, new at the time of the book's publication forty-five years ago.

Opie, Iona and Peter Opie (chosen and edited by). *The Oxford Book of Children's Verse.* Oxford University Press, 1973, 407 pp. (all ages).

This is a splendid collection of children's verse, the sort of book that becomes a family treasure. The Opies, whose lifework was the gathering and evaluating of the literature of childhood, have chosen poems of wide-ranging appeal from the fourteenth century through the contemporary era. The verses are arranged chronologically, and a wonderful "Authors and Sources" section at the end of the book provides brief biographical information about the poets and discusses the circumstances surrounding the poem's writing. This collection should not be confused with the Opies' book on nursery rhymes, listed next.

Opie, Iona and Peter Opie (chosen and edited by). *The Oxford Dictionary of Nursery Rhymes.* Oxford University Press, rev. 1998 (1951, originally titled *The Oxford Book of Nursery Rhymes*), 588 pp. (all ages).

The definitive volume of nursery rhymes, this book is a fine companion to the Opies' book of children's poetry (see above). The hundreds of rhymes in the collection represent years of research on the Opies' part. Included are the 150 most familiar rhymes, along with many others less well known. All of these are a part of our English language heritage, but aside from their literary and cultural value, research indicates that children who listen to and learn nursery rhymes enjoy more being read to and learn to read more easily. The pleasing rhythms and wide variety of sound patterns lay a helpful foundation for later facility with written language.

Plotz, Helen, editor. *The Gift Outright: America to Her Poets.* Greenwillow Books, 1977, 204 pp. (all ages).

Plotz has assembled a fine collection of poems about America by noted poets from the seventeenth century to the modern era. In addition to their literary value, many of these poems relate interestingly to American history and to the lives of famous Americans. Currently out of print but still in many libraries or available through interlibrary loan.

Prelutsky, Jack (selected by). *The 20th Century Children's Poetry Treasury.* Illus. by Meilo So. Alfred A. Knopf, Inc., 1999, 87 pp. (all ages).

An enjoyable, something-for-everyone collection. Included are more than 200 poems by thirty-six poets, all written during the 1900s and enhanced by So's lovely illustrations on each page. Humor, nature, animals, emotions, machines, food, illness, the environment, weather, sounds, music, and more—all are poetry-inspiring. Just dip in and enjoy!

Pullein-Thompson, Diana, editor. *Classic Horse and Pony Stories.* Illus. by Neal Puddephat. DK Publishing, 1999, 96 pp. (4-up).

Wonderful for reading aloud, this fine collection of stories can also provide an extra benefit for middle-grades children who have been reluctant to tackle substantial books. A number of the book's eleven stories are "stand-alone" episodes from favorite classics. "Live Cargo," for example, is from *Misty of Chincoteague,* "My Breaking In," from *Black Beauty,* and "My Friend Flicka," from the novel of the same name. (The books just mentioned are listed in this work.) These appealing selections, enlivened by the artist's superb illustrations, will charm many listeners (or solo readers) into wanting to know more about the wonderful animals, intriguing characters, and exciting events by reading the entire books the stories come from.

Also included following each story is a full page of illustrated background information related to the story's focus. After "Live Cargo," for example, the page about "New World Horses" tells how horses were brought from Europe to the New World starting in the 1500s. It is a nice touch that on all these special pages the factual material is illustrated with the realism of photographs, while the beautiful drawings that accompany the stories bring to life their world of the imagination.

16

LITERATURE: POETRY AND RHYMES

See "Anthologies" (chapter 15) for collections of poems by various writers.

Burleigh, Robert. *Goal*. Illus. by Stephen T. Johnson. Harcourt, Inc., 2001, 30 pp. (3-up).

    In the compressed language of poetry, Burleigh captures the volatile emotions, controlled focus, and hunger for victory in a school-age kids' soccer game. Johnson's vibrant in-motion drawings (done in pastels) complement the poem step by step. Enjoyable simply to read and look at, the book could also be effectively used as a model for aspiring young poets.

de Gasztold, Carmen Bernos. *Prayers from the Ark*. NAL-Dutton, 1976 (1962), 71 pp. (all ages).

    Perceptive and imaginative poems that capture the distinctives of a number of animals and birds, and use these characteristics to express a variety of ways in which the human spirit can offer itself, *its* distinctives, to God.

Folk song. *Hush Little Baby: A Folk Song with Pictures*. Illus. by Marla Frazee. Browndeer Press, 1999, 33 pp. (ps-2).

    Primary listing under *Music*

    Don't miss this singing-rhyme picture book—an instant favorite. The book was researched in the hills of West Virginia (where the song has its Appalachian roots), and the pictures are a delight as the whole family tries to coax the screaming baby to stop howling and go to sleep. Most of us remember "Hush little baby, don't say a word; Papa's gonna buy you a mocking bird." (The melody notes and all the verses are on the book's last page.) Each line of the song has its own two-page picture spread. Sing the words to a little one as you turn the pages.

Frost, Robert. *You Come Too*. Holt, 1995 (1959), 96 pp. (6-up).

    The poet chose this selection of his work to be read to, and by, young people. Frost's life included frequent contact with children, and he especially enjoyed making this collection of his poems that were their favorites.

George, Kristine O'Connell. *Little Dog Poems*. Illus. by June Otami. Clarion Books, 1999, 40 pp. (ps-up).

Small children will love this appealing book of poems—and so will older children and adults who know and love dogs. Both the brief, deftly phrased poems and the lovely watercolor illustrations reflect an understanding of dog nature and behavior and a deep fondness for these beloved companions. Thirty little poems—perceptive, humorous, loving—follow a small girl and Little Dog through a variety of doings. "Oops! Little Dog is not allowed/to have people food/Sometimes I have accidents/with my popcorn." A warm and endearing book.

George, Kristine O'Connell. *Toasting Marshmallows: Camping Poems*. Illus. by Kate Kiesler. Clarion Books, 2001, 48 pp. (3-up).

Reflective, humorous, companionable, nostalgic, awed by beauty—thirty perceptively written poems capture the essence of a family camping trip. Beautifully complemented by the illustrator's paintings, the evocative lines of the poems take the reader into a lovely wilderness of flower-strewn meadows, tall trees, and great mountains, flowing water, glimpses of wildlife, glowing campfires. Just right for reading aloud or for a cozy read-alone by a nature-loving child.

Grimes, Nikki. *Stepping Out with Grandma Mac*. Illus. by Angelo. Orchard Books, 2001, 39 pp. (3-up).

An appealing book of poems about the complex, close relationship between a feisty grandmother and a granddaughter. Grandma Mac had to struggle when she was young, scrubbing and polishing for affluent families. "So when I gripe about homework, / Grandma reminds me/ How earning a G. E. D./ Got her off her knees,/ And by the time/ She's done preaching,/ My math book gleams/ Like gold." (From "Homework.") The poem "Radio City" finds the two of them in a long line, shivering in the cold as they slowly move toward the ticket booth. "I would mind more/ Except that Grandma/ Who normally/ Avoids touching/ Grabs my hand/ Sticks it in/The warm well/ Of her coat pocket/ And holds it there/ What seems like/ Forever." Such a few words, but just the right words to say so much; it's poetry.

Hines, Anna Grossnickle. *Pieces: A Year in Poems & Quilts*. Greenwillow Books, 2001, 30 pp. (all ages).

In an inspired melding of verse and quilted art, Anna Hines has created a charming and unusual book. Moving through the seasons of a year, each of twenty poems is shown on a background of beautifully designed color and pattern. For example, the words of "Good Heavens" are seen against a deep blue sky that blends into a grassy green below. "Our lawn is astronomical/with dandelion blooms./A green sky filled/with a thousand suns/and then/a thousand moons/that with a puff/of wind become/a hundred thousand stars." Tiny triangular snippets—miniature quilt pieces in golden tones for the blossoms and white for the airy seed puffs—dot the background. On the facing page the tiny quilt repeats the sun, moon, stars motif more fully with its intricately contrived patchwork. Each double-page spread is a photographic reproduction of an actual quilt, its design reflecting the theme of a poem; an adventure in imaginative word pictures and quilted artistry. Two fascinating pages on "The Story Behind the Quilts" are included with a bibliography and an Internet location for quilting information.

Jarrell, Randall. *The Bat Poet*. Illus. by Maurice Sendak. HarperCollins Children's Books, 1997 (1964), 48 pp. (3-up).

Poet Jarrell talks about the making of poems, the lack of audience for poetry in today's world, the varied response to poetry—and does it all in a story about a bat who is also a poet. Several delightful poems are included as part of the story. A very special book—try reading it aloud and watch for individual response.

Johnson, James Weldon. Ed. by Paul Edwards. *The Creation: A Poem*. Illus. by Carla Golembe. Little, Brown, and Co., 1993, 30 pp. (ps-up).

The sonorous rhythms of the poem, written eighty years ago, have been visually imaged in striking monotype—an artist's technique that combines painting with printmaking. The writer's colorful imagery of the creation of the world is reflected in colors and forms against the monotype's dark background. Johnson wanted the poem to echo the spoken rhythms of an African-American preacher as he painted, for his congregation, vivid word-pictures of God's acts of creation—so mighty, yet so involved with varied detail. The poem's magisterial voice in company with the artist's sometimes dramatic, sometimes playful graphics indeed realizes the writer's original intent. Children will warmly respond to the rich sounds and rhythms of the poem and the unique creation-themed art.

Keats, Ezra Jack. *Over in the Meadow*. Illus. by Ezra Jack Keats. Puffin Books, 1999 (1971), 20 pp. (ps-3).

First published three decades ago, this lovely book has been reissued. Beloved children's writer and illustrator Ezra Jack Keats (1916-1983) created a wonderful series of charming and whimsical illustrations that go perfectly with the meadowland setting of an old Appalachian counting rhyme that starts, "Over in the meadow, in the sand, in the sun,/ Lived an old mother turtle and her little turtle one." Each number—up to ten—is related to a different mother-creature of the wild and her young. Excellent for counting practice, but the choice of words, the captivating rhythm, and the charming illustrations give the book a literary and artistic value quite apart from its numerical reinforcement. A wide range of each era's young children have taken it to their hearts.

Lear, Edward. *The Complete Nonsense of Edward Lear*. Dover, 1951 (1912), 320 pp. (4-6).

All of Lear's delightful rhymes, limericks, poems ("The Owl and the Pussy Cat," "The Jumblies," and "The Quangle Wangle's Hat" are probably the best known), and nonsense alphabets. Nothing else takes the place of this classic collection of fun with language.

O'Neill, Mary. *Hailstones and Halibut Bones*. Doubleday, 1989 (1961), 59 pp. (all ages).

Twelve poems about colors. The form and style of the poetry itself are not outstanding, but the metaphors used enhance sensory perception and encourage new ways of seeing. "And in the fall/When the leaves are turning/Orange is the smell/Of a bonfire burning."

Prelutsky, Jack. *It's Raining Pigs and Noodles*. Illus. by James Stevenson. HarperCollins Children's Books, 2000 (1993), 159 pp. (all ages).

Lots of nonsense, lots of fun with words and sounds. "It's raining pigs and noodles," the poem begins, "it's pouring frogs and hats,/chrysanthemums and poodles,/bananas, brooms and cats." And after another ten lines it ends, "I like this so much better/than when it's raining rain." James Stevenson's wonderful black-and-white sketches romp through the pages, whimsically picturing Prelutsky's zany images. It's all for giggles, chortles, and guffaws, but parents and teachers may want to note that the rhymes are also full of good stretching exercises for the vocabulary—and for the imagination. Great to read aloud!

Schaefer, Lola M. *This Is the Sunflower*. Illus. by Donald Crews. Greenwillow Books, 2000, 23 pp. (ps-3).

In the form known as "cumulative verse" ("The House That Jack Built" is a well-known example), this bright and bouncy rhyme describes, with accompanying illustrations, the golden, beaming sunflower. Blossom and seed-bearer, it not only delights the eye and warms the heart, but its seeds provide a favorite food for a variety of birds. A double-page spread at the book's center pictures the heads—with their "beaks sharp and strong"—of seventeen different kinds of birds as they "crack the seeds, black and brown." Young children will enjoy hearing the verse read over and over as the pages with their rural scenes, beaming golden flowers, bright green foliage, and blue sky are turned. A joyful combination of rhythmic beat, appealing language, and information about one of God's happiest creations.

Spires, Elizabeth. *The Mouse of Amherst*. Illus. by Claire A. Nivola. Farrar, Straus and Giroux, 1999, 64 pp. (3-7).

Also listed under *Literature Level III—Fantasies*

A charming book that could serve as an introduction to the work of poet Emily Dickinson (1830-1886). The whimsical fantasy of Emmaline, a white mouse who lives for a time behind the wainscot of Emily Dickinson's bedroom, deals with (among other things) Emmaline's heartfelt response to Dickinson's poems. Eight of the poet's best-loved poems are included, and seven of Emmaline's. Spires's book offers a wonderful opportunity for a young reader to learn about the poet and to read some of her distinctively created, evocative poems in an enjoyable setting.

Stevenson, James. *Just Around the Corner: Poems*. Greenwillow Books, 2001, 56 pp. (3-up).

A whimsical and imaginative collection of short poems. "Classroom" has an admission to make: "When I raised my hand in class,/ It didn't mean I knew the answer./ Far from it./ I was hoping the answer might float by,/ And I could catch it like a butterfly."

Stevenson, Robert Louis. *A Child's Garden of Verses.* Illus. by Alice and Martin Provensen. Simon and Schuster, 1951 (1885), 76 pp. (ps-up).

This beloved children's classic is still able to charm its readers. No child should be denied the opportunity to open his or her heart to "I should like to rise and go/Where the golden apples grow;—/Where below another sky/Parrot islands anchored lie,/And, watched by cockatoos and goats,/Lonely Crusoes building boats;—" (from "Travel") and all the other perceptive verses that reflect so timelessly and enjoyably the world of childhood. Because of the book's lasting popularity, there are many different editions, produced by a number of publishers. Three of the many, in addition to the one listed above, are illustrated by popular children's artists Tasha Tudor (Macmillan), Jessie Willcox Smith (Scribner's), and Brian Wildsmith (Oxford University Press).

Stevenson, Robert Louis. *My Shadow.* Illus. by Penny Dale. Candlewick Press, 1999, 20 pp. (ps-3).

Artist/author Penny Dale has taken one of Stevenson's timeless, beloved poems and wonderfully pictured the poem's narrator bringing the words of "My Shadow" to life. Sometimes alone and sometimes with other children, the lovable tot frolics through changing scenes, musing about the strange nature and changing size of that persistent shadow companion. The imaginative and widely varying shadows are not only surprising and funny; they also invite little readers to notice their own shadows and try some shadow-making themselves. This is, of course, over and above the sheer pleasure of letting the rhythms and sounds fill the consciousness: "I have a little shadow that goes in and out with me. . . ."

17

MATHEMATICS

Anno, Masaichiro and Mitsumasa. *Anno's Mysterious Multiplying Jar*. Philomel Books, 1983, 48 pp. (2-5).

Artist and scholar Mitsumasa Anno (sometimes in collaboration with son Masaichiro) writes for children about mathematics in a way that adds color and even a degree of suspense to a subject often perceived as dull and tiresome. In this account, the Annos start with a large, beautiful, imagined jar. Illustrations accompany the narrative, as a little water in the jar becomes a rippling sea, and "On the sea was 1 island." The narrative continues: There are 2 countries on the 1 island, 3 mountains within each of the 2 countries, and the story proceeds in this manner with each successive unit—walled kingdoms on the mountains, villages in the kingdoms, houses in the villages, rooms in the houses, cupboards in the rooms, boxes in the cupboards—containing one number higher of the objects until the final accumulation: "Within each box there were 10 jars." The Annos then ask, "But how many jars were in all the boxes together?" The answer (which I will refrain from giving away) is utterly astounding. A mathematical symbol for the huge total is 10! factorial and is the result of multiplying 10x9x8x7x6x5x4x3x2x1. The writers go on to explain the process step by step. It is not a game but a mathematical method of calculation used routinely—and the writers detail some of these uses. A fascinating and clearly stated account that will rivet the attention of anyone interested in figures and calculations.

Bendick, Jeanne. *Archimedes and the Door of Science*. Living History Library. Bethlehem Books, 1995 (1962), 143 pp. (5, 6-up).

Primary listing under *Biography*

Born in 287 B.C., the Greek mathematician Archimedes is considered by many to be the single most important person in the history of mathematics. The things he discovered are basic to much of all later mathematical knowledge. The writer tells interestingly, in clear, simple terms, of some of Archimedes' work and of the later knowledge based on what he first discovered. Along with discussions of mathematical concepts is background information on Archimedes' life and the culture of his time. Now in print again, this book was originally part of the wonderful old series Immortals of Science.

Caron, Lucille, and Philip M. St. Jacques. *Geometry*. Enslow Publishers, Inc., 2001, 64 pp. (5-up).

This clear and concise book is written to be used at a youngster's own pace. Some kids find mathematics fascinating and satisfying and would like to forge ahead of their grade level into more complex areas when they have already mastered all the material they have been given. They could find Caron and St. Jacques's book just the sort of thing they want to get into. On the other hand, for older students already struggling with geometry, finding it lacking in interest or difficult to understand, this well-done and simply stated book could prove helpful, especially in the hands of an assisting parent or math-inclined friend.

Charosh, Mannis. *Number Ideas Through Pictures*. HarperCollins Children's Books, 1974, 40 pp. (1-5).
   Approaching numbers through play will give many children a feel for some of the inventive possibilities in mathematics. Using small objects (or drawing them), then following the patterns in the book, children are introduced to the concepts of odd and even numbers, combinations of these, consecutive numbers, square and triangular numbers. Approaching mathematical concepts in this way is especially helpful as a supplemental resource for children who tend to feel stressed in the world of numbers.

Cole, Joanna and Stephanie Calmenson. *Rain or Shine Activity Book*. Illus. by Alan Tiegreen. Morrow Junior Books, 1997, 192 pp. (all ages).
   Primary listing under *Crafts, Hobbies, and Domestic Arts*
   The "Brainteasers" chapter in this big book that includes a variety of activities has several math-related games. See the *Crafts* entry for more details on the book's contents.

Dilson, Jesse. *The Abacus: A Brief History of the World's First Computing System & How to Use It*. St. Martin's Press, 1995 (1968), 143 pp. (5-8).
   For centuries people have used the abacus for computing. Widely used in Asia, a skilled user can operate an abacus with lightning speed—even winning contests against computers, impossible as this seems. The writer explains the principle on which the abacus is based, discusses its history, talks about its continuing use in Asia and in Soviet schools—and gives directions for making one.

Duke, Kate. *Twenty Is Too Many*. Dutton Children's Books, 2000, 45 pp. (k-2).
   This entertaining picture-book introduction to subtraction is designed to make a sometimes unpopular mathematical process both clear and enjoyable. The author/illustrator starts with a cast of twenty amusingly outfitted guinea pigs on an overloaded little boat. "But twenty sinking guinea pigs minus ten diving guinea pigs leaves ten floating guinea pigs" reads the line of text, with the large "20 -10 =10" figures shown above. From that point on, the number is reduced by subtracting guinea pigs one by one, until just one is left. Each page is full of color and interest, with the playful guinea pigs seen cavorting and playing against the background of sea, sandy shore, palm trees, chest of pirate treasure, and more. With an adult at hand to share the fun (and emphasize the subtraction), young readers should find themselves in a happy process of learning (or reinforcing) an important skill.

Froman, Robert. *Less Than Nothing Is Really Something*. Harper Children's Books, 1973, 33 pp. (1-5).

A beginning-level introduction to negative numbers. The concepts of adding, subtracting, multiplying, or dividing using both negative and positive numbers often causes students difficulty at some point in their math study. A clear grasp of some of the facts that are explained simply in this book can be very helpful. (For example, -2 is one more than -3, etc.) The number line, with its graphic representation of the fact that moving to the right from the central dividing point between the positive and negative numbers represents one more at each step, while moving to the left from the same point reverses the process, helps visually to reinforce the concept.

Gardner, Martin. *Entertaining Mathematical Puzzles*. Illus. by Anthony Ravielli. Dover Publications, Inc., 1986 (1961), 111 pp. (6-up).

A plentiful supply of old and new puzzles divided into categories: money, speed, probability, topology, and more groupings. Each section is headed with a discussion of the nature and importance of the kind of mathematics to be used in solving the puzzles in that particular group. Gardner explains the solution (shown at the end of each problem) in detail and makes suggestions as to further paths that can be pursued with this type of problem. Using a light, witty style, the writer obviously enjoys mathematics and wants his readers to share the fun.

Geisert, Arthur. *Roman Numerals I to MM*. Houghton Mifflin, 1996, 32 pp. (k-3).

This is an original and enjoyable book with a serious purpose—mastering the use of Roman numerals. Author and gifted etcher Arthur Geisert moves immediately into the basics of his subject with the statement that every number can be written in Roman numerals, choosing from just the seven possible components: I, V, X, L, C, D, and M. He then graphically illustrates the value of each one: He has the reader start counting little pigs. "Count the number of pigs to find the value of each numeral." Each number (I, V, X, and the rest) is shown clearly at the left side of an illustration of a pig farm full of all sorts of fascinating details, meticulously etched. One little pig appears for "I"; five little pigs for "V," and so on. Yes, there are a thousand piglets on the double-page spread for "M." Throughout, the key to it all is twofold. First, count, count, count, becoming completely familiar with the value of each of the numerals; then think, think, think—should you add or subtract the numerals beside each other? Second, practice using Roman numerals, becoming very comfortable with them. Great fun, worthwhile knowledge.

Gies, Frances and Joseph. *Leonard of Pisa and the New Mathematics of the Middle Ages*. New Classics Library, 1983 (1969), 128 pp. (6-up).

Italy was one of the prominent European powers during the Middle Ages, and both the scholars and traders of its wealthy, bustling cities had frequent contacts with their counterparts in the Moslem world. Thus it was that at the beginning of the thirteenth century a brilliant young mathematician, Leonard Fibonacci of the city of Pisa, had learned of the Hindu-Arabic system of numerals and eventually wrote a book on this system. This book, in time, revolutionized mathematics. It is true that small numbers of European scholars here and there had known of the

Hindu-Arabic numeration, but knowledge of it was not being developed or used in the West. (It is these Arabic numerals that we use today and on which whole areas of modern scientific inquiry rely.) The Gieses' book includes fascinating material on the two spheres of influence of the Mediterranean and European medieval world—the nominally Christian and the Moslem. This is a scholarly but lively account of the life and work of a key figure in mathematics who is little known or written about. Excellent for advanced students and for parents and teachers.

Keats, Ezra Jack. *Over in the Meadow*. Illus. by Ezra Jack Keats. Puffin Books, 1999 (1971), 20 pp. (ps-3).

Primary listing under *Literature: Poetry and Rhymes*

Reissued recently, this appealing book combines an old Appalachian counting rhyme with delightful illustrations. A mother-creature of the meadowland and her offspring—a different group for each number from one to ten—are engaged in a variety of activities: digging, swimming, singing, and so forth. Youngsters will thoroughly enjoy the rhyming count and the entertaining pictures.

Knapp, Brian and Colin Bass. *Tables and Charts*. Math Matters! Series. Grolier Educational Corporation, 1999, 48 pp. (4-7).

Effectively written and illustrated, this user-friendly supplement does an excellent job of showing students how to demonstrate number information (data) graphically. The basic concepts involved for a variety of charts and tables are clearly described, and step-by-step instructions are given for their use. Tallying, grouping data, lengths of time, rainfall totals, percentage, and spread charts are just some of the areas covered. A glossary of terms and a detailed index of the contents are included.

Leedy, Loreen. *Measuring Penny*. Illus. by author. Henry Holt and Co., 1997, 29 pp. (2-up).

Lisa learns about the mathematics of measurement by measuring a variety of the dimensions of her jaunty Boston terrier, Penny—and some of Penny's canine friends. The basics of measuring are delightfully—and effectively—described, using both standard (inches, centimeters, cups, pounds, for example) and nonstandard (paperclips, bricks, pencils, toes) units of measurement. Comparative weights, the amounts of water and food Penny consumes each day, the amount of time Lisa spends with her, and other measurable Penny-related elements are included. The author has her own real-life Boston terrier as a model, and the book's illustrations are quite irresistible, combining a posterlike simplicity with appealingly lifelike expressions and poses. Young readers will be drawn into duplicating Lisa's measuring experiences and will learn an important mathematical concept and a new skill.

Linn, Charles F. *Probability*. HarperCollins Children's Books, 1972, 40 pp. (4-6).

Examples of probability estimates are shown. The concept is illustrated; then a number of sample problems/experiments in probability are given. This is a helpful supplemental resource, one students will enjoy using.

Murphy, Stuart J. *Room for Ripley*. Illus. by Sylvie Wickerstrom. HarperCollins Children's Books, 1999, 33 pp. (2-up).

An effective combination of story and lesson. As the reader follows the preparations Carlos makes for a new pet guppy, the idea of measuring capacity is clearly explained. He puts water into a fishbowl cup by cup; two cups equal a pint, and two more make a quart. Carlos continues measuring and adding up to the half-gallon and finally the gallon quantities. All the measuring is illustrated, and the equivalencies shown clearly. The concept is amplified as the water level in the bowl rises higher with each addition. The story component moves enjoyably along. Carlos's sister Ana gets out her old fishbowl and accessory equipment; the two prepare the bowl, talk about what they are doing, and go to the pet store. Once they have put the guppy in its new home, Ana even has a special surprise for Carlos. The concluding two pages of the book are titled, "For Adults and Kids," and have suggestions for further ways of using the measuring concept presented. Colorful, lively illustrations are very much a part of this pleasing and helpful book.

Note: For readers wanting to prepare a fishbowl or tank for fish, see also *Me and My Pet Fish* by Christine Morley and Carole Orbell, listed under *Animals*.

Sitomer, Mindel and Harry. *Zero Is Not Nothing*. HarperCollins Children's Books, 1978, 34 pp. (1-3).

The basic mathematical principle of the zero is explained clearly. Its importance and historical background are discussed; then practical applications of its use are detailed. In addition to its crucial function as a place holder, the zero is also used in a variety of other important ways. Clear illustrations illumine the concepts throughout. An excellent supplemental mathematics resource.

Stonaker, Frances Benson. *Famous Mathematicians*. Harper and Row, 1966, 118 pp. (4-9).

The stories of eleven famous mathematicians down through the ages. Each account, written in a lively, popular style, is of necessity only a summary of the person's life and work. The material does offer good general information and serves as an introduction for the reader who wants to dig more deeply into a specific mathematician's achievements. For the student who does not expect to concentrate especially on math, it provides the basic identification of important mathematicians that is so beneficial to a well-rounded education. Though out of print, Stonaker's book is still available in many libraries and through interlibrary loan.

Wegman, William. *Triangle Square Circle*. Hyperion, 1995, 12 pp. (ps-k).

Using his dogs along with a variety of brightly colored basic shapes, Wegman has created an effective tool to help children recognize and name common shapes (triangle, square, for example—shapes often related to mathematical problems). The pages of this sturdy "board" book are easy for small children to turn, and the pictures' association of each shape with an amusing and appealing dog sharpens the reader's focus on exactly how each shape looks.

18

MISCELLANEOUS

Chorao, Kay. *Shadow Night: A Picture Book with Shadow Play*. Dutton Children's Books, 2001, 29 pp. (ps-1).

Primary listing under *Literature: Level I, Realistic Stories—Modern*

Chorao's comforting and cozily illustrated story of James, who is afraid of the shadows on his wall, includes a number of hand-shadow ideas and a concluding page of directions and suggestions for successful shadow-making. This simple—and very old—form of amusement is one that young children especially enjoy.

Douglas, Ann. *Before You Were Born: The Inside Story*. Illus. by Eugenie Fernandes. Photographs by Gilbert Duclos. Owl Books, 2000, 32 pp. (ps-up).

This especially well-done book personalizes for children their life before birth: "You know what you look like now," it begins. "You see yourself in the mirror every day. But have you ever wondered what you looked like *before* you were born?" Down to earth, yet never tasteless, the writer's narrative explains the remarkable process: "At the beginning of your life, you were a tiny egg that was smaller than a grain of salt." Drawings and photographs (in color) complement and illustrate each detail of the text. In addition to the prebirth sequence of growth and development shown chronologically through the book, on each two-page spread a circular inset gives further information. Even many mothers will be surprised at some of the little-known facts that will intrigue children—and often greatly amuse them. Perhaps the most endearing quality of the book, however, is the atmosphere of joy, anticipation, and love that characterizes the mother's wait for her baby to be born. Children will cherish this book, and the younger ones will want to hear it read over and over. A delightful book to give to mothers of very small children.

Kalman, Bobbie. *Games from Long Ago*. Illus. by Barbara Bedell. Historic Communities Series. Crabtree Publishing Company, 1995, 32 pp. (1-9).

Enhanced by colorful and often amusing illustrations reflecting nineteenth-century settings in this country, the text describes the games children played then. Children have played many of the same games for almost 200 years, although less frequently in recent decades. The writer has focused on each kind of game in turn. "Silly parlor games," "word games," "board games," "holiday games," and "classroom games" are just some of the many discussed. Young readers might enjoy choosing games that sound like the most fun and spend an evening playing these with family or friends—with much hilarity sure to ensue!

Lasky, Kathryn. *A Baby for Max*. Photographs by Christopher G. Knight. Charles Scribner's Sons, 1984, 48 pp. (ps-up).

Children's author Kathryn Lasky, her husband, photographer Christopher Knight, and their almost-five son, Max, await the arrival of their new baby. Lasky records Max's words as he talks about the coming child—and later after the little sister has arrived. Dad photographs everyone, recording visually the anticipation, impatience, and speculation that Max's words express as he waits—and later his reaction to tiny Meribah herself, whom he has been learning to love before her birth.

It has been sixteen years since Max's mother put together this book. Still in print, its simplicity and joy reflect an atmosphere that has been shared countless times with other families, and with other small children whose whole known world is being changed around them. This is a lovely book to read aloud and to give to still more families.

Love, Ann and Jane Drake. *Kids and Grandparents: An Activity Book*. Illus. by Heather Collins. Kids Can Press, 2000, 160 pp. (1-up).

Also listed under *Crafts, Growing Plants,* and *Outdoor Activities*

Among the book's more than ninety ideas and how-to's are a number of indoor games that kids and their grandparents will enjoy playing together: Toothpick Teasers, the old Chinese game of NIM, Tangram pictures, card games and tricks, marble games, and jacks, to name a few. Another great idea is story-taping, something that will keep the memories of the past alive for young readers now, and someday for *their* children. See the other listings given above for more about other activities suggested.

Marzollo, Jean. *I Spy Extreme Challenger: A Book of Picture Riddles*. Photographs by Walter Wick. Scholastic, Inc., 2000, 31 pp. (4-up).

Thirteen two-page-spread photographs of dozens of small objects, with a rhymed riddle at the bottom of each page, comprise the book's content. Solving the riddles and identifying all the objects is a challenging activity that stretches children's powers of observation and encourages them to widen their vision. As they seek to identify and accurately name each object, they build vocabulary. If they are encouraged to write out the names of the many pictured things, their reading, writing, and spelling can also be aided. These are not simple, easily accomplished tasks, as the selection and arrangement of the wide-ranging, colorful objects is complex and intriguing. For a somewhat less challenging level of the same format, look for some of the many other *I Spy* books of picture riddles, or those for even younger children such as *I Spy Little Animals* or *I Spy Little Numbers*, all by Jean Marzollo and Walter Wick.

Silverstein, Dr. Alvin, Virginia Silverstein, and Laura Silverstein Nunn. *Staying Safe*. Cartoon drawings by Rick Stromoski. My Health Series. Franklin Watts, 2001, 48 pp. (3-5).

A practical safety manual for kids, focusing on staying safe wherever they are— at home, at school, at play, on streets, and with people. The warnings are familiar ones, clearly stated and with reasons given for them. The chief value of such a book is not just in reading it through, but in staying alert to the reality that people need to learn early in life to practice sensible safety habits. Especially in today's culture, children often think of parents' and teachers' safety cautions as needless fussing. Seeing the same warnings in a clearly written and well-illustrated book offers support to the adults' warnings. Developing a sensibly safety-conscious lifestyle largely depends on the ongoing awareness and guidance of parents and teachers, starting when children are very small. *Staying Safe* can be used to raise the safety consciousness of both kids and adults.

Steiner, Joan. *Look-Alikes Jr.* Photography by Thomas Lindley. Little, Brown and Company, 1999, 29 pp. (k-3).

An unusual and very enjoyable book that offers hours of fun. Each vividly portrayed ensemble of look-alike objects is a challenge to identify all the items substituted for the actual components. For example, the farm scene has a number of different fabrics on the ground that in the photograph look very much like: a plowed field (corduroy pants), barnyard geese (garlic cloves), small trees (green gumdrops), barnyard fence (cinnamon sticks), and so on. A scene of a child's bedroom shows a bed with four posts (crayons), quilt (alphabet blocks), puffy pillow (bread roll), on floor, among many things, a small rug (potholder), toy basket (roll of brown twine). This written description cannot convey the charm of the photographs themselves. They are clearly not "the real thing"; yet they give such a sense of the objects they represent that they have a strong, whimsical appeal. All scenes except two have at least fifty-two objects to be identified. Great for sharpening observation and encouraging precise identification of objects.

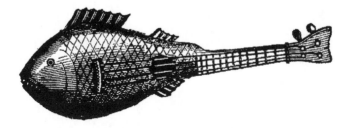

19

MUSIC

Ardley, Neil. *A Young Person's Guide to Music*. With music by Poul Ruders, in association with the BBC Symphony Orchestra conducted by Andrew Davis. DK Publishing, Inc., 1995, 80 pp. (4-7).

This attractive book, which comes with a CD, is designed to introduce young readers—and listeners—to the various instruments of a symphony orchestra. The CD features a new work by Danish composer Poul Ruders, "Concerto in Pieces." The text is coordinated with the CD, and the reader will be told when to turn the CD on to hear each specific instrument being discussed. The orchestra conductor explains different parts of the music as the CD and text are used together. In addition are sections that expand the reader's view of an orchestra and its work. Photographs show the composer at work and the BBC Symphony Orchestra rehearsing, along with the text. A brief section gives some history of significant musicians and composers, and other reference pages provide an A-Z listing of composers, a list of musical forms, and a glossary of musical terms. The book is lavishly illustrated with excellent photographs, including those of the various instruments and of specific parts of these and how they are used.

Berger, Melvin. *The Story of Folk Music*. S. G. Phillips, 1976, 127 pp. (6-up).

A survey-style discussion of folk music: its characteristics, history, and contemporary development. Prominent collectors of folk music as well as well-known performers are noted. The writer seems to have focused largely on performers known for their strong (sometimes radical) social protest, while generally ignoring less controversial folk singers. The book, however, offers the kind of overview that can lead readers to do further research and develop their own skills and interest in specific areas of folk music.

Brett, Jan (illus. by). *The Twelve Days of Christmas*. Dodd, Mead, and Company, 1986, 28 pp. (all ages).

Also listed under *Celebration Days and Seasons*

This beautifully illustrated book opens with the musical score and words of the ancient counting song that celebrates the twelve days from Christmas, December 25, to the Epiphany on January 6. This traditional carol focuses on celebrations and the giving of gifts. Each day of the twelve is shown on a two-page spread, in verse and with a picture of the gift given on that day. Surrounding the central illustration is a border (different for each day) of several small pictures of family members, their festively decorated home, and various appealingly depicted animals and birds of the home or countryside. In the lower left and right corners of each two-page spread, "Merry Christmas" is written in a different language for each day. A lovely book to add to the year's Christmas festivities—and one that insures no more racking of the brain trying to remember what each of the twelve days' gifts can be!

Danes, Emma. *The Usborne First Book of Music*. Illus. by Norman Young. Usborne Publishing Ltd., 1994, 48 pp. (all ages).

Intended for a broad, general audience, this playfully illustrated book seeks to help children make a more personal and knowledgeable connection with music. It encourages readers to get involved in the suggested musical activities and experiments: listening to music, making sounds with the voice and with any instruments available, following the explanations of how sounds are made and how different instruments work, learning how to write down and record tunes and how to make up their own. Specific suggestions and how-to's accompany the directions, all effectively illustrated. Additional sections focus on a variety of jobs that musicians do, discuss briefly the music of the past, and offer advice about how to choose an instrument to play. Music offers a lifetime of enjoyment, something that can be a part of life in many different ways, an enrichment of day-to-day experience.

Danes, Emma. *Music Theory for Beginners*. Illus. by Gerald Wood. Usborne Publishing Ltd., 1997, 48 pp. (2, 3-up).

Music theory is simply the study of how music works and is put together, how it is written down. Knowing the structure behind the sounds is important for anyone who sings or plays an instrument and who takes music seriously. Even those who don't perform themselves but who want to listen understandingly to music find that a knowledge of music theory greatly enhances their appreciation of the music they love to hear. There are many things to learn that may be entirely new to the reader. In using this book, for example, most beginners will need to take each new concept slowly, one part at a time, being sure to relate the concepts to the examples of written music given in the book, and then practice writing any symbols given or play the musical notes shown in the examples.

Note: The grade level indicated is simply a general suggestion; the actual age at which a child can benefit by the material depends on many varying factors, including whether he or she has the help of a knowledgeable adult.

Dunleavy, Deborah. *The Kids Can Press Jumbo Book of Music*. Illus. by Louise Phillips. Kids Can Press, 2001, 208 pp. (all ages).

A book of fun for kids who like the idea of getting together and making music. (Listening parents might question the term "music," but many would be the first to become an enthusiastic audience.) Thick—more than 200 pages—and unpretentious, with lots of lively cartoon-style illustrations but no fancy paper or full color, the book is full of ideas and how-to illustrations for kids. Using mostly "found" materials—stuff around the house or garage—or items purchased inexpensively from a hardware or variety store, youngsters can come up with dozens of sound-makers or sound-and-rhythm instruments: a set of panpipes, a tuba made out of a jug, several kinds of kazoos, a paint-tray rub board, a bucket bass, a penny whistle, and many, many more. Ideas abound: There are eleven kinds of bands, suggested tunes and tempos with clap and beat instruction patterns, words to songs, words and melody-line notation for twenty-two songs, instructions on how to use the instruments and put together programs. A glossary of musical terms, twenty-four simple guitar chord diagrams, and an index round out this volume.

Edens, Cooper and Benjamin Darling. *The Glorious Christmas Songbook.* Blue Lantern Studio, 1999, 77 pp. (all ages).
   Primary listing under *Celebration Days and Seasons*
   This aptly titled book is indeed a glorious addition to the celebration of Christmas. Its more than fifty selections include both beloved traditional carols and cheery secular songs, generously enhanced with appealing classic vintage illustrations from the nineteenth and early twentieth centuries. Musical notation for melody lines is given for all the songs.

Elliott, Donald. *Alligators and Music.* Illus. by Clinton Arrowood. Harvard Common Press, 1984 (1976), 67 pp. (all ages).
   A whimsical book that nevertheless does some serious informing. It is an introduction to the symphony orchestra, picturing and describing each instrument and its particular function and then addressing the qualities of the orchestra as a whole. All the instruments are shown as being held or played by elegantly dressed alligators. The book abounds with delightful touches (seats in the concert hall designed to accommodate the physical shape of alligators, for example) and subtle humor. A fine supplement in music study.

Folk Song. *Hush Little Baby: A Folk Song with Pictures.* Illus. by Marla Frazee. Browndeer Press, 1999, 33 pp. (ps-2).
   Many nights of rocking and singing to her own three little boys inspired children's book illustrator Marla Frazee to create this wonderful "singing" picture book. Most of us are familiar with the nonsense lullaby that begins, "Hush little baby, don't say a word, Papa's gonna buy you a mocking bird." (The melody notes and all the verses are on the book's last page.) Learning that the old folk song had Appalachian roots, Frazee went to the hills of West Virginia and researched the setting for the book's many illustrations. The result is wholly delightful. Each ridiculous line of the song is whimsically illustrated, with mama, papa, big sister, and a peddler with a cart full of toys and animals all trying get the robust little baby to stop howling and go to sleep. Sing (or say) each line (one to a double-page spread) to a little one as you turn the pages. What fun!

Hoberman, Mary Ann (adapted by). *The Eensy-Weensy Spider.* Illus. by Nadine Bernard Westcott. Little, Brown and Company, 2000, 25 pp. (ps-2).
   A favorite children's classic singing rhyme for years, "The Eensy-Weensy Spider" has been given eleven more enjoyable verses by poet and children's book

author Mary Ann Hoberman. Along with Westcott's delightful and wonderfully imaginative illustrations, the expanded poem will be charming more eensy-weensy fans than ever. And just inside the cover of the book readers will find the musical score and hand motion directions for the song.

Kroll, Steven. *By the Dawn's Early Light: The Story of the Star-Spangled Banner.* Illus. by Dan Andreasen. Scholastic, Inc., 1994, 40 pp. (4-7).
    Primary listing under *History*
    Music not only has the power to affect our emotions and our thoughts but often has itself been created in response to dramatic occurrences and profound feeling. No piece of music demonstrates this more fully than our own national anthem. Its story should be a familiar part of our heritage. Author Steven Kroll has given us a stirring account of how "The Star Spangled Banner" came to be written, putting it in its context of a pivotal time in the final war between Great Britain and the United States. After a long day of heavy shelling and rocketing from the big British ships and a night of land attack on Fort Henry, Francis Scott Key, by the first light of morning, had been able to see that the flag flying over the fort was still the Stars and Stripes. In a great outpouring of joy and thankfulness, Francis—a well-known Washington lawyer who had written poetry all his life—wrote the four verses of the song that was soon being sung everywhere, later becoming our national anthem. For a fuller comment on this book, see the entry under *History*.

Krull, Kathleen (collected and arranged by). *Songs of Praise.* Illus. by Kathryn Hewitt. Harcourt Brace Jovanovich, Publishers, 1993 (1988), 32 pp. (all ages).
    A splendid book that combines many excellent features to offer a selection of fifteen best-loved hymns that children and adults can especially enjoy. The songs themselves, including "Jesus Loves Me!" "Amazing Grace," "A Mighty Fortress Is Our God," "Christ the Lord Is Risen Today," and eleven more, include full musical scores for piano, with guitar chords as well, in easy-to-sing and easy-to-play arrangements. Brief historical notes accompany each hymn, and each page of music is surrounded by wonderful illustrations based on the style of an illuminated medieval Book of Hours. Details of rural life in spring, summer, fall, and winter enhance the spirit of faith, joy, and gratitude that the hymns inspire. A truly lovely book that a child will never forget as he or she remembers the hymns of praise joined with the beauty of God's world.

Langstaff, John (compiled and edited by). *"I Have a Song to Sing, O!": An Introduction to the Songs of Gilbert and Sullivan.* Piano arrangements by Brian Holmes. Illus. by Emma Chichester Clark. Margaret K. McElderry Books, 1994, 80 pp. (all ages).
    A grand introduction to the music of Gilbert and Sullivan, with sixteen songs from eight of their rollicking operettas. Absurd plots, comic characters, and hilarious songs with wonderfully catchy tunes make each operetta a fun-filled experience; *H. M. S. Pinafore, The Mikado, The Gondoliers,* and *The Pirates of Penzance* are some of the operettas from which the songs have been chosen. "Titwillow," "Three Little Maids from School," "I'm Called Little Buttercup," "I Am the

Captain of the *Pinafore*," and "The Flowers That Bloom in the Spring" are just a few of those songs. Musical scores for singing, with piano arrangements and suggested guitar chords, are provided for each song. The book is delightfully enhanced by Clark's lively comic drawings and paintings.

MacDonald, Margaret Read and Winifred Jaeger. *The Round Book: Rounds Kids Love to Sing*. Illus. by Yvonne LeBrun Davis. Linnet Books, 1999, 121 pp. (all ages).

A real find for any group that already enjoys singing rounds—or would like to try this fun-filled activity at school, camp, boys' and girls' clubs, and last but not least, at home with family and friends. Learning and singing a round is a great way to help a group to relax and get acquainted or just to share the joy of musical harmony. The book is divided into eleven sections, with each one focused on a particular subject area: the joys of nature, friendship, playful children's songs, table graces, and songs of praise, to name just five of the categories. In addition to the music itself, the book opens with helpful tips on round singing and ends with brief sections on the history of the round, suggestions for round leaders, and a bibliography of a number of other books of rounds.

Patterson, Charles. *Marian Anderson*. Franklin Watts, 1988, 159 pp. (6-up).

Primary listing under *Biography*

Marian Anderson will be recognized for all time as one of America's greatest singers, and the story of her life and career is an inspiring one. Music was the dominant element in Anderson's life; song filled her being, and that song must have an outlet, must be shared with countless others, lifting them up with her into another realm. The story of her life is the story of her relationship to music, and it offers a depth of insight into what that relationship means. In reading of Anderson's life, so filled with endless commitment, purpose, courage, determination, with long hours of study, practice, and performances, young people will become aware of what is involved in becoming a channel through which music can flow and touch the lives of others.

Reader's Digest Editors. *The Reader's Digest Children's Songbook*. Music arranged and edited by Dan Fox. The Reader's Digest Association, Inc., 1998 (1985), 252 pp. (all ages).

A potpourri of children's folk and traditional popular songs: "It Ain't Gonna Rain No More," "Frog Went A-Courtin'," "If You're Happy and You Know It, (Clap Your Hands)," "Frosty the Snowman," "Over the Rainbow," and dozens more. All songs except those in the nursery rhyme sections have a full musical score piano accompaniment; chord diagrams for guitar, banjo, et al. are given, and a little booklet inside the back cover of the book has the complete words of all the songs. A great family book to have and enjoy.

Rubin, Mark. *The Orchestra*. Illus. by Alan Daniel. Firefly Books Ltd., 1992, 45 pp. (all ages).

Written in an informal narrative style and with large, very enjoyable illustrations, this informative book is especially accessible. Opening with some general comments about the nature of music and definitions of musical terms, the book moves on to specifics about an orchestra. The several groups of instruments—strings, wood-winds, brass, and percussion—are illustrated and discussed, and the book concludes with a description of the role and work of an orchestra's conductor.

Seeger, Ruth Crawford. *American Folk Songs for Children.* Doubleday, 1980, 192 pp. (all ages).
    Especially designed as a book for children, parents, and teachers, this collec-tion of ninety-four folk (traditional) songs has more text than the usual song-book. The writer tells how the book came into being and why folk music is so valuable to use with children, gives hints on how to sing the songs and how to use them at home and at school, offers suggestions as to accompaniment (fine, but not necessary, says the author), and comments on the value of the humor in such songs.

Stevens, Byrna. *Ben Franklin's Glass Armonica.* Illus. by Priscilla Kiedrowski. Dell, 1992 (1983), 48 pp. (k-3).
    Designed for easy reading in the primary grades, this book provides surprising and interesting information about still another invention of the versatile Benjamin Franklin. Using an idea that apparently originated in China, Franklin, an accom-plished and enthusiastic musician, elaborated on it and came up with something he called an armonica—glass bowls of varying sizes that were played with the fin-gers while being rotated by a foot pedal. A delightful bit of musical trivia and another sidelight on the remarkable Mr. Franklin.

Turner, Barrie Carson. *The Living Piano.* Alfred A. Knopf, 1996, 46 pp. (4-up).
    With its comprehensive approach and attractive format, Turner's book has much to offer anyone interested in the piano and piano music, whether as a player or a listener. The book opens with concise background information on keyboard instruments and the development of the piano and its predecessors over the cen-turies to the present, followed by a section on how the piano works, is made, and is played. The body of the text focuses, in chronological order, on profiles of ten great composers, from Scarlatti to Debussy. Each of these gifted men wrote sig-nificant keyboard works. The full-length audio CD that comes with the book con-tains representative selections from the work of each of these composers. The book concludes with a picture and paragraph about each of a dozen of the great pianists of the last hundred years. The book is generously and beautifully illustrated in color.

Turpin, Nicholas and Marie Greenwood, eds. *The First Noel: A Child's Book of Christmas Carols to Play and Sing.* DK Publishing, 1998, 31 pp. (all ages).
    Primary listing under *Celebration Days and Seasons*
    This lovely book of thirteen traditional carols and accompanying reproductions of Christmas paintings by both classic and living artists is a most worthwhile addi-tion to family seasonal celebration or to a musical child's lesson repertoire. Each

carol is presented in a simplified, easy-to-follow musical score for piano (for both hands) and guitar. On each facing page is a beautiful painting, with the carol's additional verses printed below.

Yolen, Jane, editor. *The Lullaby Songbook*. Musical arrangements by Adam Stemple. Illus. by Charles Mikolaycak. Harcourt Brace Jovanovich, Publishers, 1986, 32 pp. (ps-up).

In her note at the end of this book, Jane Yolen writes, "One of the tenderest moments an adult and child can share is a lullaby. . . . These are the songs that say to the listening child: 'Go to sleep now. I am here. There is nothing you should fear. Sleep. Sleep. Sleep.'" Yolen has selected fifteen loved lullabies, offered in the context of musical scores arranged for piano and guitar. Accompanying the songs are tender, imaginative illustrations.

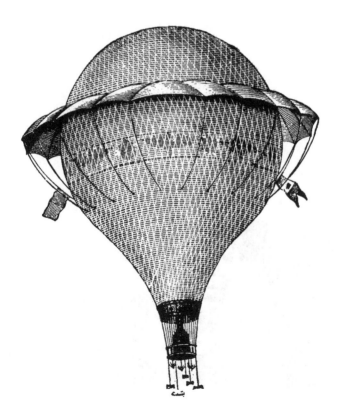

NATURE, SCIENCE, AND TECHNOLOGY

Aaseng, Nathan. *Building the Impossible.* The Oliver Press, 2000, 144 pp. (5-8).
    Primary listing under *Art and Architecture*
    In each of these fascinating accounts of builders who achieved the "impossible," the reader is introduced not only to the innovative technical breakthroughs that made the achievements possible, but to the men of extraordinary vision who were able to see and implement possibilities that others had not recognized. When Imhotep, a gifted builder, was faced with the task of trying to build a magnificent tomb for Egypt's ruler that would be huge, lasting, and protective of the royal remains, he wanted to use something better than the usual bricks that aged and crumbled and were vulnerable to break-ins. Immense, heavy blocks of stone could be the answer, and Imhotep found amazing ways to cut these out, move them to the building site, and raise them, one upon another, in the first Step Pyramid of Egypt. Marc Brunel believed he could build a tunnel under the Thames River of London—and had the vision to relate the technique of a woodworm he observed tunneling into a piece of oak to the purpose of the tunnel he wanted to build. These and five other "impossible" building projects are effectively described by the writer, achievements made possible by the creative technical innovations of men with unique vision—a combination still at the heart of great accomplishments.

Adler, David A. *A Picture Book of George Washington Carver.* Illus. by Dan Brown. Holiday House, 1999, 30 pp. (ps-3).
    Primary listing under *Biography*
    George Washington Carver, born into slavery during the Civil War and orphaned as a small child, overcame great obstacles to gain an education. He had a lifelong desire to help his people and was one of the first African-Americans to bring significant economic help to the agricultural South. Carver's genius with plants enabled him to aid countless people. He saw that the cotton farming most African-Americans did for a living was no longer meeting their basic needs. So while he did develop an improved breed of cotton, he also decided he must find other plants that would not rob the soil of nutrients, as cotton did, and that would also provide nourishing food. Carver made discovery after discovery that made it possible for farmers to grow better crops, improving their own nutrition and bringing in needed income. Carver believed that each of his discoveries was a message

to him from God, enabling him in his work, and he would not take any money for his discoveries, one of which was a very special way to use peanuts—peanut butter! This brief biography is a good way to learn about how George Washington Carver combined science and faith to improve the lives of countless people.

Ammon, Richard. *Conestoga Wagons*. Illus. by Bill Farnsworth. Holiday House, Inc., 2000, 30 pp. (3-6).

Primary listing under *History and Geography*

A forerunner of today's giant freight-hauling trucks, the Conestoga wagon is usually thought of today as the vehicle used by pioneers to transport themselves and their possessions across plains and mountains to westerly destinations. This was certainly one of the wagon's significant uses, but Conestogas (and their humbler kin) also functioned as an indispensable part of the nation's economy, primarily from 1750 to 1850. One reason for the Conestoga's lasting fame was the excellent materials and technology used in its construction. Richard Ammon's clear and carefully researched text and the splendid illustrations of Bill Farnsworth combine effectively in this account of both the construction and the storied uses of the historic wagon. Although the chief era of the Conestoga was in the 100 years mentioned above, many wagons were in use until trucks were invented, hauling goods from freight trains, for one example, to destinations away from railroad lines. A part of our nation's history, the Conestoga is a vivid reminder not only of its historic significance but of the value of technological excellence, whatever the era.

Arnosky, Jim. *Watching Water Birds*. National Geographic Society, 1997, 28 pp. (1-5).

The acclaimed artist and naturalist Jim Arnosky has chosen his favorite water birds to profile in this colorful and informative book. Most of these birds can be found in many areas across the country, a good reason to become familiar with their appearance and types of habitats. The writer has a special interest in nature education for children, and he speaks clearly and conversationally about the varied birds—loons, grebes, ducks, herons, gulls, and others—pointing out the physical characteristics to look for and presenting meticulously accurate portraits of each one. Helping youngsters to recognize and identify the birds they see can start them on a rewarding lifelong interest as well as adding another area of achievement to their lives. Arnosky brings each bird to vivid life in his wonderful paintings, including also a variety of information about the birds' habitats, choice of food, and other details.

Arnosky, Jim. *Wild and Swampy: Exploring with Jim Arnosky*. Harper-Collins, 2000, 28 pp. (1-5).

The writer loves to share with children the fascination he feels for wildlife and their habitats. Many of his books focus on settings not far from his Vermont home, but with their family now grown, Arnosky and his wife, Deanna, travel farther afield. This book finds them in the Southern swamps, a favorite destination. These quiet swamps, protected in every direction by trees, provide shelter and food for a profusion of wildlife: birds, mammals, fish, reptiles, and crustaceans. The writer's warm, conversational style as he talks about what he is seeing sets a tone like that of a little family expedition led by a favorite (and knowledgeable) family member. In an inspired combination of the artist's vivid paintings interspersed with lively pen-and-ink sketches, readers see a number of the swamp creatures the Arnoskys encounter. The settings are varied: mangrove, bald cypress, and hardwood swamps—named for the different trees that predominate in each one. *Wild and Swampy* takes readers into a world far from the places they are used to seeing— one of the things a good book can do best.

Bendick, Jeanne. *Archimedes and the Door of Science.* Living History Library. Bethlehem Books, 1995 (1962), 143 pp. (5, 6-up).
See entries for this book under *Biography* and *Mathematics* listings.

Boring, Mel. *Birds, Nests, and Eggs.* Illus. by Linda Garrow. Gareth Stevens Pub., 1998, 40 pp. (2-up).
One of a series (Young Naturalist's Field Guides), this book provides a useful and pleasant start in developing a child's interest in, and knowledge of, birds. A wise choice has been made of fourteen bird species that can be found in many areas of the country. Attractively illustrated and with a comfortably conversational style of brief text, each bird and its characteristic habits is described, as are typical nesting places and nests, food choices, eggs, and seasonal residency patterns. (The latter are often not typical for mild-climate areas, but understandably books of this kind must be written for the more typical parts of our country.) Interspersed through the book are instructions for three little projects: a simple bird-watching blind, a drip-shower for birds, and a hanging suet feeder. The observation and identification of birds can became a rewarding lifelong interest in the backyard, on walks, and on more distant travels. With an introduction such as Boring's book provides, it is an easy step to using one of the complete field guides to the birds— those by Roger Tory Peterson, for example.

Brandenburg, Jim. *An American Safari: Adventures on the North American Prairie.* Walker Publishing Co., 1995, 44 pp. (4-up).
Wildlife photographer Jim Brandenberg has taken pictures all over the world, but one kind of wilderness in his own country has a special place in his heart—the remnants of the American prairie. Until little more than a century and a half ago, the midsection of the United States—from the Canadian border to south Texas and from the east side of the Rockies to the western edge of Indiana—was grass-covered prairie. This was not a flat, uniform growth resembling a rough lawn, but a richly varied diversity of many grasses lavishly adorned with colorful wildflowers. The vast area teemed with wildlife: literally millions upon millions of bison, ante-

lope, a wide variety of smaller animals and birds, with prairie dog "towns" running underground for miles over immense areas.

The writer's splendid photographs illumine his descriptions of the prairie's former extent and nature and of the prairie preserves of today with their large herds of bison, prairie dog towns, and other wildlife brought back from near extinction by the persistent efforts of both public and private conservationists.

Brimner, Larry Dane. *E-Mail.* Children's Press, 1997, 47 pp. (1-up).

A clear, simply written book in large type, defining e-mail, describing briefly how it works and how to use it. Several screen addresses are given to which the reader may write for specific information—for example, Ask-A-Geologist@usgs.gov for questions about earthquakes or Sea.world@bev.net for questions on marine animals. A list of additional resources includes helpful books and Internet sites. Brimner's kid-friendly book is a good introduction to a splendid twenty-first-century tool.

Brown, Marion Marsh. *Homeward the Arrow's Flight.* Field Mouse Productions, 1995 (1980), 185 pp. (5, 6-up).

Primary listing under *Biography*

This excellent biography of Susan La Flesche relates to medical science in the 1880s. It is the story of the first Native American woman doctor in history.

Carey, Charles W., Jr. *George Washington Carver.* The Child's World, Inc., 1999, 39 pp. (2-6).

Primary listing under *Biography*

Written for higher grade levels than the David A. Adler listing above, Carey's book includes more details of Carver's groundbreaking work with agricultural plants. Born into slavery near the end of the Civil War and orphaned early, Carver struggled to gain the education he patiently pursued. Finally, having achieved a Master of Science degree, he took a job teaching history at the Tuskegee Institute in Alabama. Carver had a long-held desire to help his people, and he began working with agricultural plants, trying to find ways of solving the economic problems of the South. Carver's main focus for some time was on peanuts and yams. As he persisted, he made discovery after discovery with results that brought widespread economic help to both African-American and white southerners. A man of deep faith, Carver believed that every discovery was given him by God. Carver is now known as the father of chemurgy, the industrial use of plant products.

Cherman, Beverly. *The Mysterious Rays of Dr. Röntgen.* Illus. by Stephen Marchesi. Atheneum, 1994, 23 pp. (4-6).

The first Nobel Prize in physics was awarded in 1901 to German physicist William Conrad Röntgen (pronounced rent´-gen and usually spelled "Roentgen" in this country). The award was for Röntgen's discovery of one of the world's most widely used pieces of technology, the X-ray. Author Cherman's concise biography describes in a clear, simplified form the nature of the electromagnetic tests the physicist was working on and the scientific principles involved in the "mystery" ray he discovered, which he called "X" for "unknown." Röntgen's discovery that the rays could pass through flesh, wood, and other nonmetallic substances and reveal internal structures or objects met great acclaim. Over the years he developed and refined the technology to an amazing extent. Initially, much had to be learned about the nature of the ray—most crucially its potential for causing cancer. The process was intensively refined over time and today is widely used in medicine and dentistry, in the study of fossils and mummies, in investigations of the collapse of building structures, and in connection with varied types of criminal cases. As with so many great scientific discoveries, Dr. Röntgen was not striving for fame and fortune, but simply seeking to know more about his field of research when he made his discovery. Cherman has effectively presented the life and work of a notable modern scientist.

Cobb, Vicki. *Lots of Rot*. HarperCollins Children's Books, 1981, 40 pp. (1-3).
The writer provides information for the inquiring young student on what causes rot. Simple, clearly described projects result in the discovery of facts about bacteria, mold, and mildew. Most children will enjoy trying out the suggested experiments.

Cobb, Vicki and Kathy Darling. Illus. by True Kelley. *Don't Try This at Home!: Science Fun for Kids on the Go*. Morrow Junior Books, 1998, 175 pp. (4, 5-up).
An enjoyable and practical compilation of how-to's for sixty-three science projects for kids. (Some require adult supervision.) The projects are clearly explained and helpfully illustrated. Each of the book's eight chapters focuses on a different away-from-home kind of setting suitable for specific projects. Classrooms, parks, amusement parks, trains, planes, and cars, for example, are some of these settings. Written in a conversational and sometimes humorous style, the scientific information and project instructions are easy to read and understand. The graphic layout is excellent, and the projects themselves are instructive and entertaining.

Cole, Henry. *Jack's Garden*. Greenwillow Books, 1995, 23 pp. (ps-3).
Primary listing under *Growing Plants—Outdoors and Indoors*
A great little book that moves through the process of making a garden. The successive steps, the related tools, plants, and other life forms found in and above the garden are shown and identified. The illustrations are outstanding, and the book offers an appealing introduction to a wide variety of plants that can be cultivated and creatures that can be found in a backyard garden.

Coulter, George and Shirley. *Science in Sports*. Rourke Science Projects Series. Rourke Publications, Inc., 1995, 32 pp. (3-6).
Six science projects about the whys and hows of various sports-related actions. For example, two of the projects answer these questions: "What is the relationship between speed and stopping distance on roller blades?" and "How do hot and cold packs work?" Well illustrated with color photographs and drawings, the projects are clearly explained, and the final chapter suggests good ways to display a project. A glossary and index conclude this useful book. The series also offers project books on science in art, in food, in music, and in other fields.

Cousins, Margaret. *The Story of Thomas Alva Edison.* Landmark Books Series, Random Books for Young Readers, 1981, 160 pp. (5-9).

Primary listing under *Biography*

The life and work of the "Wizard of Menlo Park" make enthralling reading. Edison, inventor of the incandescent light bulb, the phonograph, the motion picture, and many other devices, is a prominent example of the unpredictable and inexplicable gift of genius that characterizes so many of the world's innovators and discoverers. Coupled with Edison's genius, however, was an almost obsessive preoccupation with his work. Once he started on an idea, he would repeat experiments, make tests, seek for better solutions literally thousands of times if necessary. From the explosion of interest the nine-year-old Edison experienced as he read his first science book, to his death at eighty-four while still working avidly on projects, his life was an ongoing experience of a curious, restless, analytical mind seeking answers to questions and practical applications of scientific truths.

Croswell, Ken. *See the Stars: Your First Guide to the Night Sky.* Boyds Mills Press, 2000, 32 pp. (3-up).

If a child you know has tried to use complicated star charts to find constellations in the night sky and become frustrated, this book will help. With a Harvard doctorate in astronomy, Ken Croswell knows thoroughly the scholarly literature of his field. But he is also interested in helping children get started in their exploration of the starry skies. This well-organized book guides the reader step by step, explaining what to do and how to do it, beginning with the section, "How to Use This Book." *See the Stars* is an introductory book, and readers who develop a lasting interest in astronomy will later go on to the more complicated star charts. For the majority, however, who simply want to be able to identify those bright and more readily recognizable star patterns, the book provides answers in a form accessible to a beginner. The book concludes with a list of the brightest stars and a chart to help the reader locate the four planets besides our own that are easy to see.

Curlee, Lynn. *Ships of the Air.* Houghton Mifflin, 1996, 32 pp. (3-7).

Flying has captured the dreams of many people through the centuries. Some simply dreamed; a few determined to apply their imagination, creativity, and relevant technology to build a machine that could lift a person into the air and move him from one place to another. Author Curlee has written a clear, briefly comprehensive account of the dreamers and makers especially fascinated by the idea of lighter-than-air machines who were able to realize at least some of their dreams. From the first hot-air balloon, built in 1783 by a pair of French brothers, Joseph and Etienne Montgolfier, to the 800-foot-long *Hindenburg,* launched in 1936 by the Zeppelin Company in Nazi Germany, a long succession of hopeful innovators tried a variety of means toward the desired end. Airships for the commercial transporting of passengers vanished after the *Hindenburg* disaster, but the little blimps are still around, and ballooning continues to capture the efforts of dedicated enthusiasts. In the last four decades interest in hot-air ballooning has grown—as seen today in the efforts of committed balloonists to set records for flights around the world and the growth of recreational hot-air balloon groups.

d'Aulaire, Ingri and Edgar Parin. *Benjamin Franklin.* Doubleday, 1985 (1950), 48 pp. (1-4).
　　Primary listing under *Biography*
　　An excellent introductory biography to use in connection with a first-level exploration of Franklin's scientific experiments and discoveries.

Ehlert, Lois. *Waiting for Wings.* Harcourt, Inc., 34 pp. (ps-2).
　　Flowers and butterflies in bursts of intense color shimmer and glow on each page. The writer tells briefly—in rhyme—of the butterfly eggs that turn into caterpillars, then encase themselves, and finally emerge as impossibly beautiful winged creatures flying among the flowers, looking for nectar to sip. In the first half of the book, an unusual arrangement of small pages that become successively larger adds to the feeling of anticipation and change that go with the story of the butterflies. The book's five full-size concluding pages identify the butterflies shown in the book, present the parts of a butterfly, and include several paragraphs of further butterfly information. A page identifies the flowers of the book, and the final page offers ideas for growing a butterfly garden.

Fisher, Leonard Everett. *Alexander Graham Bell.* Illus. by author. Atheneum Books for Young Readers, 1999, 28 pp. (4-7).
　　Primary listing under *Biography*
　　Fisher's concise and especially well-written biography of the man known the world over as the inventor of the telephone includes a substantial amount of material on his work. The book would be a helpful supplemental resource in relation to science curriculum covering the transmission of sound (as with the telephone) and the expansion of communication systems and related technologies. Bell's work with the hearing-impaired is also discussed, as are his constant efforts to encourage and help individuals and causes to which he felt his knowledge could contribute.

French, Vivian. *Growing Frogs.* Illus. by Alison Bartlett. Candlewick Press, 2000, 29 pp. (1-4).
　　Author and artist have created a charming, yet entirely accurate and doable little manual on how to grow frogs. Warning readers that frogs are becoming endangered in today's world, the writer uses a narrative form to tell children exactly how to care for frog spawn at home, how the little eggs go through their rapid stages of development, how to avoid harming the little amphibians, and what should be done with them when they have turned into tiny frogs. Just inside the

front cover of the book are the "Rules for frog-lovers," starting with, "Don't ever take frog spawn from a pond in the wild." (Spawn should be taken only from a man-made pond.) Being able to watch the "eggs-to-frogs" process is something almost every child would enjoy doing, but in order to avoid risking the tiny lives, kids need clear instructions and the help of an interested adult. Like almost every worthwhile undertaking, work and care are involved. This well-written and vividly illustrated book will not only inform but enable readers to decide whether growing frogs is something they want to undertake—and show them how to do it right.

Gibbons, Gail. *Click!* Little, Brown and Co., 1997, 28 pp. (4-up).

Being able to use a camera knowledgeably and competently is a skill a good many children would like to have. *Click!* offers a clear, step-by-step introduction to cameras and photographic know-how. The writer's accompanying illustrations are carefully labeled, and they effectively amplify the text. Gibbons describes simply the parts of a camera, the configuration of typical film (cartridge and disc), how they work, and how to use them—from inserting the film in the camera on through the taking of the pictures, to the removal of the film and its trip to the photo processor. A brief explanation of film processing itself is included. Following the basic get-started instructions, the writer then discusses outdoor and indoor picture-taking and offers suggestions on successful photographic techniques. The book concludes with some ideas for using and keeping the finished pictures and provides a mini-history of photography and a page of "Fun Photo Facts."

Giblin, James Cross. *The Amazing Life of Benjamin Franklin*. Illus. by Michael Dooling. Scholastic Press, 2000, 48 pp. (3-7).

Primary listing under *Biography*

This lively and well-researched picture biography is an excellent introductory resource to use in connection with a beginning understanding of Benjamin Franklin's scientific experiments and wide-ranging inventions.

Giblin, James Cross. *Charles A. Lindbergh: A Human Hero*. Houghton Mifflin, 1999, 212 pp. (5-up).

Primary listing under *Biography*

James Giblin's excellent biography of Lindbergh includes a significant body of material on aircraft and aviation, particularly as they first developed. Technical information is clearly and interestingly presented as the story of Lindbergh's life and close relationship with planes and flying is chronicled. For example, the design of Lindbergh's famous plane, *The Spirit of St. Louis,* was the flyer's own, and the author discusses Lindbergh's design choices and the reasons for them. An especially well-done and interest-holding volume.

Haddon, Mark. *The Sea of Tranquillity.* Illus. by Christian Birmingham. Harcourt Brace and Company, 1996, 27 pp. (ps-3).

Years ago a little boy in London was fascinated by space and the solar system. At night he would look at the map of the solar system on his wall and think of each planet spinning around the sun. But of all the round bodies moving in the sky, it wasn't a planet but earth's only natural satellite, the moon, that interested him most. He pored over an atlas of the moon and read about space exploration and astronauts' flights around the moon. And one night the thing he had been hoping for happened. Two astronauts were walking on the surface of the moon. The writer's excellent account, along with the fine illustrations, make the true story come alive; the reader is aware in a new way of the capacity a child has for sustained interest in some particular aspect of the world around him (or her). Young readers can be inspired by this record of one little boy's pursuit of his interest in an element of the natural world and the joy it brought him.

Note: In relation to the book's title, either a single or double "l" in the word *tranquility* is correct. The double "l" is more common in Britain where this book was written.

Heller, Ruth. *The Reason for a Flower.* Putnam Publishing Group, 1983 (1976), 24 pp. (k-2).

A vividly colorful introduction to the seed-forming function of flowers. The brief, rhymed text accompanies dramatic illustrations in this fashion: "Birds and bees and these, and these [butterflies, moths, a hummingbird, and a bat, are pictured] sip nectar from the flowers." Pollination is briefly described and pictured. Then: "The reason for a flower is to manufacture . . . SEEDS that have a cover of one kind or another." A beautiful array of seeds is shown, and the following pages show ways seeds are distributed in nature, some of the wide varieties of plants that all come from seeds, and finally some of the things we use that come from plants: paper, coffee, bread, cotton fabric, and more. A delightful, purposeful book.

Hightower, Paul. *Galileo: Astronomer and Physicist.* Enslow Publishers, Inc., 1997, 128 pp. (5-up).

A very clear, concisely stated record of Galileo's life, with the chief focus on the progression of his scientific discoveries and their effects on the scientific beliefs of his time and on his own life. A brilliant astronomer and physicist, Galileo (1564-1642) was involved for much of his life in issues related to the structural nature of the universe. His studies convinced him that the earth was not the center of the world, as Aristotle and others averred, but that the earth revolved around the sun. Hightower's account discusses the conflicting views (as well as other aspects of Galileo's work) in an easy-to-understand manner. Because the

Catholic church, all-powerful in Italy (Galileo's home), had adopted the ideas of Aristotle, renowned philosopher of ancient Greece, it refused to accept any other view. In 1633 the church called Galileo before the Inquisition for his disagreement with Aristotle's beliefs about the universe. Because of Galileo's international fame as a scientist, he was not treated as harshly as many, but he was convicted of heresy and sentenced to permanent house arrest. Galileo's position was, of course, vindicated centuries ago and widely accepted around the world, eventually in Italy as well, though unofficially. In 1979 Pope John Paul II had the case against Galileo reopened. In 1992, a little more than 350 years after his conviction, the Catholic church formally acknowledged their error, and Galileo's record was cleared!

Hyde, Margaret O. and Elizabeth H. Forsyth, M.D. *Vaccinations: From Smallpox to Cancer*. Franklin Watts, 2000, 127 pp. (6-up).

This comprehensive and clearly written account starts with the history of smallpox, as far as it is known. In various parts of the world smallpox killed millions of people, and eventually, here and there, fumbling attempts were being made to inoculate people against the dreaded disease. These attempts became more focused and scientific in England during the eighteenth century. The writers briefly profile some of the pioneers in this endeavor, their methods, the growing knowledge that developed, and the later amazing success that resulted in wiping out smallpox worldwide by 1977. As the principles of inoculation were discovered, they were later applied to other diseases. Most families with children are familiar with the DPT shots given to young children to protect them from diphtheria, whooping cough (pertussis), and tetanus. Today we can hardly realize what a menace these afflictions used to carry, and the writers summarize these and other conditions still dangerous in the absence of vaccines. They go on to discuss a number of other current health problems : tuberculosis, malaria, HIV and AIDS, hepatitis A, B, and C, Alzheimer's disease, and cancer. Attention is given to people's concerns over immunization available for some diseases and recurring fears that it is harmful. The text is annotated, and the book concludes with a glossary, endnotes, sources of further information, a list of helpful books, and a detailed index.

Lasky, Kathryn. *Monarchs*. Photographs by Christopher G. Knight. Harcourt Brace and Co., 1993, 64 pp. (4-up).

Most of us have a few scraps of knowledge about the monarch butterfly, that handsome orange-and-black insect with its distinctive white-spotted wing borders. Some may remember that every year large numbers of them gather in the sea coast town of Pacific Grove, California, but may be vague about what time of year this occurs or where the monarchs are before they make their impressive migration to the southern tip of Monterey Bay. The book's account is a fascinating one that involves remote villages in Mexico, habitat rescue projects, unsolved mysteries, and displays of overwhelming beauty. This is one of those books found on library shelves across the country, and if your library doesn't have a copy, request one through interlibrary loan. Just don't miss it.

Lawlor, Laurie. *Window on the West: The Frontier Photography of William Henry Jackson*. Holiday House, 1999, 132 pp. (5-up).

Primary listing under *Biography*

When, in 1869, William Henry Jackson went west "in quest of the picturesque and marvelous" to photograph, he was in the vanguard of a technology only thirty years old in America. During most of the early years, the art of picture-taking usually involved various kinds of portraits—wedding couples, children, public figures. It was only during the Civil War that photography began to be used in ways that foreshadowed its future—as a new art form, as a significant technology, and an as-yet-undreamed-of cultural influence. With the dissemination of battlefield photographs, people began to realize that seeing a picture was the nearest thing possible to being there themselves.

Jackson's passion to share the scenic wonders of the American West with others came at just the moment in the nation's history when people were hungry to see, through pictures, as much as they could of what was "out there." The first transcontinental railway had just been completed, and this became Jackson's means of reaching areas virtually no one had seen before. Lawlor has created an especially worthwhile volume, combining not only a wonderful representation of Jackson's photographs, but also information about the processes of photography itself as it was done at that time. The reader learns of the heavy, yet fragile equipment Jackson hand-hauled up mountainsides—in one instance to the top of a 13,000-foot peak— and will marvel at the commitment, skill, and artistry of a gifted pioneer in a field that now permeates every aspect of contemporary life. Check the book's listings under *Biography* and *History and Geography* for more information.

Levine, Shar and Leslie Johnstone. *Quick-But-Great Science Fair Projects*. Illus. by Emily S. Edliq. Sterling Publishing Co. Inc., 2000, 96 pp. (4-up).

A colorful, well-organized, and well-expressed guide to successful science fair projects. Its preface provides clear directions on how to use the book, hints for teachers and parents, and an encouraging "Note to Kids." In the following chapters on getting started, presenting projects, and detailing specific directions for twenty-six projects, the student is offered practical guidance. Each basic project gives "Going Further" hints for both elementary and junior high (middle school) levels. The crisp graphic layout and attractive illustrations (photographs and drawings, all in color) make the book appealing to young students who may be feeling tense about doing a science fair entry.

Macaulay, David. *Building Big*. Houghton Mifflin, 2000, 192 pp. (5-up.)

Primary listing under *Art and Architecture*

A majority of people see or hear the word *technology* hundreds of times a year because it is associated with so much that is a part of daily life. Without realizing it, most have a feeling that technology is primarily modern. In reality, however, technology has always been a part of human life. One dictionary definition is "the system by which a society provides its members with those things needed or desired." This system includes the large and the small, and Macaulay's *Building Big* is all about technology on a grand scale. From the Ponte Fabricio in Rome, a bridge built more than 2,000 years ago and still in use, to the innovative German skyscraper Commerzbank, which Frankfurt completed in 1997, the reader is immersed in the technology of thirty-four outstanding bridges, tunnels, dams, domes, and skyscrapers. Across the centuries builders have tackled the problems of spanning waterways with bridges, holding back water with dams, burrowing underground with tunnels—meeting human needs and wishes. The writer/graphic artist shows how these feats were done. In concise text and a wealth of drawings and diagrams, he explains the technology used to create notable structures that have had (in some cases for centuries) a significant impact on the lives of millions of people across the world.

Macaulay, David. Technical text by Neil Ardley. *The New Way Things Work*. Houghton Mifflin, rev. ed. 1998 (1988), 400 pp. (all ages).

This revised and updated version of the acclaimed reference volume *The Way Things Work* deals accessibly with the principles and scientific laws by which all forms of "machinery"—anything that works—operate. From can openers to camcorders, hammers to hydrogen bombs, sewing machines to synthesizers, detailed descriptions, explanations, and illustrations take the mystery out of the technology. Even preschoolers will be fascinated with the intriguing pictures and the humorous little "mammoth" stories that preface sections of the text. Even if you are a reader who usually avoids introductions, do start with this one—page 8. Commendably brief, it profiles the book's organization and focus, which lend themselves to either methodical study and research or fun-filled browsing through. A splendid addition to your family library or your kids' own bookshelves.

Mandell, Muriel. *Physics Experiments for Children*. Dover, 1968, 96 pp. (4-6).

Dozens of simple but effective experiments using readily available materials. Scientific facts about air, water, mechanical energy, heat, sound, light, magnetism, and electricity are demonstrated by experiments for which clear step-by-step instructions are given.

Martin, Jacqueline Briggs. *Snowflake Bentley*. Illus. by Mary Azarian. Houghton Mifflin Co., 1998, 26 pp. (1-6).

Primary listing under *Biography*

This enjoyable picture biography is not only the story of a man with a lifelong interest in snow and especially in the beauty and uniqueness of each lovely snowflake; it is an easily recognized example of scientific research—in an era (late nineteenth century) when a boy on a remote farm wouldn't have seen or read much (if any) about such things. First of all, Bentley had a problem to solve: He was determined to share with the world the intricately lovely patterns of snowflakes—each one different from all the others. Unfortunately, the flakes always melted before he could draw them! After reasoning out a way he could achieve his purpose, the hard work began. At first it was just one failure after another. He thought some more; he refined his technique; but most of all, he just kept on, time after time after time. Ultimately he succeeded and left a wonderful heritage of his work. Even today much scientific research is just as slow, repetitive, and painstaking. A helpful read for budding research scientists—and all the other readers. Vision, patience, and persistence are wonderfully modeled by this man of the past who loved one of nature's hidden wonders and was determined to share its beauty with the world.

Morpurgo, Michael. *The Silver Swan*. Illus. by Christian Birmingham. Penguin Putnam Books for Young Readers, 2000, 28 pp. (2-5).
    Primary listing under *Literature, Level II: Realistic Stories—Modern*
    To get to know the mute swan, which is found mainly in parks in the United States, look for this splendid book set in England. The swans in the book are wild. The boy of the story develops an intense love for a particular swan and must learn to accept the sometimes harsh aspects of nature and his helplessness to intervene. In the process, an accurate account of the characteristics and way of life of these swans is perceptively given. The artist's accompanying illustrations are breathtakingly beautiful.

Patent, Dorothy Hinshaw. *The Bald Eagle Returns*. Photographs by William Muñoz. Clarion Books, 2000, 68 pp. (4-7).
    As the book's title indicates, the preservation of the bald eagle is its primary focus. This magnificent bird and its similar-sized but less spectacular relative, the golden eagle, are the only North American eagles. Except for the California condor, they are the largest American birds of prey. The author provides an extensive account of the bald eagle itself, its habitats, patterns of life, the causes of its endangerment, and the successful efforts made to stop its decline and substantially increase the number of nesting pairs of bald eagles in the country. Many fine photographs complement the text.
    Patent's attractive book offers a great deal of worthwhile information about America's national bird, but the writer could have done a much better job of discussing the bald eagle's role as a national emblem—which the book's introduction promises will be done. Apart from that lapse, this is a useful book.

Provensen, Alice and Martin. *The Glorious Flight*. Picture Puffins, 1987 (1983), 39 pp. (k-2).
    The 1984 Caldecott Medal winner, this picture-book story is based on a significant piece of aviation history that has been largely forgotten. In 1901 Louis Bleriot, a settled family man with a wife and five children, became enthralled with the idea of flight. Eight years (and eleven airplanes) later, he became the first man to fly across the English Channel. The Provensens have told this story in beautifully chosen words, with a subtle, charming humor, and with page after page of wonderfully authentic illustrations, detailed and, in the case of the airplane scenes, shimmering with light and creating a sense of buoyancy and movement through the air.

Quackenbush, Robert. *Here a Plant, There a Plant, Everywhere a Plant Plant! A Story of Luther Burbank*. Luther Burbank Home, rev. ed. 1995 (1982), 35 pp. (1-5).
    An entertaining introduction to the work of the man who developed many new varieties of fruits, vegetables, and flowers, including the Burbank potato and the Shasta daisy.

Rockwell, Anne. *Bugs Are Insects*. Illus. by Steve Jenkins. HarperCollins Publishers, Inc., 2001, 33 pp. (ps-3).

With its amusing, larger-than-life illustrations, this beginning-level science book about insects is a good introduction to the way in which the diverse little creatures frequently called "bugs" are classified and identified. After focusing on the characteristics of a number of familiar crawlers, hoppers, and fliers, children can say with understanding, "Anything that has six legs and three body parts is an insect." They have learned about some of the insect subgroups—bugs and beetles, for example. Part of the Let's Read-and-Find-Out-About Science Series, the information in this book is theoretically intended for preschool and kindergarten levels. However, the book must be read to these young children by a teacher or parent, as the vocabulary mandates a competent reader. For this reason, the book can be profitably used by grades one to three for self-reading.

Schaefer, Lola M. *This Is the Sunflower*. Illus. by Donald Crews. Greenwillow Books, 2000, 23 pp. (ps-3).

Primary listing under *Literature: Poetry and Rhymes*

This colorful book with its cheerful, cumulative rhyme (in the familiar "The House That Jack Built" form) not only describes and pictures the sunflower in detail, but also focuses on some of the many birds that seek out its seeds. The book goes on to recount the way in which dropped and scattered seeds can root, sprout, and send up a new patch of golden sunflowers. A lovely way to add to a child's knowledge of nature and encourage interest not only in the beauty and reproduction of plants, but in noticing birds and beginning to learn about them. A book for enjoyment and for opening new doors into the natural world.

Silver, Donald M. *One Small Square: Backyard*. Illus. by Patricia J. Wynne. McGraw-Hill, 1993, 47 pp. (2-up).

Backyard is a good way to get involved with the excellent One Small Square Series of nature/science books. Readers are asked to mark off for observation just a yard-square area in a specific natural setting. In *Backyard*, young discoverers are to look for all the life forms they can find on the small backyard square's surface, underground, or seen in the air over the square. The book's colorful, delightfully illustrated pages reflect the teeming life to be found: "A backyard is . . . alive with creepers and crawlers, lifters and leapers, movers and mixers, munchers and scrapers, singers, buzzers, chirpers, climbers, builders, buriers and recyclers." The lively, well-written text includes precise directions and suggestions for how to go about exploring the one small square, and an amazing wealth of appealingly (and accurately) presented information fills every page.

Smith, Linda Wasmer. *Louis Pasteur: Disease Fighter*. Enslow Publishers, Inc., 1997, 128 pp. (4-8).

One of the foremost names in modern medicine, Louis Pasteur is responsible for some of the most effective scientific breakthroughs of the nineteenth century. Writer Linda Smith effectively discusses the background elements of Pasteur's life and follows his developing interest in science. As a very young man he evidenced the tenacity and the observation of detail that would prove invaluable to him later as he worked patiently on repeated laboratory tests. For many people today, the name Pasteur, if known at all, is related to the pasteurization of milk. A few may recall that Pasteur developed the vaccine for rabies. These are, of course, two of his most significant contributions to medical science, but he was also responsible for many more discoveries and became one of history's most honored scientists, known today as a founder of microbiology. Smith deals with formidable-sounding science in a way that makes the basics pleasantly understandable. Three simple science projects related to aspects of Pasteur's work, a chronology of his life's events, endnotes on the text, a glossary, suggestions for further reading, and a good index complete the book.

Sootin, Harry. *Robert Boyle: Founder of Modern Chemistry,* Immortals of Science Series. Franklin Watts, 1962, 133 pp. (6-up).
      Also listed under *Biography* and *History*
      From boyhood on, Robert Boyle (1627-1691) was fascinated by the natural world and its orderly laws that were slowly being discovered. Although he was born into a very wealthy family, Boyle had no interest in a life of luxury or amusement. Instead, he began to spend his time both in studying and experimenting on his own and in listening to a group of educated, intelligent men, all eager to forward the development of science. Boyle's chief interest was in chemistry and physics, and he made a number of significant advances, particularly in the field of chemistry. An important scientific concept in relation to gases is still identified today as Boyle's Law. Sootin's biography is a well-written account of Boyle's life and work, with a high level of human interest as well as much specific discussion of his experiments and discoveries. Especially helpful for advanced readers, this long out-of-print book is still worth trying to find or special-requesting through interlibrary loan.

Staiger, Ralph C. *Thomas Harriot, Science Pioneer.* Clarion Books, 1998, 128 pp. (6-up).
      Like the man who is its subject, this biography ranges far and wide in the era of Queen Elizabeth I. Ralph Staiger, in his account of the life and work of Thomas Harriot (1560-1621), offers many glimpses of the world beyond Elizabethan life as related to Harriot. This book includes a brief listing at the head of each chapter titled "These Other Things Were Happening." Harriot's life itself was not spent in isolated study. In the sixteenth and seventeenth centuries few students of the natural world (they were not yet known as "scientists") could earn a living in pursuit of their primary interests. Instead, they depended upon patrons, wealthy men who provided some degree of financial support and whom they usually served in various capacities. Harriot carried out a number of very responsible duties but also found time to pursue his interests in the application of mathematics to marine navigation, mapmaking, ship-building, ballistics, optics, gravity, and astronomy (a partial list). He also studied linguistics, the flora and fauna of Virginia, and what is now known as anthropology. Yet Thomas was not a dabbler. His studies were intensive, precise, and insightful. His discoveries made a substantial contribution

to the science of his day; not only that, but his findings continued to be used in succeeding generations. As recently as 1978 his notes and drawings on sunspots were used in a modern astronomical study of the sun's motion in the early seventeenth century. Thomas Harriot was an unusual and gifted man, and this is an absorbing account not only of his work but of his era, at a time that launched the scientific discoveries and the new vision that built, for good and ill, today's world.

Note: Some of the detailed explanations and calculations on Harriot's mathematical work may not be useful for most readers, who should be encouraged to skim over such sections and not lose the overall thread of the narrative.

Swinburne, Stephen R. *Coyote: North America's Dog.* Boyds Mills Press, 1999, 48 pp. (2-up).

"If you're reading this somewhere in North America," writes the author, "chances are good that you're closer to coyotes than you think." By 1970 those elusive members of the dog family lived in every state but Hawaii, and their territory within each state continues to expand. In the early 1990s they were seen for the first time in the Bronx, New York, and wildlife biologists estimate that at least 5,000 coyotes now live in Los Angeles. The intelligence and adaptability of the coyote have long been legendary among many Native Americans. Some Indian tribes believe the coyote has supernatural powers, but tribes differ as to their concept of the animal's role in the mythology. Many people enjoy knowing that the often-heard-but-not-seen canines are "out there" and regret it if the animals aren't close enough for their evening song of yips and barks to be heard. It is worthwhile as well as interesting to know more about these adaptable animals, and Swinburne's informative and effectively illustrated book is a good place to begin.

Thimmesh, Catherine. *Girls Think of Everything.* Illus. by Melissa Sweet. Houghton Mifflin, 2000, 57 pp. (5-8).

In a lively, conversational style, the writer tells the stories of ten women who invented such things as the chocolate-chip cookie, flat-bottomed paper bags, windshield wipers, Scotch Gard, Kevlar (as in bullet-proof vests), Snugli baby carriers, and a high-strength shield to protect satellites, shuttles, or space stations from the hazardous impact of orbital debris in space. The accounts of the varied ways in which these women became inventors are brief and interest-holding. In addition to providing worthwhile information, they support the writer's underlying theme: Thimmesh wants girls to know that becoming an inventor isn't a matter of gender or age; it's a matter of having a good idea! Further support is provided by the listing of well over 100 more women inventors over the centuries. These are shown on the book's front and back endpapers.

Trumbauer, Lisa. *Cool Sites: Homework Help for Kids on the Net.* The Millbrook Press, 2000, 80 pp. (3-8).

Primary listing under *Reference and Research/Study Skills*

Current technology offers helpful resources accessible on home, school, and public library computers. For details on this useful, wide-ranging resource aid for young students, see the primary listing shown above.

Wilson, Dorothy Clarke. *Ten Fingers for God*. Zondervan, 1989 (1965), 304 pp. (6-up).

   Primary listing under *Biography*

   The story of Dr. Paul Brand and his remarkable pioneering work in restorative surgery and rehabilitation of the victims of leprosy. While the book is written for the layperson, Wilson does go into a substantial amount of medical description and detail. Exciting reading for those interested in the medical field—and for those inspired by people who care and dare and accomplish great things. Reading aloud some of the episodes most directly related to Brand's medical work would be one good way to use the book with children's science curriculum. This is not a children's book, but advanced readers will find it fascinating. The *Biography* listing offers other suggestions for a broader use with children.

Yount, Lisa. *Asian-American Scientists*. Facts on File, Inc., 1998, 112 pp. (adv. 6-up).

   The writer has profiled twelve distinguished American scientists whose roots are in Asia—in China, Japan, or India. Some came to the United States as children, some as adults; all have become a part of the American scientific community and have contributed much in the areas of astronomy, physics, chemistry, and molecular biology to their adopted homeland. The specific work of the three women and nine men profiled is discussed clearly, providing insights into the varied scientific concepts and achievements involved. Young students interested in science will find it especially helpful to read about the ways in which the scientists prepared themselves for their careers. Well organized and researched, with a chronology and list for further reading provided for each scientist.

21

OUTDOOR
ACTIVITIES
Other Than Group Games

Burke, L. M. *Skateboarding! Surf the Pavement.* The Rosen Publishing Group, Inc., 1999, 64 pp. (4-8).

Viewed uneasily by some parents, skateboarding is not for everyone. It is, however, an outdoor activity particularly suited to some youngsters who like to acquire individual skills while engaged in an exciting and strenuous activity. Spills, scrapes, and bruises are part of the sport, and in some communities there are few good places in which to skateboard. For these reasons, parental research and decision-making are especially significant. *Skateboarding!* provides clearly stated information on the sport, details of equipment and safety gear, and specifics of the sport's techniques. Ample attention is given to safety measures and appropriate attitudes and behaviors related to skateboarding. This book is from the Extreme Sports Collection Series, which includes books on rock and ice climbing, mountain biking, snowboarding, in-line skating, and others.

Cole, Joanna and Stephanie Calmenson. *Rain or Shine Activity Book.* Illus. by Alan Tiegreen. Morrow Junior Books, 1997, 192 pp. (all ages).

Primary listing under *Crafts, Hobbies, and Domestic Arts*

A large book that offers a variety of outdoor games that include jumping rope, hopscotch, Red Light-Green Light, coin bowling, and others. See the *Crafts* listing for more information on the book's contents.

Drake, Jane and Ann Love. *The Kids' Summer Handbook.* Illus. by Heather Collins. Ticknor and Fields/Books for Young Readers, 1994, 208 pp. (3-up).

Also listed under *Crafts, Hobbies, and Domestic Arts*

A companion volume to the following entry, this handbook of summer activities is specifically geared toward things for kids to do while on vacation near the water or in the mountains (although many of the activities can also be done at home). A majority of the suggestions are for outdoor enjoyment: beach sculpting, swamp things, canoe tips and strokes, for example. Swing into summer, sweep-netting for meadow bugs, garden gone wild, hiking, camping, and star-gazing are still more ideas for outside action—with more suggestions not listed here. See the *Crafts* listing for things to make and build outdoors.

Drake, Jane and Ann Love. *The Kids' Winter Handbook.* Illus. by Heather Collins. Kids Can Press, 2001, 127 pp. (all ages).

> Also listed under *Celebration Days and Seasons* and *Crafts, Hobbies, and Domestic Arts*
>
> A full-of-fun book crammed with all kinds of winter activities. Some of them involve "real winter" weather, but many of the ideas can be used wherever the reader lives. From windsock forecasting to snow forts, winter picnicking to traditional snow games, there are twenty-five different outdoor activity ideas—and the twenty-fifth, Winter Olympics, involves fourteen more things to do. In addition to outdoor winter doings, the book includes a lot of winter-related projects for crafty kids to make, and a bunch of seasonal goodies, decorations, and around-the-fireplace fun.

Hogrogian, Nonny. *Handmade Secret Hiding Places.* Overlook Press, 1975, 48 pp. (all ages).

> Primary listing under *Crafts, Hobbies, and Domestic Arts*
>
> Ideas for making a number of different little hideaways in a hurry. A small, delightful book.

Love, Ann and Jane Drake. *Kids and Grandparents: An Activity Book.* Illus. by Heather Collins. Kids Can Press, 2000, 160 pp. (1-up).

> Also listed under *Crafts, Growing Plants,* and *Miscellaneous*
>
> Several schoolyard games that your grandparents probably played when they were kids, a plant-growing contest, and picking fruit or vegetables at a "pick-your-own" farm or orchard are some of the ideas included in this fun-filled collection. Check the listings shown above for many more how-to's and suggestions.

McManus, Patrick F. *Kid Camping from Aaaaiii! to Zip.* Avon, 1991 (1979), 125 pp. (3-8).

> With expertise and abundant humor McManus talks to kids about camping. As he so perceptively points out, there is only one requirement for kid camping: being a kid. Even when an adult has started his camping early in life and has camped frequently ever since, the adult shouldn't expect ever to recapture the unique kid-camping experience. But he can remember. It is with this memory-filled consciousness, along with current interviews with his own four daughters, that the writer plunges into this highly entertaining—and highly practical—handbook. Organized alphabetically, as the title implies, the book digs right in to such topics as bears, beds, beverages, blisters (to name just a few of the B's). Helpful and hilarious.

Silver, Donald M. *One Small Square: Backyard.* Illus. by Patricia J. Wynne. McGraw-Hill, 1993, 47 pp. (2-up).

> Primary listing under *Nature, Science, and Technology*
>
> For a good, purposeful individual activity, turn to the primary listing of this book (shown above) for more information on the procedure detailed in the book.

The series of which *Backyard* is a part is excellent and offers other *One Small Square* projects as well.

Swan, Malcolm D., editor. *Tips and Tricks in Outdoor Education.* Interstate Printers and Publishers, 1994 (1978), 260 pp. (all ages).
Primary listing under *Supplemental Teaching Resources*
A fine source book for outdoor activities. Its eighteen chapters focus on different areas: animal studies, weather, plants, and many more.

22

PHYSICAL EDUCATION AND ORGANIZED GAMES

NOTE: The skills books included in this section are not intended as a substitute for the instruction of experienced coaches. Such books serve to reinforce competent coaching and to remind readers of basic techniques.

Anderson, Dave. Foreword by Carl Lewis. *The Story of the Olympics*. HarperCollins, 1996, 168 pp. (4-8).

The Olympic Games manage to arouse interest—even excitement—not only in the sports-minded but in many people who usually care little for athletic competition. With roots in ancient Greece, its international scope, and the drama often associated with its events, the Olympics continue to capture the attention of millions. This balanced and thorough account offers a wealth of information and human interest both in its text and its accompanying illustrations. Part One opens with an "In the Beginning" summary and follows on to its seven sections focusing on the Games highlights involving personalities and events from 1900 to 1998. Part Two, also in seven sections, focuses on the different categories of events— track and field, gymnastics, swimming, and so forth. A concluding chapter suggests some answers as to why the Olympic Games are so popular around the world. A well-done and always interesting record.

Brundage, Buz. *Be a Better Hitter: Baseball Basics*. Sterling Publishing Co. Inc., 2000, 96 pp. (all ages, with adult guidance).

This generously illustrated manual does an excellent job of dealing with fundamental skills needed for success in baseball. Most crucial, says Brundage, are the player's grip on the bat, his stance, and pre-swing readiness. In words and pictures the writer describes the hows and whys of each part of the process—details that need to be fully understood and then practiced over and over again until they come naturally. The same kind of explanation and direction go on to address the swing of the bat, making contact, and understanding how the swing works. Brundage emphasizes that baseball is 90 percent a mental process. Skills in addition to batting are needed, of course, but as many teams become sadly aware, consistent success depends on players knowing what to do as they stand at the plate. Helpful guidance on the art of bunting and how to handle failure constructively conclude this informative book.

Coleman, Brian. *Basketball*. Dorling Kindersley, 2000, 48 pp. (4-7).
    A step-by-step guide through the background, rules, and skills of basketball. Beginning with a brief history of the game, the book proceeds through basic court layout to each playing technique. Thoroughly illustrated all the way through with full-color photographs, the reader can see each position and action, with accompanying explanation and instruction. Diagrams of formations, for example, are detailed and clear. A thorough understanding of a book such as this helps the young player grasp more quickly what an instructor is trying to achieve and how to accomplish this task.

Crossingham, John and Sarah Dann. *Volleyball in Action*. Crabtree Publishing Co., 2000, 32 pp. (6-up).
    A well-organized and effectively illustrated manual. The game of volleyball is clearly described, including a full-page drawing of the ball court with a game in progress, each area labeled and the functions of each official defined. Rules of the game are detailed and clothing and protective gear discussed, with the main body of the book focusing step by step on specific techniques of play. A brief section refers to the popular beach volleyball, with its variations in team numbers and rules of play. The book concludes with a glossary of terms and an index.

Gibbons, Gail. *My Football Book*. HarperCollins Publishers, 2000, 22 pp. (ps-3).
    A brief, concise beginning book introducing new players to American football. Basic rules and layouts of playing positions and movement are thoroughly illustrated. Formations on the field are labeled in detail. Terminology used in the game is explained and illustrated. The book's format is accessible and attractive.

Hammond, Tim. *Sports*. Dorling Kindersley, 2000, 64 pp. (4-7).
    A helpful overview of a wide range of recognized sports. Lavishly illustrated, the book defines the activity, illustrates and briefly explains how it is carried out, and also shows the clothing and equipment used in that particular sport. From soccer, football, rugby, field and ice hockey, basketball, baseball, cricket, tennis, table tennis, badminton, squash, and racquetball, the book moves to more individual activities: gymnastics, weightlifting, boxing, martial arts, fencing, archery, shooting, bowling sports (including mention of marbles and curling), golf, pool, snooker, athletic track (running and walking), and field track (jumping and throwing). Obviously, the material on any one sport is relatively brief, but it provides enough information to give the reader some ideas on what sport might particularly interest him or her, and also adds to the person's general knowledge so that when an unfamiliar sport is mentioned, total ignorance is not the response.

Hornby, Hugh. *Soccer*. Photographed by Andy Crawford. Dorling Kindersley, 2000, 65 pp. (4-8).
    Like others of the extensive Eyewitness Books Series, *Soccer* is a colorful montage of information about its subject area. Each of its twenty-four sections starts with a paragraph that summarizes the topic: "The Global Game," "The Field," "Tactics," "The World Cup," for example. This is followed by a variety of captioned pictures relevant to the section; taken together, the many details provide a

view of the game broader than the scope of soccer as experienced by any one community or country. While there are sections on rules, game officials, and playing techniques, the book is not a step-by-step handbook of soccer how-to's. It is, on the other hand, a lively overview of soccer's origins and development through the years; its noted players and teams; its equipment, garb, and accessories, and even some of its business aspects. An enjoyable and informative summary of soccer essentials—and trivia.

Miller, Marc. *Fundamental Tennis*. Lerner Publications, 1995, 64 pp. (6-9).

A well-done and helpful manual for young tennis players. Full-color action photographs accompanied by clear, detailed instructions give young readers a pattern of stance and motion to follow in their own efforts to master the basics of tennis. A glossary of the terms used and a resource list are included.

Ogilvie, Robert S. *Basic Ice Skating Skills*. HarperCollins Children's Books, 1968, 176 pp. (6-up).

In use for a number of years, this official handbook of the United States Figure Skating Association is still popular with ice skaters, whether skating simply for recreation or to develop competitive skills. Starting out with answers to preliminary questions (as to the recommended age for a child to begin, for example), moving on to equipment and then into techniques, the book thoroughly covers all areas of figure skating and illustrates each point with photographs and diagrams. The text explains that the term "figure skating" covers everything not falling into the ice hockey or speed skating categories.

Simmons, Richard. *The Young Golfer*. DK Publishing, Inc., 1999, 48 pp. (4-up).

Opening with a foreword by golfer Nick Faldo and a mini-history of golf, the book moves on to the essentials of equipment. Types of golf courses are then noted, followed by notes on scoring and golf etiquette. The bulk of the book is devoted to clear step-by-step instructions on each aspect of the game, with excellent photographs of girl and boy players, a picture, and explanatory text for each move and change of position. Fairway strategies, approaching the green, different kinds of shots, bunker play, putting, and even suggestions about how to deal with bad weather conditions are discussed. The book concludes with a glossary of golfing terms and a list of useful addresses of major golfing associations.

Wilson, Stacy. *The Hockey Book for Girls*. Illus. by Bill Slavin. Kids Can Press, 2000, 40 pp. (3-9).

A concise but detailed manual for girl hockey players. Starting with a brief mention of the world of women's hockey, the book moves on through all the essentials: the equipment needed and its use and care; tips for off-ice conditioning; ways to improve players' skills in specific areas—skating, shooting, passing, and so forth. Suggestions from a top Olympic coach are followed by comments on the importance of the team aspect of the game, an interview with a star player, and profiles of five top world players of women's hockey. The book is helpfully illustrated throughout with relevant photographs.

23

REFERENCE AND
RESEARCH/STUDY SKILLS

Ford, Paul F. *Companion to Narnia.* HarperSF, 1994 (1980), 512 pp. (4-up).
 A detailed guide to "the themes, characters, and events" of the seven Narnia books. Entries are arranged in alphabetical order, cross-referenced, and annotated. Maps and illustrations add to the guidebook's usefulness.

Fritz, Jean. *George Washington's Breakfast.* Illus. by Paul Galdone. Putnam Publishing Group, 1998 (1969), 47 pp. (2-up).
 A contemporary "George" with the same birthday as the "father of our country" decides to find out what our first president ate for breakfast. The story of his research (which involves his whole family) and what he learned is not only entertainingly written but opens new doors for young children as to how to go about researching a topic.

Grun, Bernard. *The Timetables of History: A Horizontal Linkage of People and Events.* Simon and Schuster, 1991 (1982), 724 pp. (4-up).
 A unique broad-spectrum view of history in which the reader can scan horizontally across the book's category columns (History, Politics; Literature, Theatre; Religion, Philosophy, Learning; Visual Arts; Music; Science, Technology, Growth; Daily Life) and see events of significance (or merely of whimsical interest) that occurred in different aspects of culture and in different parts of the world during the same time period. The book is not only most helpful for reference but is also a pleasure to browse through. The coverage begins with the year 5000 B.C., and up to 1000 B.C. events are grouped in 500-year periods—not too much was going on as to detailed recorded change and development at that time. From 1000 B.C. to 500 B.C., the time period is reduced to 100-year sections, then to fifty-year spans up to 500 A.D., and from 501 A.D. on, a separate time slot is allowed for each year. The entries run through 1990.

McDonnell, Sharon. *The Everything Internet Book*. Adams Media Corporation, 1999, 281 pp. (4-up).

An extensive guide to using the Internet. Its ten chapters start with the Internet's history and access procedures through basics for everyday use, e-mail and Internet etiquette. News groups, bulletin boards, chat rooms, and other features are discussed. Information and warnings as to protecting the user from undesirable contacts, availability of filtering software, preventing viruses, and being aware of privacy issues are all covered. With the wealth of legitimate information sources for students available on the Internet, it is unfortunate that problems are sometimes possible.

Trumbauer, Lisa. *Cool Sites: Homework Help for Kids on the Net*. The Millbrook Press, 2000, 80 pp. (4-7).

This great little book offers information on almost seventy websites that provide Internet help for homework. Some give general help, others a wide range of information on specific class-subject areas, and still others offer useful reference tools. Each page pictures a different website, and its screen address briefly describes the site's subject area and suggests ways to use it helpfully. Most entries close with a brief comment by a youngster who has used the site and found it very helpful.

Tunis, Edwin.

Note: A number of Edwin Tunis's books, published by Harper and Row twenty to twenty-five years ago, are now out of print. Those listed below were included in the original *Books Children Love*, providing excellent and generously illustrated resource material in a number of areas. It would be well worth looking for the following books in your local library and also to request them through the interlibrary loan service available in many libraries: *Colonial Living; Frontier Living; Indians; Oars, Sails and Steam: A Picture Book of Ships; The Tavern at the Ferry; Wheels: A Pictorial History; The Young United States.*

Urdang, Laurence. *The Timetables of American History*. Simon and Schuster, 2001 (1981), 560 pp. (4-up).

Using a similar, but not identical, format to Grun's *The Timetables of History* (listed above), this book is organized around American history. Its four categories are History and Politics, The Arts, Science and Technology, and Miscellaneous. Each category has a column headed "America" and one headed "Elsewhere." Each year is listed vertically in the left margin. Thus one can follow across the page for the year 1818, for example, and find listed seven significant political events (three in America and four elsewhere), nine important happenings in the arts (three in America and six elsewhere), five events in science and technology, etc. The idea behind this horizontal approach is to broaden students' concepts of history and to encourage them to see patterns and the interrelationships of events.

Dictionaries

A wider range of children's dictionaries is being offered now than was the case when *Books Children Love* was first published. In addition to several early-age picture dictionaries, a number of publishers offer a "children's" category; following that level are the ones usually designated as "student" dictionaries, some of which run to around 1,000 pages. Following these are the adult "college" or "collegiate" editions. Children who are advanced readers, interested in academic subjects, and with no vision-limiting problems may want to start early using the college editions with their smaller type and content-crammed pages.

It is helpful, when dictionary shopping, to take along a list of several words your child has encountered in reading that need to be defined. Have the student look up each word in the dictionaries you are considering and discuss ease of finding, clarity of definition, and personal reaction to each volume. (Check also the pronunciation guide and other additional features.)

All of the following are worthwhile dictionaries, and there are others not listed that are also satisfactory. "Children's" and "student" editions offer simpler language in their definitions, larger type, more illustrations, and less of the linguistic information, puzzling abbreviations, and so forth than do adult editions—the degree of their simplification based, of course, on which grade-level they represent. It is always important to check the title and publisher; many inferior dictionaries use the name "Webster" in their titles—in itself no guarantee of scholarship.

The dictionaries are listed in alphabetical order by name.

EARLY AGES

The American Heritage Picture Dictionary. Houghton Mifflin, 1998, 138 pp.

The Kingfisher First Dictionary. Kingfisher Publications, 1995, 190 pp.

CHILDREN

The American Heritage Children's Dictionary. Houghton Mifflin, 1998, 856 pp.

Merriam-Webster Children's Dictionary. Merriam Webster, 2000, 911 pp.

Webster's New World Children's Dictionary. Hungry Minds, Inc., 1999, 928 pp.

STUDENT

The American Heritage Student Dictionary. Houghton Mifflin, 1998, 1094 pp.

Macmillan Dictionary for Students. Simon and Schuster Books for Young Readers, 2001, 1190 pp.

Webster's New World Student's Dictionary. Hungry Minds, Inc., 1996, 1056 pp.

ADULT

The American Heritage College Dictionary. Houghton Mifflin, 2002, 1636 pp.

Merriam Webster's Collegiate Dictionary. Merriam Webster, 2001, 1557 pp.

Webster's New World College Dictionary. IDG Books Worldwide, 2001, 1716 pp.

It is helpful to have as many good reference books as possible in the home. *World Book Encyclopedia (World Book)* is recommended for children; the *Encyclopedia Britannica* is still the best compilation of its kind for adults, although in many cases *World Book* can be used by all ages.

The list of desirable reference books could be almost endless. A good thesaurus (several for the intermediate level are now available: for example, *The American Heritage Student Thesaurus,* Houghton Mifflin, 1999, 378 pp.), a variety of atlases, an up-to-date almanac, specialized dictionaries in the fields of music, medicine, the classics—the possibilities are as varied as the readers' interests. There are excellent geographical and biographical dictionaries, invaluable guides to literature (one is *Merriam Webster's Encyclopedia of Literature,* Merriam Webster, 1995, 1236 pp.), field guides to plants, wildlife, rocks, and minerals—and more. Many people find a large reference book on familiar quotations helpful, and for the person with a "back to the roots" interest in the English language, the multivolume *Oxford English Dictionary* (frequently referred to as the OED) is indispensable. Fortunately for the majority of people whose financial resources aren't unlimited, the OED is published in a compact edition—full contents in micro-reduced printing— and comes complete with a magnifying glass. (The micro edition used to come in two volumes but is now in one very large one.)

Having and using a wealth of good reference material in the home is one of the most effective ways of establishing invaluable research skills and encouraging wide-ranging interests in children

24

SPECIAL NEEDS

Bunting, Eve. *Jin Woo*. Illus. by Chris Soentpiet. Clarion Books, 2001, 30 pp. (ps-2).
Primary listing under *Literature: Level I, Realistic Stories—Modern*
This well-told and beautifully illustrated story provides a model for good family relationships when an adoptive child joins another child or children in a family. Mom and Dad, with a young adoptive son, David, are preparing to welcome a second son, five-month-old Jin Woo from Korea. Part of a loving, happy family, David nonetheless has fears and anxieties that need to be recognized and allayed, and this is exactly what the reader sees the wise parents doing in one little incident after another. An appealing story and a positive and helpful model.

Calvert, Patricia. *Picking Up the Pieces*. Simon and Schuster Children's Books, 1999, 176 pp. (6-up).
Primary listing under *Literature: Level III, Realistic Stories—Modern*
An appealing, well-written story of Megan, a young teenager trying to deal with life in a wheelchair after an accident has left her paralyzed from the waist down. Most young people don't meet that kind of disaster, but a number do; there are also many who do experience shattering and irrevocable changes of various kinds in their lives, or who were born with difficulties that make existence an endless struggle. The things Megan learns as she tries to confront reality and simply accept the nitty gritty of all she has to cope with in daily life make this a book potentially helpful both for those struggling with handicaps themselves and for all those who aren't, but who could extend their understanding and compassion to people around them with special needs.

D'Antonio, Nancy. *Our Baby from China: An Adoption Story*. Albert Whitman and Co., 1997, 22 pp. (1-4).
A captioned color-photo picture story of one couple's adoption of a lovely Chinese baby girl, including pictures of four other families also adopting Chinese babies. There are brief step-by-step comments on the adoption process and the Farnhams' time in China, concluding with arrival-home pictures of both sets of new grandparents and other family members.

de Paola, Tomie. *Now One Foot, Now the Other*. Illus. by author. G. P. Putnam's, 1981, 48 pp. (all ages).
Primary listing under *Literature: Level I, Realistic Stories—Modern*
Bobbie and his grandpa are close friends. After his grandpa's stroke, it is Bobbie

who is able to elicit response from him, encourage him to walk again, and help him as Grandpa once helped him.

Kaminsky, Marty. *Uncommon Champions.* Boyds Mills Press, 2000, 147 pp. (7-up).
    Also listed under *Biography*
    Teacher, writer, and sports enthusiast Marty Kaminsky has written vivid, action-filled biographical profiles of fifteen outstanding athletes who overcame extreme difficulties. Cancer, Tourette syndrome, blindness, spina bifida, and Graves disease are just a few of the major conditions they battled with persistence, hope, and tremendous courage. These accounts are not written just for the athletic or for those struggling with unusual physical challenges; the writer wants to inspire all his readers to meet whatever hardships, disappointments, and loss life brings, with the kind of "won't quit" determination and grit that characterize the people profiled. But because those with special needs can identify with others who have struggled as they do, they may find among the people of this book role models whose sense of purpose and tough endurance bring them added help and encouragement.

Kent, Deborah and Kathryn A. Quinlan. *Extraordinary People with Disabilities.* Children's Press, 1996, 288 pp. (4, 5-up).
    Biographical profiles of forty-eight high-achieving people with disabilities provide inspiring and thought-provoking material for both the general reader and also for children with disabilities (and those concerned with their needs and hopes). The emphasis is not, "Whatever your difficulties you, too, can become famous," but is rather on helping both the disabled and the non-disabled realize that having a handicap does not mean a life without purpose, opportunity, and achievement. Not only are a number of unknown people written about (along with others who are widely known), but interspersed throughout the book are six chapters of information on the development of advocacy and legislation for the disabled; the disabled and education, sports, employment, independent living, and technological aids. Of real value also are the frank comments of some of the book's biographical subjects about their own experiences in dealing with common attitudes of the non-disabled toward them. Children, especially, need to be able to put themselves in the place of the disabled they may encounter. Simply reading of the lives of the book's diverse subjects can immeasurably increase their understanding and empathy. A useful glossary and a chapter on sources of further information conclude the book.
    Note: Readers and their parents should be aware that not all the people profiled are ideal role models even though their courage and determination are admirable. Their overcoming of daunting disabilities can be recognized, whatever their chosen philosophy and lifestyle.

Little, Jean. Two books: *From Anna* and *Mine for Keeps.* HarperCollins Children's Books, 1973, 203 pp.; Viking Children's Books, 1995 (1962), 205 pp. (3, 4-up).
    Primary listing under *Literature: Level II, Realistic Stories—Modern*
    In both of these books, the central character is coping with a physical handicap—and with the related emotional and social problems. In the first book, Anna's visual impairment is finally discovered, and in *Mine for Keeps,* Sally, with

cerebral palsy, struggles with the transition from a special boarding school to life at home and in a regular school. Little writes especially well, and her books have warmth, humor, perception, and depth.

Millman, Isaac. *Moses Goes to School.* Farrar Straus Giroux, 2000, 30 pp. (k-3).

A splendid presentation in story form of the way many deaf or hard-of-hearing children communicate and learn. Moses goes to a public school in New York City that has only hearing-impaired students. They communicate in American Sign Language, often called by its initials, ASL. The writer includes many drawings showing the hand positions and movements used in ASL. Colorfully illustrated, the story shows the children in their classrooms and on the playground as they study and also sign to each other. In one class, the teacher brings in a boom box. He writes the words to a familiar song, "Take Me Out to the Ballgame," on the board and then turns on the cassette player. The children can't hear the music, but they can feel the vibrations and "sing" along—something they love to do. An especially enlightening section explains that even though ASL uses words everyone uses, it is essentially like another language because the sentences are put together differently from regular English language syntax. So in their English classes, the students write out in ASL form what they want to say, then rewrite it in the standard English arrangement of phrases and sentences. This enjoyable story is an excellent introduction to the world of hearing-impaired youngsters—a good way to increase understanding of what it means to be unable to hear.

Peter, Diana. *Claire and Emma.* HarperCollins Children's Books, 1977, 30 pp. (k-4).

This is a true story about Claire and Emma who are four and two and live in London, England, with their mother and their brother Alastair, who is six. Claire and Emma were both born deaf, and this simply written photo-story explains their handicap and tells about the things they have to do to try to learn to speak, to lip read, and to hear a little with the use of hearing aids.

Tada, Joni Eareckson. *You've Got a Friend.* Illus. by Jeff Meyer. Crossway Books, 1999, 31 pp. (1-5).

Primary listing under *Literature: Level II, Realistic Stories—Modern*

Ben and Tony are best friends before Ben is injured in an accident, losing the use of his legs and permanently confined to a wheelchair. Tony doesn't know how to bridge the gap or find things to do with Ben, who, in turn, feels he will never be part of things again where other kids are concerned. Adding to the problem, Tony himself is really down, with his dad away on business all the time and his mother completely absorbed with a new baby. The two boys need each other, but don't know how to reconnect. With some wise, unseen help from their guardian angels— nothing sensational, just a little arrangement of circumstances that gives the boys each a chance to reach out—they begin to realize that *being* a friend is the way to *have* a friend. Reaching out to others from her own life in a wheelchair, author Joni's spirit of warmth and courage lends authenticity to the atmosphere of the story, an atmosphere enhanced by Meyer's fresh, sensitive illustrations.

Warren, Andrea. *Orphan Train Rider: One Boy's True Story*. Houghton Mifflin, 1996, 80 pp. (4-7).

> Primary listing under *History and Geography*

> This appealing true account of one homeless "orphan train" boy from the past is not only a touching story, but it adds a new perspective to today's problems of uncaring homes, inadequate to sometimes harmful foster care, and the unmet needs of so many children. Virtually every school around us has its share of students who live every day with neglect and a lack of love and understanding—sometimes with frequent mistreatment. *Orphan Train Rider* is not only a well-done account of a piece of American history, but on its pages young readers from caring, loving homes can glimpse the hardships of children less fortunate than they and gain the compassion and sensitivity that are no less needed today. Archival and personal photographs bring long-ago children to life for twenty-first-century children.

Waybill, Marjorie. *Chinese Eyes*. Herald, 1974, 32 pp. (k-2).

> A little Korean adoptee growing up in a white community experiences the kind of unthinking prejudice that brings pain and a feeling of rejection into the lives of many children. She is teased by other children because her eyes are Asian instead of Caucasian, but even her Korean birth-identity is muddled in their taunting of "Chinese eyes." The way her wise and loving mother restores her sense of self-worth provides a subtle lesson for children in learning not to have hurtful attitudes toward those who happen to be "different" in some way.

Wolf, Bernard. *Connie's New Eyes*. HarperCollins Children's Books, 1976, 95 pp. (4-up).

> A fine documentary on a young woman, Connie David, who has been blind from birth. Although a full photographic sequence runs through the book, the text is much more substantial and detailed than in many such documentaries. Connie is preparing to start her first full-time job in a few months as a teacher in a school for children with special needs. For years she has wanted to have a guide dog, and now seems the ideal time to realize her dream. The reader is shown—and told about—the care and training of Blythe, the dog that will later be introduced to Connie, and about the month Connie herself spends at The Seeing Eye headquarters being trained to properly use a guide dog. The account then goes on to show Connie's life over a period of months as she enjoys the new independence and freedom brought to her by the help and companionship of Blythe. An excellent and informative book.

Wolf, Bernard. *Don't Feel Sorry for Paul*. HarperCollins Children's Books, 1988 (1974), 96 pp. (3-6).

> Paul Jockimo, an especially handsome little boy, is just turning seven; but all his life he has had to live with a problem. He was born with only stumps beyond a flexible right wrist and right heel; his left hand has an enlarged thumb and two webbed-together fingers, and his left foot just a heel and a big toe. What went wrong? Not even medical experts can say why this happened, but Paul must learn to live as fully as possible in spite of his substantial difficulty. Writer-photographer

Wolf perceptively documents two active weeks in Paul's life and accompanies the pictures with clear, detailed text. Wolf has caught just the scenes and brought out exactly the facts that help a reader to "feel" Paul's situation, to realize a little of what a struggle he determinedly carries on.

Yashima, Taro. *Crow Boy*. Illus. by author. Viking Children's Books, 1955, 38 pp. (ps-3).

Chibi, a painfully shy Japanese schoolboy, is not like the rest of the children, who scorn and avoid him. Chibi is left to live in the closed world of his own thoughts and interests through the years of his school experience. A new teacher, however, finds a way to communicate with the solitary boy and helps others to understand and appreciate his unusual gifts. Readers are made aware that they, like Chibi's schoolmates, may be jumping hastily to wrong conclusions about some of the people they see every day and that they need to look beyond outward appearances.

25

SUPPLEMENTAL
TEACHING RESOURCES

Allison, Linda. *Trash Artists Workshop*. Fearon Teaching Aids, 1981 (all ages).
Primary listing under *Crafts, Hobbies, and Domestic Arts*
A worthwhile collection of things to make from throwaway materials. Many of the objects made are more useful and creative than those in some craft books.

Gerston, Rich. *Just Open the Door*. Interstate Printers and Publisher, 1982, 112 pp.
Nearly 300 lesson plans and activities that use outdoor/environmental experiences, tying them in to classroom curriculum, relating them to various specific subjects, etc. Practical and useful. Entries are all short, but much specific guidance is given briefly. Excellent.

Macaulay, Susan. *For the Children's Sake: Foundations of Education for Home and School*. Crossway, 1984, 192 pp.
This excellent book offers a basic philosophy of education without educational jargon or the kind of textbook theory that seems remote from the realities of life and the holistic needs of children. Writing from the heart, yet with down to earth practicality, Susan Macaulay vividly portrays the mental, emotional, spiritual, and physical needs of children, their personhood and diversity. A nourishing, joyous educational program should minister to the full range of their beings. The writer makes a logical and persuasive case for a deeply thoughtful and committed approach to education, whether it means strengthening the nurture and enrichment of the home when children attend a public or private school, or whether it involves a full program of home-based education.

Moore, Jo Ellen, Ginny Hall, Leslie Tryon, and Betsy Franco. *How to Do Plays with Children*. Illus. by Joy Evans and Leslie Tryon. Evan-Moor Corp., 1994, 288 pp. (k-6).
A helpful book full of material to use in guiding children through the presentation of plays and near-plays (readers' theater, for example—see below). The opening section of the book contains rhyming plays—familiar stories have been put into simple rhyming verse that is easier for the beginning actors to memorize. The favorite folktales section focuses on everyone-has-a-part plays in which several performers do different segments of one character's part. In the readers'

theater chapter, parts are not memorized, but instead the stories are read by its characters. Sections on scenery, props, and scripts are included, and the opening page of each section offers some general suggestions about that form's particular approach.

Rowell, Elizabeth H. and Thomas B. Goodkind. *Teaching the Pleasures of Reading.* Prentice-Hall, 1982, 256 pp.

The title of this resource book is somewhat misleading. It is not a book that aids teachers/parents in getting children involved in a specific list of recommended books. What it does do is give hundreds of suggestions that involve kids pleasurably in word-related activities in five areas: humor, TV, art, music, and the outdoors. The overall concept is that if children's reading skills are developed in diverse ways, and they find that using words can be fun, they will do more reading and enjoy reading more.

In the humor section, for example, puns, jokes, riddles, paraphrasing, idiomatic expressions, writing about a favorite humorous character, and analyzing humorous advertisements are just a few of the approaches used. Without going into lengthy detail, it is difficult to adequately describe the variety of activities covered, but they are extensive. A helpful, idea-generating handbook.

Shoemaker, Kathryn. *Creative Classroom.* HarperSF, 1982.

A well-done book full of great ideas for creative activities and projects children can do in the classroom.

Sisson, Edith A. *Nature with Children of All Ages: Activities and Adventures for Exploring, Learning and Enjoying the World Around Us.* Prentice-Hall, 1982, 224 pp.

Information and suggested activities related to the natural world: trees, seeds, insects, fish, birds, mammals, etc. Some of the activities involve hiking or games; others are science experiments; still others give craft instructions for making a variety of things. A bibliography is at the end of each chapter. This is a secular book, and in some discussions the evolutionary theory is implied. Parents/teachers should be prepared to respond in the manner in which they normally deal with this issue—one their children will frequently encounter.

Swan, Malcolm D., editor. *Tips and Tricks in Outdoor Education.* Interstate Printers and Publishers, 1994 (1978), 260 pp.

A fine source for outdoor activities. Its eighteen chapters focus on different areas. "Animal Studies," "Geology and Soils," "Interpretive Trails," "Measurement and Mapping" are a few of the chapter titles; others focus on water, weather, plants, and more. Detailed instructions for many procedures are given.

INDEX